Immigration Policy in the Federal Republic of Germany

Immigration Policy in the Federal Republic of Germany

Negotiating Membership and Remaking the Nation

Douglas B. Klusmeyer

and

Demetrios G. Papademetriou

Berghahn Books
NEW YORK • OXFORD

Published in 2009 by

Berghahn Books

www.berghahnbooks.com

Library of Congress Cataloging-in-Publication Data

Klusmeyer, Douglas B., 1957–

Immigration policy in the Federal Republic of Germany : negotiating membership
and remaking the nation / Douglas B. Klusmeyer and Demetrios G. Papademetriou.
    p. cm.
Includes bibliographical references and index.
ISBN 978-1-84545-611-5 (hardback : alk. paper)
    1. Germany—Emigration and immigration—Government policy.
2. Emigration and immigration law—Germany. I. Papademetriou, Demetrios G.
II. Title.

JV8033.K49 2009
325.43—dc22

2009025361

British Library Cataloguing in Publication Data

A catalogue record for this book is available from
the British Library.

Printed in the United States on acid-free paper

Contents

Tables

Acknowledgments

═══════════

We are pleased to have this opportunity to thank the many persons who have contributed generously in different ways during the long process that this book took shape. We are indebted to Maryam Kamali, who helped lay the foundations for this project and participated actively in its early development. Our work benefited from several careful critical readings at various stages in the writing process, and for this we thank Wolfgang Bosswick, Dilek Cinar, Sophie Pirie, and James J. Sheehan. Kathleen Newland graciously shared her expertise on refugee policy when she read our chapters pertaining to this issue. Likewise, Bill Davies gave us many valuable recommendations regarding our discussion of the Maastricht Treaty and the evolution of aspects of European Union law. Claudia Diehl offered invaluable data advice. The staff of the Migration Policy Institute provided able assistance at many junctures along the way, but several persons require special mention. Celine Artal provided effective research assistance and some sharp analytical advice. The multi-talented Aaron Ehrlich and Eric Leise played instrumental roles in many different capacities from copyediting and organizing our system of references to conducting considerable supplementary research. Their hard work over long stretches proved indispensable to finishing this book.

For their help in moving this manuscript through the production process, we wish to thank Cassandra Caswell, who copyedited it, and Jeanna Cullinan, Mingzhi Chen, Gretchen Pfau, and Andrew Viteritti, who proofread it. We also are very grateful for the exceptionally fine work of Carolyn Carmody, who prepared our index, and to Shawn Kendrick, who finalized the manuscript for publication. Finally, we wish to thank Melissa Spinelli and Ann Przyzycki of Berghahn Books for their unstinting guidance, support, and patience. Although all of these individuals deserve much credit for improving the book and saving us from many mistakes, we alone are responsible for any errors and shortcomings that remain.

Parts of several chapters draw on previously published articles. Most of this previously published material has been substantially reworked here. We would like to thank the following journal publishers for permitting us to reprint here material from previously published articles: Douglas Klusmeyer, "Aliens, Immigrants, and Citizens: The Politics of Inclusion in the Federal Republic of Germany," *Dædalus* 122(3) (Summer 1993), 81–114, © 1993 by the American Academy of Arts and Sciences; Douglas Klusmeyer, "Four Dimensions of Membership in Germany," *SAIS Review* 20 (Winter-Spring 2000), 1–21, © by The Johns Hopkins University Press; Douglas Klusmeyer, "A 'Guiding Culture' for Immigrants? Integration and Diversity in Germany," *Journal of Ethnic and Migration Studies* 27(3) (July 2001), 519–532, © by the Taylor & Francis Group (http://www.informaworld.com).

Abbreviations

BAFL	Federal Office for the Recognition of Foreign Refugees
BAMF	Federal Office for Migration and Refugees
BITKOM	German Association for Information Technology, Telecommunications and New Media
BSHG	Federal Social Assistance Law
CDU	Christian Democratic Union
CSU	Christian Social Union
COE	Council of Europe
DGB	German Federation of Labor
DM	German Mark
DVU	Democratic People's Union
EBP	European Border Patrol
EC	European Community
ECJ	European Court of Justice
ECHR	European Court of Human Rights
ECPHR	European Convention for the Protection of Human Rights and Fundamental Freedoms (or the European Convention on Human Rights)
ECSC	European Coal and Steel Community
EEC	European Economic Community
EU	European Union
Euratom	European Atomic Energy Community
FDP	Free Democratic Party
FRG	Federal Republic of Germany

GB/BHE	All-German Bloc/German Fellowship Bloc of Expellees and Victims of Injustice
GDR	German Democratic Republic
NPD	National Democratic Party
PDS	Party for Democratic Socialism (formerly SED)
QMV	Qualified Majority Voting
REP	*Republikaner* Party
SED	Socialist Unity Party of Germany
SPD	Social Democratic Party of Germany
TEU	Treaty on European Union (or Maastricht Treaty)
USSR	Union of Soviet Socialist Republics
ZDJ	Central Council of Jews

Introduction

Despite the reception of many millions of foreign-born persons since the late nineteenth century, the Federal Republic of Germany (FRG) for most of its history has declared itself officially to be "not-an-immigration-land."[1] In reality, nothing could have been further from the truth. Between 1950 and 1994, approximately 80 percent of the increase in the West German population resulted from migration. This proportion amounted to 12.9 million persons (Münz and Ulrich 1997: 65–66). In 2006, the Federal Statistical Office, counting the second and third generations of immigrants in Germany, reported that nearly one-fifth (19 percent) of the population in Germany had a migration background (*Migrationshintergrund*). This number did not include the approximately 12 million ethnic German refugees and expellees, who came to Germany as a result of World War II and its aftermath, and the even larger number of their offspring, whose roots also lie outside of modern Germany. Recognizing this reality, most analysts over several decades rejected the FRG's official self-characterization and routinely described the FRG as a de facto immigration land long before the federal government did (Bade 1994a). Nonetheless, governmental policy has been slow to address the civic, legal, and sociocultural ramifications of this fact.

As Christian Joppke observed in 1999, the most striking feature of the government's response to the FRG's post-war migration experience was not its persistent reluctance to acknowledge the reality of large scale immigration,

---

1. This stance was first officially adopted in a 1977 policy report of a joint commission of the federal government and the states on migrant workers. The report recommended that future policies be guided by (among others) the fact that the "Federal Republic of Germany is not a country of immigration. West Germany is a country in which foreigners reside for varying lengths of time before they decide on their own accord to return to their home country" (translated excerpts of this report are contained in Katzenstein 1987: 239–240).

but rather its continual insistence on grounding its policy on a self-conception of national identity defined by a perceived counter model, namely, the immigration land.[2] For decades, German government policy was framed around a portrait of national identity that highlighted the absence of characteristics associated with a presumed opposing type of society. This kind of dichotomy always presupposed a polar model that is all the more striking in an era that some have labeled "the age of migration." In their study of this era, Castles and Miller have emphasized the ways that the international movement of people has constituted a "key dynamic" within that complex of sweeping transformative changes associated with "globalization" (Castles and Miller 2003: 1). While sharing some general common features, the causes, character, and impacts of these movements have varied considerably according to time, place, and local conditions. In his history of the modern European migration experience, Klaus Bade identifies the period from the late 1950s as a pivotal moment in the "historic transition from a continent of emigration to one of immigration," which has had profound effects on the economy, politics, and cultures of the receiving states (Bade 2003: 217). Trying to come to terms with such changes through the lens of a starkly drawn dichotomy between immigration societies and non-immigration societies obscured far more than it illuminated the nature of these changes.

The concept of an "immigration land" can be understood as an "ideal type" in the manner that Max Weber had advocated (Weber 1973a: 201–205; 1973b: 535–540). Ideal-typical models are deliberately constructed in a one-sided fashion to accentuate certain features of the phenomenon under investigation while obscuring many other features in order to clarify particular causal relationships and facilitate comparative analysis. But for Weber, such analytical constructs are intended as heuristic devices that provide a means for sharpening lines of empirical inquiry and thereby do not stand as ends in themselves. Employed properly, they are not to be treated as descriptive representations of reality, but rather must be understood as informed theoretical fictions. In other words, they are highly stylized conceptual artifices that—by design—grossly oversimplify the complexity and contingent variability of actual phenomena as they exist in different empirical contexts. When such models are divorced from their role as analytical guides for social science research, they entirely leave the ground of facts and enter the realm of political ideology and public myth. At this level, they may prove effective as a rhetorical tactic and may find resonance in popular sentiment, but they do so at the expense of abandoning any claim to social science validity. To the extent that one believes that sound

2. "While Germany is not alone in Europe in not defining itself as a nation of immigrants," Joppke writes, "it is the only country that has not become tired of repeating it, elevating the no-immigration maxim to a first principle of public policy and national self-definition" (1999: 62).

policymaking requires a strong social science foundation, basing policy on the juxtaposition of fictions with counter fictions seems like a political strategy more calculated to evade hard facts than to address them.

The German government's perception, that managing migration well poses significant political challenges, is hardly unusual. Its long arch-defensiveness in response to these challenges, however, crippled its ability to chart a positive policy agenda and to build public support for that agenda. As a result, major government policy initiatives in this area too often have been reactive rather than proactive. Senior German migration scholars such as Klaus Bade have long lamented this failure, observing in retrospect: "Ethno-national thinking and the jus sanguinis tradition had severely retarded the general course of development, leading to a quite belated acceptance of social reality on the levels of programmatic and legal declarations" (Bade 2001: 42). During the 1990s, for example, the government liberalized highly restrictive naturalization rules, but only after all other perceived alternatives had long since failed and continued inaction had become untenable. The sudden, rapid pace of reunification at the outset of the 1990s understandably caught the government unprepared, but it also offered an unprecedented opportunity to reassess its post-war experience in charting a positive, new direction for the future. Only in the late 1990s did the federal government fully begin to take up this challenge.

Starting with the reform of the FRG's citizenship law in 1999, the federal government has begun to come to terms with the challenges and opportunities and has begun to craft more proactive policy strategies—albeit all too slowly. This reassessment has led to rethinking the legal basis for immigrant incorporation and the fundamental terms in which both the challenges and rewards of immigration are understood. In a remarkably thoughtful and candid 2001 report, a well-balanced Independent Commission on Immigration, impaneled by the Social Democrats but chaired by a distinguished Christian Democrat, former Minister and Bundestag President Rita Süssmuth, opened its report by flatly declaring, "Germany needs immigrants." It pointed out that Germany has actually been an immigration land for a long time, but lacked a positive integration strategy to reap the full benefits from this fact. Shortly after the federal government submitted a draft of an immigration law for the first time in the FRG's history based largely on the Commission's report, Wolfgang Thierse (SPD), President of the Bundestag, recognized that, "after denying and ignoring it for decades, we have finally reached a consensus that Germany is a country of immigration and that we must bear the consequences of this" (Thierse 2001: 7).

A few years and many missteps later, the law that emerged bears little resemblance to the Commission's vision and insights. Although this new approach is a major step in the right direction, changing fifty years of history and ninety years of self-identification cannot be done overnight. In understanding the challenges that lay ahead, it is as important to stay mindful of how such problems as immigrant integration took their current shape, as it is to address pragmatically the realities of the present and the needs of the future. There is no better place to start exploring such issues than by reexamining the formulation of membership in the German constitutional order.

This study is divided into four main parts. Part 1 offers a critical reading of the FRG's constitution to distinguish five different, and sometimes conflicting, dimensions of membership. These aspects are an international dimension, a federalist dimension, a civic/political dimension, a social dimension, and an ethnonational dimension. Part 1 argues that any coherent migration policy must take all these different dimensions into account to comprehend the FRG's experience with migration and to assess reform alternatives. By distinguishing among these dimensions, it seeks to underscore the importance of an ethnonational perspective for understanding the character, barriers, and opportunities for membership in the FRG. But this section also seeks to emphasize that this perspective has hardly been the sole determinant of German membership policy and that the normative basis for a more inclusive policy already exists.

Part 2 provides a concise history of immigration to West Germany in the post–World War II era to emphasize the powerful impact of this history and to offer those new to German studies a solid foundation for understanding the FRG's current migration dilemmas. The section begins by tracing West Germany's experience in receiving millions of ethnic German refugees and expellees. To situate the FRG's approach to ethnic German minorities in Eastern Europe and Russia, this section also looks back at German diaspora politics and the problem of minority rights in Europe from the foundation of the Second Empire in 1871 through to the end of World War II. It then compares and contrasts the integration of refugees and expellees with West Germany's uncomfortable shift to a country of imported labor against the historical background of a much longer tradition. Paying particular attention to the development of German law, part 2 then moves to examine the implementation of the guestworker model. As this model became increasingly untenable during the 1970s, the FRG began to grapple with the problems of integration. However, the struggle to reform aliens and citizenship policy were repeatedly stymied by partisan politics, leaving the Federal Constitutional Court as the most influential agent of reform. By the late 1980s, the FRG was facing not only mounting integration challenges, but also rapidly rising numbers of asylum seekers and *Aussiedler*. The FRG's attempts to come to grips with migration and the growing diversity of its society had always been tied to its overarching goal to reunify the German homeland. This section concludes by looking at the achievement of this goal.

Part 3 discusses the importance of EU institutions in the development of the German migration regime in the post-reunification era. The section takes a dual approach by placing the development of German migration policy within the evolving framework of EU-level migration policy. The section illuminates the problems that Germany faced after the collapse of the Soviet Union and the implosion of Yugoslavia, which generated massive flows of both those claiming ethnic German status and refugees. It also highlights the FRG's critical stance toward the European Commission's attempts to "harmonize" migration policy and the FRG's resistance to adopt forward-thinking, long-term policy initiatives on migration and immigrant integration. This section concludes by examining Germany's demographic dilemma and the contributions immigration can make to mitigate this dilemma.

Part 4 addresses the migration issues facing Germany at the beginning of the twenty-first century, including the need for high-skilled labor and the challenge to integrate new and earlier generations of immigrants. This section begins by looking critically at the ethnonationalist rhetoric that reemerged around the concept of *Leitkultur*. The failure of this kind of culturally focused approach to come to grips with the integration and migration challenges facing the FRG becomes clear when the discussion turns to an examination of Germany's demographic problems and the bold report of the Independent Commission on Immigration. Unfortunately, many of the Commission's most promising reform proposals were sharply truncated in the making of the 2005 Migration Law. Whatever its shortcomings, however, the enactment of this law represents the end of an important phase in the FRG's long struggle to rethink its approach to migration and to develop a constructive policy basis for managing its rewards and costs. This section concludes by considering the ramifications of this new law for integration policy.

Part 1

Membership and
the Basic Law

The Basic Law of 1949 established the Federal Republic of Germany (FRG) as a liberal-democratic polity that is subject to the rule of law. While originally conceived as a provisional document, the framers intended this constitution to establish a supreme, authoritative set of norms for the new political and legal order they were seeking to construct. Because all policymaking is guided by normative considerations, we begin by examining some of these foundational principles and values to establish the framework for our analysis. This section uses the Basic Law as a starting point to investigate five fundamental dimensions of membership in the FRG: an international (or transnational) one grounded on universal human rights; a federal one that more fully reflects the complex character of German political traditions than any abstract notion of unitary national sovereignty; a civic/political one that distinguishes between citizens and foreign residents; a social one that provides collective insurance against individual risk; and an ethnonational one based on shared descent and cultural affinities. These dimensions express both complementary and conflicting membership norms. The ambiguous relationships among these norms reflect not only the particulars of German history, but also the multiple modes of membership that every modern liberal-democratic polity must confront. These norms have framed the debate over membership issues in the FRG, and have determined the constraints and alternatives available to public policymakers dealing with these issues.

Chapter 1

The International Dimension

The drafters of the Basic Law inserted their catalogue of fundamental rights at the beginning of their document rather than the end, as the authors of the Weimar Constitution had done, to signify its paramount importance. Article 1 of the Basic Law provides,

1) The dignity of man shall be inviolable. To respect and protect it shall be the duty of all state authority.
2) The German people therefore acknowledge inviolable and inalienable human rights as the basis of every community, of peace and of justice in the world.
3) The following basic rights shall bind the legislature, the executive and the judiciary as directly enforceable law.[1]

The wording of this Article bears a striking resemblance to the preambles in the United Nations Convention of 1945 and the Universal Declaration of Human Rights of 1948.[2] The Article establishes the principle of respect for human dignity as the highest constitutional value and anchors this principle on the recognition of universal human rights. Although the first two paragraphs are written as programmatic statements, the third makes them binding on all component parts of the federal government. Article 2 expands on the

1. A translation of the Basic Law text is contained in Hucko (1987: 194). Paragraph 3 rendered as amended by federal law of 19 March 1956.
2. The Charter's preamble begins, "We the people of the United Nations determined … to reaffirm faith in fundamental human rights, in the dignity and worth of the human person, in the equal rights of men and women and of nations large and small." The Declaration's preamble begins, "Whereas recognition of the inherent dignity and of equal and inalienable rights of all members of the human family is the foundation of freedom, justice and peace in the world." (Brownlie 1992: 3, 21). In framing their catalogue of rights, the authors of the Basic Law cited the Declaration as one of the sources for their work (Spevack 1997: 420–421).

meaning of its predecessor: "(1) Everyone shall have the right to the free development of his personality in so far as he does not violate the rights of others ... (2) Everyone shall have the right to life and to inviolability of his person. The liberty of the individual shall be inviolable" (Hucko 1987: 194). Both Articles can only be read as a repudiation of Hitler's National Socialism and all other particularistic ideologies that deny the equal dignity of every human being. By making it the cornerstone of their constitutional edifice, the framers set forth an explicit commitment to international human rights standards.

This interpretation is buttressed, in 1952, by the FRG's ratification of the European Convention on Human Rights (ECPHR), which came into force in 1953. As stated in its preamble, this convention "aims at securing the universal and effective recognition and observance of the Rights therein declared" (Brownlie 1992: 327). As the wording suggests, the norms set forth in the convention are at once both aspirational and formally binding as statements of principle. Article 1 declares that these norms apply not simply to the citizens of State Parties, but to "everyone" within the jurisdiction of a State Party (Brownlie 1992: 327). As a matter of law, the European Convention was clearly intended to be "subsidiary to national protection," that is, "a system of 'outer protection' for the traditional range of civil and political freedoms which, by and large, are already protected under the legal systems of the participating states" (Hannum 1992: 136). The Convention also established the first supranational mechanism of international human rights law through the creation of the European Commission of Human Rights and the European Court of Human Rights (ECHR). The latter's decisions are binding on the domestic courts of the signatory state parties, including the FRG. More recently, Protocol 11 to the Convention has given individuals, groups, and other nongovernmental organizations the right to apply directly to the ECHR.[3] Convention provisions specifically addressing the rights of immigrants were not adopted until Protocol 4.[4] Article 2 of this Protocol guarantees the right of free movement to "everyone lawfully settled within the territory" as well as the "freedom to choose his residence." The construal of these rights is subject to rather broad restriction as determined "by the public interest in a democratic society" (Brownlie 1992: 346–347).[5] Article 4 of this Protocol prohibited the collective expulsion of aliens. Article 1 of Protocol 7 of the Convention went a step farther in prohibiting the arbitrary

---

3. Protocol 11 (ETS no. 155) was opened for signature in 1994 and entered into force on 1 November 1998. For its text, see: http://www.echr.coe.int/NR/rdonlyres/F55E9400-69A0-4306-851C-7911B06AF9B0/0/P11ENReport.pdf (accessed 16 April 2009).

4. Protocol 4 (ETS no. 046) was opened for signature in 1963 and entered into force in 1968.

5. Under this Article, such restrictions may be justified "in the interests of national security or public safety, for the maintenance of 'ordre public', for the prevention of crime, for the protection of health and morals, or for the protection of the rights and freedoms of others."

expulsion of individual aliens without due process.[6] Over time, the ECHR developed the position that the European Convention on Human Rights had not merely the status of an international treaty, but also that of a "constitutional instrument of the European Public Order."[7] However, in its judgment of 14 October 2004, the German Federal Constitutional Court disagreed with this expansive interpretation of the Convention and its Protocols. It ascribed them the status of statutory law within the German national legal order, thereby subordinate to norms of the Basic Law.[8] The Court held that German judicial and administrative organs are obliged to observe the Convention, its Protocols and ECHR case law as a guide to interpreting the scope and content of domestic fundamental rights, but reserved to the German courts the competence for integrating ECHR case law into the domestic legal order.

In honoring its commitment to universal rights and mindful that the Nazi state had driven many German citizens into exile, the framers of the Basic Law included another Article that applied universally to anyone suffering political persecution irrespective of his or her ethnicity, national origin, gender, religion, or relationship to the FRG. The Article codified that "[p]ersons persecuted on political grounds shall enjoy the right of asylum."[9] This right gave foreigners an important claim of protection under West German constitutional law by reinforcing the international norms expressed in Article 1 of the Basic Law. It also paralleled the right of asylum recognized in Article 14 of the 1948 Universal Declaration on Human Rights. As we will discuss later in the text, the exercise of this constitutional right of asylum was restricted drastically through an amendment to the Basic Law in 1993.

The most extensive international dimension of membership in the Federal Republic has been the FRG's progressive integration into a supranational union of European states. Article 24 of the Basic Law authorizes "the Federation … by legislation [to] transfer sovereign powers to intergovernmental institutions" and to "consent to such limitations upon its rights of sovereignty as will bring about and secure a peaceful and lasting order in Europe and among

---

6. Article 1 provides, "1. An alien lawfully resident in the territory of a State shall not be expelled therefrom except in pursuance of a decision reached in accordance with law and shall be allowed: (a) to submit reasons against his expulsion, (b) to have his case reviewed, and (c) to be represented for these purposes before the competent authority or a person or persons designated by that authority. 2. "An alien may be expelled before the exercise of his rights under paragraph I.a, b and c of this Article, when such expulsion is necessary in the interest of public order or is grounded on reasons of national security" (Brownlie 1992: 352). Protocol 7 (ETS no. 117) was open for signature in 1984 and entered into force in 1988. The FRG has signed but not ratified this Protocol.

7. Case No. 40/1993/435/514, *Loizidou v. Turkey* [1995], ECR, para. 75.

8. BVerfG 111, 307, 2 BvR 1481/04.

9. Article 16(2) (see Hucko 1987: 200).

the nations of the world."[10] Consistent with this article, the FRG became a founding member of the European Coal and Steel Community (ECSC), of the European Economic Community (EEC), and of the European Atomic Energy Community (Euratom). The Treaty of Paris of 18 April 1951, which established the ECSC, also created the European Court of Justice (ECJ) to interpret the treaty and subsequent Community laws.[11] The Treaty of Rome of 25 March 1957 established the EEC and Euroatom. Together these founding acts created a set of supranational institutions to coordinate the construction and enforcement of a common market. The Treaty of Rome provided for the free movement of workers among Member States by 1970 and prohibited "any discrimination on grounds of nationality between workers of the Member States as regards employment, remuneration and other conditions of work and employment."[12] The rights of the worker as expressed in the treaty ensured the equality of all workers within the emergent European labor market, but it fell short of defining workers as European citizens by limiting their status to "functionally specific factors of production" (Joppke 2001: 48). In this regard, a worker's rights encompassed issues of entry into and residence in another EC (European Community) Member State.

Even though the language in the treaty was unequivocal about a worker's right to free movement, EC regulations and treaties failed to define precisely the definition of "worker" (Mancini 1992: 68). The ECJ clarified the matter in a 1986 ruling when it established that a worker is "any person performing for remuneration work the nature of which is not determined by himself for and under the control of another, regardless of the legal nature of the employment relationship" (quoted in Mancini 1992: 68).[13] In court cases leading up to the 1986 decision, au pairs and professional athletes had been included under the original conceptualization of the worker (Mancini 1992: 8–69).[14] Beyond a legal conceptualization of the worker, a precise definition also had important implications for the discussion about rights. Since workers enjoyed a privileged status as migrants within the EC area, clarifying the menu of workers'

10. (Hucko 1987: 203). Articles 23 and 24 were amended in 1992 to provide a broader constitutional foundation for this transfer.

11. The ECJ's innovations have played an important role in promoting European integration. For example, although not provided for in any treaty, the ECJ set forth its doctrine of direct effect of Community laws in Case 26/62, *Van Gend en Loos*, [1963] ECR 1. The ECJ first articulated its doctrine of the supremacy of Community law over conflicting domestic law of Member States in Case 6/64, *Costa v ENEL* [1964] ECR 585.

12. Article 48 (see Joppke 2001: 48; Rudden and Wyatt 1993: 28, 48).

13. The ECJ case referred to here is Case 66/85, *Lawrie-Blum v. Land Baden Württemberg,* [1986] ECR 2121.

14. The ECJ cases referred to here are, respectively, Case 118/75, *Watson and Belmann,* [1976] ECR 1185 and Case 13/76, *Donà v. Montero,* [1976] ECR 1333.

rights remained a matter of contention (Joppke 2001: 49, 51). The tension between the ECJ, in particular, and Member States about workers' rights centered on the Member States' insistence on protecting their authority to grant specific rights to their citizens and withhold others from non-citizen workers from other EC Member States (Joppke 2001: 49). Until the introduction of citizenship at the European level in the Maastricht Treaty, questions about workers' rights relating to economic welfare benefits such as equal access to education and social welfare benefits, including protections against immediate deportations, clouded the distinction between an EC worker and a Member State citizen (Joppke 2001: 50–52; Mancini 1992: 74–76).

The necessity to maintain this distinction lost importance when the Maastricht Treaty of 7 February 1992 established citizenship at the level of the European Union (EU) for "every person holding the nationality of a Member State."[15] Besides turning the EC worker into an EU citizen, this treaty gave EU citizens, who reside in a Member State of which they are not a national, the right to vote and stand for office in both municipal elections and European parliamentary elections.[16] The treaty also extended to EU citizens the right to petition the European Parliament on matters that involve their personal interests and that fall within the scope of EU jurisdiction.[17]

Building upon the work done at Maastricht, the 1997 Treaty of Amsterdam affirmed the status of fundamental human rights among the founding principles of the European Union.[18] In the wake of this affirmation, critics pointed out that the EU had yet to translate its rhetoric of human rights into a comprehensive, coordinated human rights policy with adequate institutional mechanisms to support it (Alston and Weiler 1999). At its 1999 meeting in Cologne, the European Council took the "view that, at the present stage of development of the European Union, the fundamental rights applicable at Union level should be consolidated in a Charter and thereby made more evident" (European Council 1999a). It pointed out the EU's obligation to respect these rights as specified by the European Court of Justice. "In order to make their overriding importance and relevance more visible to the Union's citizens," the Council prescribed that a body be established to draft such a Charter, composed of Heads of State and Government and of the President of the Commission, and that it

---

15. Article 8 (see Rudden and Wyatt 1993: 30). The 1997 Treaty of Amsterdam reconfirmed the status of an emerging EU citizenship without significantly strengthening it.

16. Article 8b (see Rudden and Wyatt 1993: 31).

17. Articles 8d and 138d (see Rudden and Wyatt 1993: 31, 118).

18. In its case law the ECJ had recognized fundamental rights as among these principles, and inferred the content of these rights from the ECPHR, its protocols, the European Social Charter and the constitutional traditions common to Member States. See, for example, 124 Case 36/75 *Rutili [1975]* ECR 1219; Case 44/79 *Hauer [1979]* ECR 3727.

include members of the European Parliament and national parliaments (European Council 1999a). Four months later at Tampere, the European Council agreed upon the practical arrangements for convening this body, which took the name "Convention" (European Council 1999b). After the Convention had finalized a draft text, the Presidents of the European Parliament, the Council, and the Commission adopted the Charter on behalf of their institutions at the European Council's meeting in December 2000 at Nice.

Like Germany's Basic Law, the Charter reaffirmed the universalistic character of the rights it recognized against the background of shared European "common values." As stated in its preamble, the Charter elaborated, "Conscious of its spiritual and moral heritage, the Union is founded on the indivisible, universal values of human dignity, freedom, equality and solidarity; it is based on the principles of democracy and the rule of law. It places the individual at the heart of its activities, by establishing the citizenship of the Union and by creating an area of freedom, security, and justice."[19] The reference to EU citizenship qualifies the preceding language emphasizing the centrality of the "individual" in this scheme of rights by narrowing the application to leave out even lawfully resident third-country nationals. Despite the growing willingness that the European Council had shown at its 1999 Tampere meeting to address precisely such questions, the Charter did little to strengthen recognition of the rights of aliens in the EU, and did not deal with the issue of access to citizenship.

The authors of the Charter had no mandate to introduce any new rights, but rather had been commissioned to combine "in a single text the civil, political, economic, and social rights hitherto laid down in a variety of international, European or national sources" (European Council 2000a). The Council left the actual legal status of the Charter to be determined later, so it had no independent force of its own. The Charter was designed to be complementary and consistent with the earlier European Convention on Human Rights. This complementarity is reflected in Article 52(3) and Article 53, which provide that those rights enumerated in the Charter corresponding with the rights covered in the Convention shall have the same "meaning and scope." At the same time, the Charter's provisions make clear that it applies only to EU law, and not to the law of Member States. Article 51 stipulates that they are "addressed to the institutions and bodies of the Union with due regard to the principle of subsidiarity and to the Member States on when they are implementing Union law."

At its 2001 meeting in Laeken, the European Council began considering seriously the question of whether the Charter should be incorporated into the basic treaty as well as whether the "European Community" should accede to the European Convention on Human Rights (European Council 2001). It set this question within the larger one about whether the EU should adopt a

---

19. See http://www.europarl.europa.eu/charter/pdf/text_en.pdf (accessed 16 April 2009).

constitution, and, mindful of the need for internal reform of the EU institutional framework brought to the fore by the prospect of enlargement, decided to create a Convention under the chairmanship of former French President Valéry Giscard d'Estaing. Like the Convention that had drafted the Charter, this one, the Convention on Europe's Future, was composed of fifteen representatives of the Heads of States and Governments of each Member State, thirty members of national parliaments, sixteen members of the European Parliament, and two Commission representatives. The resulting Convention on Europe's Future drafted a constitution for the EU,[20] which incorporated the Charter of Fundamental Rights. Giscard d'Estaing submitted the Convention's 200-page draft to the European Council at its 2003 meeting in Thessaloniki. The Council described the proposed constitution as a "good basis for starting [discussions] in the Intergovernmental Conference" (European Council 2003a), but Council approval of the Convention's much amended product did not occur until the waning moments of the Irish Presidency, a year after the Thessaloniki Council.

During the drafting and ratification process, the German government stood out as one of the strongest advocates for an EU constitution. In a speech at Humboldt University on 12 May 2000, German Foreign Minister Joschka Fischer (Green) outlined his personal vision of a federal system as the next step to complete European integration, which could be achieved through the adoption of a formal constitution. Likewise, in a speech before the European Parliament on 4 March 2001, German President Johannes Rau (SPD) called for transforming the EU into a "federation of nation-states" by means of a constitution. In May of that same year, Chancellor Gerhard Schröder (SPD) proposed his own plan for creating a federal system through constitutional reform (Pond 2001: 31–33). All of the major German political parties came out in support of the d'Estaing constitution. On 12 May 2005, the lower house of the German parliament voted to ratify the European constitution with 569 yes votes against 23 no votes and 2 abstentions. Two weeks later, the upper house also approved the constitution by a nearly unanimous vote. Although the issue was not subject to a popular referendum in Germany, a March 2005 Eurobarometer report indicated that 54 percent of the German electorate supported ratification, while only 17 percent opposed it (Leonenko 2006). Despite the German endorsement of the constitution, momentum behind its adoption quickly collapsed after voters in France and the Netherlands rejected it by substantial margins.

By the time Germany's Chancellor Angela Merkel (CDU) became EU Council President in January 2007, it was clear that no new effort would be undertaken to push through the adoption of a constitution. As an alternative path toward the same goals of structural reform, she made it a priority to achieve agreement

---

20. The European Constitution failed the referenda in France and the Netherlands in May 2005, blocking the constitution's enactment indefinitely.

on a new reform treaty. Her efforts proved successful. At a meeting in Berlin on March 23 to mark the fiftieth anniversary of the EU's founding, EU leaders issued the "Berlin Declaration," which expressed their intention to establish a new legal basis for the EU by 2009. At the EU Council's June meeting in Brussels, Merkel guided negotiations to an agreement over the basic form of a new treaty. On December 13, the 27 EU Heads of State and Government signed the Lisbon Treaty with the goal to ratify the treaty by the end of 2008. Although extremely complicated by potential ramifications that will require years to assess, the treaty is designed to streamline the EU's governing process to make it more efficient. Having learned from the failure of the proposed constitution, nearly all Member States planned to ratify the treaty in parliament rather than through popular referenda. Ireland was the lone exception to this ratification process, and on 13 June 2008, the Irish public voted against the treaty in a popular referendum by a vote of 53.4 to 46.6 percent (Lyall and Castle 2008). As of this writing, the repercussions of this defeat are unclear.

Unlike the proposed constitution, the treaty (assuming its main provisions are ratified in some form) will amend existing treaties rather than replace them. Nevertheless, the content of the Lisbon Treaty is almost identical to the defeated constitution. Among its significant structural reforms, the treaty would create the post of an EU President to run for two-and-a-half year terms with the possibility for a second term. This new position would replace the current system whereby EU Council Presidencies rotate between the Member States on a six-month basis. A new EU foreign relations representative would be created and hold the official title "EU High Representative of the Union for Foreign Affairs and Security Policy." Both the office of the EU President and the High Representative would be empowered to represent the EU abroad as a single, legal entity. The EU Commission would be reduced in size, which would eliminate the automatic right of each Member State to have its own Commissioner. Once the change takes effect, only two-thirds of Member States would be able to hold a Commission post at a time, but a rotation system will be defined in order to ensure fair representation of all EU Member States in the Commission over time. The treaty would also redistribute voting weights among Member States in the European Council. In that regard, it would introduce a double majority voting procedure on the majority of EU Commission proposals, which would allow measures to be adopted if they carry 55 percent of the vote, and if those states voting affirmatively represent 65 percent of the EU population. In addition, the treaty would expand the powers of the European Parliament and the European Court of Justice in areas such as justice and home affairs, while moving most policy areas from the decision rule of unanimity (providing all members with veto powers) to the qualified majority rule mentioned above. Finally, the treaty would make binding the Charter of Fundamental Rights, but, unlike the proposed constitution, the Charter is not part of the treaty text.

Chapter 2

The Federalist Dimension

The restrictions on the Federal Republic's external sovereignty and the openness of the Basic Law to transfer significant sovereign powers to supranational institutions have been only the most obvious expressions of the FRG's "semi-sovereign" character. As Peter Katzenstein has argued most influentially, this character has also been reflected in the FRG's internal organization of state power. In contrast to the traditional Hobbesian understanding of the sovereign as an absolute, indivisible, and monopolistic bearer of political authority, the internal sovereignty of the FRG is highly decentralized, with a strong system of checks and balances as well as a high degree of power sharing across levels of government. "It is implausible to view the West German state," Katzenstein observed in 1987, "as an actor that imposes its will on civil society" (1987: 372).[1] In place of this image, Katzenstein describes a paradox in which the "ability of the West German state to impose its objectives on other actors is ... weak. But because it has drawn so many 'private' actors into its political orbit, it is at the same time strong" (Katzenstein 1987: 372; see also Schmidt 2003: 44–46; Glaessner 1992). This paradox is explicable in that the very channels enabling social forces to influence policymaking also provide the means through which state norms, practices, and goals may be diffused effectively within civil society. Seen against the background of the failure of the Weimar Republic, the brutal Nazi dictatorship, and the military occupation of a defeated, divided, and devastated Germany, the creation of this system has proven to be a remarkably effective integration and democratization strategy.

Cooperative federalism is one of the three main "institutional nodes" that Katzenstein identifies as central to the semi-sovereign character of the FRG in

---

1. Our discussion here follows Simon Green's similar formulation of the analysis (Green 2004: 9–22).

its internal order. Article 20(1) of the Basic Law defines Germany as a "federal state," and Article 79(3) makes this core principle unalterable by constitutional amendment. The constitutional design of this federal system imposes a high degree of intergovernmental consultation, policy coordination, and legislative competence sharing. Article 74, for example, stipulates a long catalogue of legislative domains in which the *Länder* and federal governments exercise concurrent authority, though most legislation in practice is federal. As prescribed by Articles 82 through 85, the *Länder* governments are chiefly responsible for implementing federal legislation and collecting taxes. They also exercise primary functions in such areas as the administration of justice, the police, and the regulation of the media. The Bundesrat (Council of State Governments) guarantees the representation of particular territorial interests of the *Länder* at the federal level. All federal legislation that affects state competences and any constitutional amendment require Bundesrat approval. Federal revenue sharing helps to offset economic differences among the *Länder*. This revenue sharing takes two main forms: vertical payments from the federal government to the poorer states (as well as to compensate for some of the costs of administering federal law); and horizontal transfers from the richer states to the poorer ones. The accession of five new economically dependent *Länder* in 1990 has put significant strains on this revenue sharing arrangement.

This federal system has helped to promote the integration of diverse political interests and the stability of the FRG. For example, opposition parties who lose at the national level have the opportunity to gain ground in state elections. Success in state elections can translate into a party's majority in the Bundesrat, guaranteeing them an important voice in federal policy even if they are a minority party in the Bundestag. "This possibility," Manfred Schmidt has pointed out, "has major effects: it reduces the intensity of political struggles, eases the acceptance of defeat, allows for integrating the opposition party and their followers rather than alienating them from the polity, and is thus conducive to a high level of social cohesion" (2003: 241). This form of integration suggests that having institutional means of representation gives different groups a clear stake and voice rather than mere shared cultural affinity, which is an essential ingredient in building cooperation across contending interests and binding them together behind a common allegiance to the democratic system. It often requires contending political interests to negotiate with one another to achieve key objectives and thereby creates a (not insurmountable) bias in the system toward incrementalism in policymaking. It can also lead at times to policy fragmentation, drift, and stalemate (Renzsch 2002). For member constituencies of the FRG, the viability and attractiveness of this form of integration presupposes effective access to party structures as well as to being part of a voter constituency or well-funded interest group that the major parties seek to cultivate. At the same time, this manner of integration has made no guarantee of political harmony. Over the last decade, the degree of adversarial politics, party competition, and ideological conflict has intensified at both the federal and the state levels.

Where the Basic Law provides for a decentralized political system, observers have long emphasized the "densely organized" character of German civil society, through which members pursuing an extensive variety of sociocultural purposes and private interests have been able to find representation in the policy process (Conradt 2005: 146). Ranging considerably in their activities and scope, the number of associations in German civil society has been estimated to total 544,000 in recent years. Among these associations only a small share are organized as political interest groups, but their influence in the policy process can be considerable (Schmidt 2003: 160–161). "The dispersion of state power among competing institutions," Katzenstein observed prior to reunification, "contrasts sharply with the concentration of private power in large social groups" (1987: 15). Both business and labor interests, for example, are highly organized into large umbrella associations, such as the Confederation of German Employers' Associations, the Federation of German Industries, the German Federation of Civil Servants, the Federation of German Trade Unions, the German Farmers' Association, and the German Salaried Employees Union. There are also major semipublic institutions, such as social insurance funds and the Federal Labor Institute, that combine significant public and private functions.

The tight organization of private interests in such associations has frayed a bit in recent years, but they continue to provide important avenues of influence into the parties and the civil bureaucracy in many policy domains. Not surprisingly, non-nationals have always been marginalized in their access to these policy networks and modes of representation. Simon Green, who has explored most thoroughly the implications of this semi-sovereign policy framework for *Ausländerpolitik*, has commented recently that "direct representation of non-nationals has so far been fragmented, difficult and largely unsuccessful. Their membership in political parties remains possible but unusual, while unions have been slow to integrate their considerable foreign membership fully into their leadership structure. Other attempts to develop dedicated structures of interest representation have so far, gone little further than 'tokenism'" (Green 2003a: 18). The lack of representation has meant that non-nationals have been subjects of policy rather than active agents at the various bargaining tables across the German policy networks. For German public interest groups, such as churches and welfare organizations, addressing the specific needs and interests of non-nationals are only one set among many in their agendas. Foreigner associations tend to organize around ethnic or nationality lines that underscore their separation from the mainstream as well as from one another. Without the right to vote, non-EU nationals have had political representation at the local government level only through consultative committees (*Ausländerbeiräte*) that have been organized in many municipalities, but their influence has been modest at best (Green 2003a: 17–18).

The federal character of the FRG is also expressed in its citizenship law, which was based on the 1913 Imperial Citizenship Law (*Reichs- und Staatsangehörigkeitsgesetz*). The German Democratic Republic (GDR) also adopted this law as its own. This law "still determines the structure of the new German Staatsangehörigkeitsgesetz of 2000" (Gosewinkel 2002: 70). The 1913 law reaffirmed the principle of the 1870 Citizenship Act of the (short-lived) North German Confederation that had stipulated that federal citizenship derives from the possession of Member State citizenship and that only Member States are empowered to confer citizenship through naturalization (Fahrmeir 2000: 40–42). Within its federal system, the states have developed different immigrant integration policies, especially in the areas of education, culture, and naturalization. Bavaria alone, for example, has instituted a practice of bilingual education, while each state deals with the issue of religious instruction differently (Heckmann 2003: 55). With respect to naturalization, state policies range from liberal in Berlin and Hamburg to restrictive in Bavaria, Baden-Württemberg, North Rhine-Westphalia, and Bremen. Because the naturalization rules under federal law are fairly general and abstract, the Federal Ministry of the Interior can only prescribe administrative guidelines in agreement with the Interior Ministers of the states (Bultmann 2002).

"Federalism is not a static, but a dynamic notion," the historian Thomas Nipperdey observed in an essay surveying Germany's own long historical experience with a variety of federalist arrangements. "It describes not primarily a legally fixed condition, but rather a process, a movement, in which ever changing [tendencies toward] integration and disintegration and situations of equilibrium are formed between unity and diversity" (Nipperdey 1986: 60). The deep roots of this "process" in the German past reflect the fact that the manifold challenges of balancing cohesion and fragmentation have always been a predominant theme of German history. In this history, the idea of a unitary sovereign German nation-state has far more often been an aspiration, if that, than a reality (Sheehan 1981; Langewiesche 2000). The federalist system of the Basic Law is much more pronouncedly functionalist in design than Germany's previous experience with such systems. With notable exceptions, such as Bavaria, most of the *Länder* comprising the Federal Republic were not historically shaped autonomous states, but rather post-war creations that nevertheless reflect the existence of long established regional, economic, and cultural differences in Germany. To the extent that federalism is recognized as a means for accommodating diversity amidst unity, it implies a greater respect for differences among members than any abstract notion of collective democratic or shared ethnonational identity ever has. Viewed from the standpoint of integration strategy, federalizing may be understood as a "process by which a number of separate political units, be they states or other associations (churches, trade unions, parties, and so forth), enter into and develop arrangements for working out solutions together, that is to say, making joint decisions, and adopting joint policies on common problems" (Friedrich 1968: 177). For the FRG, the dispersion of power across a polycentric, multilevel system of governance has played an important integrative role for the diverse elements incorporated within it, but one fundamental prerequisite for incorporation has always been German nationality or, more recently and to a lesser extent, the nationality of another EU Member State.

Chapter 3

The Civic/Political Dimension

Modern societies qualify as "liberal" to the extent that they guarantee their members a menu of basic liberties, such as freedom of conscience, freedom of speech, and freedom of association. The formal membership status of individuals is determined by the packages of rights and duties they hold in these societies. Rights afford fundamental protections and create legal conditions for agency through which individuals are able to participate more fully in the social, civic, economic, and political life of a society. The recognition of rights as vested in individual persons is also a chief means through which respect for human dignity is accorded. Although integration into the EU has expanded the rights available to EU citizens in some significant ways, the rights guaranteed by its Member States remain the most important both to their nationals and to the non-nationals who reside there. Citizenship within the EU still derives from the citizenship conferred by Member States. The so-called "democratic deficit" in the EU reflects, among many other things, the weak authority of the European Parliament, but also the reality that Member States remain the primary locus of substantive political participation. As Christian Joppke has argued, since the World War II, there has been a trend among most Western liberal states toward the expansion of the rights conferred upon aliens. This trend has not been uniform and has been subject to reversals, but Joppke's larger point is that the main source of this trend has been the work of domestic courts (interpreting their own state's constitution) and legislatures (Joppke 2001).

The framers of the Basic Law incorporated a broad catalogue of fundamental rights. This catalogue divided these rights into two classes: general rights that apply to all persons and particular rights reserved for citizens. The first of these classes include the right to the inviolability of the person (Article 2); equality before the law for both men and women (Article 3); freedom of faith, conscience, and creed (Article 4); freedom of expression (Article 5); the establishment of private schools (Article 7); and the right to petition the government (Article 17). The second of these classes include the right to peaceful assembly (Article 8); freedom to form associations (Article 9); freedom of movement (Article 11);[1] freedom to choose one's trade and occupation (Article 12); the right to vote (Article 20); and equal eligibility for public office (Article 33).

Such a dichotomy between these two classes of rights is hardly distinctive to the FRG. All modern liberal states distinguish between rights applicable to persons generally, and thereby to both aliens and citizens, and rights that only citizens enjoy. The most obvious rationale for this distinction is that certain rights, such as voting, are necessary for citizens of a democratic polity to participate in the political process, but are not extended to aliens who have not committed themselves fully to the polity. Not all of the Basic Law's reserved rights, such as freedom of occupational vocation, can be justified on this basis. They are recognized as a simple entitlement of citizenship (Goerlich 1988: 47). Some commentators have argued persuasively that the Basic Law's dichotomy of rights affords aliens greater legal protection than do constitutions, such as the United States', that do not specify which guarantees apply only to citizens. The Basic Law's explicit dichotomy thereby "avoids the textual ambiguity that has plagued American debates over the constitutional rights of aliens" (Neuman 1990: 78–81).

Among its catalogue of general rights, the Basic Law also contains a broad nondiscrimination clause. Article 3(3) provides, "No one may be prejudiced or favoured because of one's sex, one's parentage, one's race, one's language, one's homeland and origin, one's faith, or one's religious or political opinions" (Hucko 1987: 194).[2] This provision is binding at every level of federal, state, and local government, but it has only an indirect effect on discrimination in transactions among private parties. The provision is designed primarily to give individuals rights of redress against their governmental bodies, but not against other private parties. Nigel Foster points out that Article 3 "is not an absolute right and seeks to establish equal treatment under the law rather a complete prohibition on any discrimination, however justified ... The concept of discrimination includes dissimilar treatment of like cases and similar but unfair treatment of dissimilar cases" (1993: 120). Among its criteria of nonpermissible discrimination grounds, Article 3 does not include the ground of alienage.

The status of citizen in the FRG is naturally much more secure and is vested with more rights than the status of alien, and citizenship within EU Member

---

1. This right has been extended to all persons after the FRG ratified Protocol 4 of the ECPHR. Article 2 of the ECPHR provides, "Everyone lawfully within the territory of a State shall, within that territory, have the right to liberty of movement and freedom to choose residence." Article 4 further stipulates, "Collective expulsion of aliens is prohibited" (Brownlie 1992: 346–347).

2. We have altered the translation, substituting "one's" for "his" as appears in the original.

States is the gateway to a slowly developing EU citizenship. The differences in legal status between citizen and alien mark a boundary between full and partial membership that can help codify an enduring relationship of inequality if alienage is not treated as a transitional stage toward citizenship. The Imperial Citizenship Law of 1913 that the FRG founders reaffirmed was based on the principle of descent (*jus sanguinis*), and treated the prospect of naturalization as an exception rather than a regular procedure.[3] Under this law, German citizenship was acquired through descent from a German citizen (originally the father, but subsequently amended to include the mother), by legitimatization, by adoption, or by naturalization. The founders sought to retain the Imperial Citizenship Law to preserve the FRG's claim as the sole legitimate representative of the German people as a whole (the *Volk*) and its claim to national unity despite the division between East and West. Since 1989, the rules governing naturalization have been considerably liberalized. Broadly, and as a first step in 1990, the rules were amended (as part of a comprehensive reform of the Aliens or Foreigners Law) to provide state officials with the discretionary authority to grant naturalization in the general case where certain minimum qualifications were met. This approach still treated naturalization on a case-by-case basis rather than as a means of collective incorporation. In 1993, as part of the constitutional compromise on asylum, a legally enforceable entitlement to naturalization was conferred.

This modification signified a basic change from a practice of treating naturalization as an exception to establishing it as a permanent rule. As part of this general trend toward seeing the acquisition of citizenship as an integrative measure, the federal government in 1999 enacted a major reform of the citizenship law by introducing the *jus soli* principle to supplement the traditional *jus sanguinis* basis for acquiring citizenship. Under this new law, a (legally resident) child of a foreign parent who has been a lawful and habitual resident of Germany for eight years acquires German citizenship. To discourage an increase in dual nationals, the law introduced the "options model" whereby children are required to choose which nationality (their German or their parent's foreign) to retain upon the completion of their eighteenth year.

---

3. Scholars are divided on whether the name of law should be translated as a "citizenship" or "nationality." In a technical sense, "nationality" may be closer to its actual meaning, because *Staatsangehörigkeit* in German literally means membership in a state, but because voting rights depend on possession of this membership we use the term "citizenship."

Chapter 4

The Social Dimension

In his famous essay on citizenship, the British sociologist T. H. Marshall sought to justify the provision of social rights by linking their development with earlier established civic and political rights (Marshall 1950). He emphasized the ways that social rights complement civic and political rights, and that the combination of all three is essential for any one cluster of rights to be fully effective. Marshall depicted the emergence of these three clusters in different historical epochs as part of a common evolution toward a fully realized model of modern social-democratic citizenship. He viewed the broad extension of shared social rights as a significant source of collective solidarity in alleviating class antagonisms and in giving all citizens a common framework of civic experience. But Marshall did not consider the issue of social rights with regard to the admission, terms of work, eligibility for entitlements, and integration of large numbers of migrants.

The extension of social rights to migrants inevitably magnifies the stakes involved in their admission and continued residence, because it directly involves questions about the distribution of collective material benefits within a polity. Broad public support for the distribution of collective resources depends on some shared sense of common identity as polity members. Even when it can be shown that aliens are on balance contributing more in taxes than they are receiving in public benefits or that their contributions are crucial to support domestic social insurance systems, their eligibility for benefits can nonetheless arouse enormous controversy. The denial of these benefits, however, can also have serious consequences both in exacerbating the exploitation of alien workers and in lowering compensation standards for the native labor force.

The Basic Law defines the FRG as a "social federal state."[1] The meaning of the term "social" is not elaborated elsewhere in the document, and the framers

---

1. Article 20 (see Hucko 1987: 201). This term is used again in Article 28(1), which provides, in part, that "The constitutional order in the *Länder* must conform to the principles of republican,

did not generally incorporate specific social rights into their catalogue of rights as had been done in the Weimar constitution.[2] But this lack of specification does not mean that the term is a mere constitutional adornment or wishful aspiration. The underlying principle of the social state recognizes that the government has a responsibility to promote the general welfare and to provide for individuals in need. As a constitutional norm, the principle does not prescribe the policies by which the government should promote social justice, but it does legitimize state intervention in the economy, the redress of gross inequalities, and the implementation of measures that promote public welfare measures. This norm is also grounded on the catalogue of rights contained in the Basic Law. Echoing Marshall here, one commentator has concluded that "the state is obliged by the mere existence of basic rights to bring about conditions, under which these basic rights may be enjoyed" (Kunig 1988: 197).

As the history of the FRG amply demonstrates, domestic welfare systems presuppose a logic of closure that confines the distribution of benefits to members, but these systems are situated within a global market economy that continually exposes them to the movement of foreign labor, capital, and goods. Distribution within a polity is limited to members, because the public resources available are scarce and is based normatively on a—perceived—shared obligation of cooperative assistance among members. The boundaries of modern welfare systems then are closed in principle but—at least—partially open in practice (Freeman 1986: 51–63; Faist 1994: 50–71; Kitschelt 1997: 257–273). This openness raises the immediate problem of determining criteria for distinguishing members from nonmembers and eligible beneficiaries from ineligible ones. Using citizenship as such a criterion suggests a simple straightforward rule, but often conflicts with the structure of domestic social insurance systems that base benefit eligibility on contributions from earnings and that may offend elementary notions of fairness.

The FRG has developed a social insurance system that seeks to allocate legally mandated entitlements to pensions, unemployment benefits, and health insurance according to contributions calculated from earnings levels. Insurance funds are segregated by occupational category. In addition, the Federal Republic has noncontributory welfare measures to help individuals on a temporary basis. In its classification of migrants for welfare policy purposes, the

---

democratic and social government based on the rule of law, within the meaning of the Basic Law" (Hucko 1987: 203).

2. Thus, for example, the Weimar Constitution imposed on the state affirmative duties with respect to supporting maternity and families with a large number of children (Article 119); public education (Articles 143–146); and social insurance, including health, unemployment, old age, and general infirmities (Articles 161, 163). The one exception in the Basic Law is a provision for maternity (Article 6).

FRG has also divided them by group (such as, refugee/expellee, guestworker, ethnic German, and asylum seeker) and has allocated different menus of rights and legal entitlements accordingly.

Under this system, the allocation of social rights depends much less on a distinction between citizen and alien than on residential status and economic contribution. This basis for distribution contradicts any simple formula that links civic, political, and social rights in a singular tripartite membership model (as Marshall had envisioned). It also means that the criterion for measuring a substantial membership connection to a modern liberal-democratic polity cannot be reduced to one set of links, such as any one designated legal status might imply. In light of the legal and cultural barriers to full membership, Friedrich Heckmann has recently observed that "the main feature of the German mode of immigrant integration has been and is the inclusion of migrants into the general welfare state and social policy system" (Heckmann 2003: 74).

Chapter 5

The Ethnonational Dimension

Alongside the international, federal, and social dimensions of membership, the Basic Law also affirms a strong national dimension. Depending upon how the latter is construed, the first three may stand sharply at odds with it. The international dimension attaches primacy to the dignity of the individual in a universal sense as a guiding constitutional norm. It also is reflected in the FRG's aspiration to be a partner in broader, supranational associations. Supported by a rich historical legacy, the federal dimension creates a strong basis for a polycentric understanding of both membership and sovereignty. The social dimension conditions benefits on territorial residence and contributions to the society rather than on nationality. In this sense, it uses non-ascriptive criteria to calculate the benefits and burdens of membership. By contrast, the national dimension emphasizes the qualities of collective identity that distinguish one people from another and are understood to be transmitted across generations. It presupposes nationality as the fundamental criterion for the exercise of political authority and the allocation of political rights on this basis. It has been used to justify highly illiberal naturalization policies and remains a barrier to fashioning a positive immigration policy.

The idea of national identity is an important source of civic solidarity in all modern liberal-democratic states and citizenship always has been used as a vehicle to exclude as much as to include. But the FRG's long history of restrictive naturalization policies and its conferral of automatic citizenship to those designated "Status German" reflect an ascriptive understanding of nationality as an ethnocultural community. This understanding has been a strong barrier to the integration of immigrants and conflicts with other dimensions of membership recognized by the Basic Law.

The problem with reconciling the particularistic character of the nation with commitments to international individual rights goes back to the birth of the modern nation-state in the French Revolution. As Hannah Arendt observed, the grim "paradox" of the classic eighteenth-century human rights statements, such as the US and French Declarations, is that they proclaimed these rights in principle to be universal, while in practice they implemented them only on the national basis of state citizenship. The Basic Law offers a case in point for Arendt's thesis, which is about the effects of the nationalization of rights that followed the French Revolution. By her account, this nationalization undercut the very premise of international human rights insofar as it implied "that only nationals could be citizens, only people of the same national origin could enjoy the full protection of legal institutions, that persons of different nationality needed some law of exception until or unless they were completely assimilated and divorced from their origin" (Arendt 1979: 275). Individuals learned that they effectively could claim their rights not by virtue of their common humanity, but only collectively as members of a particular nation that achieved sovereignty (Arendt 1979: 230–231). The association of the realization of rights with national self-determination was thereby forged. This identification of rights with nationality proved fatal to the whole program of universal rights, because, as Arendt wrote, "no human dignity is left if the individual owes his value only to the fact that he happens to be born a German or a Russian" (Arendt 1979: 235). The moral status of individuals is thereby displaced by the assertion of the transcendental value of the nation as a collective actor on the world stage. As the idea of the nation became identified with the model of the ethnically homogeneous national community, the membership status of minorities became increasingly problematic and vulnerable (Arendt 1979: 238, 261). The full consequences of these developments, Arendt argued, only became apparent in the first half of the twentieth century.

The original preamble to the Basic Law expressed the twin aspirations for the restoration of national unity and partnership in a "united Europe." Its framers intended their work to serve as a provisional constitution until national unity had been achieved and they included Article 146 with this end in mind. Their strong commitment to this goal was not surprising in the wake of military defeat, Allied occupation, and the emerging divisions between East and West Germany. However, the framers also wove into the Basic Law an understanding of FRG membership based on shared cultural and historical ties as privileged over ones based on actual residence and direct contributions to civic and economic life in the Federal Republic.

Although this ethnonational understanding of membership had definite exclusionary implications, the framers designed the Basic Law's citizenship provisions to be inclusive. For example, the framers stipulated in Article 116(2), "Former German citizens who, between 30 January 1933 and 8 May 1945, were deprived of their citizenship on political, racial, or religious grounds, and their descendants, shall be regranted German citizenship on application" (Hucko

1987: 255). This provision guaranteed the recovery of German citizenship to Jews and other minorities who had been stripped of it under the Third Reich. In approaching citizenship issues, the framers were then not thinking of foreign migrants yet to come, but rather of integrating the millions of refugee/expellee Germans who had already come or yet might come, of protecting the rights of citizens of the former Reich, and of denying a permanent division of Germany.

By trying to frame a definition of citizenship that would be broadly inclusive of Germans affected by the war, the framers invested the idea of Federal Republic citizenship with a distinctly ethnonational understanding of Germanness. Thus, Article 116(1) defines "a German within the meaning of the Basic Law [a]s a person who possesses German citizenship or who has been admitted to the territory of the Reich within the frontiers of 31 December 1937 as a refugee or expellee of German stock (*Volkszugehörigkeit*) or as the spouse or descendant of such person" (Hucko 1987: 255). The term *Volkszugehörigkeit* defies any direct translation into English. As a legal concept, it applies to persons who feel a self-identification with a people, an identification that is manifested through visible markers, such as language, customs, and other characteristics associated with defining ethnicity. In using this term as a basis for the recognition or conferral of FRG citizenship, the framers introduced ethnicity as an important—but not a necessary—criterion of citizenship into the Basic Law.

The deep tensions between the Basic Law's recognition of respect for individual dignity as a universal principle and the ascription of rights to German nationals came to the fore in the debate over alien suffrage in the 1980s. The presence of a large population of long-term, lawfully settled aliens combined with a highly restrictive naturalization policy had created a near permanent subclass of residents without voting rights that extended across generations. In 1989, the Social Democratic state governments of Schleswig-Holstein and Hamburg extended local voting rights to resident aliens who met certain conditions. In Schleswig-Holstein, this extension was confined to aliens who had resided in the FRG for at least five years and either had a residence permit or who were not legally required to have one. It further restricted this grant to those foreign nationals whose home countries recognized a reciprocal right for German nationals. In practice, this limited the local franchise to Danish, Swedish, Dutch, Irish, and Swiss citizens. By contrast, Hamburg granted local franchise to all foreign nationals who had lawfully resided in the FRG for at least eight years.

In response, the Christian Democratic Union (CDU)/Christian Social Union (CSU) faction of the Bundestag petitioned the Constitutional Court in Karlsruhe to strike down these measures.[1] Among their chief arguments,

---

1. The Constitutional Court delivered separate opinions in these two cases. The discussion here of the facts and positions of the parties is based on these two opinions. Judgment of 31 October 1990 (Schleswig-Holstein), 83 BverfGE 37–59; Judgment of 31 October 1990 (Hamburg), 83

the complainants contended that the extension of local alien suffrage violated the democratic principle of the Basic Law, specifically Articles 20 and 28. Under this principle, all state authority emanates from the people or nation (*Volk*), and the complainants interpreted this under the Basic Law as specifically denoting the *German* people. Resident aliens do not belong to this collective entity, whose membership is defined through citizenship. In their view, the bond of citizenship not only constitutes the state inwardly as an association, but also outwardly as an association among a plurality of similar state associations.

From the CDU/CSU's standpoint, citizenship is the indissoluble personal legal bond between the citizen and the state. The character of this bond incorporates the citizen into a shared "political community of fate" (*politische Schicksalsgemeinschaft*), because it is an inescapable bond for the individual citizen, who must therefore bear the consequences of any democratic decision made by the people. By contrast, aliens always have the option to return to their homelands. This understanding of a democratic people, they concluded, is consistent with both Germany's own democratic traditions as well as those of other Western states.[2]

In addition, the complainants argued that the granting of local voting rights to aliens violated the "homogeneity clause" (Article 28) of the Basic Law. This article provides:

> (1) The constitutional order in the *Länder* (states) must conform to the principles of republican, democratic and social government based on the rule of law, within the meaning of the Basic Law. In each of the *Länder*, counties (*Kreise*), and communes (*Gemeinden*), the people must be represented by a body chosen in general, direct, free, equal, and secret elections ... (2) The communes must be guaranteed the right to regulate on their own responsibility all the affairs of the local community within the limits of the law. The associations of communes (*Gemeindeverbände*) shall also have the right of self-government in accordance with the law and within the limits of the functions assigned to them by law. (Hucko 1987: 203–204)

In their interpretation of this article, the complainants contended that voting rights cannot be parceled out by different levels of government by applying different definitions of the term "people." Rather, the term "people" must be understood as a singular, monolithic unit from which all political authority derives, and out of which different subsets are represented at various levels of government in a federal system. Levels of government within the constitutional order have different functions and spheres of competence, but constitute

---

BverfGE 60–81 (*Entscheidungen des Bundesverfassungsgerichts* [Tübingen: J.C.B. Mohr, 1991]; abbreviated as "BverfGE").

2. 83 BverfGE 39–41.

a completely integrated whole. Moreover, extending political rights to resident aliens devalues the institution of citizenship as provided under the Basic Law.

Against these arguments, defenders of local alien suffrage contended in their briefs that the extension of franchise did not violate either the democratic principle or the concept of the people in Article 20.[3] They also rejected the view that the homogeneity clause of Article 28 barred this extension; nothing in it expressly prohibits the granting of suffrage to resident aliens at the local level. By their interpretation, the basis for the constitutional order is a democracy of discrete individuals, not a collective nation. From this basis, a "state people" is any collection of individuals subject over time to governmental authority. This expansive understanding of the democratic principle is especially appropriate given the growing share of the FRG's resident population that is non-German. Moreover, they argued, Article 20(2) merely stipulates that "all state authority emanates from the people" as a general principle without expressly referring to German nationals in particular.

Defenders of alien suffrage insisted that these arguments were even more compelling when applied to local voting rights. The basis for democratic legitimacy of local government in their view differs from that of the federal or state governments, because it has a different function, structure, and jurisdictional competence. Self-administration at the local level can only be effective if all residents affected by government policy are represented. The enfranchisement of aliens does not impair the democratic underpinnings of the constitutional order whose authority derives from the citizenry as a whole, because the federal and state governments still regulate the exercise of local government authority through their laws and administrative oversight. Adherence to the Basic Law's homogeneity clause does not require uniformity in the application of the democratic principle across all layers of government. Rather, different sources of democratic legitimacy may be appropriate for different forms of government. From this perspective then, enfranchising resident aliens augments, rather than compromises, the democratic basis for the FRG's political order as a whole.

Not persuaded by such arguments, the Federal Constitutional Court struck down the alien suffrage provisions in both Schleswig-Holstein and Hamburg. In explaining its grounds, the Court declared in its opinion on the Schleswig-Holstein case that the FRG is

> constituted in Article 20(1–3) of the Basic Law as a democratic, social and federal state within a rule-of-law/division of powers structure; and as a democratic state it cannot be imagined without the totality of persons, who are the bearer and subject of state authority, which is exercised through its organs. The totality of persons forms

3. 83 BverfGE 42–48.

the State-people from which all state authority emanates. Art. 20(2i) of the Basic Law therefore does not mean that the decisions of state authority must be legitimated by reference to those who are concerned; rather [it means that] state authority must have as its subject the Volk as a group of people who are linked into a unit.[4]

In the Court's view, the preamble and Article 146 of the Basic Law make it clear that the framers intended the state people of the FRG to be understood as the German people (or nation). Likewise, Article 116 shows that this quality of German nationality can be stretched to include those recognized as "Status German." Therefore, the Court concluded, "since according to the conception of the Basic Law the quality of being German is the connecting point for belonging to the *Volk* as the bearer of state authority, then this quality is also a precondition for voting rights, by exercising it, the people primarily exercise their state authority."[5]

According to the homogeneity clause of Article 28, the idea of the *Volk* is a unitary one that applies uniformly across all levels of government. Although this clause does permit some leeway, the introduction of alien suffrage by Schleswig-Holstein and Hamburg does not meet the minimum requirements of homogeneity. To address the problem of voting rights for long-settled aliens, the Court recommended liberalizing the naturalization rules. At the same time, it left open the prospect that the Basic Law could be amended to permit alien suffrage, which was then being contemplated by the European Community.

In explaining its decision, the Court's opinion embraced a holistic conception of a democratic national community while recognizing the need to reduce barriers to the admission of resident aliens into that community, and to adapt the constitutional order to further European integration. To articulate this holistic conception, the Court leaned heavily on the abstract language of political and legal theory, which favors logical over empirical analysis. Through this kind of sanitizing abstraction, the Court could avoid employing the organic metaphors of a discredited nationalist tradition while achieving the same effects of positing some sort of essentialized bond of shared national identity. The Court's emphasis on the collective basis for political rights encapsulated the dominant pole of the "paradox" that Arendt had traced back to the French Revolution. By vesting popular sovereignty in the nation, the Revolution had made the nation the supreme, collective agent in a moral, political, and cultural sense, but this inevitably undercut the universalistic individualism of the 1789 French Declaration of the Rights of Man and of the Citizen. Summing up this paradox, Arendt observed that "man had hardly appeared as a completely emancipated, completely isolated being who carried his dignity

---

4. 83 BverfGE 50–51.
5. 83 BverfGE 51.

within himself without reference to some larger encompassing order, when he disappeared again into a member of the people" (1979: 291). The Court's abstract language exemplifies how this disappearance could transpire through the reification of the nation and the demos, which then provided the rationale for denying even minimal political rights to lawfully settled non-nationals. By endorsing the liberalization of naturalization rules, the Court pointed the way through which legal reform could proceed, while preserving the unitary idea of a national community. Even with the Court's encouragement, it would be a long road before major steps were taken in this direction. The Court handed down its decisions in these two cases shortly after formal reunification of the two Germanys in 1990. Though the Court took no express account here of reunification, this event would remove much of the earlier pretext that had been invoked to justify a highly restrictive naturalization policy.

The issue of reconciling the Basic Law's national and supranational dimensions soon reappeared in the Constitutional Court's 1993 decision on the Maastricht Treaty. The Court determined that the Treaty did meet the constitutional requirements, but sought to strike a balance between the Basic Law's openness to supranational integration and its nationalist understanding of the democracy principle. In striking this balance, the Court emphasized that as presently constituted the EU was no more than an international "alliance of states," in which members retained their own independence and sovereignty. The Court also recognized that the EU is a work in progress that aspires to deeper integration; however, the Court set some limits or conditions based on its reading of one part of the democracy principle guaranteed in Article 38.[6]

The Court's analysis of the application of Article 38 began with the question of whether, by transferring competences to supranational institutions beyond the control of the German people, the Federal government had violated the principle that all political authority emanates from the people. The Court concluded that the Treaty did not contradict this principle, but emphasized the inadequacy of the democratic infrastructure within the EU. At present, the Court observed, the EU does not derive its democratic legitimacy from its own institutional modes of political representation. It obtains its strongest democratic validation only indirectly through the assent of the national parliaments of Member States. Until it develops the necessary infrastructure, such as through the growth of trans-European political parties, trade associations, and media, there will remain distinct limits to the extent that competences can be permitted to accrue to its governing bodies. The Court reserved for itself the

---

6. Article 38 of the Basic Law stipulates, "The deputies to the German Bundestag shall be elected in general, direct, free, equal, and secret elections. They shall be representatives of the whole people, not bound by orders and instructions, and shall be subject only to their own conscience" (Hucko 1987: 208).

authority to decide when these limits had been overstepped in matters pertaining to the German people.

The Court's ruling can be plausibly read in two ways, which are not necessarily mutually exclusive. On the one hand, it can be interpreted as an honest assessment of the so-called "democratic deficit" in the EU and as a prod to encourage its leaders to address this deficiency more resolutely before integration proceeded much farther. On the other hand, it can be read as misapplying the conditions of a state model of democratic governance to the supranational level of the EU and thereby creating an insurmountable barrier to decoupling nationality from membership at this level. The key passage from this opinion supporting this interpretation reads:

> If the peoples of individual States (at present) impart democratic legitimacy by means of national parliaments, then limits are imposed, by the principle of democracy, on an extension of the functions and powers of the European Communities. State authority in each of the States derives from the people of that State. The States require sufficient areas of significant responsibility of their own, areas in which the people of the State concerned may develop and express itself within a process of forming political will which it legitimates and controls in order to give legal expression to those matters which concern the people on a relatively homogeneous basis spiritually, socially, and politically.[7]

Here, in contrast to its earlier opinions in the Schleswig-Holstein and Hamburg cases, the Court applied the criterion of homogeneity, not as a formal principle of political organization, but as a character of a people as a unit. The prospect that the peoples of the EU will converge into one substantive whole that remotely satisfies these criteria seems dim and, if possible, probably not desirable. In suggesting this standard, the Court implied that there was no alternative between the EU conception of a mere alliance of independent sovereign states and becoming a megastate in its own right. These alternatives preclude recognizing the EU as a supranational framework that is predicated on the diversity of the individuals and groups that compose it, not as unitary state peoples, but as subscribers to a common set of political values, aspirations, and trans-European loyalties. It thereby can provide a different basis for commonality, cooperation, and the guarantee of individual rights that is independent of nationality and the collectivized concepts of state will.

---

7. Judgment of 12 October 1993 (Maastricht), BVerfG 89 BverfGE 186.

Chapter 6

Debating Concepts of
National Membership

Policy debates over the reception and the integration of immigrants are often driven less by disputes over "facts" than by rival conceptions of membership. Assumptions behind these conceptions determine how the facts are weighed and sorted. Discussions about national identity are often one of the clearest places to see these assumptions expressed in issues over the incorporation of newcomers, which invariably implicate different national self-understandings. To appreciate the significance of such assumptions in policy debates, we must consider carefully how national identity arguments are made and used in them. Here, we will focus on one of the most frequently used arguments, whose influence made it possible to avoid the concrete realities of immigration for a key period in the 1980s and 1990s. In considering these arguments, we will begin by examining Kay Hailbronner's use of them, because he has long been a preeminent German scholar of migration law and policy and, during the period in question, a close adviser of the CDU/CSU-led German federal government. Notably, Hailbronner was also appointed a member of the Independent Commission on Immigration established by the Social Democratic Party (SPD)/Green coalition government.

"The rationale of German naturalization law and policy," Hailbronner has written, "can be understood only in historical context" (1989: 72). From this context, the fundamental outlines of the German national self-understanding have emerged to guide policy formulation in the present. "The German idea of nationhood," he explained,

> is basically not a political one but a cultural, linguistic, and ethnic one. For most of its history, it has been politically fragmented ... In the eighteenth and nineteenth century, political fragmentation led Germans to think of their nation not as a political unit

but as a cultural, linguistic, and ethnic unit. This traditional ethnocultural element remains alive today, reinforced by the postwar division of Germany … Citizenship law and naturalization policy reflect in part this romantic understanding of nation-hood as ethnic and cultural community—an understanding enshrined in certain provisions of the Basic Law. (Hailbronner 1989: 74)

Hailbronner is clearly correct in finding this conception of German national identity contained "in certain provisions of the Basic Law." But here one must pause to ask, what about the other provisions that unequivocally base the German constitutional order on respect for the inviolability of human dignity and on an explicit recognition of universal human rights? How much weight do these norms bear as a moral standard against which policy should be held accountable? Hailbronner allows little place for moral norms in deciding such matters of policy. "'Moral' claims to citizenship," he explains, "… are generally inappropriate. There are no moral and therefore generally applicable criteria in judging a nation's citizenship policy apart from the principle forbidding a state to deprive a citizen arbitrarily of his citizenship" (Hailbronner 1989: 74–75). By reading the Basic Law this way, its ethnonational norms do provide a justification for a highly restrictive citizenship policy, while its universalistic, liberal-democratic norms are simply ignored.

Despite his explicit reference to the importance of historical context, Hail-bronner glosses over the long historical experience that German governments have had with systems of imported foreign labor. From his extensive research into this experience, the German historian Ulrich Herbert has concluded that "the history of dealing with foreign nationals in this country has been chiefly a history of efforts to prevent the permanent settlement of foreigners and to define and regulate their stay as *temporary*—solely for one's own benefit, based more on *Volkstum*—political or economic criteria, depending on the state of the economy. The effects of this tradition have been deeply ingrained in the imagination and mentality of the West German population" (1990: 257). Hailbronner's explication of the rationale for German policy was clearly used to justify what was being done until the late 1990s, rather than to consider what else could (or should) be done in light of the actual circumstances. As a result, Germany found itself completely unprepared to deal with an unsus-tainable reality on the ground, let alone to prepare for a future of more, rather than less, immigration. In his strident defense of the ethnonational model of membership, Hailbronner provided the intellectual ammunition for Ger-man government officials to deflect growing criticism from "North American" analysts who questioned the wisdom of the FRG's restrictive naturalization policies. Hailbronner dismissed such criticisms as coming from persons liv-ing in "nations composed of immigrants from a variety of cultures, [who] have conceptions of citizenship differing sharply from those prevailing on the Continent" (Hailbronner 1989: 72, 75). In effect, by positing that historical contexts—German and presumably European—are determinative for understanding the nuances of German policy and the FRG's experience with migration, Hailbronner's work provided comfort to political and social actors who resisted change and were, thus, blind to the building body of evidence of growing convergence in migration policies as well as citizenship policies among Western liberal-democratic states on both sides of the Atlantic.[1]

How should the dichotomy between ethnonational communities and "immigration" societies be considered from a normative standpoint as a policy rationale? In an essay exploring different dimensions of the German national self-understanding, the sociologist M. Rainer Lepsius, for example, sharply contrasts the differences between an immigration land and an ethnonational community with respect to their formation, bonds of allegiance, social composition, and political development (Lepsius 1985: 43–64). A state whose national self-understanding is based on an ethnonational identity, he contends, derives its bonds of allegiance from a myth of common descent and a shared sense of common language and other cultural attributes. The formation of an ethnonational community is a "prepolitical" phenomenon, because it precedes in time any eventual achievement of statehood. The claim of ethnic unity provides the basis of legitimacy for such a community's assertion of statehood, and shared ethnicity becomes the fundamental criterion for political membership in the state. Their ties of common ethnicity bind members of such a state more than their devotion to shared political principles or ideological creeds. Indeed, he observes, *Volk* nations can be "indifferent" to the form of political constitution the state assumes, and place their collective ethnic interests over respect for individual rights. The idea of a *Volk* nation, he concludes, "implies a latent potential for degrading other peoples as inferior" (Lepsius 1985: 51; see also Wehler 1995: 952–953).

By contrast, countries of immigration, Lepsius argues, can only achieve unity through their collective allegiances to shared political principles and ideological creeds. "As regards immigration societies, like the United States," he explains, "the idea of the folk nation cannot even pretend to be responsible for the formation of the national state. The concrete experience of ethnic heterogeneity requires criteria for classificatory and normative self-legitimation that are other than ethnic" (Lepsius 1985: 49). Immigration societies, he argues, are founded on a political basis that is anchored in a shared commitment to individual rights, general civic equality, and a common volitional creed.

1. Thus, for example, James F. Hollifield concludes his study, finding "considerable evidence of a convergence of immigration and refugee policies in Western Europe and the United States, despite important cultural and institutional differences" (1992: 232). See, more recently, the conclusions that Patrick Weil draws from comparative survey of the nationality laws of twenty-five different states (Weil 2001).

Belonging to a nation conceived in such political terms, he concludes, makes membership independent of shared ethnicity. The people are bound together as a "nation of citizens," whose ideals are embodied in such documents as the US Declaration of Independence and Bill of Rights.

Drawing sharp distinctions between societies that operate with templates of a *Volk* nation, on the one hand, and an "immigration land," on the other hand, inhibits understanding because the realities were never so simple.[2] Until recently, Germany has been the most prominent example within the EU of a state whose migration and citizenship policies have been strongly shaped by a community based on a descent (*Abstammungsgemeinschaft*) type of national self-understanding. Moreover, as the French sociologist Dominique Schnapper has observed, "any national construction is elaborated from ethnic elements which its strictly national institutions later operate to reinforce" (Schnapper 1998: 63; see also A. Smith 1998: 125–127, 210–213). In the case of the United States, restrictive, exclusionary categories of membership—such as those often associated with a "*Volk* nation" understanding—historically have deeply informed its citizenship policies.[3] In the German case, the notion of a *Volk* nation as a distinguishable, continuing entity historically traceable through time is a myth that masks a much more complex, multiform past.[4] When used only to denote linguistic boundaries, the applicability of this idea is still highly problematic (Sheehan 1989: 4). "Although the German national movement in the nineteenth century soon aimed at political unification," the historian Dieter Gosewinkel has observed, "the concept of belonging to the nation was initially based principally on diversity of cultural and ethnic criteria of adherence" (Gosewinkel 2001b: 23). Moreover, given the confederal structure of German politics of this era and the fact that both Prussia and Austria were multinational states, an ethno-national idea of German identity was more a threat than a means to consolidate

---

2. Lepsius himself recognizes this point. He does not treat a particular variant of ethnonational solidarity as the representative expression of the modern German self-understanding, but rather as one dimension of it. In the FRG (as elsewhere), this dimension persists alongside others. As Lepsius explains, "we find that the idea of the nation of citizens therefore rests on predemocratic political socialization processes which have already developed an historically formed idea of national solidarity" (Lepsius 1985: 60).

3. The pervasive impact of this influence on citizenship policy has been exhaustively recounted in R. Smith (1997). For his reflections on the cogency of this book's themes for public policy issues today, see R. Smith (1998). See also here Dittgen (1998: 256–285).

4. In his study of German citizenship from the early nineteenth century to the creation of the FRG, Gosewinkel concludes, "A strong assimilationist-skepticism, ethnic-cultural base line is characteristic for German citizenship law. The development of this basic idea occurs, however, much later, is much more defensive and less dominant than it has been perceived so far. This basic line is not a natural, quasi-genetic constant of the German nation, but rather was to a decisive extent dependent upon a specific political constellation of [factors affecting] state instability" (Gosewinkel 2001a: 433).

state citizenship. Even Rogers Brubaker, who has advanced an influential argument for the continuity of a Romantic "idiom" in the modern German national self-understanding from its origins in the wars of liberation against Napoleon, has acknowledged that "German citizenship law developed without reference to German ethnocultural nationality in Prussia and other German states in the first half of the nineteenth century" (Brubaker 1992: 51).

To recognize that all modern nation-states have some mixture of civic and ethnic dimensions of membership is not to deny the significance of national differences among states. Such differences can play a significant role in shaping the climate for the reception and integration of immigrants. However, it does underscore the problem in invoking any specific national self-understanding as a basis for justifying a particular policy agenda. By what criteria do we privilege one over another? Even if it could be empirically demonstrated that a majority shares a common national self-understanding, it remains at best unclear why that in itself should be a decisive consideration. Consider, for example, the case of the white majority in the US South during the 1950s. It appeared to share a broad consensus in favor of segregation and the denial of equal rights to their fellow black citizens on the grounds that the existing arrangement was fundamental to their heritage and to the structure of their way of life. Should that definition of collective identity have been regarded as decisive in determining membership policy? Likewise, twentieth-century European history is replete with examples of nationalist groups appealing to some version of a majority culture to justify oppression, expulsion, persecution, and mass murder of various minorities (Naimark 2001). Unless one is prepared to defend such cases, one simply cannot invoke collective national identity as some sort of higher guiding norm for justifying membership policies. If one is not prepared to do so, then we are forced back to the problem of specifying a set of membership norms that are distinct from any particular national self-understanding or even a specific democratic expression of the majority's will.

But times change and politics has a tendency to "facilitate" the reconsideration of the most deeply held views. In an essay published in 2002, Kay Hailbronner acknowledged that the "basis of German nationality can no longer be seen in the attachment to the idea of the nation with a homogeneous cultural identity, primarily transferred by descent" (Hailbronner 2002: 130). This statement reflects a significant evolution in his views on German national identity as set forth in his 1989 essay. Similarly, he has come to advocate a much more tolerant approach to dual nationality as well (Martin and Hailbronner 2002). This evolution in Hailbronner's thinking underscores just how arbitrary national character arguments tend to be when invoked in immigration and integration debates. Is he really suggesting that in a mere decade the basic national self-understanding in the FRG has fundamentally altered? Or, as seems more likely, is it the case that his perception of the problem of immigration in the FRG has changed, and from this new perspective he perceives the character of national identity substantially different in order to reach a more constructive accommodation with that reality?

Whatever the case, the change exemplified by Hailbronner is indicative of a larger shift in the official government position on the issues of immigration and citizenship that occurred during the second half of the 1990s (Heckmann 2003: 55–56). However, if this shift is going to move beyond a mere grudging admission of contemporary demographic reality into a positive embrace of the pluralistic dimensions of the German past and future, then the myths of an older "homogeneous" model of nationhood need to be squarely confronted. This kind of reexamination requires taking into account the full spectrum of migrants that have entered the FRG since the end of World War II, and not simply those migrants who were officially designated as "foreigners" or "aliens" at the time they entered.

Recent reform of the citizenship law, the adoption of a modest immigration law in 2004, and the subsequent policy changes in Germany's posture on immigration in 2007 represent important steps toward creating a more positive climate for immigrants. However, it is important that the legacy of decades of officially fostered restriction, denial, and marginalization is not overlooked because changing long-set habits, expectations, and attitudes requires a more profound transformation than any legislation can immediately effect. Consider, for example, Hailbronner's conclusion from more than a decade of reflection: "The fact that Germany has become a *de facto* country of immigration does not necessarily argue in favour of changing its basic rules as to who should be admitted to German citizenship ... One may object that the requirement of being born in Germany in connection with residence rights of parents should be sufficient to indicate integration. Recent experience, however, shows that this assumption is not always correct. An increasing number of foreigners are deliberately rejecting any attempt to integrate into German society" (Hailbronner 2002: 130–131).

On its face, Hailbronner's last point appears to have some merit. In fact, his concern that many immigrants choose not to become assimilated into receiving societies and choose to retain many more of the customs and connections to their countries of origin than they used to is now a phenomenon that is found throughout the world. This new reality is of concern to some conservative analysts and politicians. The way that Hailbronner constructs his argument, however, once again aids those who seek to blame immigrants for policy mistakes. These mistakes have come out of a stubborn society's unwillingness to appreciate how its attitudes and the government policies that reflected them nurtured a generation of immigrants that have had to look to other institutions to find the acceptance and protection that the German government and much of German society had aggressively withheld for so long. Hailbronner's writings thus abet a point of view that, while accepting of some of the "facts on the ground," nonetheless continues to gloss over a critical issue. Namely, that it is the behavior of the German state and society that merits closer—much closer—examination in the attempt to explain the behavior of foreigners "who are *deliberately* rejecting *any* attempt to integrate" (Hailbronner 2002: 131).

In trying to understand better the reasons so many immigrants in Germany and elsewhere in Europe appear to resist assimilation, one must confront two fundamental realities. First, the integration of immigrants into host societies is a long-term process that often spans more than a generation. Hence, "recent experience" is simply too narrow a time frame to reach any clear conclusions about the process now taking place in Germany and elsewhere. Second, it ignores what anthropologist Andrea Klimt has described in her ongoing study of Portuguese residents in Germany as the "negative baggage of history as well as the expectation of assimilation and suppression of cultural difference" that "German citizenship still carried" even after the 1999 reform (Klimt 2002: 136). If this history of marginalization is ignored, it becomes all too easy to overlook continuing barriers to integration within the host society and to attribute the immigrants' "sense of protracted liminality as they lived and worked in a country that resolutely rejected the incorporation of non-ethnic Germans into the national polity" as a simple matter of volitional choice to reject the new options available to them (Klimt 2002: 117).

Chapter 7

Integration, National Identity, and the Quest for Homogeneity

The challenge of integration has been a continuous issue throughout the history of the Federal Republic of Germany. This challenge has taken on a myriad of forms: from the incorporation of the refugees and expellees in the 1950s, through the unification of the two German states, to the FRG's active partnership in building an integrative European state system. This challenge has been no less fundamental or enduring where the FRG has been least successful in meeting it, namely, with respect to immigration. Its defensive approach to immigration—as a perceived threat to national cohesion and to the integration of foreigners as a one-sided process of assimilation—is closely tied to an ideal of national homogeneity. Of course, this ideal is not specifically German. The drive to homogenize populations has long been considered fundamental as a generic attribute to the modern state-building process. The republican tradition, as exemplified in both France and the United States, has developed its own models of national homogeneity (Smith 1997: 83–85; Lefebvre 2003).

Here, we will examine the German variant to argue that the anti-pluralism of this variant has not provided an effective basis for promoting national integration and has lent itself to extreme applications. The ideal assumes an abstract, essentialized definition of national identity, and thereby obscures the degree to which national identities are the product of negotiation, contestation, and revision. It sharpens boundaries between inclusion and exclusion, making it more difficult to find middle ground for the accommodation of differences within a shared polity. By very selectively examining the history of this variant, we will concentrate on the era in which this ideal became ascendant in shaping state policy toward integration, citizenship, and immigration; namely, in the Second German Empire (1871–1918).

To render homogeneous is "to unite into a single whole of uniform composition."[1] It is used in mathematics to denote terms of the same kind or dimension. When applied to people and their cultures, it may be best understood as a kind of Weberian ideal type that abstracts and accentuates those characteristics of a population most consonant with state objectives and categories of measurement (Scott 1998: 1–8, 32). The drive to homogenize populations has long been understood to be a generic feature of the state-building process (see Tilly 1975: 43–44, 77–79; 1992: 106–107, 115–117; McNeill 1986: 33–56, 84–85; Hechter 2000: 56–67). This process entails the construction of a common national identity from above. As the historian John Breuilly has observed of this construction, "the identity of the nation will be related to 'tradition' and to existing cultural practices, but the decisions as to what is relevant and how it should be used in establishing the national identity will rest with the state. In this way, nationalism becomes purely arbitrary" (Breuilly 1994: 390; see also Hobsbawm 1994: 10–11).

The drive for national homogeneity in the state-building process creates a powerful structural bias against any accommodation of minorities within national cultures. Hannah Arendt examined this problem in her critique of France's 1789 Declaration of the Rights of Man and of the Citizen. She argued that vesting absolute sovereignty in the nation and making the nation-state the supreme guarantor of individual rights makes the presence of national minorities anomalous and leaves them exceedingly vulnerable to the loss of any legal protection. Her critique demonstrates the importance of the perspective from which we frame the issue of minorities, namely, whether we see it from the standpoint of the state's requirements for national integration or from the standpoint of the homeless minorities caught in a modern international system of increasingly exclusivist nation-states. As she expounds upon in her analysis of inter-war Eastern Europe, for Arendt it is the horrible mismatch between the homogeneous nation-state model and the stubborn reality of human cultural multiplicity that helps to generate many of modernity's political pathologies. The more extreme the measures that a state may use to solve its integration problems domestically can generate enormous externalities, such as massive refugee flows or the spread of violence across state borders, which can be destabilizing not only for only neighboring states, but for the international system as a whole (Arendt 1979: 267–302).

Likewise, in his study of ethnic cleansing in twentieth-century Europe, Norman Naimark points to the "modern sovereign state's inability to tolerate large minorities within its borders." Drawing on the work of Zygmunt Bauman, he observes that the modern state "insists on identifying ethnic groups and concretizing difference and otherness with the goal of banishing it (Naimark 2001:

---

1. *Oxford English Dictionary*, 2nd ed., s.v. "Homogenize."

8; Bauman 1989: 61–62). In an essay emphasizing the historically problematic relationship between political democratization and ethnic homogenization in Germany and East Central Europe, Philipp Ther has sought to show how state policy aimed at political democratization has obstructed and corrupted efforts to realize ethnic homogenization, pointing out that "the measures necessary to substantially accelerate the assimilation of an ethnically diverse population are incompatible with a democratic system and a state that respects the rule of law" (Ther 2005: 90–91). The structural bias of modern nation-states against minorities does not inevitably lead to systematic discrimination, forced assimilation, expulsion, and massive refugee flows, but it does help to explain how such practices so often accompany the modern state-building process (see also Zolberg 1985).

Heather Rae has categorized such extreme national integration strategies as forms of "pathological homogenization," which "state-builders have employed to signify the unity of their state and the legitimacy of their authority through the creation of an ostensibly unified population" (Rae 2002: 5). In explaining why states resort to these strategies, she emphasizes the pivotal role of political elites who make the critical choices in defining the national identity of their state in either exclusive or inclusive terms.[2] State elites do not construct these collective identities out of thin air, but rather selectively draw upon the cultural symbols and national discourses of the majority whose support they seek to win by stigmatizing particular minorities. In advancing this argument, Rae examines a series of case studies extending from early modern Spain and France to the Armenian genocide during World War I, and, more recently, to the divisions of Yugoslavia and Czechoslovakia. She does not include any German examples among the case studies she explores to advance her argument. This omission underscores her point that such strategies are not the outgrowth of any particular national culture or even late nineteenth-century nationalism. To the contrary, Rae argues that such strategies are an extreme expression of a more generic state-building process and have been used selectively by elites, especially under conditions in which state authority was weak, "to construct the bounded political community of the modern state as an exclusive moral community from which outsiders must be expelled" (Rae 2002: 3, 41, 305; see also

---

2. Similarly, Naimark concludes from his study, "Although the modern state and integral nationalism have [been] critical to ethnic cleansing in this century, political elite nevertheless bear the major responsibility for its manifestations. In competing for political power, they have exploited the appeal of nationalism to large groups of resentful citizens in the dominant ethnic population. Using the power of the state, the media, and their political parties, national leaders have manipulated distrust of the 'other' and purposefully revived and distorted ethnic tensions, sometimes long-buried, sometimes closer to the surface. They have initiated campaigns of ethnic cleansing by their orders and intimations; they have held the power to stop them if they wished, and they did not" (Naimark 2001: 10).

Snyder 2000: 45–69). This kind of weak central authority is often the hallmark of new nation-states, where the task of consolidating a political normative order and promoting a shared conception of national membership is also likely to seem most acute (see also Geertz: 259–276, 306–310; Brubaker 1996: 79–106).

The second German Empire offers a case in point. Prussian Minister President Otto von Bismarck established the Empire through a series of successful military wars against Denmark in 1864, against Austria and her German allies[3] in 1866, and finally against France in 1870. "After a unified [German] state was achieved," Hans Ulrich Wehler has observed, "the 'wars for [national] unity' would be carried out as 'internal campaigns' with the goal to compel internal homogeneity" (1995: 953). The new empire's federal constitution rested on a compact among sovereign Member States, who retained considerable powers within their own jurisdictions. While the empire established a German nation-state, it excluded some significant German populations, such as the Austrians, and included a small share of national minorities in its border regions, most notably the French-speaking populations of Alsace-Lorraine, the Danish of Schleswig-Holstein, and the Polish in Prussia's eastern provinces. Comprising more than half of the Empire's population and territory, Prussia was by far the dominant state. Bismarck became Imperial Chancellor, while retaining his post as Minister President of Prussia. The Prussian King William I became the German Emperor.

The most pronounced divisions in the Empire existed between German Protestants and Catholics. "Few lines of division so clearly cut to the quick of people's identities," Helmut Walser Smith has observed, "so self-evidently defined their cultural horizons, and so deeply determined their political loyalties as the line that separated the two major religious groups" (Smith 1995: 13; see also Gross 2004: 246). Catholics constituted approximately one-third of the Empire's population, while Protestants comprised, roughly, two-thirds. The liberal party representatives in the new Empire saw themselves as the enlightened representatives of the Protestant majority. Liberals, as Thomas Nipperdey has observed, were committed to a "unitary (and modern) national culture on the basis of a national-civil religion, to homogeneity of the nation against such profound pluralisms as those of religion" (Nipperdey 1992: 254). The immediate achievement of national unity and the introduction of universal male suffrage magnified tensions and conflicts across this religious divide rather than diminished them. The introduction of universal male suffrage helped not only to politicize these fault lines, but enabled opponents of the government, including regionally based national minority protest parties, to mount resistance through the election and parliamentary process. It also opened the door to new forms of mass political mobilization (Nipperdey 1992: 323).

---

3. Baden, Württemberg, Bavaria, Saxony, Hesse, and Hanover had all supported Austria's side against Prussia.

Waged as a "battle of culture" (*Kulturkampf*), Imperial Chancellor Otto von Bismarck and his (then) liberal allies launched a campaign in the 1870s to consolidate national unity and marginalize the (perceived) retrograde Catholic element. The suspicions that Bismarck and his liberal allies harbored against the Catholic minority as an internal threat to the Empire centered on questions about the inferiority of Catholic educational backgrounds, their social and economic backwardness, their subservience to local religious authorities, and their divided loyalties toward the Empire and toward a foreign power represented in the Papacy (Nipperdey 1990: 428–467). The liberal conception of the *Kulturkampf* reflected a "highly Manichaean view of the world." In explaining this 'view,' David Blackbourn has pointed out that "liberal discourse on the subject of Catholics, was organized around a set of metaphors (darkness/lightness, flood/canalization, stagnation/progress" (1987: 148). For his part, Bismarck branded German Catholics as "enemies of the Empire" (*Reichsfeinde*), an epithet he also applied to non-German nationalities and Social Democrats within the Empire.[4]

The first legislative act of the *Kulturkampf* was an Imperial Reichstag law in 1871 that amended the criminal code to prohibit the clergy from using the pulpit for illicit political purposes, such as preaching sermons supporting particular candidates or parties. The *Kulturkampf* reached its apex between 1872 and 1878. In 1872, the Reichstag enacted legislation to expel the Jesuits from German territory, while the Prussian parliament passed legislation to replace clerical inspectors in schools with state inspectors. In the spring of 1873, Articles 15 through 18 of the Prussian constitution that had guaranteed ecclesiastical autonomy were amended to pave the way for the legislation that followed.[5] In May of that year, the Prussian parliament approved four laws aimed at placing the Catholic Church under tighter state control and weakening the internal administrative authority of the Catholic ecclesiastical hierarchy. The most important of these laws introduced, as a requirement for ordination, that candidates must attend a German university and pass a cultural examination in history, philosophy, literature, and history. Other measures gave the state veto power over all church appointments and created a royal court for ecclesiastical affairs with final jurisdiction over all internal matters of church discipline. Another measure sought to simplify the procedures through which church members could separate themselves from their church. To buttress the Prussian legislative efforts, the Reichstag adopted a law the next year empowering

4. In 1878, Bismarck prevailed on the Reichstag to enact an anti-socialist law to ban the newly formed Social Democratic party. The legislation outlawed all socialist clubs and organizations, including any trade unions affiliated with them, throughout the Empire.

5. The Imperial constitution contained no catalog of fundamental rights, so it did not require amendment.

the Imperial government to incarcerate or to denaturalize and exile any clergy member who refused to comply. On 22 April 1875, the Prussian government also adopted the so-called "Breadbasket Law," which cut off all state funding to the Catholic Church and salary payments to the Catholic clergy. It provided for the resumption of funding and salary payments on the condition that the responsible Episcopal administrator or individual clergyman promised to obey the state laws governing the church. On 31 May 1875, the Prussian government enacted a law banning all monastic orders except those engaged in medical service (Nipperdey 1992: 373–374; Wehler 1995: 892–897).

Over the course of the campaign, the church officials were subject to all manner of harassment, intimidation, and censures. Fines were levied against recalcitrant clergy and priests were removed from their parishes. Many clerical offices fell vacant, because the church would not submit to appointment requirements. Considerable efforts were made to repress the Catholic press through censorship, confiscation, fines, and jail for editors and journalists. The Prussian government purged large numbers of Catholics officials from the local level to the highest echelons of its administration. By the end of the *Kulturkampf*, 1,800 priests and all eleven of Prussia's bishops had been imprisoned or exiled. The government confiscated DM 16 million of church property (Nipperdey 1992: 374–375; Wehler 1995: 892–897; Blackbourn 1998: 162; Smith 1995: 42).

Despite such punitive measures, the campaign to impose a national German identity defined in the terms of Protestant, or majority, culture called forth stubborn and effective Catholic minority resistance. "Large-scale arrests and persecutions," Ronald Ross observes, "in fact promoted rather than impeded Catholic militancy" (Ross 1998: 181). The campaign deepened divisions among Germans by polarizing cultural differences between Protestants and Catholics. In the face of derision and discrimination, David Blackbourn observes, Catholics "responded by holding to the faith, closing ranks and wearing their religion as a badge of identity" (Blackbourn 1998: 302). Both the Catholic laity and clerics showed no reluctance in refusing to comply with the laws directed against their faith (Ross 1998: 121–122). The *Kulturkampf* helped to consolidate electoral support, among Catholics, for the confessionally based Center Party in those *Länder* where Catholics were geographically concentrated and in the Empire as a whole. In the 1874 Reichstag elections, for example, the Center Party more than doubled its popular vote. From 1870 to 1880, Catholic newspapers grew significantly in number and readership. The *Kulturkampf* also strengthened and helped perpetuate the influence of the Catholic Church in German politics. "[N]owhere else in Europe or America," Margaret Anderson has observed, "did clerical influence become so widespread, so continuous, so coordinated, and so effective as in Catholic Germany. Nowhere else was it institutionalized in a powerful political party" (2000: 108). The *Kulturkampf* then not only failed to achieve its advocates' aims, but also produced the opposite effect.

Bismarck's suspicions toward the Empire's Catholic subjects were compounded by his fears about the loyalties of the national minorities occupying the Empire. In Prussia, for example, approximately one-tenth of the population was Polish.[6] Prussian Poles were also Catholic, and Bismarck's anti-Polish policy goals were initially a core dimension of his *Kulturkampf* campaign (Blanke 1981: 18–19). However, Prussia's Polish minority posed distinct challenges of its own. With some cause, Bismarck had long worried about the aspirations of Prussian Poles for a national state of their own, and he dismissed the prospect that Polish loyalties to the German Empire could be won by any strategy of appeasement. Beginning with the *Kulturkampf* legislation of 1872, Bismarck and his successors implemented a series of steps designed to crush any potential Polish opposition to state authority in Prussian provinces with high Polish concentrations. The long anti-Polish campaign amounted to a program of internal colonization. This program reflected not only security concerns, but also traditional German perceptions of the inferiority of Poles and a duty of more advanced people to civilize them. The 1872 legislation was aimed at diminishing the influence of the Polish Catholic hierarchy by eliminating clerical supervision over elementary schools. Additional laws soon followed mandating that all teaching in Posen, West Prussia, Silesia, and East Prussia be conducted in German rather than in Polish, with the exception of religious instruction. In 1876, the Prussian parliament passed a law requiring that only German be used in the courts and in the civil administration. These measures did not have their intended effect, but rather provoked a strong counter-mobilization, such as through the creation of an extensive network of self-help organizations, to preserve Polish identity and to defend Polish interests (Blanke 1981: 106–109, 211–212; Hagen 1980: 128–131, 139–142). Moreover, the demographic and economic trends in these border regions undercut the effectiveness of the policies aimed at Germanization and supported the continued expansion of the Polish population (Blanke 1981: 41–44; Hagen 1980: 208–224).

In response, Bismarck introduced more forceful measures. From 1883 to 1885, the Prussian government expelled 32,000 Poles and Jews living in the eastern provinces. They had not violated any law, but could not prove they possessed German citizenship. The Reichstag formally condemned these expulsions, but they were only one prong of a more systematic effort to Germanize these provinces (Hagen 1980: 131–135). In 1886, the Prussian Landtag established the Royal Prussian Colonization Commission to purchase Polish properties for the purpose of facilitating the settlement of German peasants and workers in the provinces of Posen and West Prussia. Beginning in the 1890s, the Prussian government also began taking administrative steps to make the

---

6. Other Slavic groups, such as Sorbs, Mazurians, and Kashubians, were also longstanding subjects of the Prussian state.

naturalization of Poles and Jews more difficult. Additional Germanizing measures, such as a new school policy aimed at eliminating religious instruction in Polish, were also implemented. In 1908, the Reichstag enacted laws to facilitate the expropriation of Polish-owned properties and to restrict the use of Polish in public assemblies (Hagen 1980: 183–184, 188–190; Nathans 2004: 139–142).

Just as their campaign to homogenize German Catholics had failed, the Imperial and Prussian governments' concerted efforts to Germanize their Polish regions proved unsuccessful. "By attacking a minority on nationalist grounds," the historian John Kulczycki has observed, "the government actually armed the minority" (Kulczycki 1981: 220; see also Blanke 1981: 232–233; Hagen 1980: 176–177, 192, 225–226, 320–321). Each stage in the anti-Polish campaign provoked an effective counter-response from the Poles. Pressures from groups espousing *völkisch* ideologies to intensify internal colonization efforts sharpened Polish nationalist consciousness and spurred the growth of a Polish national independence movement. The nationality conflicts drove a wedge between German and Polish Catholics, while polarizing local social life in these borderland Prussian provinces. Measured in absolute and proportional terms, the Polish population in these borderland provinces was larger in 1914 than in 1870, while their local economies remained dependent on a steady supply of seasonal workers from the Polish areas of the Russian and Austrian-Hungarian Empires. The number of seasonal workers in Prussia rose from more than 25,000 in 1894 to 900,780 in 1914 (Hagen 1980: 146–148, 233–236, 260–262; Nathans 2004: 125; Smith 1995: 169–205).

The German Empire not only contained non-German nationalities at its inception, but, from the 1880s onward, increasingly became a magnet for immigration in the wake of industrialization. Between 1880 and 1914, the number of foreigners in the Empire more than quadrupled from 276,057 to 1,259,873. The largest share by far came from Austria-Hungary, followed by (in descending order) Russia, the Netherlands, Italy, and Switzerland (Herbert 1990: 21). Fears about the disloyalties of the Empire's national minorities, including not only Poles, but also Danes and Alsace-Lorrainians, among others, carried over into citizenship policy toward immigrants. Perceived attributes indicating a clear disposition toward embracing German political loyalties and culture became increasingly important as a naturalization criterion. In its administration of naturalization from the early 1890s to 1914, the Prussian government became increasingly discriminatory toward applications from Jews, Poles, and other nationalities deemed undesirable, such as Czechs and Danes. It was most severe in its policy toward Jews on both religious and racial grounds. Where the Prussian government's policy assumed that Jews were inassimilable and therefore as a presumptive rule should be denied citizenship, it was somewhat more open to the prospect that Poles and other nationalities could be assimilated. Prussian government policy was most favorable toward Poles who had learned German and had been born in Prussia, and least favorable to those who were deemed most likely to promote Polish national loyalties, such as Catholic clerics.

Against this background, the concept of an "inner homogeneity of the nation" emerged as a guiding idea for German citizenship policy (Gosewinkel 2001a: 265; see also Hagen 1980: 167–168).[7] The 1913 Imperial Citizenship Law was designed as a defensive measure to prevent the naturalization of foreigners deemed inassimilable and culturally inferior rather than as a means to promote the integration of foreign residents. It was intended to preserve barriers between those who belonged and those who did not. This defensiveness reflected a fear of migration pressures from the east and, more specifically, the influence of the nationality conflicts in Prussia's eastern provinces. It also reflected deeply chauvinistic attitudes toward Jews and Poles. In the debates over the enactment of the new law, Prussian administrators in the eastern provinces had strongly objected to Social Democratic party proposals to introduce the territorial principle (*ius soli*), because they feared that it would make it more difficult to deter the unwanted settlement of migrants from Russia and Austria-Hungary (Brubaker 1992: 114–134; Gosewinkel 2001a: 263–277, 317–327; Nathans 2004: 146–154). Instead, the new law sharpened the application of the principle of descent (*ius sanguinis*) as the basis for acquiring citizenship. "The principle of the inheritance of citizenship through descent," Gosewinkel has observed, "corresponded to ideas of ethnic homogeneity, which proceeded from the 'objective,' genetically transferable qualities of Germanness. As a result, the ethnic-*völkisch* ideas of the nationalistic associations as opposed to the political-utilitarian conception of the parliamentary left had prevailed" (2001a: 324–325). Proponents of these nationalistic ideas seized upon the principle of *ius sanguinis* as the basis for justifying and translating their agenda into law and policy.

In affirming this principle, the new law attenuated the link between citizenship and residence in a double way. Removing the ten-year limit that had existed, it now permitted Germans living abroad to retain their citizenship indefinitely and to transmit it to their descendants, though with one significant qualification. Men who emigrated abroad could only retain their citizenship if they had fulfilled their military service obligations. At the same time, it supported the administration of a naturalization policy aimed at preventing Jews, Poles, and other undesirables from acquiring citizenship, irrespective of their lengths of residence. It conferred no right or entitlement to naturalization if certain conditions were met, but rather treated the grant of naturalization as an exception

---

7. Gosewinkel uses the term "homogeneity" to characterize a particular conception of "nationhood," explaining that his use of this conception "refers not merely to a group, but also to the totality of qualities, images, and ideas ascribed to a nation and its members by defining what is called the 'homogeneity of the nation'" (Gosewinkel 1998: 126).

to the general rule. It prescribed several broad criteria for eligibility, such as residence, socioeconomic self-sufficiency, and good character, but the vagueness of the criteria allowed an enormous amount of administrative discretion in their application by the states. In administering naturalization, Prussia and the other states maintained their own secret criteria that used factors such as religion, nationality, political orientation, family background, and occupation as the basis for assessing the assimilation potential of an applicant (Gosewinkel 2001a: 246–263, 268–277, 310–327; Nathans 2004: 146–154, 176–179).

The Imperial Citizenship Law did not enshrine a racialized understanding of national belonging as the Nazis later would conceive it. The Nazis would have to introduce their own fundamental reforms of the German citizenship law to achieve their much more extreme aims of purifying the German *Volk* and establishing it as the master race (Gosewinkel 2001a: 369–420; Majer 2003: 98–128; Nathans 2004: 217–234). That the *Kulturkampf* failed and political parties representing minorities could emerge effectively in opposition are indicative of the categorical difference in the use of coercion between Bismarck's Germany and Hitler's. However, starting with the emergence of national homogeneity as a guiding ideal of citizenship policy, important precedents were established in Imperial Germany that would later find a more radical application. As Gosewinkel observes about the policies used to wage the *Kulturkampf*, "denaturalization, the most extreme means a state can authorize aside from physical annihilation in order to expel unwelcome people out of a community, was introduced and used against the Catholic clergy" (Gosewinkel 2001a: 222). Similar plans were contemplated against the Social Democrats, but were never implemented. Moreover, Bismarck's tactic of designating 'enemies of the empire' to mobilize majorities against stigmatized minorities established a dangerous legacy that appeared in more extreme forms after 1933 (Wehler 1970: 198–199; Kershaw 1995: 225). During the post-Bismarck era, an extreme form of nationalism emerged, whose exponents advocated "the mastering of antagonisms through the inner completion of national unity. All enemies and foreigners should be either excluded or assimilated, so that the purified nation could meet the challenges of the day as a monolithic block" (Wehler 1995: 956). The popular movements advocating this ultranationalist vision sought to finish the task they believed Bismarck and his liberal allies had failed to complete. Nevertheless, it was only the profound impact of World War I and the subsequent crises of the Weimar Republic that created the conditions and opportunities for exponents of this kind of vision to gain ascendency (Bartov 1996: 15–50; 2000: 9–43; Naimark 2001: 9–11; Hamilton 1982: 361–474).

The Nazis brought the radicalized ideal of a homogeneous national community to its pathological apogee. From the beginning, their party program advocated uniting all Germans in a greater Reich consistent with the principle of national self-determination, and excluding all non-Germans from citizenship according to a blood-based criterion. They effected "the transition from an ethno-cultural conception to a racial conception of homogenization" (Gosewinkel 2002: 71). As a matter of ideological discourse, the jurist Ernst Forsthoff provides an instructive example of how this radicalized ideal was understood in his 1933 book, *The Total State*. Forsthoff, who would become a leading authority of constitutional and administrative law under the Nazis, explained that *Volk*

> is a community based on homogeneity within life and species [*seinesmässigen, artmässigen Gleichartigkeit*]. The homogeneity arises from the sameness of race and national destiny [*volkliches Schicksal*]. The *political people* forms in the final unity of will that grows from the awareness of homogeneity within life. The awareness of homogeneity within species and national identity [*volkliche Zusammengehörigkeit*] becomes actual in the ability to recognize the difference of species and distinguish friend from enemy. The issue is recognizing the difference of species when it is not automatically visible through membership in a foreign nation, for example, in the Jews, who successfully attempted to create the illusion of homogeneity within species and of national solidarity by participating in the cultural and economic life. The rebirth of a politically German people had to end this illusion and to take away the Jew's last hope of living in Germany other than in the consciousness of being a Jew. (Forsthoff 2000: 322–323)

This understanding of national identity obviously did not bode well for the Jews or other vulnerable minorities within Germany, but it is also important to recognize how it ignored long-standing qualitative differences in identity between Catholic and Protestant Germans. It did not posit a new framework of accommodation based on mutual toleration and respect for those differences, but rather it brushed them aside behind a nationalist vision of organic unity. Because the whole notion of homogeneity presupposes some sort of essentialized uniformity, the flattening discourse of homogeneity lends itself to precisely this kind of usage. In other words, the idea of an authentic homogeneous national culture is an oxymoron, but it does provide a powerful conceptual means to demarcate between putative insiders and outsiders.

Forsthoff had been a student of the radical conservative legal theorist Carl Schmitt, whose own assaults on the normative foundations of the Republic began from the premise that democracy presupposes the homogeneity of a state's people. In his writings before joining the Nazi party in 1933 and becoming initially the Nazi's most prized jurist, Schmitt had elevated the friend-enemy distinction from a demagogic political tactic into the defining core of his theory of politics. Against pluralistic, parliamentary systems of government that he regarded as dangerously outmoded and fatally flawed, he developed a model of homogeneous democracy. His model rested on a putative "identity" of the ruling and the ruled, with the people themselves consigned to play a passive role under the firm hand of a ruling elite and executive-centered government. Equality among citizens was fundamental to his conception of democracy, but citizenship was to be reserved only to those deemed substantially similar. If national minorities must be tolerated, then they must be strictly subordinated within a hierarchical membership structure. A state, he observed, "can exclude one part of those to be governed without ceasing to be a democracy" (Schmitt 1996: 9). While this is indisputably true from a historical perspective, the same argument can be invoked to justify slavery.

Consistent with this view of national homogeneity as essential to political unity and vitality, he argued that a "democracy demonstrates its power by knowing how to refuse or keep at bay something foreign and unequal that threatens homogeneity" (Schmitt 1996: 9). To meet this threat, Schmitt pointed out that states have a range of options from peaceful assimilation to more expedient and coercive methods such as segregation, direct oppression, and resettlement. Rejecting any universalistic understanding of individual rights, equality, and freedom as a valid normative criterion for state policy, he considered all such methods from the standpoint of how they served "to assure and achieve national homogeneity" (Schmitt 1970: 232). From this standpoint, he argued that the migration controls and citizenship restrictions that the United States, Australia, and South Africa utilized to deter "undesirable foreign elements" in the 1920s all illustrate the logical or necessary "consequences" of the same underlying principle. Likewise, he called attention to "the development of special forms and methods of domination of regions with heterogeneous populations" under various Western colonial regimes as further instructive examples of how this principle is applied in practice (Schmitt 1970: 232). The guiding idea behind these "special forms" is to make a subject people dependent without ever giving them a share in the wealth and in the rule of the governing power.

A Schmittian approach provides a clear nationalist rationale to justify discriminatory membership policies. However, Schmitt never pretended that such policies are reconcilable with universal norms of individual rights, freedom, and dignity as guaranteed by the FRG's Basic Law or by the types of international human rights conventions that the FRG has ratified. The Basic Law stands as an impressive bulwark against the strategies of pathological homogenization that modern states have proven too apt to pursue. The Federal Constitutional Court's jurisprudence on aliens has demonstrated the effectiveness of the Basic Law's guarantees. Nevertheless, the Basic Law has also provided constitutional sanction for an exclusivist ethnocultural conception of national membership. Likewise, in his critique of the Federal Constitutional Court's 1993 Maastricht opinion, the legal scholar J. H. H. Weiler has called attention to the Schmittian overtones of the Court's conception of the nation-state model that reflected the "old ideas of an ethno-culturally homogeneous *Volk*" (Weiler 1995: 223). Ulrike

Davy, an eminent legal scholar on immigrant integration, argues that much of German integration policy retains what Schmitt considered necessary "ingredients of democracy," namely, the "annihilation of all heterogeneity" (quoted from Davy 2005: 125). The idea of Germany as a homogeneous nation still echoes throughout the political discourse on immigration and integration, especially from the political right (Hell 2005: 83–87, 111–113, 138–140).

As a policy norm for states that have experienced large scale immigration, the concept of a homogeneous culture compounds the difficulties in promoting integration, because it confronts immigrants with an all or nothing choice in terms of their understanding of their own cultural identities in relation to their host state. Such an approach simply ignores the multilevel, trans-generational character of the integration process. In the theoretical literature, older concepts of "assimilation" that presupposed a linear, one-sided process have been largely rejected. Instead of understanding the assimilation of immigrants as a "shift from one homogeneous unit to another," Rogers Brubaker writes that it is now increasingly recognized to involve "a shift from one mode of heterogeneity—one distribution of properties—to another mode of heterogeneity, that is, to a distribution of properties more similar to the distribution prevailing in some reference population" (Brubaker 2001: 543; see also Castles et al. 2002). The best evidence for the failure of the older approach is the FRG's own poor record in promoting the integration of its immigrants. Successful integration will require a respect for pluralism that the concept of a homogeneous national culture denies at its core.

As we have sought to emphasize, the FRG norms of membership are multidimensional and cannot be understood from the one-sided standpoint of any one particular dimension. The tensions between different sets of membership norms are hardly unique to the FRG, but emphasizing these tensions underscores the role of choice to be made by state governments in deciding how conflicts among diverging membership criteria are to be addressed. As in all states, membership in the Federal Republic involves a much more complicated set of elements than any singular model of collective identity can capture. Moreover, as Ulrich Preuss has observed, the "quest for ethnocultural homogenization" is only one of a much broader menu of "responses" that Germans have crafted in their long historical experience with "constitutional, political, religious and social fragmentation." This multifaceted experience with accommodating plurality extending from the Middle Ages through today offers a strong heritage for promoting "an attitude of openness towards the multiplicity of political identities and the tendency towards multiple commitments and loyalties that all Member States of the European Union must find ways to address" (Preuss 2003: 48, 53; see also Sheehan 1981). Surely, the FRG's more immediate historical experience with immigration and integration demonstrates the failure of homogeneity as a guiding norm for twenty-first-century policymakers.

Part 2

Laying the Foundation for Managing Migration, 1949–1990

In this section, we examine the legacy of the FRG's immigrant past from its inception in 1949 through reunification in 1990. With regard to this past, the FRG's Independent Commission on Immigration aptly observed in its 2001 report:

> Throughout its recent history, Germany has experienced literally every conceivable form of cross-border migration: immigration, emigration, transit migration, labour migration as well as migration of persons fleeing and people forced to migrate, either from Germany or to Germany. In this context, not only did people migrate across border; borders were also moved to divide resident populations. Within Germany, individuals and groups have also been isolated and persecuted on the grounds of their political and religious beliefs or ethnic origin. In the light of these historical experiences, Germany has a great responsibility to promote an immigration policy that is based on humanitarian motives. (Independent Commission on Immigration 2001: 119)

It is this extensive and multivariate historical experience that gives German policymakers a concrete choice to decide now which parts of their migration tradition they want to build upon and which parts they want to depart from when charting a new course in the twenty-first century. In facing these choices today, the findings of the Independent Commission on Immigration are encouraging, but much of the political discourse since 2001 and the resulting legislative response in 2004 are disappointing, if not troubling.

Chapter 8

The Descent of the *Aussiedler* and the Politics of the German Diaspora

The privileged admissions and reception granted to the *Aussiedler* were emblematic of the ethnonational character of the FRG's membership policies, but it is a mistake to explain this character simply as an intrinsic expression of the German national self-understanding. The original policies toward the *Aussiedler* arose from a particular set of circumstances and political choices. As these circumstances have changed, such as with reunification and the end of the Cold War, the choices and the policies have also changed, as illustrated by the more restrictive rules applied, since 1993, toward the *Spätaussiedler*. Moreover, the official image of the *Aussiedler* as returning settlers of German descent glossed over the many concrete historical and cultural differences that distinguished various groups of *Aussiedler* from one another as well as from the native-born Germans in the FRG.

The whole issue of the *Aussiedler* arose from the diasporic character of historical German settlement patterns throughout Central and Eastern Europe. German ethnonational discourses reflect this dispersion of German minorities across different states, but the bearing this diaspora has had on different conceptions of national belonging and Germany's understanding of its place in Europe has proven to be highly contingent. From the establishment of the Second Reich in 1871 to today, German state policies toward external German minorities and the national self-understandings of these minorities have been subject to continuous and sometimes radical change. In analyzing the general factors shaping such changes during the twentieth century, Rogers Brubaker (1996) has emphasized the importance of the "triadic nexus" between nationalizing states seeking to homogenize their populations, the national minorities in these states who typically resist pressures to assimilate, and the homeland nationalism of external states through which ethnic kinship with these minorities is construed. Changing definitions of ethnic and national identity become objects of contest in the "dynamic interplay" that is a hallmark of these "triangular relationships" (Brubaker 1996: 55–69). Likewise, the whole issue of minority rights becomes entangled in this same interplay.

To explore these complicated interrelationships, this chapter will focus on two examples: the Volga Germans and the multi-ethnic Silesians. In considering Germany's own changing role in the politics surrounding the German diaspora, it will focus on the Weimar Republic and its role as the foremost champion of minority rights during the inter-war period. The failure of the League of Nations' minority protection system during this period had a powerful effect not only on post-war approaches to minorities in Central and Eastern Europe, but also on the emergence of human rights as international norms as a substitute for this system. In looking at this historical background, we seek to situate the FRG's own policies toward external German minorities as part of a much longer story.

German Minorities in Russia: The Example of the Volga Germans

The *Aussiedler* are the descendants of colonists who first began to migrate eastward from German lands in the twelfth century, and in several subsequent waves through the middle of the nineteenth century. In the twelfth century, colonists pushed the frontier of German settlements from the river Elbe to the Vistula, reaching as far north as the Baltic Sea and as far south as Transylvania. The colonists established their own communities, which were perpetuated as linguistic islands amidst neighboring groups. The relative prosperity of these German communities would strengthen the colonists' desires to preserve their own separate identities and to guard jealously their rights and privileges. After the twelfth century, German migration eastward penetrated into the heart of Russia in a series of waves that continued into the nineteenth century. The Germans were only one of many other nationalities that migrated eastward, but they made up the largest share (Conze 1992: 8–9, 67–92; Rady 1999: 11–37).

During the eighteenth century, several Eastern European states, including Prussia and Austria, sought to recruit immigrants for their under-populated territories. To advance his attempts to westernize Russia, Peter the Great (reign: 1682–1725) successfully sought to recruit Germans with specialized skills and knowledge. Many of the new arrivals settled in Russian cities, and some received important posts in the civil administration and military. He also conquered and annexed the Baltic States, which had a large and prosperous German population. Through her Manifestos of 1762 and 1763, Catherine the

Great (reign: 1762–1796), invited an even larger wave of migration. To attract German settlers, she offered special tax immunities, exemption from military service, freedom of worship, and material assistance in establishing their settlements. In contrast to the overwhelming majority of Russian peasants, immigrant German farmers were not subject to serfdom. These privileges gave the immigrants and their descendants enormous economic advantages, but also encouraged their insularity in relationship to the general Russian populace. The new immigrants established their largest base of colonies in the Volga region, where they established agricultural colonies. New waves of migration to Russia followed (Fleischhauer 1986a: 30–64; Bartlett 1979: 31–49, 58–65, 95–105; Bartlett and Mitchell 1999).

The segregation of the Volga German colonies enabled them to maintain their own customs, traditions, and dialect, but, after 1860, the material and institutional basis of their autonomy began to erode. During the nineteenth century, the rapid growth of their population created severe land shortages for colony members, which would drive many to emigrate. In 1798, the Volga German population comprised nearly 40,000 persons. By 1850, their number had soared to 165,000. It would almost treble over the next 60 years to reach 480,589 by 1912 (Long 1988: 12). Denied access to financial credit, the ability of the colonists to acquire new land did not nearly keep pace with their population growth. A series of reforms beginning with the abolition of serfdom in 1861 and the Volga Germans' loss of their exemption from military service in 1874 undermined the special protected status that had preserved the relative autonomy of the Volga Germans. The emancipation of the serfs created new competitors for landownership. Subsequent government reforms aimed at encouraging private ownership of rural land undercut the communal ownership practices of the colonies. Military conscription and school reforms served as instruments of assimilation, which began to undermine the cultural insularity of the Volga Germans. Assimilation also brought benefits, and the Volga Germans recognized the need to adapt their communities to the forces of modernization. For example, they supported the teaching of Russian in their schools as a necessary accommodation (Long 1988: 110–137, 170–179). However, these same forces were rendering the viability of their established patterns of life ever more precarious.

Despite these pressures, the Volga German colonies maintained their distinct identities as a minority within the Russian Empire. These identities reflected the German heritage they had brought with them in the eighteenth century as well as their subsequent exposure to Russian culture. Anyone visiting a Volga German settlement at the end of the nineteenth century would have been struck by how isolated the Volga Germans had been from social, cultural, and political developments in Germany. As James Long has explained, there would be "no works of Fichte, Schleiermacher, Goethe, Schiller, or Herder on the shelf with the family Bible, and not even a copy of the Grimm folktales lying on the table. Mentioning the name of any these great figures of German civilization would only have drawn blank stares, and those educated few who could understand these classics would have learned about them in Russian! The only 'Kaiser' they knew was Alexander or Nicholas, whose picture hung in the schoolhouse and sometimes adorned the walls of private cottages" (1988: 61). By the close of the nineteenth century, the Volga Germans had developed a distinct identity with a blending of Russian and German cultural elements, but not one that they were able to express in any sophisticated manner. They developed no literary tradition of their own. There were no organized circles of Volga German intellectuals who could articulate their particular cultural sensibility, mount a defense of their institutions and customs, or write the histories of their settlements. Having left Germany long before any unitary national state existed, they thought of the places from which they had come in highly local, rather than national, terms. Throughout the nineteenth century, their horizons were too limited to see themselves as part of a larger pan-German cultural community. Their sense of shared national belonging was based on "a constructed historical memory designed to appeal more to the state of Germany for help than to the colonists themselves" (Bridenthal 2005: 189). The Volga Germans identified their patriotic homeland with Russia and with their own Volga region, and not with Imperial Germany.

Bismarck was not only indifferent to the situation of German minorities outside of the Reich, including the Russian Germans, but he also saw them as a "potential threat to his attempts to stabilize the settlements of 1866 and 1871" (Chickering 1984: 26–27; Long 1988: 54–57, 61, 213, 250). Beginning in the late 1880s, efforts were made to recruit Russian Germans to settle in Prussia's eastern districts, but the number (4,900 families) immigrating prior to World War I remained small compared to the numbers of foreign Poles admitted during the same period (Oltmer 2005: 142). During the war, the Imperial government recruited more than 30,000 Russian Germans from the Eastern European and Russian territories it occupied. Of those Volga Germans who left Russia after 1871, the vast majority chose to immigrate to the Americas, not to Germany. From 1870 to 1914, approximately 116,000 Russian Germans went to the United States (Oltmer 2005: 140; Giesinger 1988: 228).

By the beginning of the twentieth century, the Volga Germans were facing the threat of a growing xenophobic Slavic nationalism, whose exponents were attacking German minorities in increasingly strident terms. The Volga Germans were also struggling to cope with the Russian government's growing encroachments on their communities. Resentment against these encroachments was reflected in their support of the Revolution of 1905 (Long 1988: 192–199). Nevertheless, when World War I broke out, the Volga Germans supported their Tsar. A quarter of a million Russian Germans fought in the Russian army and they occupied leading positions in both the military and civilian administration. However, this service to the Tsar did not save the Russian Germans living near the front lines from being classified as "enemy subjects." The Russian government shut down the German-language press and German organization. It adopted a law to expropriate the Volga German's lands and deport them, but it was never able to execute it. Mistrusting the loyalties of its many national minorities, the Russian government forcibly transported large numbers of Russian Germans, together with other national minorities to interior regions, including the Volga. These mass transfers established contacts among different Russian Germans, whose individual communities had formerly been relatively insular. In participating in relief efforts for their fellow Russian Germans, Volga Germans helped to create new organizational networks through which Russian Germans could work together on a national level. Only at this time did Volga Germans begin to develop a broader identification with other Russian Germans as a collective national minority, though this identification remains limited to the most urbanized and educated (Lohr 2003: 129–137, 156–157, 169; Long 1988: 223–231).

While Bismarck had never shown any interest in the *Auslandsdeutsche* in the Russian Empire or elsewhere, a new generation of radical nationalists arose who did show interest. The example of the Pan-German League (*Alldeutscher Verband*) offers a case in point. Founded in the early 1890s, the League was a populist pressure group with a largely middle class membership. It considered the German Empire to be an "incomplete" nation-state, because of the German minorities the Empire excluded outside its borders as well as the many non-German nationals it included. As Roger Chickering has explained, the League embraced ethnicity as the defining basis of national identity, and regarded the "the function of politics, of the state," as simply providing "organized expression and protection to the ethnic community." For the League, "the claims of the *Volk* were accordingly higher than of those of the state" (Chickering 1984: 72). Despite its relatively small size, the League was able to exert considerable influence on the Imperial government. Pressure from the League and other patriotic societies in the 1890s reopened a debate over the Imperial Citizenship law, which then culminated in the new 1913 law. The League's twofold aim was to restrict the acquisition of citizenship to ethnic Germans (*deutsche Volksgenossen*), while extending it as an automatic right to *Auslandsdeutsche*. In this way, it sought to use citizenship as an instrument to strengthen the preservation of Germanness among its people inside and outside the Reich. However, the 1913 Imperial Citizenship did not satisfy this aspiration. First, it did not offer any special accommodation for *Auslandsdeutsche* who had had no legal connection to the Reich, but were German merely by ancestry and by certain shared cultural characteristics. Second, in requiring that emigrant Germans fulfill their military service obligation in order to retain their citizenship, the law put statist concerns about the defensive needs of the territorial Reich before any concern about preserving links with a globally dispersed German community (Brubaker 1992: 115–119; Gosewinkel 2001a: 278–327; Nathans 2004: 172–175).

Consistent with the growing imperialist competition among the European powers, the League advocated an aggressive expansion of German dominion over Central and Eastern Europe. Reflecting the influence of the nationality conflict in the Prussia's eastern provinces, it emphasized the specific threat to Germany and the "outposts" of German culture to the east posed by a rising "flood" of immigrating Slavic peoples, especially the Poles. At the core of its ideological vision, the League saw conflict as fundamental to the existence of peoples as they competed with one another for territory and mastery (Chickering 1984: 77–86, 122–125). Thus, in contrast to Bismarck's statist approach, pan-national movements emphasized the opposition between state membership and ethnonational membership, and subordinated the former to the latter. The growing perception of such an opposition posed a serious challenge to any concept of the German nation-state as a politically and geographically bounded unit (Arendt 1979: 222–243).

Major interest in the Russian Germans remained largely confined to radical nationalists during the pre-war era, but World War I dramatically changed this picture. Proponents of large-scale annexations in the east, such as the Pan-German League, used the plight of *Auslandsdeutsche* in the Russian Empire to build critical support behind their objectives. The German government looked upon the *Auslandsdeutsche* as a potential source of badly needed labor for the war economy and as future settlers to populate the annexed regions. By 1915, German and Austria-Hungarian military forces had advanced deeply into the western provinces of the Russian Empire. Under the 1918 Brest-Litovsk Treaty, the Russian government, now in Bolshevik hands, ceded to Germany 1.3 million miles of territory that comprised 62 million people. In May of 1918, the German government created the Office for German Return Migration and Emigration[1] to establish more effective controls over the migration of Germans pursuant to labor needs and future settlement plans. Subsequent German defeat would annul these territorial gains, but a strong link had now been forged between the *Auslandsdeutsche* and German expansionist ambitions (Oltmer 2005: 151–182).

During the war and upheavals that followed, approximately 120,000 Russian Germans emigrated, the majority of whom eventually settled in the Americas (Brandes 1992: 124). The war experience undermined the Russian Germans' loyalty to the Tsarist government, and most supported the February revolution in 1917. As they grew disillusioned with the Provisional government, their political support shifted leftward. After seizing power in October, the Bolsheviks wooed

1. *Reichstelle für deutsche Rückwanderung und Auswanderung.*

the Volga Germans with promises of greater autonomy, but their policies were initially aimed at encouraging revolution in Germany rather than from any commitment to the principle of national self-determination. Establishing a Volga German socialist commune not only served their propaganda objectives, but also could provide a potential channel for attracting Western capital investment (Long 1988: 251; Fleischhauer 1986d: 34–37). At the same time, this general approach toward the Volga Germans was not exceptional, but part of a broader ethnoterritorial federalist system the Bolsheviks constructed to establish their control over the multinational conglomeration they had inherited from the Romanov Tsars. They used promises of autonomy to national minorities as a means to differentiate their own rule from the Russification policies of the Tsarist government and as a means to entice these minorities to buy into their new order. Between 1918 and 1921, the Bolsheviks began implementing their policy of creating autonomous national republics around Russia's borderlands (Smith 1999: 43–65). In 1924, they established the Autonomous Soviet Socialist Republic of Volga Germans.

Whatever the advantages the Volga Germans gained from this autonomy, they had also suffered enormous hardships during this period. This suffering reached its apogee in 1921 when widespread famine devastated their communities. Brought on by bad harvests combined with ruthless confiscations of grain and livestock, the famine killed at least 10 percent of the Volga German population and sent many more into flight. Between late 1920 and August 1921, the population in the Volga German region fell from 452,000 to 359,000. Although Soviet collectivization policies would bring new hardships to the Russian Germans, the vast majority would find that emigration was no longer possible, because of the Soviet government's tight border controls. Overall, the Russian German population declined from 1,621,000 in 1918 to 1,238 million by the end of 1926 (Long 1992: 511–513, 523; Oltmer 2005: 186–187).

The Weimar Republic: Minority Rights, the *Auslandsdeutsche*, and Homeland Nationalism

After World War I, the issue of the *Auslandsdeutsche* remained a major political issue in Weimar Germany. The loss of territories as a consequence of defeat had drastically diminished the number of foreign nationals and foreign-speaking residents in the Reich, but it had also expanded the number of German minorities outside of it. Although many hundreds of thousands of Germans from the ceded territories resettled in the Reich, there remained nearly 10 million external German minorities across Europe and Russia, not including Austrian and Swiss Germans (Lumans 1993: 22). Those Germans who continued living in the ceded territories lost their Reich citizenship, but many Germans on both sides of the new borders saw those without Reich citizenship as no less than members of the German nation. No major German political party accepted the legitimacy of the territorial borders imposed at Versailles. As a result of the territorial losses, Dieter Gosewinkel observes, the idea of state citizenship as a designation of national belonging was devalued. "In the 1913 Imperial Citizenship law," he points out, "the word 'German' had been used as a synonym for 'Reichsangehöriger' (citizen of the Reich) in the Imperial Citizenship law of 1913, because the contents of both concepts were largely co-extensive in the political reality and ideological world view of the Kaiserreich. This was no longer the case after 1918" (Gosewinkel 2001a: 342). The dissolution of the Austrian-Hungarian Empire had demoted Germans living in the successor states from a ruling nationality in most parts of the Empire to the status of a vulnerable minority. In Poland, for example, a beleaguered German minority looked to Germany for protection and support against the encroachments of the nationalizing Polish state. In Czechoslovakia, the majority of Sudeten Germans sought autonomy. Some identified more with Austria, others more with Germany, but the majority seemed willing until after 1933 to cooperate with the Czech government under the right conditions. Hitler's designs on the Sudeten region would ultimately render the matter moot (Komjathy and Stockwell 1980: 17–41, 157–158; Lemberg 1999: 186–190). For their part, the Austrians had sought annexation into the German Reich. Despite the fact that the proposed *Anschluss* would have been consistent with the principle of national self-determination, the Allied Powers decided otherwise. The peace settlement not only intensified Germany's feelings of victimization after a bitter defeat, but also magnified an understanding of the German nation as an ethnic community whose collective identity transcended existing state borders (Brubaker 1996: 117–120, 160–166; Mazower 1999: 41–64).

The broad resonance this irredentist ethnic understanding of nationhood found during the Weimar era is reflected in the numerous new associations established to promote German culture abroad, to defend the interests of external German minorities, and to support compensation claims for Germans who had suffered damages. New organizations, such as the German Protective League for Border and Foreign Germans,[2] the Organization for German Ethnonational Groups in Europe,[3] and the Society for Volga Germans,[4] worked alongside pre-war ones, such as the Association for Germans Abroad.[5] Membership in the Association for Germans Abroad, for example, rose from 100,000 in 1914 to 2,000,000 by the mid 1920s (Komjathy and

2. *Deutscher Schutzbund für die Grenz- und Auslandsdeutschen.*
3. *Verband der deutschen Volksgruppen in Europa.*
4. *Verein für Wolgadeutsche.*
5. *Verein für das Deutschtum im Ausland.*

Stockwell 1980: 3).[6] The Reich government contributed millions of Reichsmark (RM) in support of these organizations, and some functioned as semi-official bodies while attracting broad mass-based constituencies. The organizations helped create networks, which connected representatives of German minorities throughout Europe as well as another level of political friction that cut across foreign and domestic policy realms among European states (Brubaker 1996: 120–123, 131–134; Komjathy and Stockwell 1980: 1–6). The strength of this interest in external German minorities was indicative of the internal weaknesses of the Weimar Republic, whose capacity to represent the German nation had been crippled by its association with defeat, revolution, and economic crises. The suffering of German minorities outside the Reich became a potent symbol for the perceived victimization of the German nation as a whole. Among the external German minorities, the Russian Germans acquired a special symbolic importance. Weimar Germans "came to understand the Russian Germans," James Casteel observes, "as emblematic of Germany's fate—as innocent, hard-working farmers who were loyal to Germanness and who worked tirelessly to expand German culture in the world" (Casteel 2007: 429). The growing identification with the *Auslandsdeutsche* was symptomatic of popular dissatisfaction with the Weimar Republic in its existing political form and geographical boundaries.

The reorganization of Europe after World War I, far from establishing the foundations for a new stable order, instead seemed to underscore the artifice and contingency of this configuration of states, while creating fresh sources of grievances for a plethora of groups dissatisfied with their place in the new order. The collapse of the Austrian-Hungarian, German, Ottoman, and Russian empires in the wake of World War I had made some form of reorganization necessary, but the ethnographic distribution of peoples in Central and Eastern Europe made drawing state borders so as to be congruent with the nationality of peoples impossible. The huge number of refugees persisting during the inter-war period was symptomatic of this problem. It has been estimated that as of 1926, there were at least 9.5 million refugees in Europe (Marrus 1985: 51). Applying the principle of national self-determination as the basis for state organization had significantly reduced the number of national minorities in Central and Eastern Europe living under the rule of another dominant nationality, but dividing up territory according to this principle could only be followed so far if the new states were to have sufficient size to be viable entities. During the inter-war years, all of the successor states in Eastern Europe "had at least a 15 percent minority population, while four states—Czechoslovakia, Yugoslavia, Poland, and Romania—had a minority population that comprised more than 33 percent of the total population" (Skran 1995: 39). Moreover, basing statehood

6. Membership in the Pan-German League declined sharply during the Weimar era, and it ceased to be an influential organization during these years.

on the principle of national self-determination accentuated the sense of ownership and entitlement that many dominant nationalities felt toward their states,
while underscoring the anomalous status of national minorities within those
same states (Arendt 1979: 269–278).

In grappling with the anomalous status of minorities, the Allied Powers
gave international sanction to two contrasting approaches as part of the Paris
peace settlement process. On the one hand, the Treaties of Neuilly (1919) and
Lausanne (1923) established the legitimacy of mass population transfers as a
means to promote national homogeneity and reduce the potential for ethnic
conflict. Under the Treaty of Neuilly, Bulgaria and Greece "exchanged" more
than 135,000 persons as part of a territorial settlement. Although the transfer
was described as "voluntary," both governments exerted "considerable political, economic, and social pressure" to effect the arrangement (Pearson 1983:
140). All pretense of voluntariness was dropped in the Convention of Lausanne, which established modern Turkey's territorial borders. More than 1
million Greeks were forcibly expelled from Turkey with little more than the
clothes on their backs, and 380,000 Turks were forcibly expelled from Greece
(Pearson 1983: 140). Whatever the benefits for regional stability, the Treaty
established a dangerous precedent for solving minority issues that took no
account of individual consent of the affected persons. At this time, international law did not recognize individual human rights, and "the only 'rights'
of individuals allowed in the Convention are ... rights which are incidental to
the exchange but do not frustrate it" (Thornberry 1991: 51; Meindersma 1997:
338–351). On the other hand, the Allied Powers imposed Minorities Treaties
(1919–1921) on the successor states as a condition for the recognition of their
sovereignty. The Treaties required these polyglot states to guarantee minorities
their basic rights, such as access to citizenship, equality before the law, the use
of their language in public communications, freedom of religion, and control
over the organization of the education of their children. The states subject to
the Treaties bitterly resented this imposition on their sovereign independence,
and many had irredentist aims of their own. Nevertheless, these Treaties established the basis of the inter-war minority protection system under the League
of Nations. This system encompassed fifteen states with fifty different minorities, but it was hardly universal. First, no universal standards prescribing the
rights of minorities or rules to govern their treatment were ever promulgated.
Second, all of the Allied Powers exempted themselves from being bound by it
(Fink 2004: 267–283; Jackson Preece 1998: 86–87).

Although it had played no role in the establishment of this minority protection system, the Weimar government became a champion of minority
rights. From the outset, its concerns over the protection of minorities were
closely associated with its ambitions to revise the Versailles settlement. At
the Versailles peace negotiations in May of 1919, the German delegation had

demanded "assurances for those German minorities which, by cession, will pass over to alien sovereignty" and that they will "be afforded the possibility of cultivating their German characteristics." At the same time, the delegation expressed Germany's "resolve to treat minorities of alien origin in her territories according to the same principles" (Luckau 1941: 325). Accordingly, Article 113 of the 1919 Weimar Constitution prohibited restrictions on the free ethnonational (*volkstümliches*) development of minorities who speak a foreign language, especially with regard to the use of their mother tongue in school, as well as in matters before public officials and before courts. Similar to Article 118 of the 1849 Frankfurt Constitution, this provision was not designed to promote inclusion, but rather to preserve distinctions between the majority and minority cultures (Gosewinkel 2001a: 343).

Although often stymied in its efforts to strengthen minority rights in the Reich by opposition from *Länder* governments such as Prussia, the German foreign ministry believed that protecting the cultural autonomy of minorities at home would enhance its credibility in defending German minority rights abroad. As foreign minister from 1923 to 1929, Gustav Stresemann played the leading role in crafting the Weimar Republic's policies toward external German minorities. Although a member of the Pan-German League during the pre-war era and an advocate of annexations during the war, Stresemann may have seized upon the minorities cause as little more than a political and diplomatic card to play in pursuing broader foreign policy objectives. However, having elevated the issue of protecting the *Auslandsdeutsche*, his failure to achieve any notable successes merely gave more fodder to right-wing critics of the Republic. Under his leadership, the Weimar government pressed the League of Nations to reform the enforcement of the Minority Treaties, and became the only major state actively supporting the minority rights protection system (Fink 1972; 1979; Blanke 1993: 129–137). By 1932, the Foreign Ministry was spending 8,059,000 RM per year "for the preservation of Germandom" abroad, with most of these funds directed at Silesia, Pomerania, Posen, and Danzig (Komjathy and Stockwell 1980: 14).

The Weimar government's interest in protecting the rights of external German minorities was rooted less in any humanitarian concern than in a determination to discourage their resettlement in the Reich. Groups representing these minorities advocated admitting these minorities on both humanitarian and ethnonational grounds, but, for the Weimar government, other domestic and foreign policy considerations proved decisive. First, when facing problems of structural unemployment and other economic difficulties, the government did not feel equipped to take on the additional costs and burdens of integrating a continuing influx of migrants (Oltmer 2005: 182–217). Second, the government regarded preserving a German presence in the territories lost at Versailles as indispensable to its irredentist objectives. To uphold Germany's claims to these regions, it was not simply a matter of deterring their emigration to the Reich or to third countries, but also of discouraging their assimilation—voluntary or otherwise—into the majority culture of their respective states. With respect to other external German minorities, the government was equally instrumental in its calculations. Through the Rapallo Treaty of 1922, it established diplomatic and commercial ties with the Soviet Union, and looked to the Volga German region as an entry point for penetrating the Soviet market. For the more radical nationalist groups, concern for the *Auslandsdeutsche* was tied to more aggressive expansionist ambitions. Whatever the agenda driving different interests in the *Auslandsdeutsche*, James Casteel points out, "the language of national belonging was part and parcel of a German discourse on empire" (Casteel 2007: 435). The Nazis would exploit the full imperialist potential of this discourse.

After coming to power in January 1933, Hitler quickly began implementing his party's own radical approach to the minorities issue. In October 1933, he withdrew Germany from the League of Nations. Through a series of anti-Semitic legislative measures between 1933 and 1935, the Nazi government moved to strip Jews of their rights of citizenship, purge them from the professions, education, and the civil service, and vilify them in the media. "Europe and the entire world reeled from the shock," Carol Fink observes, "of a self-proclaimed champion of minorities transformed suddenly into a persecutor of its own citizens" (Fink 2004: 330). During these early years in power, the Nazis quickly co-opted all of the Weimar associations dedicated to the protection of German minorities and the promotion of the German cultural mission abroad in the service of their imperialistic ambitions. After German troops had overrun Poland and in early October 1939, Hitler declared that Germany would make no further territorial demands and expressed his desire for peace. He outlined his plan for resettling the German minorities from the east into the conquered territories. Because it promised to remove "a potential source of friction and conflict," the Nazi press praised his plan as the "'Magna Carta' for eastern Europe" (Lumans 1993: 130). As part of this resettlement effort, Nazi officials began negotiations with a number of eastern states in 1939 to reach an agreement on the transfer of ethnic Germans. Overall, 500,000 ethnic Germans were uprooted and transferred between 1939 and 1941 (Fleischhauer 1986b: 96; Koehl 1957: 91–96, 100). However, Hitler was making preparations, even in October 1939, to expand his war of conquest in an attack on the Soviet Union (Craig 1978: 716).

In Nazi ideology, the Russian Germans occupied a special symbolic role. The Nazis emphasized their stalwart virtues as honest, hardworking tillers of the soil to depict them as archetypical representatives of the uncorrupted German *Volk*. Bolshevik mistreatment of them provided useful propaganda fodder to dramatize the communist menace. Their victimization was attributed to their Germanness, and their victimhood was raised as an exemplar of the collective suffering that the German *Volk* had endured. The Nazis invoked the cause of the Russian Germans in justifying war against the Soviet Union (Casteel 2007: 462–463). When Hitler launched his invasion of the Soviet Union on 22 June 1941, Stalin wasted little time in moving against Soviet Germans. Mass deportations began in Ukraine. Approximately 100,000 ethnic Germans were deported, but the process was interrupted by the swiftness of the German advance. Over the course of the summer, some 400,000 Volga Germans were forced to evacuate their Republic, which was then dissolved as an autonomous political unit. The methods of transportation were brutally harsh, and many died along the way. Estimates suggest that between 650,000 and 700,000 ethnic Germans were deported altogether (Fleischhauer 1986c: 66–91).

When the Soviet forces withdrew before the rapid German advance, they left behind several hundred thousand ethnic Germans, mainly in the Ukraine and the Black Sea region. As early as January 1942, Nazi authorities began transferring groups of ethnic Germans westward. The evacuations continued until May 1944. Overall, the Nazis' records suggest some 350,000 persons were transferred (Fleischhauer 1983: 193, 208–224). The homecoming proved to be of short duration for the vast majority of the evacuees. Most had been settled temporarily in territory on the eastern rim of the greater German border. When Soviet forces arrived, they had little difficulty tracking them down. Soviet troops captured 200,000 of the evacuees and returned them to the Soviet Union. In their return passage, between 15 and 30 percent of the evacuees died along the way. Under a post-war agreement, the Allies sent back another 80,000, whom the Soviets placed in settlement camps with the earlier arrivals. Of the 350,000 evacuees, then, only about 70,000 were able to remain (Fleischhauer 1986b: 101–102). After all the resettlements had been completed by 1945 to 1946, the population of Soviet Germans numbered 1,250,000, which was almost 300,000 less than in 1941 (Pinkus 1986: 103).

Where Borders Intersect: The German Minority in Silesia

Today, Upper Silesia is located in southwestern Poland along the borderlands Poland shares with Germany and the Czech Republic, but it has been a major source of the *Aussiedler* from Poland since the 1950s. The multi-ethnic character of the region reflects its history as a borderland frontier fought over by competing nationalizing powers. Upper Silesia was populated not only by Germans and Poles, but also by a mixed segment of groups of Slavic extraction. During the inter-war years, the population in this multicultural region was caught between Germany's irredentist agenda and the Polish government's homogenizing ambitions. The nationalist presumption that collective cultural identity should be singular and exclusive left little room for accommodating the ethnic diversity of this region. To the consternation of both German and Polish nationalists, the mixed segment of indigenous groups oscillated in their professed cultural loyalties between Poland and Germany, depending on circumstance. This pattern of oscillation reflects the multi-ethnic affinities of this segment, whose core identity had long been syncretistic and rooted in an attachment to their own region. These groups displayed a pragmatic willingness to adapt their cultural orientations to the majority culture so that it did not require sacrificing their own regional identities. In competing for possession of Upper Silesia, both the Polish and German governments sought to impose their own definition of nationality upon these groups (Linek 2002: 137–144; Ther 2002: 183–184).

After World War I, both Poland and Germany asserted claims to Upper Silesia, while a separatist group of Silesians sought autonomy, if not outright independence. The autonomy movement had as many as 350,000 members, and probably represented the strongest preference of the indigenous Silesians, but it was never given serious consideration by the Allied Powers (Ther 2002: 176). However, applying the principle of national self-determination to settle the question would also prove highly problematic since the Silesian's national affinities were in continuous flux and variegated according to one's socioeconomic status, religious affiliation, and linguistic and cultural sensibilities (Kamusella 2002: 49–55; Ther 2002: 172–174). The Allied Powers agreed to hold a plebiscite in 1921 that would allow Upper Silesians to decide whether they wanted to be a part of Germany or Poland. In the plebiscite, almost 60 percent of the region's inhabitants had voted in favor of Germany, including 40 percent of the Polish-speaking voters. After the plebiscite, a League of Nations' panel divided the province, and assigned the different parts to Germany and Poland in rough proportion to the percentage of the vote. As a result, Poland acquired approximately two-fifths of Upper Silesia, the most urbanized and industrialized part encompassing 46 percent of its population (Blanke 1993: 26–31, 245; 1975: 247). These territorial changes brought continued outmigration on both sides of the border. Between 1918 and 1925, some 117,000 to 170,000 persons left the Polish quarter of Upper Silesia to resettle in Germany, while during the 1920s, some 90,000 to 100,000 persons relocated from the German region to the Polish quarter (Kamusella 1999: 56).

In dealing with their respective minorities in Upper Silesia, the Polish and German governments faced very different situations. In contrast to the non-German minorities in German Upper Silesia, the German minority in Polish Upper Silesia had traditionally occupied a dominant role among the educated and economic elites. The relative strength of the German economy compared to its Polish counterpart enhanced the appeal of accepting German rule. Moreover, whereas the Polish government lacked the resources to provide much assistance to its kin minorities in German Upper Silesia, the German government not only had more resources, but also saw supporting its ethnic kin as essential to its irredentist ambitions. In the face of these challenges, the Polish government set out to marginalize the German minority in Upper Silesia through such measures as the liquidation of German-owned property, manipulating the public educational system to close minority schools, imposing controls on the ecclesiastical administration of German churches, prohibiting the use of German in communicating with public officials, suppressing German political organizations, and censuring German-language newspapers. However, just as the Polish government sought to de-Germanize its part of Upper Silesia, so too did the German government seek to de-Polonize its part. In some cases, there were striking parallels. For example, while the Polish government began in the early 1920s to undertake the Polonizing of place and family names, the German government in the 1930s pressed to replace Slavic names with German ones.

Although the Polish government's policies toward its German minority was subject to the 1919 Minority Treaty imposed on Poland by the Allied Powers as well as the 1922 Geneva Convention that Poland had concluded bilaterally with Germany, these constraints did not alter the nationalizing thrust of these policies. These two legal instruments had proved ill-equipped to do more than curb the extremes of these efforts at nationalization. The League was always reluctant to meddle much in the internal affairs of its Member States, and was more concerned with appeasing its Member States than in redressing injustices that had been inflicted on minority petitioners (Blanke 1993: 132; Fink 2004: 282, 361). The Polish government learned quickly, as Christian von Frentz's research has shown, that through various obstructionist tactics, it could "create irreversible economic and demographic facts within a significantly shorter time than the League needed to react" (Frentz 1999: 141–145, 238). In 1934, the Polish government repudiated its obligations under the 1919 Minorities Treaty, and the Geneva Convention lapsed in 1937. On 5 November 1937, the German and Polish governments issued a Joint Declaration pledging to respect the cultural autonomy of their respective minorities, but it had little practical effect. That same day Hitler held a secret meeting in the Reich Chancellery at which he told his top military officials to prepare for war within a year and revealed his radical plans for conquest to acquire "living space" (*Lebensraum*) in the east. For its part, the Polish government continued pursuing the same aggressive policies toward its German minority (Blanke 1993: 126–137, 215–218).

After 1933, the overwhelming majority of the German minority in Poland had thrown their support behind the Nazi movement, looking to Hitler as their last best hope as a vindicator of their rights. Since Poland had been living under a dictatorship since a coup in 1926, the authoritarianism of Nazi rule did not detract from their appeal. Given the precariousness of their situation inside Poland, the German minority was also drawn to the Nazi ideological vision of a broad national community that transcended state borders and promised to include them on an equal footing in a Greater Germany (Blanke 1993: 163). The mixed groups also identified more with the German-held part of Upper Silesia than with the Polish state. Like the German minority, they resented the government's Polonization policies, which threatened to reduce them to the status of second-class citizens. They saw greater possibilities for social and economic advancement in being associated with Germany than with Poland. In German-held Upper Silesia, the Nazis saw these mixed groups as racially tainted and opportunistic (as opposed to manifesting an authentic attachment to German culture), but they were suitable for Germanization. Under the new two-class Reich Citizenship Law of 15 September 1935, the Nazi government classified these mixed groups as *Reichsbürger* rather than *Staatsangehörige*. The former category was reserved for those persons deemed members of the German *Volk* in a biological and cultural sense. Aimed initially at Jews and gypsies, the latter applied to those of non-Aryan descent, and denied its bearers any political rights, including the right to vote and to hold public office (Kamusella 2000: 99; Majer 2003: 111–113).

After Nazi Germany had attacked and defeated Polish forces in September of 1939, Hitler absorbed western Poland into the Reich as the annexed eastern territories. The Nazis created a system of concentration camps in Silesia, most notably Auschwitz. To integrate the territories, the Nazi government sought to Germanize the territories by eliminating all visible traces of a Polish presence. From 1939 to 1942, some 81,000 Poles in the newly acquired quarter of Upper Silesia were driven out. At the same time, the Nazis moved to resettle ethnic Germans from Eastern Europe into the annexed lands (Kamusella 1999: 57). Cognizant of the ethnically mixed character of Upper Silesia and the other annexed territories, the Nazis sought to determine the racial composition of the occupied territories. Despite their ideology of racial purity, they thought that some portion of this mixed population could be assimilated into the *Volksgemeinschaft*. To this end, the Nazis developed elaborate procedures to identify, categorize, and rank groups based on the four part classificatory scheme of the German National List (*Deutsche Volksliste*). Category 1 (*Volksdeutsche*) applied those persons who had actively demonstrated their Germanness culturally or politically before the war, such as through participation in German organizations. Category 2 (*Deutschstämmige*) applied to those persons of German descent who had not openly expressed their German identity during the inter-war era. Those persons enrolled in these first two categories became eligible for *Reichsbürgerschaft* under the 1935 Nazi Citizenship Law, while those in Category 3 were limited to become only *Staatsangehörige*. Category 3 (*Eingedeutschte*) designated those persons suitable for Germanization, meaning those persons of at least partial German descent or married to persons of German descent. Most of the mixed groups in Upper Silesia were registered in this category. Category 4 (*Rückgedeutschte*) denoted those persons of German descent who had been assimilated into Polish culture, but may be capable of re-Germanization. Everyone who did not qualify for one of these four categories was assigned to the general class of "protected person," though this was a little more than a administrative euphemism (Linek 2002: 154; Majer 2003: 123–124, 238–241). Those who were not under any of the categories were subject to deportation or incarceration in a concentration camp.

As the Soviet armies advanced toward Berlin, many ethnic Germans in Poland fled westward in front of them. From the summer of 1944 to the spring of 1945, hundreds of thousands of civilians died from malnutrition, cold, disease, and other hardships in this first mass exodus. Beginning in the summer of 1945, the Polish military and other civilian authorities followed this phase with their own brutal expulsion campaign. They sought to cleanse Poland of its German minorities before the Allied Powers imposed their own peace settlement. At the same time, the cruelty of the Nazi occupation had aroused an intense hatred among Poles toward Germans, and the Poles now took their revenge on the Germans in their midst. Even Germans who had taken no part in the Nazi atrocities were subject to beatings, robbery, murder, and rape. German minorities living in the borderlands, including Upper and Lower Silesia, were a particular target of this campaign. While roughly 100,000 persons were deported to the Soviet Union, most were stripped of their citizenship and sent to occupied Germany. The displaced Germans had to leave behind most of their property, and many were interned in labor camps formerly used by the Nazis as concentration camps. In the wake of the Red Army's advance, the homes and possessions of the indigenous Silesians were plundered not only by Soviet troops, but also by roving gangs of criminals, the so-called "szabrownicy." The plunderers typically came from central Poland and often acted with the connivance of Polish authorities (Ther 1998: 38–50, 52–66, 126–130).

Building on agreements reached at the Yalta conference in February 1945, the Allied Powers at the Potsdam Conference in August 1945 assigned to Poland all of the territories east of the Oder and Neisse rivers, the southern part of East Prussia, and the former free city of Danzig, in exchange for Poland losing its eastern territories of southern Lithuania, western Byelorussia, and the western Ukraine to the Soviet Union. Under these terms, Lower and Upper Silesia became a part of Poland. The Polish and Czech expulsions of their German minorities forced the hands of the Allied Powers at the meeting at Potsdam. While Stalin actively supported mass expulsions, the Western Allies sought to limit them. Nevertheless, the Potsdam Treaty established a legal sanction for the forced population transfers (de Zayas 1979: 80–104). Following the conference, Polish authorities continued the expulsions of Germans through the spring of 1947, but in a somewhat more orderly and organized fashion. Although no consensus exists over the numbers, one estimate suggests that from June 1945 to December/January 1947, 1,770,000 persons were driven out of Lower Silesia and 310,000 from Upper Silesia (Kamusella 1999: 58n38). The German population in Lower Silesia declined from roughly 1,234,000 in 1946 to 51,000 in 1950 (Kamusella 1999: 58). From the middle of 1945 to 1947, nearly 2 million Germans were displaced from the Polish borderland regions. In total, approximately 2 million Germans died in the process of being driven from their ancestral homes (de Zayas 1979: 103).

Territorial changes and forced population transfers had made Poland far less ethnically diverse than before the war. While most of the resident population in Lower Silesia was expelled, with the exception of those with skills that made them economically useful, the Polish government sought to keep the majority of the population in Upper Silesia. However, it required the indigenous Silesians to certify their "Polishness" by submitting to a procedure of verification and rehabilitation. From 1945 to 1949, the Polish government employed the Nazis' classification list as a rough basis for determining the status of the Silesian population, but applied the categories in inverse order. Those persons registered in Categories 1 and 2 were deemed as unequivocally German, and therefore subject to expulsion, prosecution for war crimes, and/or internment in a labor camp. The vast majority registered in Categories 3 and 4 were required to take a loyalty oath in order to obtain Polish citizenship. Even after completing the verification process, indigenous Upper Silesians remained targets of discrimination, suspicion, and ostracism. They found themselves doubly stigmatized in the minds of Poles as untrustworthy, disloyal, and pro-German: first, from the fact that they had been enrolled on the German National List, and second, from the subsequent fact that their "Polishness" had required certification through a verification procedure (Jonderko 2002: 210–211).

In seeking to consolidate and legitimate its hold over its new western territories, Polish authorities depicted their efforts as a matter of reclaiming lands that had historically belonged to Poland. They immediately set out to re-Polonize the newly acquired territories, and re-Polonization also entailed de-Germanization of Silesia. They also moved aggressively to eradicate any sign or memory of German cultural influence. Both teaching in German and speaking it in public were prohibited. Polish authorities also revived the policy of Polonizing place names, and prohibiting the public display of German writing. Even German inscriptions on tombstones were not exempt (Linek 2000: 140–141).

Re-Polonization also meant first repopulating the areas with Poles. Settlers arrived from devastated parts of central Poland, drawn by the prospect of claiming abandoned houses and farms. Poles repatriated from Western Europe also came to the area. In addition, forced migrants from the eastern territories of Poland annexed by the Soviet Union were also directed to Poland's newly acquired western territories. The Polish government saw these incomers as "pioneers and missionaries of Polishness," and the indigenous Silesians as "the receptors of the Mission" (Ther 1998: 304). Accordingly, the government gave the incomers preferential treatment over the indigenous Silesians. Together, these groups came to comprise the overwhelming majority of the population in Lower Silesia and approximately one-third of the population in Upper Silesia (Kamusella 1999: 59). The arrival of these newcomers created new rifts with the indigenous population in Upper Silesia. The indigenous Silesians associated the incomers with those who had plundered their homes. The newcomers were disposed to see the indigenous Silesians as crypto-Germans. The resettlers from central Poland fared best because they had arrived sooner than the forced migrants from the territories annexed by the Soviet Union, and so had been able to claim the best available housing for themselves. Because they were often better educated and more staunchly anti-German than other groups, the Polish government gave them a disproportionate share of the posts in the new civil administration in Upper Silesia. At the same time, indigenous Silesians were denied positions in local government and the civil administration, and found it difficult to obtain jobs commensurate with their training and education (Ther 1998: 314–320).

The harsh repressive measures the government applied in its de-Germanization and re-Polonization campaigns did not have the intended effect. Although officially declared to be Polish, the indigenous Silesians were alienated from the exclusivist Polish nationalism pressed upon them. "The indigenous Silesians," Philipp Ther observes, "reacted then to Polish nationality politics the same as they had earlier to National Socialist [politics]. They withdrew into the private sphere and confined themselves predominantly to contact with their fellow Silesians" (2002: 196). With long-standing historical ties to German culture, they began to increasingly identify with it as a defensive measure. Continued discrimination and dissatisfaction with communist rule reinforced this trend. The new communist government sought to use an exclusivist Polish nationalism as the basis for consolidating its authority and homogenizing the population. Its approach assumed a sharp dichotomy between a German and Polish national self-understanding, and so made little accommodation for the region's mixed cultural heritages or the multi-ethnic character of its indigenous residents (Linek 2000: 133). Administrative officials treated the indigenous Silesians as second-class citizens, and their local dialects and often poor knowledge of Polish made them conspicuous targets for discrimination. They found themselves trapped at the lower end of the labor market with few opportunities for advancement. The curriculum in the local schools was oriented around vocational training to provide workers for the industry in the region, so the indigenous Silesian youth did not receive the kind of education that would facilitate upward mobility. For the most part, the teachers in the local schools were resettlers from central Poland, and not favorably disposed toward the indigenous residents (Jonderko 2002: 213–217).

The FRG's impressive economic achievements during the 1950s made the German lure ever more attractive. The remaining German minority in Lower Silesia was given the option of obtaining Polish citizenship in 1951 and they were offered some modest minority rights, but they would emigrate instead in large numbers as soon as they could. De-Stalinization helped to open that emigration window in 1956, and the need for Western goods and commercial ties that the FRG could provide kept it open. Between 1956 and 1959, some 48,000 so-called "indubitable" Germans emigrated from Lower Silesia to the FRG, while another 7,000 emigrated to the GDR. From 1960 onward, the FRG would continue to press successfully for the release of more 'ethnic Germans,' but the majority who emigrated came from the ethnically mixed indigenous population of Silesia. They had any number of reasons to seek to emigrate—from feeling a cultural affinity with German culture and alienation from communist rule to materialistic aspirations for greater social and economic security. Given their subordinate, marginalized status in Polish society, they had many fewer reasons to identify their allegiances with it. From the standpoint of the majority culture, the explanation was much simpler. "Polish society saw in the emigration," Franciszek Jonderko observes, "exclusively a disloyal behavior toward the Polish state, not ... a reaction to the problems with which the indigenous population were confronted" (Jonderko 2002: 217). With few opportunities for voice in Poland, the indigenous Silesians chose to exit. By 1989, the number of Silesians that had resettled in the FRG and the GDR approached 4.5 million (Kamusella 1999: 70).

Minority Rights and the FRG's Policy toward the *Aussiedler*

After World War II, the principle of minority group rights was eclipsed by a focus on individual human rights. A general consensus had emerged that the inter-war Minority Treaties had been a failure. The Allied Powers' sanctioning of forced population transfers at the Potsdam Conference (1945) was not only indicative of this perceived failure, but also of a widely shared belief that minorities pose a chronic threat to any stable order of states in Eastern and Central Europe. Appraising how states coped with the problems of ethnic diversity from the end of World War I through to the immediate post–Cold War era, Aviel Roshwald observes that "state-organized violence proved the preferred method for resolving East Central Europe's intractable demographic dilemmas" (Roshwald 2005: 77). At the end of World War II, Eastern and Central European states, such as Poland and Czechoslovakia, made it clear that they would never again accept being subject to minority treaties. Private individuals and groups put forward proposals to create a universal system of minority protection to remedy the problem of partiality that had afflicted the inter-war minority system. However, the Allied Powers recoiled from any prospect that they might be bound by such a system, and recognized their own self-interest in keeping minority issues as a matter of domestic sovereignty. At the same time, they could not completely turn their backs on the idealistic rhetoric, such as President Franklin Roosevelt's "Four Freedoms," that had been used to justify the war. A focus on individual human rights had the advantage of not entailing any commitment to preserve the cultural autonomy of minorities, such as through provisions guaranteeing education in a minority's mother tongue. It could also neatly sidestep issues of national self-determination that any recognition of a national minority's collective rights often implicates. In contrast to the inter-war Minority Treaties, the 1948 Universal Declaration of Human Rights was purely a statement of principles with no monitoring procedures or enforcement mechanisms. Together with the United Nations Charter, it was carefully crafted so that prerogatives of state sovereignty within domestic jurisdictions would not be impinged. Affirming the promotion of individual human rights as the aspirational goals of the international society of states was consistent with the core principles of Western liberalism, but it was also compatible with a homogeneous nation-state model that is predicated on the absence of minorities with distinct group claims, rights, and interests (Thornberry 1991: 113–120; Jackson Preece 1998: 95–106; Mazower 2004).

The FRG's Basic Law reflects this change in approach. The Basic Law not only specifically elevates respect for universal human rights into a guiding normative principle, but in contrast to the Weimar Constitution and the 1849 Frankfurt Constitution, it contains no provision regarding minority rights. The Basic Law was designed as a constitution for a homogeneous nation-state, not a multinational empire, but it was also predicated on an overarching commitment to reunification and on a self-understanding of the FRG as a national homeland. Consistent with this homeland self-understanding, the FRG took a strong protective interest in the welfare of external German minorities. The relentless lobbying of German refugee and expellee groups reinforced this commitment (Wolff 2005: 291–292). However, aside from its *Aussiedler* admissions policy and providing some humanitarian assistance, the Federal Republic had little maneuvering room to deal with such issues during the early decades of the Cold War. In the early 1950s, for example, Denmark refused to sign a bilateral treaty with the FRG that would guarantee rights for their respective German and Danish minorities. Only the prospect of the FRG's accession to NATO in 1955 induced the Danish government to agree to reciprocal Declarations of rights of the German and Danish minorities (Heintze 2000: 206–208). In light of their experience with Germany's external minorities policy after World War I, many suspected the FRG of harboring irredentist aims (Wolff 2000: 188–191). Since expellee groups were by no means reconciled to German territorial losses, there was some basis for these fears. During the 1950s, the expellee demands for a restoration of the 1937 borders enjoyed broad support among the West German political leadership and the public (Moeller 2001: 35). This support was reflected in Chancellor Konrad Adenauer's public declaration in 1950 that "one day Silesia will again be German" (quoted in Moeller 2001: 37).

On his first visit to the Soviet Union in September 1955, Adenauer pressed his hosts on the issue of German minorities. The Khrushchev government would not budge from its position that all Russian Germans were Soviet citizens over whom the FRG had no jurisdiction. But as a gesture of goodwill, the Khrushchev government subsequently issued three decrees that granted amnesty to Soviet Germans imprisoned for war crimes and removed most of the legal restrictions that Stalin had imposed on them during the war. These decrees did not offer the German deportees any compensation for the losses they had suffered. In addition, the decrees did not rescind the charges of treason that Stalin had made to justify his deportation policies. The Khrushchev government finally acknowledged that these charges were unfounded nine years later by a decree in August 1964 (Pinkus 1986: 108–112).

The FRG's *Aussiedler* policy during the Cold War operated from the assumption that kin minorities in the Eastern Bloc and the Soviet Union were suffering discrimination and persecution on account of their German ancestry. At the same time, repressive communist policies toward German minorities were eroding their ability to preserve their German cultural heritages and practices. For example, from the first post-war census in 1959 to the 1979 census, the number of Soviets identifying themselves as German rose from 1,619,655 to 1,932,000. During this same period, the number of Soviet Germans who claimed German as their mother tongue declined from 75 percent to 57 percent. From 1968 to 1972, Benjamin Pinkus reports, "the percentage of German pupils learning German as their mother tongue can be stated as 35 percent in Kirgizia, 25 percent in Kazakhstan, 10 percent in the Russian Federal Republic and less than 10 percent in Tajikistan" (1986: 127; Stricker 2000: 168–170). In addition to the bonds of a common language, religion was traditionally a critically binding element in the cultural lives of Russian Germans. Church services conducted in German reinforced a community's shared linguistic heritage. But by the mid 1980s, Pinkus estimates, only 25 to 30 percent of Soviet Germans retained their religious beliefs (Pinkus 1986: 139–143; Heitman 1980: 32–51). The erosion of these German cultural heritages and practices meant that for ever larger numbers of *Aussiedler*, their admission to the FRG would be predicated on the principle of descent rather than on any demonstrable knowledge of German culture, participation in German cultural activities, or even the ability to speak the German language.

In the early 1970s, Chancellor Willy Brandt's *Ostpolitik* would help to defuse tensions with the FRG's eastern neighbors. Brandt's policy of constructive engagement resulted in a series of bilateral treaties with Poland (1970), the

Soviet Union (1970), the GDR (1972), and Czechoslovakia (1973). Opposed by the expellee organizations in the FRG, these agreements essentially recognized the post-war status quo, but also established a framework for closer coopera- tion. In the treaties with Poland, the Soviet Union, and Czechoslovakia, both sides renounced any territorial claims on one another and accepted the invio- lability of the existing borders. With respect to Poland, this agreement entailed explicitly acknowledging the Oder-Neisse boundary line. In entering its treaty with the Soviet Union, the FRG sent a formal letter to the GDR making clear that this agreement in no way signified that it had abandoned its political aim to reunify the German nation within a broader peaceful European order.

Chapter 9

The Federal Republic as German Homeland

The framers of the Basic Law were concerned with establishing the FRG as the sole sovereign representative of the German people whose overriding political goal was to restore national unity. This understanding would have significant implications for the FRG's subsequent policies toward immigrants as well as toward external German minorities. It meant, in Arendt's words, that the state was conceived as the "instrument of the nation," so that the state would "recognize only 'nationals' as citizens, to grant full civil and political rights only to those who belonged to the national community" (Arendt 1979: 230). This idea of 'national community' was defined in ethnic terms that not only transcended state borders, but also in fact presupposed that the existing configuration of state borders was only provisional, just like the Basic Law itself claimed. The self-understanding of the FRG as a homeland for ethnic kin arose not simply from the partition of the two Germanys and the loss of German territories, but also from the need to provide a basis for incorporating the millions of German refugees and expellees who had entered the FRG in the wake of World War II.

This self-understanding was reinforced by the continuing presence of external German minorities in the Eastern Bloc states and the Soviet Union, who were subject to discrimination and persecution on the basis of their perceived German ethnicity. These "ethnic Germans," Daniel Levy has observed, "exemplify the notion of the ethno-cultural nation ... expressed by shared language and culture (*Kulturnation*) and the principle of descent (*Ethnonation*)" (Levy 2002b: 222). The laws and policies the FRG adopted toward its ethnic kin have had a profound and enduring effect on its understanding of membership and immigration. This chapter examines these laws and policies with respect to the German refugees and expellees, the *Übersiedler* and the *Aussiedler*.

German Refugees and Expellees

Given the decades-long struggle that the FRG would experience in fashion-ing any comprehensive approach to the integration of subsequent immigrant groups, its remarkable success in integrating—culturally, politically, economi-cally, and socially—its first and most massive wave of immigrants during the 1950s is all the more striking. The ingredients of this success then merit some special attention. From the end of World War II until the erection of the Berlin Wall in 1961, approximately 12 million ethnic German refugees and expellees immigrated to the Federal Republic and formed by far the largest group of migrants that entered West Germany.[1] In 1950, they composed 16.7 percent of the population and this percentage rose steadily to 23.9 by 1960 (Herbert 1990: 196). The rapid and successful integration of this staggering number of migrants in the western region of the former Reich offers an instructive counterexample to the FRG's handling of the incorporation of many subse-quent migrant groups. Beginning with the inclusive citizenship provisions of the Basic Law, one of the keys to this success was the extensive measures that the Federal Republic took to facilitate their integration. Another crucial fac-tor was the German "economic miracle" that provided jobs, rising incomes, and money for recovery. If these refugee and expellee groups were counted as "immigrants," that is, as persons residing in a country other than that of their birth (the commonly accepted UN definition), then by the end of the 1950s, the FRG would have been considered as a preeminent land of immigration in both absolute and per capita numbers.

In order to resolve the citizenship status of the German expellees and refu-gees who had arrived between 1945 and 1949, Article 116 of the Basic Law extended citizenship not only to all those persons who had been nationals of the Reich within its 1937 frontiers, but also to all persons of German descent (*Volkszugehörigkeit*) who had been expelled or fled from Eastern Europe. In 1953, the federal expellee law (*Bundesvertriebenen und Flüchtlingsgesetz*) clarified and expanded the categories of persons who qualified as an "expel-lee" under this article. Article 6 defined an "ethnic German" as "someone who acknowledged himself to belong to the German people, in so far as this acknowledgement can be confirmed through such specific characteristics as descent, language, upbringing or culture" (Koppenfels 2002: 103). This defini-tion of 'ethnic German' combined subjective and objective criteria, though the very broad formulation of each left broad discretionary room in their application. The expellee law also guaranteed that that the newcomers would enjoy the same

1. Of the 12 million German refugees and expellees, almost 65 percent resettled in the west-ern part of Germany and about 32 percent in the eastern part. Smaller numbers stayed in Austria (Fassman and Münz 1994: 521–523).

entitlements as the native-born, such as with respect to social insurance and pensions. The 1955 Law on Regulating Questions of Citizenship (*Gesetz zur Regelung von Fragen der Staatsangehörigkeit*) conferred an entitlement of almost automatic naturalization to ethnic Germans residing beyond the 1937 borders. This extension applied to all persons who had been registered in the first three classes of the German National List and to those ethnic Germans whom the Nazis had recruited as part of its resettlement policy for the greater German Reich, but generally it did not apply to those persons whom the Nazis had given Reich citizenship in Austria, Belgium, France, and Luxembourg (Wolff 2003: 73). The term *Aussiedler* was applied to this group of ethnic Germans who were admitted to the FRG after 1950, and the statutory policy established during this decade continued largely unaltered until the end of the Cold War. However, only a small number of *Aussiedler* were expected to come to the FRG under this policy (Groenendijk 1997: 462–463; Koppenfels 2002: 103–106).

The common "Germanness" that the refugees and expellees shared with their fellow citizens greatly assisted their full inclusion into Federal Republic life, but, like many later migrant groups, they initially encountered a cool, and sometimes hostile, reception from native West Germans. Living in precarious circumstances themselves, many West Germans worried that the new arrivals would merely bring new burdens. Moreover, the shared "Germanness" did not preclude deep differences in culture, regional identification, and local experience. From our perspective today, it is all too easy to view these differences as rather minor relative to contemporary forms of cultural diversity, but it did not seem so to many observers at the time. The perception of difference, after all, is deeply rooted into one's frame of reference.

In early studies on the integration of the expellees and refugees, some of the same concerns are found and are raised over dealing with cultural diversity, which reappears in connection with subsequent migrant groups. Comparing the areas from which the refugees and expellees had come to their new home, Egon Lendl emphasized the differences: "Above all the land east of the Elbe presents ... an essentially different picture than the west" (1959: 461). Not only is the natural landscape of the west different, he observes, but its social and political characters are also different. The west has a more socially variegated population than the east; the urbanization process and patterns of mobility had progressed farther in the west; industry was more highly developed in the west than in the east; and, the large-landed estates that had controlled agriculture in much of the east did not exist in most of the west. In short, the social, political, and economic structures in the west were far more "modern" than in the east.

The influx of refugees and expellees also changed the religious map of West Germany. Historically, German territories had been divided deeply along confessional lines by region and by community. The dispersion of the refugees and expellees across the FRG created new enclaves of Protestant minorities in predominantly Catholic areas and new enclaves of Catholic minorities in Protestant domains. In the more confessionally mixed urban centers, the settlement of expellees and refugees substantially increased this intermixture. Remarking on the cumulative effect of this dispersion, one commentator observed, "The remaining confessional homogeneity that had survived to a large extent through four hundred years has now been broken through everywhere" (Menges 1959: 197).

Sensitive to the regional and historical differences of the German territories, Heinrich Rogge cautioned native West Germans in 1959 against asking the expellees and refugees to adopt the particular culture of the *Länder* in which they settled. "When say Silesian or Sudeten German refugees are legally integrated in Bavaria," he observed, "it cannot be expected of them to become Bavarians, that is, to be assimilated into the Bavarian ethnic folk (*Stammestum*). Rather the Federal Republic and the Bavarian state are obligated to support ... these groups in their efforts to preserve their Silesian or Sudeten German ethnic identities (*Stammestums*)" (Rogge 1959: 197). To preserve these identities, Silesian Germans, Sudeten Germans, and other German groups began very quickly after World War II to organize Homeland Associations (*Landmannschaften*). The activities and structures of these associations varied, but their main original purpose was to provide social and economic assistance and to maintain cultural traditions, customs, and rituals. Among their cultural activities, they funded research on their former homelands, developed education programs, sponsored festivals and other ceremonies, and organized outings and banquets (Boehm 1959: 521–605).

The task of integrating the refugees and expellees involved not just finding room for fellow Germans, but also accommodating pronounced differences in religion, dialect, customs, and heritage. These differences often made them seem dangerously "foreign" in the eyes of many native inhabitants, who routinely criticized their unwillingness to work, their general uncleanliness, their proneness to criminality, and their lack of gratitude (Schulze 1997: 53–72; Oberpenning 1999: 302). Government leaders also expressed doubt about the genuineness of the asylum motives of many of the refugees (Levy 1999: 72–73). For their part, the responses of refugees and expellees often displayed "disappointment and even bitterness, caused by the feeling of being rejected by the native inhabitants" (Schulze 1997: 64). Paradoxically, reports about the victimization that the expellees had endured in the hands of the advancing Red Army toward the end of the war and in the forced population transfers that followed received enormous attention. For West Germans, the expellees and the missing German POWs became important symbols as martyrs signifying that Germans had suffered collectively as much as any people from the war. As West Germans struggled to come to terms with the devastating losses that the war had brought them, this symbolic role helped to facilitate the expellees' integration into a new society bonded by common suffering and shared sacrifice. This powerful sense of collective victimhood also provided a means through which they could reassert a German national identity disassociated from the Nazi past (Moeller 2001: 4–7, 12–14, 32–35; Levy 2002a: 223).

To assert and defend their particular interests in the integration process, the refugees and expellees benefited considerably from the advantage of having full and equal citizenship, which enabled them—together with their sheer numbers—to compete effectively in the new West German political system. This advantage ensured them the right to organize politically, to hold elective office, and to vote. In January 1950, the expellee politician Waldemar Kraft established the German Fellowship Bloc of Expellees and Victims of Injustice (*Gesamtdeutscher Block der Heimatvertriebenen und Entrechteten*, or BHE). "Because the large numbers of expellees and refugees in some *Länder* made the electoral success of the BHE very likely," Franz Neumann has observed, "the [other] parties from the beginning took [these voters] strongly into account" (Neumann 1968: 21; Ahonen 2003: 56). In 1950, the BHE gained 23.4 percent of the vote in Schleswig-Holstein Landtag elections and 12.5 percent of the vote in Bavaria Landtag elections (Ritter and Niehuss 1991: 158, 174). The emergence of the BHE posed a real threat to the electoral coalition that the CDU/CSU hoped to build across the center-right spectrum. Remembering how the fragmentation of the party system in the late 1920s had helped to undermine the Weimar Republic, CDU/CSU leadership viewed the forging of a broad coalition as critical to the stability of the Federal Republic. During the 1950s, the CDU/CSU assiduously wooed BHE's supporters. Federal Republic Chancellor Konrad Adenauer even included Waldemar Kraft and other expellee leaders in his cabinet.

The example of the BHE vividly demonstrates the importance for immigrants to have the legal and institutional means to represent their own interests in the political process. As Franz Neumann concluded from his intensive study of the BHE, the refugees and the expellees owed this party a considerable debt for the improvements in their economic circumstances in the 1950s (Neumann 1968: 383). The very presence of the BHE could on occasion give refugee and expellee leaders a strong bargaining chip. In May 1952, for example, the Bundestag was preparing to enact the Equalization of the Burdens Act (*LAG*).[2] The law was designed to spread the economic losses suffered from the war by providing monetary compensation to expellees, refugees, and other Germans who had lost property, businesses, and other material assets. By early May, the legislation appeared to be headed for passage without further debate. But Linus Kather, a CDU parliament deputy and chair of the Association for Expelled

---

2. *Lastenausgleichsgesetz.*

Germans (*Bund der vertriebenen Deutschen*), launched an attack on the bill for offering too little compensation. He threatened to defect from the CDU and, taking his followers with him, join the BHE. Adenauer had little choice but to reach an accommodation with Kather, because the Chancellor needed the 20 to 30 votes Kather could swing in the Bundestag. These votes were crucial to Adenauer's effort at that time to amend the Basic Law, so that the FRG could rearm. By virtue of his threat, Kather was thus able to extract over DM 2 billion in additional compensation monies (Baring 1969: 156–57).

The inclusiveness of the FRG's democratic process then enabled the expellees to exert effective pressure in shaping the law's final form, while the successful negotiations over it showed that all sides were prepared to exercise in the end some pragmatic restraint in their approach to such an extraordinarily contentious issue (Hughes 1999: 129–150, 161–164, 172–178). Moreover, "even though the LAG aid was not substantially higher than earlier welfare payments," Daniel Levy observes, "it marked a significant symbolic shift from treating expellees as welfare recipients to their shared participation in a recovering economy" (2002b: 27). The willingness of their fellow citizens to help compensate them for their losses demonstrated to the expellees that they were recognized as members of a shared national community. This moral recognition became a key turning point in their integration into West German society, while the ability of the FRG government to put through such important social legislation did much to bolster the credibility and legitimacy of the new republican order in the eyes of all West Germans.

The CDU/CSU's efforts to win over BHE voters proved highly successful, and the latter's electoral following declined markedly during the 1950s. Although internal strife within the BHE hastened its demise, the shrinkage of its electoral base clearly showed that the expellees and refugees were becoming assimilated into their new home. In this process of assimilation, they received a great deal of help and had many channels through which to articulate their interests. "From the beginning," Hans Schoenberg observed of this assimilation process, "the government geared its organization on all levels to the existing economic and social needs of the expellees and refugees; on the federal level, also to their political aspirations" (Schoenberg 1970: 133). Along with the CDU/CSU, both the Free Democratic Party (FDP) and the SPD supported policies to help integrate the expellees and refugees. The federal and *Länder* governments created special boards, cabinet ministries, and other agencies for refugee and expellee affairs. Throughout the 1950s and 1960s, the federal, state, and local governments gave millions of Deutsche Marks annually to expellee and refugee groups to support their cultural and organizational activities. In the Bundestag, expellee and refugee representatives sat on important legislative committees, including the budget and foreign affairs committees. They controlled the parliamentary committee for expellee and refugee affairs. However, possessing the means to represent their interests did not solidify divisions between these immigrant groups and native West Germans; rather, it forced the ruling government parties to address the interests of these groups and thereby to integrate these groups into the political life of the Federal Republic.

The successful integration of the refugees and expellees in the FRG depended on their ability to participate in national politics. Contrasting the refugees' and expellees' experience in the FRG with the experience of those living in the GDR reveals how important this political participation was to those in the FRG. In the FRG, the refugees and expellees enjoyed the equal rights of citizenship, which ensured them responsive political representation at all levels of government and showed the possession of broad support among the party elites across the political spectrum (Süssner 2004: 5). Philipp Ther has also emphasized the critical difference it made for expellee groups to have the freedom to organize themselves into independent associations, have institutional channels through which to articulate their grievances and demands, and to participate in the decision-making about public matters affecting their interests. The contrast between the GDR and the FRG is telling, especially when considering the lack of political representation of expellees and refugees in the former. The absence of such opportunities in the GDR precluded expellee groups from "taking their fate into own hands" in the same way. The vast majority of these expellees never came to identify their loyalties with the GDR, and they remained underrepresented in the upper ranks of the party, government, and industry (Ther 1998: 332–333, 340–342). Approximately 40 percent of the expellees that had been admitted into the GDR migrated out again by 1961 (Wolff 2003: 69). Additionally, owing to the refugees' and expellees' political representation in the FRG, the government provided considerable assistance to facilitate their settlement and incorporation into West German life. This assistance included not only tolerance of their distinct cultural heritages and practices, but also material support for the preservation of these heritages and practices. By contrast, even though the refugees and expellees had rights equal to the GDR's resident population, they nevertheless became "people without pasts" because "they were forbidden to combine their regional identities with their new societies" (Wille 2001: 278). Soviet integration policy made ideological reeducation a priority to discourage any resistance and to encourage acceptance of the communist model. The forced migrants "were supposed to integrate themselves into their society as ahistorical beings, officially forbidden to keep memories of their homelands alive or preserve their cultural and intellectual heritages" (Wille 2001: 271–272). Also, a rising economy in the FRG created a growing demand for labor and diminished fears that the newcomers would be a long-term burden. Some expellees and refugees were able to start their own businesses, while many others found employment in businesses eager to make use of this labor resource. The comparison between the political status of refugees and expellees in the FRG and GDR demonstrates that to a great extent, political participation enabled these people to share the benefits of the FRG's growing affluence with the resident population.

The example of the refugees and expellees from the 1950s calls attention to how much migration has shaped the population of the Federal Republic from its outset and testifies to its institutional capacity to promote the integration of migrants when the political will to do so exists. The influx of guestworkers that began modestly in the mid 1950s removed the remaining barriers to the full acceptance of the expellees and refugees as full members of West German society. "The outsider function," Daniel Levy observes, "was assumed by the new group. The 'refugee problem' was replaced by the 'foreigner problem'" (2002b: 28). Since neither the expellees nor the guestworkers were considered immigrants but rather were perceived as categorically different, German policymakers did not draw lessons from the first experience and apply them to the second, especially with regard to an integration policy. The FRG's remarkable achievement in integrating the expellees and refugees did not make West Germans any more confident in their society's capacity to absorb large numbers of newcomers or to accommodate cultural diversity. In most respects, the FRG would approach guestworker policy in direct converse to the approach it had fashioned for the expellees and refugees.

The Reception of the *Aussiedler* and *Übersiedler* in the Federal Republic

Between 1949 and 1992, about 5.3 million GDR citizens migrated to the Federal Republic; another 0.5 million migrated from the FRG to the GDR (Fassman and Münz 1994: 526).[3] The category of German refugees from the GDR was called *Übersiedler*. During roughly this same period, 3 million *Aussiedler* immigrated to Germany, most of them from Poland (51.4 percent), Romania (17.5 percent), and the former USSR (24.6 percent) (Fassman and Münz 1994: 526). During the 1980s, the number of "ethnic" Germans entering the Federal Republic soared. Between 1984 and 1988, the number of *Übersiedler* fluctuated annually from 14,000 and 41,000, but then soared to well over 300,000 in 1989 and 1990. From 1983 through 1986, approximately 40,000 *Aussiedler* came on average per year to the Federal Republic. This number rose to over 78,000 in 1987 and nearly reached 400,000 in 1990 (OECD 1993). Prior to 1989, the overwhelming majority of the *Aussiedler* came from Poland, but this pattern

3. According to the 1993 SOPEMI report (OECD 1993: 78), the number of migrants from the GDR to the FRG is as follows: 1950–1959: 220,300; 1960–1969: 61,800; 1970–1979: 14,900; 1980–1989: 58,500; 1988: 39,800; 1989: 343,900; 1990: 381,300.

would change dramatically thereafter. During the 1990s, the majority would come from the former Soviet Union (Dietz 2006: 122).

Although the *Aussiedler* were entitled to German citizenship and were immediately eligible to work and receive social assistance, training (including language education), and assistance with housing, they generally encountered greater difficulties than the *Übersiedler* from the GDR when integrating into the Federal Republic.[4] One major factor behind this difference was the lower competency of the *Aussiedler* in German. In addition, while both groups came from socialist systems and had to adapt to the conditions of a market economy, the historical and cultural backgrounds of the *Aussiedler* made the gap between the familiar and unfamiliar even wider after arriving in the FRG. "Almost all investigations on the socio-cultural background of the Aussiedler," Barbara Koller observed in 1994, "find that they maintain conservative, traditional, patriarchical values more frequently than the local population." As a result, she concluded, "they are not very open to change or co-existing competing values and standards which are typical for our pluralist society. Such basic attitudes make it difficult for Aussiedlers to adapt to the new living conditions" (Koller 1994: 11–12). However, the *Aussiedler* did not regard returning to their countries of origin as an option, so they were committed from the outset to the idea of permanent settlement in the FRG. This commitment was most directly expressed in their desire to improve their competency in German.

Although the West Germans in the 1980s increasingly balked at the rising costs of integrating the *Übersiedler*, they at least accepted them to be "German" (Pratsch and Ronge 1989: 904–912; Ronge 1990: 39–47). Opinions about *Aussiedler* were far more divided. In a 1988 survey, only 38 percent of West Germans viewed the *Aussiedler* as Germans, while 36 percent of the respondents labeled them as "foreigners"; the remainder was undecided. West Germans over the age of sixty were much more likely (53 percent) to look upon the *Aussiedler* as German than those under the age of thirty (29 percent) (Herdegen 1989: 913, 920). A 1988 survey found that only 14 percent of West Germans reported having a negative opinion of the *Aussiedler*, while 36 percent expressed a positive view, and 51 percent was undecided. Those who had had personal contacts with the *Aussiedler* were more likely to have a positive attitude (Herdegen 1989: 921). Nevertheless, in contrast to the opportunistic economic motives often attributed to non-ethnic German refugees, the migration motives of the

---

4. Integration programs for the *Aussiedler* have included German language training, vocational training, assistance in finding jobs, social welfare programs run by organizations operating through churches and youth groups, refunds of travel costs, "welcome" payments per head, and settling-in loans repayable over ten years at low rates of interest. In addition, each *Aussiedler* becomes a participant on arrival in the country's social security system, including health care, unemployment benefits, and pensions (Jones 1990: 252).

Aussiedler were subject to less skepticism. As scholars examining this issue have observed, "the great part of the German public interpreted the migration decision of the *Aussiedler* as a response to political and social discrimination as well as [expressing] a clear commitment to German ethnicity and the political system of the Federal Republic" (Münz, Seifert, and Ulrich 1997: 24). For their part, many *Aussiedler* doubted that their host society regarded them as "German," and were inclined to see themselves as a minority rather than identify with the majority culture (Koller 1994: 13)

During the late 1980s and early 1990s, growing public fears over absorbing more immigrants and refugees were exacerbated by the sheer number of *Aussiedler* and *Übersiedler* who came to the western *Länder*. By 1990, the Federal Republic was experiencing a housing shortage of one million units, which was especially acute in large cities and industrial areas. Many *Aussiedler* and *Übersiedler* could not afford to pay for their own dwellings, and had to be assigned to public housing. The shortage of public housing meant in practice that many had to live in emergency shelters, such as gymnasiums and barracks. One estimate suggests that by 1990, there were more than 800,000 homeless persons in the western *Länder*. Of that number, 130,000 had no shelter at all, 300,000 were living in homeless shelters (*Obdachlosenunterkünften*), 100,000 were staying in commercial lodgings, 100,000 were in hostels (*Heimen*) and psychiatric institutions, and 200,000 *Übersiedler* and *Aussiedler* were housed in provisional accommodations (Ulbrich 1993: 24–25).

Overall, both the *Übersiedler* and the *Aussiedler* faced a much easier path to integration in the FRG than the guestworkers prior to 1989. However, during the 1990s, the newly arriving *Aussiedler* would encounter much greater integration challenges. The German government cut back on the amount of assistance it provided to facilitate their incorporation. In addition, changes in the labor market made it harder for *Aussiedler* to obtain employment. The types of jobs in mining, agriculture, and textiles to which they had gravitated declined as the German economy became more service-oriented (Koller 1994: 11). Finally, the new arrivals were handicapped by an even lower competency in German than their predecessors. Rather than assimilating, the *Aussiedler* by many measures would become more segregated in their own enclaves, associations, and networks during the 1990s (Dietz 2006: 129–134).

Chapter 10

A Tradition of Imported Labor

Despite the massive influx of refugees and expellees, the West German economic recovery proved so successful that, by the mid 1950s, there were regional labor shortages. From 1953 to 1960, German unemployment dropped from 1,259,000 or 7.5 percent to 214,300 or 1.2 percent (International Labour Office 1959: 17; Korte 1985: 31). To fill these labor shortages, the federal government embarked on a policy to recruit foreign workers on a temporary basis. The policy aimed to sustain economic growth while keeping inflation low. The government developed no comprehensive policy plan to guide the recruitment process, and there was little public debate over its implementation. In choosing the guestworker model for labor importation, the government was adopting a policy with a long tradition, and did not envision that it was opening the door to immigration. However, looking at the FRG's practices against the historical background of Germany's earlier experiences with imported labor is problematic because there are as many substantial discontinuities as continuities. From the Imperial era through the founding of the FRG, Germany passed through several markedly different regimes, two world wars, and major changes in its territorial boundaries. Its policies toward foreign labor across these eras reflect these sharp differences in context, but also reflect a common pattern to treat the recruitment and deployment of foreign nationals as an expedient measure to serve immediate economic objectives rather than to treat their admission as part of an immigration process. This pattern was predicated on the discrimination of the guestworkers by various criteria of ethnicity, race, nationality, and other cultural markers of identity.

Germany's Tradition of Imported Labor: A Background Sketch

The precedents for the FRG's guestworker model can be traced back to the system that Prussia began developing in the 1890s to regulate the entry, residence, work, and exit requirements of Polish workers from Russia and Austria-Hungary. This system was designed to allow temporary or seasonal migration, but also to prevent permanent settlement. The stringency of the controls was driven by fears that the Polish would overrun Prussia's eastern provinces. The system came to be administered by the German Worker Agency (*Deutsche Arbeiterzentrale*), a semi-official labor exchange that operated under the auspices of the Prussian Ministry of Agriculture. The Agency acquired exclusive authority for identifying and registering all foreign workers, and the Prussian government persuaded other German states to accept this system of mandatory registration. However, only Polish workers were subject to specific restrictions and, more specifically, to the policy of compulsory return. Polish workers were admitted for a fixed duration that required them to return to their home territory each year. If they overstayed the prescribed period, they were subject to deportation. They had to reapply for admission each time, and they were not allowed to bring family members with them. Their work permits were tied to jobs with specific employers, and they could not move to another job without their original employer's approval. The system gave enormous leverage to the state and employers to control the lives and work of foreign Polish laborers, while depriving the latter of any significant bargaining power with respect to wages and working conditions (Bade 1987: 65–76; 2003: 157–164; Herbert 1990: 9–23, 30–45).

When World War I broke out in August 1914, this policy of compulsory return was transformed into a policy of prohibiting return, because the mobilization of millions of German men to fight at the fronts created huge labor shortages. When the war began, Germany was employing roughly 700,000 foreign workers in industry and 500,000 in agriculture (Herbert 1990: 93). During the first few months of the war, Germany imposed prohibitions on the return of Russians and Poles. Since foreign workers could not be expected to submit willingly to the demands of their wartime roles, they became subject to increasingly repressive regulations. By December 1914, Germany began to employ prisoners of war to work in mining, manufacturing, and the metal industry.[1] In 1915, Germany started recruiting workers from occupied territories in the east and from Belgium. The German war economy was then heavily dependent on foreign laborers, whose numbers by the end of the war in Germany exceeded two million (Herbert 1990: 121). In comparing German policies and practices toward foreign labor in the two world wars, Ulrich Herbert has emphasized some striking similarities: "Imprisonment as a punishment for refusing work, docking of rations, reports of special police legislation, maltreatment, armed guard units, housing in fenced camps—all recurred in 1939. Indeed, measures

---

1. Germany was hardly alone in utilizing POWs as forced labor during World War I. Austria-Hungary, Britain, France, Russia, and, in far smaller numbers, the United States and Australia also employed them in this fashion (Spoerer and Fleischhacker 2002: 170; Lohr 2003: 178).

often thought to have been invented by the Nazis, such as compulsory badges for the Poles, were already in practice, or at least envisaged, back in 1915" (Herbert 1997: 26). Of course, as Herbert hastens to point out, forced labor would be exploited on a much more massive and brutal scale under the Nazis than in World War I and would be applied in tandem with policies of annihilation. However, he sees continuities in the "logic" of forced labor introduced in World War I that later would be radicalized under the Nazis.

After the war, the number of foreign workers in Germany dropped to 260,000. Demobilization released millions of men onto the labor market, while the German economy struggled to adjust from war to peacetime production under the additional weight of considerable reparation obligations. Confronting these circumstances, the new Republic moved swiftly to return foreign workers to their homelands. However, the demand for foreign labor did not cease entirely, though it varied according to economic circumstances. During the economic crisis of 1923, the number of foreign workers decreased to 177,000, but climbed again to 263,000 in 1925. Foreign laborers with long work records in Germany became eligible for permanent work permits and residence visas. While Prussia had had to cede some of its eastern territory to the newly created Polish state as part of the war settlement, its East Elbanian landowners continued to insist on the need for seasonal Polish workers. The pre-war Prussian compulsory return policy aimed at the Poles was applied in principle until 1926, but it was not observed in practice. In 1927, Germany and Poland entered a bilateral treaty to regulate the recruitment of seasonal workers on German terms. Nevertheless, looking only at the sheer numbers of workers involved, foreign labor comprised only a marginal component of the domestic workforce (Herbert 1990: 124–126; Bade 2003: 192; Oltmer 2001: 56).

Racial and *völkisch* arguments for exclusion figured prominently in debates over the admission and deployment of foreign workers. These arguments were also clearly visible in the highly restrictive Bavarian policies toward naturalization directed against Jews and other immigrants from the east. Led by the conservative Bavarian People's Party (*Bayerische Volkspartei*), an offshoot of the Center Party, Bavaria assumed Prussia's pre-war role as the defender of German homogeneity. Conversely, Prussia, governed by combinations of the SPD, the Center Party, and liberal parties, eased the naturalization requirements set forth in its formal administrative guidelines, which allowed for the naturalization of Jews, Poles, and other foreign nationals from the east on a case-by-case basis. Throughout most of the Weimar era, Bavarian and Prussian state governments repeatedly quarreled with one another over naturalization requirements, and more specifically over the Jewish applicants for citizenship that Prussia sought to approve (Nathans 2004: 204–209; Gosewinkel 2001a: 353–368).

The most significant development in this era involved the newly expanded role of the government in the labor market. As a result, foreign labor policy became an adjunct to labor market policy for the first time. Whereas pre-war Prussian measures to regulate foreign Polish labor had sprang from national security concerns, the Weimar government's efforts to control the admission and deployment of foreign labor were driven by concerns over problems of unemployment and economic instability. The government's highest priority was to shield the national labor market from an influx of foreign laborers, while leaving open some discretionary room for utilizing foreign labor in a supplemental role to fill specific shortages in typically the most undesirable jobs. Thus, new regulations were promulgated that guaranteed preferential hiring for Germans and parity in pay between Germans and foreigners. At the same time, the government sharply increased its administrative capacity to regulate and intervene in the labor market much more extensively than in the past. Control over the deployment and regulation of foreign labor was centralized in the hands of a new Reich Employment Office (*Reichsamt für Arbeitsvermittlung*). The pre-war German Workers Agency continued to oversee recruitment (Oltmer 2001: 55–57; Bade 2003: 192).

When the Nazis assumed power in 1933, the German economy was mired in depression, and thus the number of foreign workers had declined considerably, growing only slowly over the next several years. Nevertheless, the Nazis inherited a well-developed, centralized administrative infrastructure and legal policy framework for managing the recruitment, deployment, and control of foreign workers. Given the insignificant presence of foreign workers in their early years of rule, the Nazis were initially content to merely expand and tighten existing regulatory measures. Between 1936 and 1938, the number of foreign workers rose from 220,192 to 375,078 (Herbert 1997: 43–44, 51). In August 1938, the Nazis promulgated a new police ordinance (*Ausländerpolizeiverordnung*) that "broadened criteria for residence eligibility for foreigners, so that the police now had the option of deportation at their disposal as a handy means of pressure and intimidation" (Herbert 1997: 56). After launching Germany into war on 1 September 1939 against Poland, the Nazi government moved quickly to expand police authority to an almost unlimited degree over all foreign workers (Majer 2003: 178–183). Although the Nazis moved quickly to exploit the newly available reserve of Polish workers, it was intended as a short-term measure of expediency. Poland became the laboratory in which the Nazis experimented with the whole of range of measures that they would use elsewhere, and also proved to themselves that forced labor could be effectively exploited. Nevertheless, the integration of foreign labor on a large scale into the domestic workforce was hardly a war goal and had not been anticipated in any pre-war planning. In many respects it conflicted with Nazi racial ideology (Herbert 1997: 57–94).

As the Nazi regime learned, sustaining the war over six years would not have been possible without the massive recruitment of foreign labor from throughout Europe. The Nazis used foreign workers to replace 11 million German men withdrawn from the labor force for military service between May 1939 and September 1944 (Homze 1967: 231). While some foreign workers were recruited through agreements made with such "friendly and neutral" countries as Italy, Slovakia, Bulgaria, Hungary, Romania, Croatia, and Spain, most were recruited by force in the occupied areas and 1.8 million were prisoners of war (Castles and Kosack 1973: 23–24). In their recruitment and deployment of foreign laborers, the Nazis applied different standards to different nationalities. Nationals from western countries, such as France or Belgium, received the best treatment, especially during the early years of the war. Nationals from the east, such as Poland or the USSR, received immeasurably harsher treatment. However, such generalizations are misleading because the Nazis developed an enormously complex hierarchical system that differentiated treatment for a variety of grounds and contingent circumstances (Herbert 1997: 314–317; Spoerer and Fleischhacker 2002).

By August 1944, Greater Germany was employing more than 9,500,000 foreign workers (including 1,930,087 prisoners of war). Foreign workers comprised 25 percent of the total domestic force. Of that total, foreigner workers comprised 46.4 percent of the workforce in agriculture, 33.7 percent in mining, 30 percent in metals, 28.4 percent in chemicals, 32.3 percent in construction, and 26 percent in transportation (Herbert 1997: 297, 314–317; Spoerer and Fleischhacker 2002). The Nazis also conscripted nationals from many countries into their armed forces, including the SS divisions. Given the extent to which the foreign workers had been integrated into the domestic work force, their presence was conspicuously visible almost everywhere in Germany. Many ordinary Germans had close contact with them at work, but within a structural framework that had institutionalized discrimination, exploitation, and persecution on a systemic basis. Within this same framework, German industry also acquired considerable experience in employing foreign workers across a broad range of occupations (Herbert 1997: 124–136, 187–189, 222–225).

The FRG and Imported Labor

The founders of the Federal Republic never confronted this part of the Nazi legacy. As Herbert has observed, the scale of other Nazi crimes, such as the Holocaust, obscured the brutal record of their treatment of foreign labor. In the interval between the defeat of the Nazis in 1945 and the FRG's resumption of foreign labor recruitment in 1955, memories of the former receded (Herbert 1990: 201; 1997: 3–4). For those who did remember, their recollections centered on personal experiences that showed little awareness of the larger role and character of the Nazis' use of foreign labor. There were also memories from the war's end of roving gangs of liberated foreign laborers who raided villages for supplies, robbed houses, raped women, and exacted revenge on their German hosts. Such memories created an enduring association between foreigners and criminality in the minds of many Germans (Herbert 1997: 2, 364–370, 378–381; Chin: 2007: 42). "As far as the deployment of *Fremdarbeiter* (foreign workers) during World War II," Herbert concluded in the mid 1980s, "there is not now—nor has there ever been—any feeling of guilt in Germany, any widespread perception that there was some sort of injustice and crime perpetrated here" (Herbert 1990: 191–192). Policymakers were sensitive to any comparison that might be drawn with Nazi practices, and did seek to establish some distance from a tainted past by designating its imported laborers as "guestworkers" rather than as "*Fremdarbeiter*." However, the FRG revived the 1938 *Ausländerpolizeiverordnung* in the early 1950s, and it remained the primary legal basis for regulating foreign labor in the Federal Republic until the Foreigner Law of 1965 (Herbert 1990: 207; Joppke 1999: 66; Nathans 2004: 243).

The FRG signed its first employment contract with Italy in December 1955 to import workers for the agricultural and building sectors. The number of Italian workers recruited remained relatively small, from less than 19,000 in 1955 to approximately 49,000 in 1959. The contract became the model for subsequent agreements with other countries. It assigned the Federal Institute of Labor in Nuremburg and the Italian Labor Administration responsibility for the selection and recruitment of Italian workers. German enterprises placed their orders for labor with these two agencies, which then located the appropriate workers to fill these jobs. In response to demands from German labor unions, the agreement stipulated that foreign laborers had equal rights in the workplace and would receive pay equal to their German counterparts within a job category. It further guaranteed the term of employment, promised provision of adequate housing, and permitted the return of earnings to the home country. Finally, the agreement left open the opportunity for foreign workers to bring their families with them subject to the approval of German authorities (Rist 1978: 61; Herbert 1990: 205–206).

Although the West German government treated the recruitment of foreign labor as a temporary expedient, it did not implement a strict rotation model of labor importation, such as Prussia's earlier compulsory return policy had sought to enforce, to block long-term settlement. From the inception of its recruitment initiatives, it began accepting limitations on its discretion to enforce any such model. Upon entering the 1957 Treaty of Rome with Italy and the other original founding states of the EEC, the FRG committed itself to the goal of free movement as a general principle for EEC Member States. As defined under Article 48, achieving this goal mandated "the abolition of any discrimination based on nationality between workers of the Member States as regards employment, remuneration and other conditions of work and employment" (Rudden and Wyatt 1993: 28, 48). Under the EEC Association Accords signed with Greece in 1961 and with Turkey in 1963, their nationals obtained the same rights to the freedom of movement that the Treaty of Rome provided the nationals of EEC Member States (Feld 1965: 223, 233). However, while the EEC framework helped to equalize the legal status of applicable foreign nationals on par with German nationals in the FRG labor market, the FRG's acceptance of this framework did not significantly alter the government's approach to foreign labor, which remained averse to the prospect of permanent settlement. This approach would be reflected in the 1965 Foreigner Law.

During the 1960s, the demand of the FRG's economy for new labor continued to grow. In 1960, more than 144,000 Italian workers had entered the Federal Republic. That same year, the West German government concluded employment agreements with Greece and Spain, and the next year with Turkey. The erection of the Berlin Wall in 1961 largely stopped the influx of refugees from the GDR, removing an important source of new labor. At the same time, unions were demanding a shorter workweek, more young people were delaying entry into the work force to acquire education, and the older generations were opting for earlier retirements (precipitated in part by an increasingly generous pensions system). Additional agreements were signed with Morocco in 1963, Portugal in 1964, Tunisia in 1965, and Yugoslavia in 1968. By the mid 1960s, it had become obvious that Germany's reliance on foreign workers was becoming structurally entrenched. The labor shortages and raised expectations were making Germans increasingly reluctant to accept low wage jobs carrying low social status, much risk, and few opportunities for advancement (Kühl 1976; Rist 1978: 61–63; Münz and Ulrich 1997: 78).

The number of foreign workers rose as they spread into new occupations. The first Italian workers had been concentrated in agriculture, but in the 1960s, the great majority of foreign workers moved into the fields of manufacturing, construction, mining, and services. Despite this shift in occupations, foreign workers remained employed largely in semiskilled or unskilled positions. Most of the guestworkers were single men between the ages of 20 and 40. The great advantage of this age cohort was that as wage earners they paid taxes in considerable excess to the social spending they required in return. The initial investment in recruiting workers was not insignificant, and included such expenses such as providing transportation, housing, and job training (Völker 1975: 21). However, these costs were relatively minor compared to the savings that the FRG made from not having to pay for their education from childhood. The foreign labor recruits included women as well as men. From 1960 to 1973, the number of women rose from roughly 43,000 to more than 706,000, representing 30 percent of all foreign laborers. Women worked primarily in the textile, food, clothing, and electronic sectors of the economy. The lives of most guestworkers were insulated from close contact with Germans. They lived clustered together in their own neighborhoods, and often far from urban centers. Many large German companies provided housing for their workers near their place of employment, but these places were often in industrial areas. The housing was usually very modest in the form of a dormitory, barrack or hostel. Both men and women came with the expectation that their sojourn in the FRG would be a temporary one, and so maintained close personal links with their homelands. Because earning opportunities were so much higher in the FRG than in their homelands, their primary motive was economic. They sought to make money that could be used back home (Herbert 1990: 215, 220, 237–240; Chin 2007: 40–44).

By 1965, the FRG was employing more than one million foreigner laborers that comprised nearly 6 percent of the domestic workforce (Rist 1978: 62). That same year the federal government adopted a new foreigner law to supersede the 1938 *Ausländerpolizeiverordnung* and other pre-war legal measures as the domestic legal basis for regulating the terms of entry, residence, work, and exit of guestworkers. Although the new law was depicted as a significant improvement over its Nazi predecessor, some commentators have argued that by expanding the discretionary authority of administrative officials, the law represented a step back (Franz 1975: 50–52; Chin 2007: 51). Others attach importance to the new law because of its centrality to the legislation on foreigners law that followed from it. Simon Green has argued that because this was the first immigration law drafted since World War II, it set the foundation for how German policymakers viewed matters of immigration until today (Green 2004). Significantly, policymakers at the time emphasized the impression that immigration would be temporary and intended to fulfill the needs of the German labor market. As we will discuss later in the volume, removing this foundational assumption in the FRG's immigration laws would require decades of political entanglement and popular debate.

One of the surviving precedents set by the 1965 Foreigners Law is the authorities' discretionary power. The new law sought to give the government maximum flexibility as a policy instrument to manage its foreigner worker population in the interests of the state and the national economy. Under this law, any foreigner not from an EEC Member State, other than tourists, seeking admissions to the FRG for any period of time was required to obtain a residence permit. Section 1, paragraph 1 of the law provided that "the residence permit may be granted if the presence of the foreigner does not adversely affect the interests of the Federal Republic of Germany" (quoted in Rist 1978: 136). This kind of elastic criterion left open an almost unlimited degree of discretion to administrative officials in interpreting its application, which led to wide variations across the *Länder*. The notion of 'interests' could encompass economic, political, cultural, or social considerations in any possible configuration. The vagueness of this notion was also reflected in the broad grounds that the law authorized for deportations. Residence permits were only granted for one year and holders had no entitlement to a renewal. Moreover, residence permits could be revoked after they were issued. Typically, residence permits were issued to workers who had signed contracts with a German employer before entering the FRG, and its validity was conditional on remaining with that employer. In the event that the worker left his job for whatever reason, his residence permit could be voided. Because of EEC conventions, the new law applied differently to nationals from Common Market states. Their foreign nationals were not required to have a residence permit to enter the FRG to look for work and housing (for up to three months). After securing a job, they were entitled to a residence permit extending to a minimum of five years, and they were not required to have work permits (Franz 1975: 51–55; Rist 1978: 135–140; Joppke 1999: 66–67).

By the middle of 1966, clear signs of an economic downturn had appeared, and the coming recession would shake the German public's immediate confidence in the FRG's economic growth model that had been predicated, in part, on the recruitment of foreign labor. In December of 1966, the CDU and the SPD formed a "Grand Coalition" to govern the FRG. Its overriding priority was to end the recession. However, it soon had to confront serious opposition on both the left from the student movement and the right from the National Democratic Party (NDP). Formed in 1964, the NDP's core membership contained a high share of former Nazis. In November 1966, the NDP won 7.4 percent of the vote in Bavaria state elections and 7.9 percent in Hesse state elections. It took 8.8 percent of the vote in Bremen in October 1967 and 9.8 percent in Baden-Württemberg in April 1968. No small share of this popular support was probably given more as a protest vote reflecting concerns over the economy rather than as an endorsement of the NDP's radical right-wing ideological program. Nevertheless, the NDP's anti-foreigner appeals did speak to some growing public sentiment against the increasing number of foreign laborers in their midst. The rise in negative attitudes among the German public was also reflected in the media, which increasingly portrayed foreigners as a threat to jobs and a source of criminality. When strong economic growth resumed in 1968, the NDP's own rise faltered. It proved unable to score the necessary 5 percent of the vote in the 1969 Bundestag elections to acquire seats. It never recovered from this loss. That same Bundestag election marked the end of the Grand Coalition. After the election, the SPD and FDP formed a new ruling coalition under new Chancellor Willy Brandt (SPD). The coalition would continue in power until 1982. Joining the CSU in opposition, the CDU shifted its rhetoric to the right, and the two parties absorbed most of the NDP's former voters (Nagle 1970: 88–90; Kolinsky 1984: 257–271; Stöss 1989: 140–147; Chin 2007: 60–61).

During the recession, many foreign laborers had returned to their homelands while prospective recruits had not come to the FRG. After the recession ended, recruitment resumed on a major scale. From 1968, the number of guestworkers more than doubled from 1,011,400 to 2,595,000 in 1973, accounting for 11.9 percent of the total workforce (Herbert 1990: 230). By 1972, Turkish workers comprised the largest share, and as the largest foreign minority they became the most prominent symbol of the guestworker in the eyes of the German public. In the process, "the 'Polish Question' of the 1890s," Peter Katzenstein has observed, was "transformed to the 'Turkish Question' of the 1980s" (Katzenstein 1987: 214). Between 1968 and 1973, the workers' average length of stay and percentage of unemployed foreigners also rose. For their part, employers had found that they often preferred retaining experienced foreign laborers rather than having to train a steady supply of new ones. However, these developments also kindled fears over the potential social costs that this settlement of foreign workers and their nonproductive dependents would mean (Herbert 1990: 231–233). In the summer of 1973, foreign workers shocked German management, labor union leaders, and political authorities by staging a series of wildcat strikes at the Ford and Hella automobile manufacturing plants, among others. The strikes demonstrated that the quiescence of the foreign labor force could no longer be taken for granted, and might even be the harbinger of more serious unrest in the future (Castles 1989: 38).

The federal government had not been blind to these developments or the need to address them, but faced some daunting choices. On the one hand, there was growing concern over how much longer West German society could continue to absorb high levels of foreign labor recruitment. On the other hand, there were also worries about the impact of any cut off of this recruitment on the economy. The SPD and FDP leadership publicly opposed the adoption of a strict rotation model favored by the CSU, but the Brandt Cabinet remained divided in the early 1970s over possible alternatives. Federal Interior Minister Hans Dietrich Genscher (FDP) advocated imposing sharp restrictions on the admission of new foreign workers coupled with major new measures to promote the integration of the existing foreigner population. Such measures would involve strengthening the rights of the foreigner population, including the right to acquire German citizenship. However, Federal Labor Minister Walter Arendt (SPD) opposed any such moves. He was most concerned with protecting job opportunities for German workers, whom he believed should have a priority over foreign nationals. Chancellor Willy Brandt expressed doubts about easing naturalization requirements because of the possible reaction of the sending states to the prospect of their nationals becoming citizens of another country. The ambivalence of the Brandt Cabinet toward any major reforms was compounded by more general foreign policy concerns. The Brandt government saw immigration as not just a domestic matter, and preferred to work in tandem with its European partners (Schönwälder 2006).

The Brandt Cabinet managed a few interim steps toward reform before the OPEC oil embargo in the October of 1973 decisively changed the political calculations. During the following month, the Cabinet resolved to suspend indefinitely the recruitment of all foreign workers, but acted with no clear strategic vision in mind. It did not realize that this act would become the "decisive policy turn" marking the end of the guestworker era (Schönwälder 2006: 261–262). The new policy emphasized return and restriction by encouraging departures; by denying work permits to the spouses and children of migrants who arrived in Germany after 1 December 1974 (a policy in effect until 1978); by encouraging voluntary return; and by permitting cities to declare themselves overburdened with foreigners and deny residence permits to migrants who wanted to move in (Martin 1994: 203). As a result of the oil embargo, the FRG's economy plunged into a recession. For the next several years, the number of foreign workers dropped sharply as the government had anticipated, but by the end of the decade it had began to rise again. The number of resident foreigners, however, never experienced a similar decline. By 1980, there were one million more resident aliens in the Federal Republic than there had been in 1972 (Herbert 1990: 231–235). In short, many of the foreign workers and their families who had entered the Federal Republic as guests were now (de facto) immigrants. The failure of Brandt's Cabinet to move as decisively on integration policy as it did on restriction was a harbinger of things to come.

Chapter 11

Between Retreat and Reform

Naturalization Laws and the Challenge of Integration

In contrast to an immigration model that explicitly links the admissions of foreigners to the prospect of acquiring permanent residence and eventually citizenship on a path to full membership, the FRG's guestworker model had been predicated on the assumption that the number of foreign workers could be flexibly adjusted according to labor market needs and employers' interests. The sharp decline in foreign workers during the 1966/67 recession seemed to vindicate this assumption. The model aimed to maximize the economic benefits of labor recruitment FRG while minimizing the potential social costs by rotating foreign workers back to their homelands after temporary stays of varying lengths. Given the assumptions and objectives of the guestworker model, policymakers were inclined to view the long-term settlement of foreigners as a disagreeable anomaly and to treat policy accommodations as grudging concessions to an outcome they had sought to avoid. As a result, they were slow to adapt to changes on the ground in general and to address the challenges of integration in particular.

The growth in the foreign resident population over the course of the 1970s made it clear that these challenges now had to be faced, but it came at a time when the social burdens of the foreign resident population now seemed to outweigh whatever economic benefits the labor recruitment programs had brought. Among the burdens most tangible to native West Germans was the high financial cost of educating the children of foreign workers who were entering the FRG school system in increasing numbers year after year. In 1961, for example, only 20 percent of the foreigner population consisted of family members. By 1975, that percentage had risen to over 50 percent. The birthrate of guestworker families was also higher than that of the native German population. Numbering more than one million persons by 1975, Turks comprised the largest proportion (27 percent) of this foreign population, followed by

Yugoslavs (17 percent), Italians (15 percent), Greek (10 percent), and Spanish (6 percent) (Wilpert 1977: 473–475). In addition to these rising education costs, by the mid 1970s, leading newspapers had also begun to draw an unfavorable link between the unemployment of native Germans and the presence of foreigner workers. Observing that the unemployment rate of foreigner workers was higher than that of native workers, they also called attention to the public costs incurred by unemployment and welfare benefits paid to foreign workers. The perception of such problems raised questions about the limits of the FRG's capacity to absorb the long-term settlement of its foreigner population during an era when the German economy appeared to be faltering (Chin 2007: 145).

At the same time, it was also becoming increasingly clear that the guest-worker model was no longer viable as the governing policy framework. The difficulties that the FRG would have in moving away from this model were reflected in the 1977 joint Federal and State Commission's recommendations on employment policies for foreigners (*Bundesminister für Arbeit und Sozialordnung* 1997: 3–4). Caught between the failed assumptions of the guestworker model and a refusal to accept an immigration model, the Commission sought to find some middle ground between them, but this effort resulted in contradictory policy prescriptions. On the one hand, the Commission reaffirmed the long-standing official position that the FRG was not a country of immigration, and insisted that the recruited workers have routinely demonstrated a desire to return to their countries of origin. Observing that the German labor market had now become oversaturated with foreign workers, the Commission advocated making the suspension of new recruitment permanent and reducing over time the proportion of foreigners in the labor market. To facilitate this reduction, it called for new measures to enhance the willingness and ability of foreign workers to return to their homelands. Such policies, it reasoned, would serve the national interests of not only the FRG, but also of the workers' homelands. On the other hand, the Commission recognized that the FRG would continue to need some foreign workers for the foreseeable future and recommended against any compulsory measures of repatriation. In other words, lawfully settled foreign residents should not be returned against their will. For those foreign workers and their families who remained, it emphasized the importance of ensuring the security of their social and legal status in a manner that would promote their full integration into West German society. The Commission singled out the employment problems of the second generation as a particularly pressing issue. Taken as a whole, the muddled character of the Commission's recommendations lay in trying to combine policy proposals that would serve two conflicting goals, namely, to simultaneously promote the immediate return as well as the long-term integration of foreign workers and their families. Indeed, policies of return would be used as an alternative to integration and as a palliative to rising public anti-foreigner sentiment.

One of the key differences between a guestworker model and an immigration model turns on the issue of acquiring citizenship. Rhetoric about enhancing the security of rights and promoting integration often provided a convenient way of sidestepping this crucial issue. In fact, so long as the policy was predicated on a categorical rejection of the immigration model the rules governing the acquisition of citizenship would remain highly restrictive. This approach to citizenship is reflected in the 1977 federal naturalization guidelines, which flatly declared that "the Federal Republic of Germany is not a land of immigration. It does not aspire to increase the number of its citizens through naturalization" (Hailbronner and Renner 1991: 626; see also Meier-Braun 1988: 14; Ibrahim 1997: 97).[1] The guidelines treated naturalization as the exception rather than the rule. They delineated basic criteria that applicants needed to satisfy to be eligible for naturalization and assigned considerable discretion to local administrative officials in determining how to apply those criteria. One of most basic criterion for naturalization required the applicant to possess a basic understanding of liberal-democratic norms in Germany and express an acceptance of and sufficient integration into everyday German life (*die deutschen Lebensverhältnisse*) (Hailbronner and Renner 1991: 626–627). Other guidelines compelled local authorities to consider the applicant's duration of stay in Germany and economic standing when evaluating the naturalization application (Hailbronner and Renner 1991: 627–628).[2]

The continued prohibition on dual nationality is also indicative of the guidelines' reinforcement of the exceptionality of naturalization. In this regard, one of the criteria allows authorities to consider the citizenship of an applicant's family members. If most are German citizens, then leniency in evaluating the application is encouraged. At the same time, however, when familial considerations were not applicable, dual nationality was not to be granted except in cases where the applicant's natal country did not allow the denunciation of citizenship (Hailbronner and Renner 1991: 630). While restrictions on dual citizenship were consistent with treating naturalization as an exceptional event, they were also part of broader agenda throughout Western Europe to decrease instances of multiple nationalities (Green 2004: 41).[3] Naturalization fees as

---

1. In Section III, Appendix A (Anhang A), Hailbronner and Renner present the guidelines as published and released by the Federal Ministry of the Interior 15 December 1977 (1991: 624). This statement is a quote from the Interior Ministry's publication.

2. For a broader discussion of the naturalization guidelines, see Green (2004: 39–40).

3. The traditional aversion of states to dual nationality was reflected in the 1963 Convention on Reduction of Cases of Multiple Nationality (Plender 1997: 131–142). In a 1974 opinion, the Federal Constitutional Court labeled dual and multiple nationality as an "evil that should be avoided or eliminated in the interests of states as well as of the affected citizen" (Opinion of 21 May 1974, BVerfGE 37, cited in Plender 1997: 217).

high as DM 5,000[4] also discouraged many foreigners from applying for German citizenship (Green 2004: 41). The Federal Republic's general aversion to dual nationality would continue to play an important role in later debates about citizenship laws and immigrant integration.

Confronting the Challenges of Integration

By the mid 1970s, integration had become an issue that all of the major parties felt they needed to address. Under the SPD-FDP coalition, the federal government began to move toward devising and implementing a comprehensive integration policy strategy. However, these efforts in the end produced few tangible results. The failure of the reform efforts in this period would prove especially unfortunate, because only after the turn of the century would a new attempt be made to develop a comprehensive integration policy strategy. In 1978, Chancellor Helmut Schmidt (SPD) took two tentative steps toward reform. The first step strengthened the legal status of aliens by facilitating the acquisition of unlimited residence permits (*unbefristete Aufenthaltserlaubnisse*). Inspired by a Federal Constitutional Court ruling in the same year, which provided for the extension of a foreigner's residency permit,[5] the 1978 amendment to the legal code for residency permits granted aliens a right to unlimited residence permits after five years of continuous residency (Green 2004: 39; Meier-Braun 1988: 14). The amendment also stipulated that after eight years, legal residents would be eligible for a residence entitlement (*Aufenthaltsberechtigung*) if they met certain conditions, such as language competence. In both cases the specified conditions for eligibility remained sufficiently general enough to leave room for administrative discretion in their application, which, in turn, would occasion court intervention narrowing this use of discretion. The second step involved the creation of a new federal office, the *Ausländerbeauftragter* (Commissioner for Foreigner Affairs), to represent the interests of foreigners and to advise the Chancellor on alien policy. This post had limited powers and was designed to study the situation of foreign workers and their dependents in the FRG, but had no power to implement policy or did not have direct access to the Cabinet. The office was apportioned a small budget and attached to the Ministry of Labor and Social Affairs (Düding and Kühn 2002: 314). Schmidt appointed Heinz Kühn (SPD), the former Minister President of North Rhine-Westphalia, as the first Commissioner.

---

4. Staatsangehörigkeits-Gebührenverordung (StAGebV) from 28 March 1974, §2 (in Hailbronner and Renner 1991: 557).

5. See judgment from 26 September 1978. BVerfG, 1 BvR, 525/77. We discuss the case in more detail in the following chapter, titled "Aliens Policy and the Federal Courts."

In 1979, Kühn issued a memorandum that called upon the government to recognize that the FRG had become a de facto immigration land and sharply criticized the contradictions of the FRG's approach to integration. The report emphasized that immigration of foreign workers and their families was now irreversible, and predicted a growing crisis if the government fundamentally did not change its policy approach. Kühn condemned the one-sided character of the earlier policy for focusing too narrowly on labor market considerations and for ignoring the ramifications of long-term settlement. He contended that future policy should take into account a broader range of perspectives, including those of the resident foreigner population. Criticizing the inconsistent pattern of partial integration measures that had been adopted, he called for a new comprehensive set of policies that would promote permanent integration on an unconditional basis. Among his recommendations, he proposed liberalizing naturalization regulations to take into account the interests and needs of the potential applicants. He also advocated granting foreign residents who had lived in the Federal Republic a requisite number of years to have the right to vote in municipal elections. Highlighting the acute situation of the second and third generations, he called for the complete integration of all educational and training programs to eliminate the segregation between German and foreign students. Integration should not, he insisted, be equated with Germanization, so school curricula should be reformed to reflect the multi-ethnic character of the students and to enable students from different heritages to learn from one another. He proposed that all youths born and raised in the Federal Republic should be offered the choice of citizenship. Given his starkly pessimistic assessment of the integration problems facing the FRG, Kühn, not surprisingly, advised strongly against allowing further immigration (Kühn 1979: 2–4, 10–11, 15, 18–25, 59).

Kühn's memorandum aroused considerable public controversy. Critics focused on the projected high funding costs necessary to implement his policy proposals and more specifically focused on his call for integrating the classroom as well as for liberalizing the naturalization code (Herbert 2001: 246–247; Meier-Braun 1988: 17). Nevertheless, his report might have marked a fundamental turning point in the development of the FRG's approach to migration, integration, and citizenship. While his memorandum offered the most comprehensive attempt to come grips with the problems and the challenges of integration, Kühn was not alone in promoting this effort. German trade unions, for example, had been making important contributions to this effort since the 1960s, albeit often out of self-interest rather than from a commitment to protecting the interests of the recruited foreign workers. Beginning in the late 1950s, the unions had participated in the negotiations over the original recruitment agreements. To prevent employers from cutting wages or replacing native workers with cheaper foreign ones, pressure from German trade unions had been instrumental in guaranteeing foreign workers equal pay for equal work.

They had also played an indispensable role in improving the housing for foreign workers. By the 1970s, the unions had emerged as an important supporter of integration in the workplace and created information distribution offices to help foreign workers outside the workplace, such as through providing legal advice. From 1974 to 1982, the proportion of foreign workers who belonged to unions rose from 25 to 35 percent, and accounted for 10 percent of the Federation of German Trade Unions (DGB) membership in the mid 1980s. However, foreign workers remained seriously underrepresented in union leadership positions, such as on works councils. Likewise, differences in language and ethnicity remained a source of friction between German and foreign workers. On balance, so long as German union members saw foreign workers as contributing to national economic growth and not threatening their own employment prospects, they supported integration efforts. For their part, foreign workers found in unions one of the few institutions in the FRG that would defend their rights and interests (Rist 1978: 120–132; Katzenstein 1987: 222–223).

The Kühn memorandum received some of its strongest support from the Catholic and Protestant churches. Along with trade unions, the charity organizations of the Catholic and Protestant churches long had been providing important social services to foreign workers. In the late 1970s, the churches began holding an annual *Tag des ausländischen Mitbürgers* (Day of the Foreign Co-Citizen).[6] Against the official stance that the FRG is "not a land of immigration," its organizers started from the premise that the Federal Republic had indeed become one. They aimed to promote dialogue between Germans and the foreigner population, so that each could learn more about the cultures of the other. In this way, they sought to change the prevailing native perception of this population from an instrumental one that identified them with their economic roles in the host society to a more humanistic one that respected their distinctive cultural identities as well as their cultural contributions. The recognition that successful integration would involve a two-sided process of adaptation, communication, and learning on the part of both the immigrant communities and the host society was important. In her study of Portuguese migrant workers, for example, Andrea Klimt found, that they "understand that 'being German' does not rest on such mutable characteristics as legal status, political loyalty, or acquired knowledge. 'Germanness' is not perceived to be an open or permeable category" (Klimt 1989: 70; see also Brubaker 1992: 79). This kind of perception cannot be changed unless a respect for, and not simply the tolerance of, cultural diversity becomes a norm of the host society.

By the early 1980s, the term "multiculturalism" had emerged in public debates as a concept for challenging monocultural understandings of national identity and validating the preservation of cultural differences in the integration of

6. In 1984, this annual event was expanded into a "Woche [week] der ausländischen Mitbürger."

foreign minorities. The newly formed Green party was its strongest proponent, but it also received important support from the churches, segments of the SPD and FDP, and the trade unions. It even found influential advocates within the CDU, most notably Heiner Geißer.[7] However, the concept of multiculturalism is so open-ended that its actual meaning remained subject to a wide range interpretations and competing partisan uses. Some conservatives adopted it to emphasize the unbridgeable character of the immutable differences between the majority culture and the minority cultures within the FRG. Where group cultures are understood as holistic, homogeneous entities, the term is equally serviceable to frame an argument for permanent separation and segregation as it is for one supporting dialogue, toleration, and respect.

In their 1982 "Heidelberg Manifesto," a group of 15 prominent professors set out the most extreme version of the conservative standpoint.[8] Pointing with alarm to a declining birthrate among native Germans and a growing foreign resident population, they called for the return of foreigners to their countries of origin to preserve the integrity of German national culture. They condemned the emergence of a multicultural society within the FRG as a symptom of national degeneration and predicted that, if the trend was not reversed, it would lead to a catastrophe. They described nations as autonomous biological systems with distinct cultural identities as much a product of genetic inheritance as of historical tradition and with a "natural right" to self-preservation. In seeking to root cultural differences in the biology of peoples, the authors of the Manifesto went much farther than the overwhelming majority of Germans were prepared to support. Their appeal won little favorable public notice, but it was indicative of a much broader public reaction against the new rhetoric of integration (Dirke 1994; Klopp 2002: 23–26).

The emerging debate over multiculturalism was an important step toward coming to terms with the reality of immigration, but it tended to focus attention on identity issues rather than on the more concrete legal and social dimensions of integration. The Kühn memorandum had put forward many specific policy proposals to encourage integration, but the Schmidt government declined to act on most of them. With the 1980 national campaign in mind, Schmidt acknowledged that reforms to promote integration cut "against the instincts of our core voters" (Thränhardt 1984: 124). After being reelected, the SPD-FDP coalition did introduce in December 1981 the so-called *Optionsrecht*, the right of citizenship for the German-born children of foreign parents resident in the FRG, but the CDU/CSU-dominated Bundesrat blocked the initiative (Meier-Braun 1987: 39–40). Suffering from health problems, Kühn resigned

7. Geißer was General-Secretary of the CDU from 1977 to 1989 and Federal Minister of Youth, Family, and Health from 1982 to 1985.
8. See "Heidelberg Manifest," *Die Zeit*, 5 February 1982, p. 13.

as Commissioner for Foreigner Affairs in the fall of 1980, and was replaced by Liselotte Funke (FDP). In its remaining years in office, the Schmidt government turned away from addressing the problem of integration and focused its policy efforts on restricting entry of foreigners through tightening eligibility provisions for family reunification (Joppke 1999: 79).

During these years, West German public opinion turned decidedly against integration. As measured by opinion surveys, given a choice between sending foreign workers back to their countries of origin or promoting their integration into West German society, public support for the former rose from 39 percent in 1978 to 68 percent in 1982 (Herbert 1990: 243–244). This negative reaction against integration had multiple causes. To shift the policy framework suddenly from a guestworker model based on the principle of rotation to a quasi-immigration model that emphasized integration was an abrupt change. The fact that the FRG officially and continuously had insisted that it was not an immigration land could only reinforce the perception of native West Germans that foreigners had no legitimate claim to permanent residence and that they had breached the original conditions of their admission, irrespective of their compliance with the law (O'Brien 1988: 117). The guestworker model had targeted for labor recruitment the least skilled and educated foreigners to do the least desirable, lowest paid jobs, so they became identified with the most menial occupations and were ill-prepared to adapt to structural changes in the labor market (Castles 1985: 519–520). Moreover, the FRG school system during late 1970s and early 1980s encountered its worst problems to date in handling the influx of the children of resident foreigners. On the one hand, foreign students were severely underperforming as marked by a high dropout rate that not only precluded their advance in the labor market, but also made them the most vulnerable to unemployment. On the other hand, German parents began to grow anxious that their own children's education would suffer by being in class with other students who had a poor command of German (Wilpert 1997: 475–476). So it was hardly surprising that the West German public was not inclined to support bold new integration policies at time when the social costs and failures of past policies seemed most acute.

In the face of these integration challenges, the native German public increasingly saw their resident foreigner population as an unnecessary burden and the FRG as losing control of its own migration system. In 1980, the Federal Interior Ministry had begun to incorporate figures for foreign residents into its demographic projections. It predicted that the foreign resident number would reach approximately 7,000,000 in the year 2000 and over 12,000,000 in the year 2030, and told the West German public that the "foreigner problem" was not going to melt away (Leenen 1992: 1046). The perception that the FRG's migration control system was broken and that the influx of new foreigners would continue was dramatically reinforced by the steady climb in the number of asylum seekers from approximately 10,000 in 1975 to approximately 51,000 in 1979. These totals soared past the 100,000 mark in 1980. Of this number, 57,900 were Turks, compared with 7,900 in 1979.

These problems were significantly compounded by a deteriorating national economy that had never fully recovered from the 1974/75 recession. Economic growth in the second half of the decade was slower than in the first half. After the 1974/75 recession, both government deficit spending and unemployment had remained high compared to previous levels. In the early 1970s, unemployment had been no higher than 1 percent. It had risen to 4.7 percent in 1975, and then declined to 3.8 percent in 1979. However, by 1982, it had risen to 7.5 percent for the labor force as a whole and 11.9 percent for foreigner workers. The second oil shock in 1979 helped drive the FRG economy into another recession from 1980 to 1982. A faltering economy not only deepened public concerns about the FRG's absorption capacities with respect to its foreigner population, but also helped to awaken a broader debate over German national identity. In examining the cycles of this debate since the late eighteenth century, the historian Harold James has called attention to the strong degree that German national identity has been legitimated through economic achievement and thrown into question by economic reversals. The pivotal role that rapid economic growth played during the 1950s in consolidating the foundations of the new West German state is a case in point. The economic problems of the late 1970s and the early 1980s threatened this source of pride, security, and satisfaction, opening the door to another resurgence of political and cultural nationalism. As James points out, the trouble with renewing a debate over "What is German?" is that the very formulation of this question "seemed to demand only one right answer" (James 1989: 209). This kind of essentialism promotes exclusion, not inclusion, in dealing with the realities of social and cultural diversity. However, rather than attributing this exclusivism to some fundamental, immutable core attributes of the German national self-understanding, James's analysis underscores the importance of how changes in context, especially economic ones, shape the expression of this collective self-understanding.

Playing Nationalist Politics with the Foreigner Issue

By the beginning of 1982, Schmidt's government was facing major problems, including an economic recession, which would bring it down in October. The immediate cause behind this fall was the growing rift between the SPD and its coalition partner, the FDP. At a party congress in April, SPD members voted to support a policy agenda considerably to the left of Schmidt's own preferred course that aroused strong opposition from the FDP leadership. Divisions between the coalition partners proved impossible to repair, and the FDP left the Schmidt government in September. Lacking a majority in the Bundestag, Schmidt maneuvered unsuccessfully to have new elections called. After losing a confidence motion in the Bundestag on October 1, the Schmidt government was replaced by a new CDU/CSU-led coalition under the chancellorship of Helmut Kohl and in partnership with the FDP. When national elections were held in March of the next year, the CDU/CSU emerged as the biggest winner with nearly 49 percent of the vote, while the FDP's vote declined to just over 6 percent and the SPD's share dropped below 39 percent (Bark and Gress 1993: 376–379, 382–383).

Although it could only be expected that parties out of power would use the upsurge in negative public attitudes toward foreign residents to their own advantage against the incumbent government, the CDU and CSU also helped to shape these attitudes by dramatizing the foreigner threat and demanding a radical change of course to meet it. In 1979, Dietrich Thränhardt observed that "a massive campaign developed, concentrating on Turks and asylum seekers and carried on by important media sources, particularly the elite paper *Frankfurter Allgemeine Zeitung* in a flagrant interplay with CDU politicians. In some Land elections this became a central issue; the Hessian CDU, for example, proposed a law to reduce the number of foreigners in Germany by a million. In Baden-Wüttermberg, the CDU campaigned for a 'rotation system' or 'Swiss system' for foreign workers which would bring 'young fresh' guestworkers to Germany, instead of the old ones" (Thränhardt 1995a: 327).

During the 1980 national campaign, Franz Josef Strauss (CSU) concentrated on Cold War themes rather than the foreigner issue, but after losing to Schmidt's coalition, the CDU and CSU resumed their attack on this issue. Contending that recent government measures to restrict family reunification had not gone nearly far enough to cut off this source of immigration, the CDU/CSU had in late 1981 "launched one of the most inflammatory politicization campaigns in the history of German foreigner policy" against the Schmidt government (Joppke 1999: 80). Party leaders, such as Alfred Dregger, sharply criticized the government's irresponsible handling of the foreigner problem. A leader of the most conservative wing of the CDU in the Bundestag, Dregger argued that government had done far too little to curb the growth of the foreigner population. He called for the restoration of the rotation principle and opposed granting any rights to foreign residents to acquire German citizenship. Contending that naturalization should remain restrictive and conditioned on full cultural assimilation, he observed that certain groups, most notably Turks, had demonstrated over the years that they would never abandon their own national identities to adopt a truly German national self-understanding. Nationalities coming from non-Western countries of origin, he insisted, could not be assimilated, so the FRG was at risk of being overrun by foreigners (*Überfremdung*), if the size of their presence in the FRG was not tightly controlled (Schönwälder

1996: 167–168; Chin 2007: 150–152). With such arguments, CDU and CSU representatives not only attacked any move away from the guestworker policy model, but also called into question the whole premise behind promoting the integration of the largest contingent of the FRG's foreign resident population.

In September 1982, Helmut Kohl (CDU) called for a reduction of foreigners. Upon becoming Chancellor in October, Kohl announced that the reform of foreigner policy would be one of his government's priorities (Thränhardt 1984: 125; 1995a: 327). He set out three basic policy objectives: the integration of foreign workers and their dependents who long had settled in the FRG; restricting the entry of new immigrants; and the reduction of the number of foreigners by promoting their return to their countries of origin. Like its predecessor, the new government would focus its policy efforts on exclusion and return rather than integration. Accordingly, the Kohl government made few tangible policy changes beyond a new return policy that offered higher financial incentives for foreigners to repatriate, but this policy achieved little success (Hönekopp 1987). It dropped the heated rhetoric about the foreigner problem even before the new national elections in March 1983.

The failure of the Kohl government to introduce more substantive measures has invited accusations that the party's rhetoric was prompted by little more than a political opportunism in a quest to reclaim the chancellorship (Thränhardt 1995a: 327–328; see also Faist 1994: 57; Schönwälder 1996: 168–169). Little distinguished the actual policies of the preceding Schmidt government from the new Kohl government. Even if it had had the will, the Kohl government could not move the policy agenda forward to address issues of integration without compromising the rhetorical position of the CDU and CSU on the foreigner problem, but it also had no feasible policy alternative to which it could turn. The primary practical effect of the CDU/CSU's approach to *Ausländerpolitik* was to postpone any serious reform efforts for years, to further politicize the issue of immigration, and to shatter any prospect for forging a policy consensus among the parties to tackle the problems of integration. The "new approach," Rita Chin has observed, "marked a dramatic shift in the political discourse away from SPD discussions about how best to facilitate integration and toward the question of whether guest workers possessed the *capacity* to integrate" (Chin 2007: 153, italics in the original). Behind this reformulation of the issue lay the assumption that integration is a one-way process and that the cohesion of German national culture depends on preserving its homogeneity.

The Politics of Stalemate and Procrastination

Despite the conservative turn, or *Wende*, of 1982, the change in the governing coalitions' marked support for reform would grow over the course of the decade.

As the number of asylum seekers declined from its 1980 peak and the German economy moved out of recession, public attitudes toward the foreigner population became more positive (Leenen 1992: 1049).[9] Even within the CDU and CSU, support soon emerged for at least a modest liberalization of the FRG's foreigner policy. By 1984, for example, there was general agreement on the need to reduce restrictions on the naturalization of second-generation foreigners. However, party members remained divided over issues of broader reform. Conservatives, such as Interior Minister Friedrich Zimmermann (CSU) and Alfred Dregger (CDU), continued to insist that the acquisition of citizenship as a general policy should be conditioned on the applicant's demonstration of a strong orientation toward German culture. They also opposed any relaxation of the rules barring dual citizenship. A younger group of moderates, such as the Berlin Commissioner for Foreigner Affairs, Barbara John (CDU) as well as Heiner Geißer (CDU) and Rita Süssmuth (CDU), advocated a much more flexible stance on citizenship acquisition as a means to promote integration. They did not share the conservative's fear of multiculturalism as a threat to the preservation of German national identity. Throughout the remainder of the decade, disputes over reform within the coalition remained a serious obstacle to achieving Kohl's declared aim in 1983 to revise the Foreigner Law in order to simplify and unify its requirements and procedures (Castles 1985: 531–532; Murray 1994: 22–32; Chin 2007: 194–195).

Along with reconciling differences within the CDU/CSU over reform, the Kohl government also had to take into account the FDP's liberal position on the foreigner issue. This position reflected the party's commitment to the principles of legal equality, individual rights, civil liberties, and tolerance. During the last years of its coalition partnership with the SPD, the FDP had supported the latter's legislative initiatives to grant citizenship rights to second-generation foreigners. After the *Wende*, in partnership with the CDU and CSU, the FDP consistently advocated liberalizing the FRG's naturalization rules. Liselotte Funke (FDP) remained the Commissioner of Foreigner Affairs, and supported reducing the barriers to citizenship acquisition, including the prohibition against dual citizenship. In general, the FDP sought to distinguish its more inclusive liberal position on *Ausländerpolitik* from the conservative, exclusivist stance of its coalition partners (Meier-Braun 1987: 41–43). As a small party, the FDP used *Ausländerpolitik* as a way to stake out an independent identity from its coalition partners. During the 1980s, FDP party members openly warned their coalition partners against playing upon anti-foreigner themes, pointing out that these themes could be exploited by extremist, right-wing groups (Murray 1994: 40–41; see also Chin 2007: 98–99).

9. By the end of the decade, asylum applications will have increased sharply, which gave way to a new policy discussion about how to stem the flow of asylum seekers into the FRG. For exact figures, see Table 13.1.

The opposition to the left of the ruling party coalition, the SPD and the Greens, had throughout the Kohl administration advocated more sweeping reforms to liberalize the Federal Republic's citizenship policies than the CDU/CSU leadership would accept. The SPD remained committed to the *Optionsrecht* to facilitate the acquisition of citizenship by second and third generation foreigners. By 1986, the SPD forwarded proposals not only for permitting dual citizenship, but also for conferring citizenship automatically at birth if at least one parent had been born in Germany (which would have introduced the principle of *jus soli* into German citizenship law). Despite indications that their position was costing them votes in regional elections, SPD leaders held fast. They saw such liberalizing measures as necessary to combat anti-foreigner sentiment in West German public opinion. In their advocacy for reforming the FRG citizenship law, the SPD enjoyed general support from the West German trade unions. But the party leadership proved much bolder than their trade union counterparts. The trade unions officially endorsed a general liberalization of the FRG citizenship law, but never openly embraced proposals to give the children of foreign migrants the right to citizenship or the incorporation of *jus soli* provisions into the citizenship law (Murray 1994: 32–35).

During the 1980s, the Greens emerged as the staunchest advocates of an egalitarian, multicultural society and opponents of assimilation requirements. Critical of the exclusionary biases built into the sovereign nation-state model, the Greens championed a post-national conception of membership grounded on the principles of international human rights. They opposed any substantive naturalization criteria, such as language and ethnicity, as redolent of Nazism. They favored granting foreign residents political voting rights independent of acquiring German nationality. Likewise, they remained the strongest defenders of the FRG's liberal asylum policies as a moral debt Germany owed for its Nazi past and as an important continuing symbol of its break with that past. During the 1980s, they advocated the extension of municipal voting rights to resident aliens, and proposed the adoption of a *Niederlassungsrecht* (right of permanent settlement) after eight years of residence, which would establish greater parity in the rights of citizens and aliens. By the late 1980s, they began to advocate the introduction of citizenship rights for foreigners who lived in the FRG for five years. More radically, they came out against any immigration law that would limit the admissions of foreigners in favor of an open borders policy (Murray 1994: 43–44; Markovits and Gorski 1993: 182–183). As they must have known, such a policy proposal stood no chance of being seriously considered.[10]

With respect to enacting formal legislation, the FRG did very little during the 1980s to address in practical terms the challenges of integration that had

10. Joseph H. Carens (1987) has made the most cogent theoretical argument for open borders in his "Aliens and Citizens: The Case for Open Borders."

come to a head by the late 1970s. The decade stands out as the most significant missed opportunity for reform before reunification. However, despite the meager record of concrete policy achievement during this era, support for reform was growing across much of the political spectrum. At the same time, the path to reform was complicated by the emergence of a new political challenge from the far right that, in its nationalist rhetoric on the foreigner problem, moved to outflank the CDU and the CSU.

The Challenge of Right-Wing Extremism

The CDU's and CSU's anti-foreigner rhetoric was indicative of broader public anxieties over the economy and the prospect of integration, but, as SPD leaders contended, in sensationalizing the foreigner threat such rhetoric had also encouraged the spread of xenophobia. This contention was borne out in a *Politbarometer* poll that showed in 1981, 66 percent of respondents believed there were too many foreigners living in Germany. A year later, in 1982, this figure rose to 77 percent, while 85 percent of respondents agreed that the number of foreign residents should be curbed (cited in Green 2004: 43–44). Although the CDU and CSU expressed concern about *Ausländerfeindlichkeit*, their own rhetoric had emphasized the ineradicable differences between Germans and non-European foreigners that could never be accommodated within Germany. Giving their imprimatur to anti-foreigner ethnonationalist discourse, they had insisted on the imperative of reducing the presence of foreigners in the FRG. After taking power, however, they took little concrete action to redress the very problems against which they had inveighed. In the disparity between their rhetoric and their results, the CDU/CSU opened the door for more extremist groups to build their own case for action and to provide a new avenue for protest (Faist 1994: 58; Murray 1994: 36–37).

The first clear sign of right-wing disaffection with the governing CDU/CSU alliance came with the founding of the *Republikaner* party (REP) in 1983.[11] Two of its leading founders were former CSU representatives Franz Handlos and Ekkehard Voigt. The third founder was Franz Schönhuber, a Bavarian television personality and member of the Waffen SS in World War II. The party was organized in Munich and gathered supporters from the CSU who were unhappy with the CSU Bavarian Minister-President, Franz Josef Strauss's policies of accommodation toward the GDR (*Der Spiegel* 1989). They positioned themselves as the "German party," the true representative of the

11. According to membership figures (probably inflated) given by the REP, they began with 150 members in 1983, which rose to 2,500 in 1985, 5000 in 1987, 7,832 in 1988, and 17,000 in June of 1989 (Haller and Dieters 1991: 259).

German people's interests. This posture was used to imply that the main line parties had been compromised by their association with 'foreign' interests, be they other European countries through the EC, or the US through NATO. *Republikaner* literature championed the principle that "Germany is not an immigration state," advocating that "Germany is for Germans." Accordingly, the party opposed term-free foreign labor contracts, voting rights, and social expenditures for resident foreigners. From the mid to the late 1980s, the party's rhetoric against foreigners in the Federal Republic grew more strident. *Republikaner* leaders blamed crime, unemployment, and housing shortages on the presence of foreigners. They warned ominously of the threat foreigners posed to the preservation of German national identity and to the incitement of social unrest in the Federal Republic (Stöss 1990: 68–73).

The REP's two main competitors for right-wing support in the 1980s were the National Democratic Party of Germany (*Nationaldemokratische Partei Deutschlands*, NPD) and the Democratic People's Union (List D) (*Deutsche Volksunion*, DVU). Having originally been founded in the 1960s, the NPD emerged reorganized in this period with a new generation of leaders, who specifically sought to attract support from the young (Schönekäs 1990: 285–286). In 1986, the NPD began to move into an alliance with the DVU, which had been founded in 1971 by the Munich publisher, Dr. Gerhard Frey. The DVU was not established as a political party in the traditional sense and did not field any candidates for many years.[12] Its array of right-wing publications, however, did provide an ideological home for many on the extreme right during the years of rightist stagnation in the 1970s and early 1980s. During this period, the DVU was critical of the NPD, and refused to endorse its candidates until the growth of the rival REP pushed the DVU into the alliance with the NPD (Schönekäs 1990: 286; Stöss 1989: 184–191). Along with the REP, the NPD and the DVU shared a common hostility to foreigners in the Federal Republic, and like the REP, their rhetoric against foreigners sharpened during the 1980s.

With some exceptions, neither the REP nor the NPD attracted much electoral support at the national level through most of the 1980s. Nor did these two parties find much success in Landtag elections throughout most of this period. For example, the NPD won 6.9 percent of 1967 Rheinland-Pfalz vote, but in the 1983 and 1987 elections, the party received 0.1 percent and 0.8 percent respectively (Ritter and Niehuss 1991: 170). By the end of the 1980s, however, some disturbing signs had emerged that suggested that the electoral appeal of at least the REP might be growing. In the 12 December 1986, Bavarian Landtag

12. In November 1986, Frey established his group as a political party under the name, *Deutsche Volksliste*. He renamed this party in March of 1987, *Deutsche Volksunion—Liste D* (Haller and Dieters 1991: 265).

elections, the REP won 3 percent of the vote; that number rose to 4.9 percent in the 14 October 1990 election (Ritter and Niehuss 1991: 174; 1995: 31). The vote declined to 3.9 percent in the 25 September 1994 election. In the 29 January 1989 elections for the West Berlin House of Deputies, the REP scored an impressive 7.5 percent of the vote (Ritter and Niehuss 1991: 178).[13] Finally, the REP duplicated this showing in the nationwide direct elections for the European parliament in 1989, gaining 7.1 percent of the vote and over 2,000,000 of the votes cast (Ritter and Niehuss 1991: 202).

The European parliamentary elections showed that the REP's highest support came from males, with young voters slightly more represented than other age cohorts. The party took between 50 and 60 percent of its vote from the CDU/CSU and 15 to 20 percent from the SPD. It showed support in both rural regions, such as Bavaria, and large urban areas, such as Hamburg.[14] Opinion surveys pointed to a common cluster of concerns among REP voters. They generally expressed a higher-than-average degree of pride in being German, and a more positive view of Hitler and the Third Reich. Slightly over half (52 percent) of REP supporters had a negative opinion of the Jews compared to 18 percent of all those surveyed. While 65 percent of respondents overall expressed acceptance of the Oder-Neisse line as the Federal Republic's permanent eastern boundary, 62 percent of REP supporters opposed it. In addition, 72 percent of the party's adherents disapproved of racial intermixing and supported Germans preserving their purity. The overwhelming majority (92 percent) advocated permitting guestworkers to remain in the Federal Republic for no more than a year, and then sending them back to their home countries (Stöss 1990: 96–101; Backes 1990: 6).

In competing for votes with the REP, the CSU had since the 1986 Bavarian Landtag elections resumed campaigning against the foreigner threat, focusing particular attention on the asylum issue. Although the CDU also campaigned on these themes in the European parliamentary elections of 1989, the CSU was much more vulnerable to losing votes to its far right competitors, especially after the death of its popular leader, Franz Josef Strauss in 1988. In the 1989 European parliamentary elections, the REP received its highest support in Bavaria, 14.6 percent. Their tally in Baden-Württemberg was 8.7 percent, in Hesse 6.5 percent, and in Hamburg 6 percent. The party did least well in Nordrhein-Westfalen, polling 4.1 percent, and Bremen with 4.5 percent (Ritter and Niehuss 1991: 203–205). To drain away popular support for the REP, CSU leaders sought to contest the foreigner issue on the same nationalist terms

13. In 1988, there were 220,000 foreigners living in West Berlin out of a population of 1.8 million. In addition, approximately 20,000 ethnic Germans from the GDR and elsewhere settled in West Berlin that year (*Der Spiegel* 1989; Childs 1991: 79).

14. Before unification, West Berlin did not take part in European parliamentary elections.

as their rival. This strategy made it more difficult for Kohl's coalition government to reach any accord on a common *Ausländerpolitik* (Thränhardt 1995a: 330–331; 2000: 164–165).

The Renewal of Reform: The Adoption of a New Foreigner Law

One of the most visible effects of the Kohl's government's policy paralysis was the long delayed reform of the FRG's Foreigner Law, which regulates matters of residence, entry, exit, and legal status for aliens. In its original form, the 1965 *Ausländergesetz* had reflected the assumptions of the guestworker model, giving the FRG a flexible legal instrument through which to recruit foreign laborers as needed and to deport them when no longer needed. Subsequent Constitutional Court rulings, federal administrative guidelines, and regulations had improved the legal security of resident foreigners, but this incremental process of amendment had created a complicated legal patchwork, leaving enormous room for administrative discretion. In designing a replacement for the 1965 law during the 1980s, Interior Minister Friedrich Zimmermann (CSU) initially had the decisive voice. However, his first draft of a new *Ausländergesetz* had been defeated in 1984 by determined opposition from the FDP and members of CDU. Four years later, his newly proposed draft surfaced in the press. It not only incorporated those features of the old draft—imposing sharp new restrictions on family reunification, which had aroused opposition—but also proposed limiting residence to eight years for all foreigners. In explaining the rationale behind his proposals, Zimmermann invoked the traditional ethno-nationalist motifs: "The self-understanding of the Federal Republic of Germany as a German state is at stake. A continuing ... migration of foreigners would deeply change the Federal Republic of Germany. It would mean to abandon the homogeneity of society, which is defined by membership of the nation ... The Federal Republic of Germany would ... develop into a multinational and multicultural society, which would be permanently plagued by minority problems ... The national interest commands to stop such a development in its very beginning" (Schneider 1988: 9; quoted in Joppke 1996: 471). But both the rhetoric and the proposals proved too extreme. A leak of the draft to the press provoked a storm of protests from the SPD, FDP, Greens, welfare organizations, trade unions, employer organizations, the churches, the media, and even many members of the CDU (Bade 1994c: 61–63; Chin 2007: 199–200).

In the face of this loud chorus of protest, Kohl removed Zimmermann from office in January 1989, and appointed the more moderate Wolfgang Schäuble (CDU) as his successor. In cooperation with the FDP and other groups, such as the churches, Schäuble swiftly completed a revised draft by September of 1989. In contrast to Zimmermann's, Schäuble's draft did not attempt to promote the reduction of foreign residents or to treat their presence as a cultural threat to national homogeneity. While accepting that earlier immigration could not be reversed, his draft still did not embrace immigration as a policy. Emphasizing that the guestworker experience should be understood as a historical exception rather than a norm or precedent, the new draft strengthened the legal means for managing the control of migration. Despite some continuing opposition, most notably from the Greens, the legislation was enacted in April of 1990, at a time when the questions surrounding reunification had come to command public attention. More than a decade after the Kühn memorandum, the new law became effective on 1 January 1991.

The new law made some significant changes, most notably by giving foreigners greater security in their residence rights and easing restrictions on the acquisition of citizenship. However, in many respects, the new law, as Christian Joppke has observed, "essentially ratified what constitutional court rules had long established" (Joppke 1999: 84). With respect to residential rights, the new law established four resident alien categories to reduce room for administrative discretion and standardize rules across the *Länder*: *Aufenthaltserlaubnis* (AuslG § 15), *Aufenthaltsberechtigung* (AuslG § 27), *Aufenthaltsbewilligung* (AuslG § 28), and *Aufenthaltsbefugnis* (AuslG § 30). The first two residence permits were designed for long-term stays and permanent settlement in the FRG, while the latter two provided for a temporary legal residence status. The *Aufenthaltserlaubnis* was designated primarily for new immigrants arriving in the FRG under family migration or spousal unification regulations (AuslG §17–§20). It was broken into two different permits, the limited or temporary (*befristet*) and unlimited or indefinite (*unbefristet*) (AuslG §15–23 and §24, respectively). The categories of limited and unlimited *Aufenthaltserlaubnis* in the 1990 law liberalized some provisions from earlier legislation by allowing women and children under eighteen years old to receive a legal residence status independent from the rest of their family members' statuses.[15] The limited permit usually allowed for a three to five year stay in Germany. Under certain conditions, those possessing this permit could reapply for it after having left and returned to the FRG (AuslG §16). Those holding the limited permit under regulations of familial and spousal reunification could apply for periodical extensions, usually every five years (AuslG §17–23). The unlimited residence permit, by comparison, granted the resident a permanent legal status. The criteria for this permit included five years of continuous residency in the FRG, sufficient ability to speak German, gainful employment, and financial security (AuslG §24). The *Aufenthaltsberechtigung* was the most permanent of all of the categories of legal residence. Foreign residents would qualify for this type of residence permit after an eight-year stay in the FRG if during

15. Ausländergesetz vom 9. Juli 1990. BGBl. II S. 889, 915. § 17–20.

that time they were gainfully employed. At the time of application, the foreign resident would have to prove a sufficient ability to speak German and to provide for the well being of their family members (AuslG §24). In order to earn this status, the foreign resident also would have had to possess the unlimited *Aufenthaltserlaubnis* for at least three years. Together, the *Aufenthaltserlaubnis* and *Aufenthaltsberechtigung* transition the foreigner from a temporary resident to a permanent one in the FRG.

The last two types of permits were intended to provide foreigners with a short-term, non-permanent legal residence status. The *Aufenthaltsbewilligung* restricted one's stay in the FRG to a maximum of two years and, in most circumstances, was not renewable (AuslG §§28.2; 28.3). Foreigners residing in the FRG with an *Aufenthaltsbefugnis* were generally those asylum seekers who were awaiting a decision on their application or who for legal or political reasons could not return home even though authorities rejected their case for asylum. Even though the law stipulates a maximum period of two years residency under the *Aufenthaltsbefugnis* (AuslG §30), it was not uncommon for foreigners in this category to earn repeated renewals (AuslG §32), but they seldom qualified for permanent residence status. In most cases, foreign residents with this type of permit became "tolerated" (*geduldet*) asylum seekers and, because of repeated renewals, became tied up in a state of legal limbo referred to as the "chain toleration" (*Kettenduldung*).

While some have regarded the 1990 law's clear legal codes for residency as progressive and greatly important for improving the conditions of immigrants in the FRG (Nathans 2004: 247–248), the law's most important changes concerned the acquisition of citizenship. It made it easier for young persons between the ages of 16 and 23 from second and third generation-resident families to obtain citizenship.[16] Targeting this cohort for citizenship was particularly important considering their overwhelming interest in attaining German citizenship. In 1993, for example, over 60 percent of non-citizens between 16 and 25 years of age and more than 50 percent of those between 26 and 34 expressed a desire to become German citizens, whereas less than 40 percent of those between the ages of 45 and 64 expressed interest (Thränhardt 1995b: 70). This change did not amount to an automatic right to acquire citizenship, such as that which had been granted to *Aussiedler*, and set several conditions for eligibility.[17] To be eligible, applicants must (1) have lost or renounced their former citizenship; (2) have legally resided in the FRG for eight years; (3) have never been convicted of a serious criminal act; and (4) have attended school for six years in the FRG, of which at least four years must have been in a school of general education.

16. Ausländergesetz vom 9. Juli 1990. BGBl. II S. 889, 915. § 85.
17. Ausländergesetz vom 9. Juli 1990. BGBl. II S. 889, 915. § 85.

The new law also liberalized naturalization requirements for all aliens who had resided legally in the FRG for fifteen years, and applied for citizenship before 31 December 1995. To be eligible for citizenship under this "rule," applicants were required to (1) have lost or renounced their former citizenship; (2) have not been convicted of a serious criminal offense; and (3) have the ability to support themselves and dependent family members.[18] The new law also reduced the barrier of dual citizenship to naturalization. It provided certain exceptions to the requirements that aliens must relinquish their citizenship before acquiring German citizenship, when, for example, (1) their country of citizenship refuses to accept the renunciation of citizenship, or (2) renunciation of citizenship would cause unreasonable hardship for specific groups (such as political refugees).[19] In other areas, the new law tightened requirements for obtaining certain residence rights, such as requiring applicants to have made contributions into a social insurance fund for sixty months to obtain the right to unlimited residence (*Aufenthaltsberechtigung*).[20] In addition, the new laws still left administrative officials considerable discretionary room with respect to the issuing of residence permits and for the ordering of expulsions.

No such law could remove the fundamental dividing line in FRG law and politics between foreigner (or alien) and German, nor compensate for a decade lost in the politicized debates over the foreign problem in the 1980s. However, the new law, with further amendments in 1993, did encourage a steady increase in naturalizations over the next decade from an exceptionally low base. Throughout the 1980s, between 30,000 and 35,000 non-citizens naturalized annually, but under the new regulations the number jumped to over 60,000 by 1989 and to nearly 130,000 by 1991. On average, the naturalization rate as a percentage of the total foreign population for the FRG averaged 0.3 percent in the 1980s and 1 percent in the 1990s.[21]

Despite rising naturalization rates in the late 1980s and early 1990s, scholars have cautioned against using this figure as a stick against which to measure the acceptance of foreigners in Germany. Complementing research that judges the status of foreigners in Germany according to their socioeconomic and educational achievements, Suzanne Worbs (2003), Joel Fetzer (2000), and Jerome Legge (2003) have demonstrated that measures of individual contact between native Germans and foreigners, including ethnic German returnees, Turks, and Jews, tell us more about the status of foreigners living in the Federal Republic than can naturalization rates. Comparing the level of acceptance of foreigners

---

18. Ausländergesetz vom 9. Juli 1990. BGBl. II S. 889, 915. para. 86.
19. The new law did recognize Ausländergesetz vom 9. Juli 1990. BGBl. II S. 889, 915. para. 87.
20. Ausländergesetz vom 9. Juli 1990. BGBl. II S. 889, 915. para. 27.
21. The naturalization rate average for the Federal Republic drops substantially if ethnic Germans are excluded from the calculation.

Table 11.1. Annual Number of Naturalizations, 1945–2006*

Year(s)[a]	Number	Year	Number
08.05.45–31.12.1950[1]	2,024	1980	37,003
1951	2,357	1981	35,878
1952	8,430	1982	39,280
1953	9,554	1983	39,485
1954	9,832	1984	38,046
1955	16,515	1985	34,913
1956	37,924	1986	36,646
1957	37,540	1987	37,810
1958	33,073	1988	46,783
1959	31,028	1989	68,526
1960	24,071	1990	101,377
1961	19,621	1991	141,630
1962	18,125	1992	179,904
1963	17,799	1993	199,443
1964	17,943	1994	259,170
1965	19,194	1995	313,606
1966	18,433	1996	302,830
1967	21,929	1997	278,662
1968	19,142	1998	291,331
1969	17,818	1999	248,206
1970	18,586	2000	186,688
1971	18,914	2001	178,098
1972	18,645	2002	154,547
1973	18,858	2003	140,731
1974	24,744	2004	127,153
1975	24,925	2005	117,241
1976	29,481	2006	124,566
1977	31,632		
1978	32,710		
1979	34,952		

* Since 1991, naturalizations in (unified) Germany.
[a] Including *Aussiedler* until 31 July 1999.
[1] Not including West Berlin

Source: © Statistisches Bundesamt, Wiesbaden, 2005. Vervielfältigung und Verbreitung, auch auszugsweise, mit Quellenangabe gestattet.

by citizens of the FRG and the former GDR, Legge observes that "the more negative attitude toward foreigners that is expressed consistently by residents of the former GDR may be in large part attributable to their long years of isolation, inexperience with foreigners living in their midst, and lack of democratic institutions and predispositions" (Legge 2003: 103). Fetzer employs the contact theory in a reverse fashion to explain why an increase in casual contact between Germans and immigrants within neighborhoods may increase negative attitudes toward foreigners (2000: 135–139). Fetzer concludes, "our best guess in that this difference [between German and French versus American attitudes toward foreigners] stems from the possibly greater segregation of immigrants in Germany" (2000: 139). Regardless of what one learns from theories of contact, studies like these suggest that easing immigrants' access to citizenship is only one mechanism of integration and that such political maneuvers alone cannot achieve inclusion or compensate for periods of hostility toward foreigners in Germany. As will be seen, throughout the 1990s, and especially after reunification in 1990 and the adoption of the Maastricht Treaty in 1993, the German government would begin recognizing that a more holistic and cooperative approach to controlling immigration and regulating integration is necessary if the divide between Germans and foreigners was to be overcome.

Chapter 12

Aliens Policy and the Federal Courts

"Judged by the principles of German foreigner law and policy alone," Christian Joppke has observed, "the status of settled foreigners in Germany would be exceedingly precarious" (Joppke 1999: 69). The persistent reluctance that German executive and legislative bodies have displayed to remedy this status highlights the limitations of majority-based forms of democratic governance to extend adequate protections to vulnerable minorities, especially those who have not been enfranchised. In remedying this status, the federal courts have produced a substantial body of cases relating to the law of aliens. In particular, the Federal Constitutional Court has often had a significant role as the main governmental body to expand the rights of aliens. Its jurisprudence in this area shows a trend of protecting aliens' rights through a process of balancing individual rights against government interests, as well as guaranteeing to aliens some of the fundamental rights generally designated to persons by the German Constitution.[1] The pivotal role the Constitutional Court has played in this process is indicative of its power within the German federal system, although by institutional design the Court's[2] approach to such issues is reactive rather than proactive.

Expanding aliens' rights through legislative changes and the Constitutional Court's jurisprudence has been part of a broader trend among Western liberal-democratic states. Germany's comparatively restrictive naturalization policy makes the issue of aliens' rights all the more significant because this is the only area where the Court is able to lessen the rights of the Federal Republic's resident population, whereby citizens enjoy a broader set of rights than non-citizens (Neuman 1998: 272). Where the legislature and the executive have

---

1. According to Article 93(I)(4a) of the Basic Law, any person may enter a complaint of unconstitutionality if one of his or her fundamental substantive or procedural rights under the Basic Law has been violated by public authority (Kommers 1989a: 16).
2. Unless otherwise stated, "the Court" always refers to the Constitutional Court.

dragged their heels, the Court has repeatedly stepped in to protect and expand the rights of aliens and their legal security as residents (Guiraudon 1998: 297).[3] It has, thereby, set clear boundaries that at times have constrained the policy alternatives open to the other branches and levels of government in dealing with aliens.

The Federal Court's decisions have enhanced the protection of the rights of aliens in many areas, including rights of residency, family rights, the legal rights of guestworkers, and in cases of discrimination. This brief chapter draws on representative cases from each of these areas to analyze the Court's contribution to recognizing aliens' rights.

Continuance of Residence Cases

The 1973 "Palestinian case" provides an early example of the Constitutional Court's willingness to safeguard an alien's right to continue his residence in the Federal Republic.[4] In this case, two members of the General Union of Palestinian Students were served deportation orders on grounds of national security concerns, in accordance with Article 10 of the Aliens Act. In its initial statement, the Court explained that the deportation orders would be justified in this case "only if the state has a particular interest in carrying out [the complainants' deportations]."[5] However, in ultimately reversing the deportation orders, the Court relied instead on a more basic interpretation of the complainants' rights (Neuman 1990: 52).[6] Since the two students had not been accused previously of terrorist activity, the Court had no reason to believe that they endangered the state's security. Therefore, it reasoned that a "general suspicion" about a security threat did not justify their deportation (Neuman 1990: 53).

In a 1978 case, a man from India, who had resided legally in the Federal Republic since 1961, sought to extend his right of residency.[7] The lower court found that the man's wish to settle permanently in the FRG interfered with the state's interest and thereby denied this man a residency renewal—thus, effectively barring him from naturalization in the Federal Republic (Neuman 1990: 48). The Constitutional Court overturned the lower court's ruling by finding that since the man was brought from India to work in the Federal

---

3. Guiraudon writes that "a large body of jurisprudence has developed on alien rights that highlights the importance of courts as 'quasi-legislators'" (1998: 297).
4. See judgment from 18 July 1973. BVerfGE 35, 382.
5. See judgment from 18 July 1973. BVerfGE 35, 382, 3rd Sent. and Section A, I.
6. See judgment from 18 July 1973. BVerfGE 35, 382, 4th and 5th Sent.
7. See judgment from 26 September 1978. BVerfG, 1 BvR, 525/77

Republic, received continual residency renewals, and had integrated into German society, the state had created a "reliance interest," which protected the complainant's right to extend his residency in the Federal Republic (Neuman 1990: 49).[8] In its decision, the Court also invoked Article 2 of the Basic Law, which specifies the alien's right to reside in Germany.[9] This ruling, and others similar to it, indicates that in cases of residency, the state's absolute ability to deport foreign residents is limited by the individual's constitutional right of residency in the Federal Republic.

Family Rights

In the late 1970s, the Constitutional Court extended its reach into alien rights' issues by examining questions of an alien's family rights, although not always in a consistent or predictable manner. For instance, the Court delivered a decision in 1979 that upheld a lower court's decision to temporarily deport a Turkish man who was convicted of selling drugs to an undercover agent.[10] In this case, the Court examined the issue through the lens of Article 6 of the Basic Law, which guarantees familial rights. In doing so, "this foreigner [*sic*], who is married to a German woman with whom he has a child, may be deported from the Federal Republic of Germany on grounds of deterrence because of his criminal conviction for selling illegal drugs."[11] The Court ended up supporting the temporary deportation of this man on the grounds that the deportation would deter others from criminal activity (Neuman 1990: 57). While the Court did not prohibit the alien's deportation, it did recognize the alien's explicit family rights as guaranteed by the constitution.

The Court delivered another decision on family rights in 1987, when questions were raised about the constitutionality of residency and waiting period requirements for first- and second-generation immigrants to be united with their spouses from abroad.[12] The dispute in the 1987 case, which combined three previous decisions about an alien's right to family reunification, centered around three policies: (1) the initial eight-year residency requirement for the sponsoring spouse and the one-year waiting period following the marriage; (2) the three-year waiting period for the second-generation immigrants in Baden-Württemberg; and (3) the addition of a three-year waiting period for

---

8. See judgment from 26 September 1978. BVerfG, 1 BvR, 525/77, Section A III, §1.
9. See judgment from 26 September 1978. BVerfG, 1 BvR, 525/77, Section B I.
10. See judgment from 18 July 1979. BVerfGE 51, 386.
11. See judgment from 18 July 1979. BVerfGE 51, 386, Section A, 1st sentence.
12. See judgment from 12 May 1987. BVerfGE 76, 1.

first-generation immigrants in Baden-Württemberg (Neuman 1990: 59).[13] The Court upheld the eight-year residency requirement and one-year waiting period as a means of preventing "sham marriages," but found the extended three-year waiting period in Baden-Württemberg unconstitutional because of its deterrence effect, which impinged on the right to family reunification (Hailbronner 2000a: 523). In its final decision, the Court recognized the alien's right to family reunification, but upheld the state's interest by insuring that the alien employs this right legitimately.

The Legal Rights of Guestworkers

The case of guestworkers in Germany provides a unique example of the way the law was applied to people who were not German citizens, but who had lived for an extended period of time in the Federal Republic. The Court's activism on behalf of guestworkers was limited to questions about whether the *Länder* treated guestworkers fairly in cases of residency allowances. These cases required the courts to balance the guestworker's constitutional rights against the interest of the state in protecting "order and security."[14] In a 1983 ruling, the Federal Administrative Court forced the *Länder* governments to consider the constitutional right of residency for guestworkers when they faced deportation for committing minor offenses such as traffic violations.[15] Similarly, in a 1984 decision, the same court established the precedent that the longer the guestworker resides in Germany, the stronger his or her constitutional rights should be (Ansay 1991: 837).[16] While these judicial interventions safeguarded the guestworkers' rights to residency and to be treated equally by *Länder* authorities in cases of criminal activity, protection was not extended to a guestworker's basic political rights, such as the right to peaceful assembly and to form associations (Ansay 1991: 838). However, as we saw in an earlier chapter, the citizenship laws and voting rights for foreign residents prohibit the federal court from establishing new political rights for aliens because this is a matter of federal policy, which the courts cannot control. For this reason, the Federal Administrative Court was only able to ensure that guestworkers enjoyed the rights to which they were entitled as legal residents in the Federal Republic.

13. See judgment from 12 May 1987. BVerfGE 76, 1, Section A.
14. "The Legal Rights of Guestworkers: The Case of West Germany," *Columbia Journal of Transnational Law* 24: 311–338. The author of this article is unattributed.
15. See judgment from 4 August 1983, BVerwG (cited in "The Legal Rights of Guestworkers," p. 323).
16. See judgment from 14 February 1984, BverwG. See also "The Legal Rights of Guestworkers," p. 323.

Discrimination against Aliens

In more recent cases, like the 2003 "headscarf case," the Court broadened its reach to include cases of discrimination against naturalized citizens who are entitled to the same set of rights and protections as German citizens. The "headscarf case" concerned an Afghan woman with German citizenship who was trained as a teacher in Germany.[17] When she sought employment as a teacher in Baden-Württemberg, the government regarded her as unqualified for the appointment as a civil servant because she wore a headscarf. The initial decision by the Federal Administrative Court[18] forbade the teacher from wearing the headscarf at work based on Article 33(5) of the Basic Law, which limited a civil servant's right to religious expression as a means of upholding the state's neutrality in religious matters (Mahlmann 2003: 1103). The Constitutional Court, however, found no evidence to support the lower court's argument that "teachers may be subjected to duties as to their appearance and conduct at school, restricting their individual fundamental right of freedom of faith, in connection with the preservation of the ideological and religious neutrality of the state."[19] The Court ruled in favor of the complainant, and thereby demonstrated that it places the individual's right to religious freedom over the state's religious neutrality.[20]

Despite ruling in favor of the complainant, the "headscarf case" revealed the limitations of the Court's ability to protect the rights of German citizens of different ethnic and religious backgrounds. In its decision, the Court added the caveat that since the constitution delegates the responsibility for education-related policies to the *Länder*,[21] they are free to adopt regulations barring female teachers from wearing the headscarf or any other religious symbols in schools.[22] This ambiguous decision by the Court paved the way for many *Länder* to ban teachers from wearing the headscarf, but not the crucifix or other religious symbols, in the classroom. In this regard, the Court's action to protect minority rights was constrained by the constitutional organization of the Federal Republic,[23] which allowed the *Länder* to adopt legislation that placed boundaries on the religious freedoms of a specific minority group.

17. See judgment from 24 September 2003. BVerfG, 2 BvR 1436/02.
18. See judgment of 4 July 2002. BVerwG 2 C21.01
19. See judgment from 24 September 2003. BVerfG, 2 BvR 1436/02, §48–49.
20. See judgment from 24 September 2003. BVerfG, 2 Bvr 1436/02, §36, 37, 40, 43.
21. The Court points to the *Länder's* competencies in education policy as a means of the Constitutional Court's limitations: "The Basic Law gives the *Länder* a broad freedom of organisation in education; in relation to the ideological and religious character of state schools too, Article 7 of the Basic Law takes account of the fact that the *Länder* are to a large extent independent and within the limits of their sovereignty in education matters may in principle organise compulsory schools freely" (BVerfG, 2 BvR 1436/02, §47).
22. See judgment from 24 September 2003, BVerfG, 2 BvR 1436/02, §47.
23. See judgment from 24 September 2003, BVerfG, 2 BvR 1436/02 §13.

The Constitutional Court's involvement in discrimination cases has also included limitations on the rights of the *Aussiedler*, whose rights are supposed to be on par with those guaranteed to German citizens. In its 2004 decision in the "*Spätaussiedler* case," the Court concluded that restricting the freedom of movement for the *Spätaussiedler*, pursuant to the *Wohnortzuweisungsgesetz* (Residence Assignment Act), as amended in 1996, was constitutional.[24] The complainants, a woman and her son from the former Soviet Union who had immigrated to the Federal Republic in 1996, lodged a case with the Court when their welfare benefits were withdrawn in 1998 after they moved out of the town in which they were assigned to live upon entering the Federal Republic. The Court ruled that the woman was not in a position to take the decision to move as long as she received welfare assistance. In order to restrict the freedom of movement of *Spätaussiedler* who avail themselves of Germany's welfare programs, the Court applied a general understanding of Article 11(2), which allows the freedom of movement to "be restricted only by or pursuant to a law, and only in cases in which the absence of adequate means of support would result in a particular burden for the community" (Koppenfels 2004: 762). The Court found that the Residence Assignment Act did not violate Article 11 because the *Spätaussiedler* could move and simply forego welfare assistance—or accept the subsistence minimum that they would still be eligible for if they moved.[25] The Court also justified the distinction between the *Spätaussiedler* and other Germans on welfare, stating that the restriction on the *Spätaussiedler* is justified because they are in particular need of integration (Koppenfels 2004: 776–778).[26] This suggested that the *Spätaussiedler* had to forego their right to move freely in order to become more integrated into their new community.[27] In its decision, the Court recognized the *Spätaussiedler*'s basic right to freedom of movement within the Federal Republic, but it limited this right to those who are not legally required to reside in a predetermined location.[28]

Critics of the Constitutional Court's decision have viewed it as disturbing in that it treats the *Spätaussiedler* differently than other German citizens (Koppenfels 2004: 762). This decision, coming on the heels of the "headscarf case," suggests a possible trend in the Court's legal interpretations whereby German citizens of different ethnic origins may be treated differently under the Basic Law, which raises concerns about the Court's ability to protect minority groups living in the Federal Republic from discrimination.

24. See judgment of 17 March 2004, BVerfG 1 BVR 1266/00.
25. See judgment of 17 March 2004, BVerfG 1 BVR 1266/00 § 14.
26. See judgment of 17 March 2004, BVerfG 1 BVR 1266/00 § 54.
27. See judgment of 17 March 2004, BVerfG 1 BVR 1266/00 § 16.
28. See judgment of 17 March 2004, BVerfG, 1BvR 1266/00, § 34.

Although the Court has not always been able to grant aliens and minorities rights equal to those enjoyed by other German citizens, in general, Germany's courts have been responsible for much of the expansiveness and inclusiveness toward foreigners (Joppke 1999: 75).[29] The Constitutional Court, in particular, has tried to ensure that the variety of laws administered by the federal government and the various *Länder* are applied uniformly and in conformity with the basic human rights embodied in the Basic Law.[30] Furthermore, the Court's decisions established the floor below which legislative reforms affecting aliens' policy cannot sink. The decisions show that the liberal-democratic norms in the Basic Law have strong effect and are not just policy goals as was often the case under the Weimar Constitution (Kommers 1999a: 135).

The Federal Republic's liberal-democratic norms and their application by the Court have often been supported by the European Court of Human Rights and the European Court of Justice. The Court referred to the ECHR in a 1987 case to establish that "the process of interpretation of the Basic Law should take into account the content and state of development of the European Convention on Human Rights, provided that this does not lead to a limitation or reduction of the level of protection under the Basic Law" (Huber 2001: 172). The ECHR allowed the Court latitude in cases involving deportation by ruling that, in some instances, deportations of second-generation immigrants violate Article 8 of the Convention (Davy 2005: 139). Likewise, in 2004, the ECJ stated that "it is for the competent national authority to take into account, in its assessment where lies the fair balance between the legitimate interests in issue, the particular legal position of persons subject to Community law and of the fundamental nature of the principle of the free movement of persons."[31] In terms of protecting aliens from discrimination, the ECJ has increasingly applied the prohibition of nationality-based discrimination to the Turks living in Germany by invoking the EU Association Treaty with Turkey (Joppke 1999: 191). It remains to be seen, however, whether the Constitutional Court will continue the trend toward the protection of aliens' rights in Germany or whether it will succumb to pressures at the federal, state, and local level to limit the rights of aliens.

29. Joppke adds that "the political process only caught up with positions that had long been established and determined by the legal process" (1999: 75).

30. But see Joppke (1999: 76) where he writes that even from a legal viewpoint, German foreigner law is not that inclusive of non-discriminatory norms and the principle of source-country universalism because distinctions are made between non-privileged foreigners and privileged foreigners (EU nationals and special-treaty nationals).

31. ECJ Case C-482/01, *Orfanopoulos v. Land Baden-Württemberg*, Judgment of 29 April 2004 § 96 (cited in Davy 2005: 140).

Chapter 13

The FRG's International Refugee Challenge

The magnitude of international refugee movements in the twentieth century was unprecedented in world history. While mass migration is hardly new, the growth of effective state management of this movement dates only as far back as World War I. Not coincidentally, the challenge posed by large-scale refugee movements first attracted sustained international attention during the inter-war years. In a world presumed to be organized on the principle of nation-states, refugees are an inconvenient anomaly for most governments. They are typically not wanted anywhere, not by the states that produce them and even less by the states that end up hosting them. As Hannah Arendt observed, the clearest sign that refugees are usually regarded as little more than an unwelcome burden is that no host state wants to exploit them; they just want them to leave, if they cannot deter them from coming in the first place (Arendt 1979: 295–296). The trouble is that, typically, no viable place is available to send them, and once admitted into a host country they can be difficult to expel. In assessing international efforts to deal with the refugee crisis during the inter-war years, she observed, "all discussions about the refugee problem revolved around this one question: How can the refugee be made deportable again?" (Arendt 1979: 284). This question was central to political debates over refugees in the period of which Arendt wrote and since the late 1980s has in many ways reemerged as an overarching concern of states.

Refugees constitute a unique category of migrant as an object of law and policy, because the admissions criteria of refugees are predicated on humanitarian (as opposed to economic or social and sentimental) grounds. This domain is also unique because it is one of the few areas of migration law and policy over which many states have agreed—if more in principle than in practice—to surrender some portion of sovereign control. Much of the debate in Europe over refugees has revolved around the degree to which persons seeking asylum meet the sanctioned criteria. In part, this debate reflects the fact that the number of eligible persons who seem to meet these criteria vastly exceeds the number of available admissions slots of any receiving state. As a result, even the most generous state faces difficult choices in equitably rationing its willingness to resettle refugees. This rationing involves not only the distribution of limited admissions slots, but also the allocation of financial resources used more broadly for refugee measures. As David Martin has pointed out, the same expenditure necessary to resettle one refugee can be used to shelter and feed "many dozens of persons in a refugee camp" (Martin 2005: 13). However, the record of such camps is at best mixed, and they often leave refugees vulnerable to gross human rights abuses (Newland 2001: 519–520).

The financial expenditures needed to underwrite the asylum system in EU Member States, such as Germany, have been many times higher than those associated with the planned resettlement systems of countries such as the United States, because of the protracted nature of Germany's asylum adjudication process and recurrent prohibitions against asylum seekers obtaining employment. Where US resettlement policy strongly encourages employment as a means to protect its domestic welfare system, the German asylum system has been driven by a determination to protect its labor market and to discourage foreign nationals from primarily seeking employment or from abusing the asylum channel to gain entry.

The humanitarian character of refugee policy brings to the fore fundamental normative questions concerning a state's responsibilities toward foreign nationals in need of assistance in one form or another. States have a range of options to address deteriorating situations likely to produce refugee flows, including diplomatic suasion, public censure, trade and other sanctions, and support for human rights monitoring. The control over the admissions of aliens to a state's territory traditionally has been considered a core attribute of a sovereign's authority, and one to which state sovereigns have understandably attached great importance (Fourlanos 1986: 55, 137–139). Perceived national interests have always strongly influenced the generosity of states toward refugees and, until terrorism became a principal international preoccupation, states had usually shown considerable receptivity toward refugees originating from enemy states. Furthermore, refugee groups identified as sharing ties of kinship and/or culture with the dominant population of the receiving state have always received preferential treatment in refugee determination systems. The FRG's policies toward the *Aussiedler* and *Übersiedler* are a case in point here. National interest arguments emphasize that refugee admission is, by necessity, a scarce good, because of the financial costs of asylum and refugee settlement and of the administration of admission procedures, as well as the social and political limits of any receiving country's capacity to absorb large-scale refugee flows. All of these considerations must be weighed in the balance, though as of yet no consensus exists over the criteria for measuring such factors as integrative capacity.

In most respects, the modern nation-state is premised on the principle that it owes primary responsibility to its own members. By any liberal-democratic standard, one of the most fundamental purposes of the state is to promote the welfare and security of its members, which includes preserving the viability of the political, economic, and social institutions that sustain this welfare and security. Likewise, it seems almost universally true that people recognize a higher duty of care toward those with whom they share ties of affiliation than toward those with whom they have no such ties. However, states are not isolated units, as a strict application of the normative logic of democratic theory or communitarian cultural nationalism seems to presuppose (Gibney 2004: 32–57). They are units within an international system of sovereign states, and the sovereign authority of each depends, in part, on mutual recognition by others. The jurisdictional scope of their sovereignty is delimited by those of other state sovereigns. The rising tide of dual nationals is indicative of how, even in so fundamental a domain as the definition of state membership, these jurisdictions have increasingly interpenetrated one another. More broadly, states are closely interconnected through their roles in the global migration economy as producers, receivers, channels, territorial owners, and gatekeepers. That debates have raged in many receiving states about unwanted migration is indicative of how deeply embedded the receiving states are in this global economy and how dependent upon cooperation with one another they have become for making any policy of control effective.

These connecting linkages take a variety of different forms. With respect to the problem of "failed states," for example, it is important to remember that when the European powers withdrew their colonial regimes from Africa they left behind a host of dysfunctional political, administrative, and legal systems (Betts 1998: 65–77; Castles 2002: 178–179). In more recent years, the major advanced industrial, liberal-democratic states have exerted influence in developing countries through economic reforms supervised by the IMF and the World Bank, two institutions that seek to export their economic models. Whether beneficial in the long run or not, these reforms have often been highly destabilizing for the countries affected (Castles 2002: 176, 182; Chimni 2000: 13–14). States also implicate themselves in the violence that engenders refugee flows by merchandizing weapons to unstable parts of the world and to regimes with poor human rights records. As a recent NGO briefing paper reports, "six of eight of the G-8 countries are among the top 10 largest global arms exporters, and all of the eight export large amounts of major conventional weapons or small arms" (Amnesty International, IANSA, and Oxfam

2005: 3). The Federal Republic is fifth on that top 10 list. "In 2003, Germany licensed small arm exports to many countries, including Egypt, Kazakhstan, Kuwait, Malaysia, Mexico, Saudi Arabia, Thailand, Turkey, and the United Arab Emirates, all countries where serious human rights abuses have been committed" (Amnesty International, IANSA, and Oxfam 2005: 12). While the degree of responsibility remains very much open to debate, states who are major suppliers in the global arms market are not mere innocent bystanders to the uses to which these weapons are put.

States also directly implicate themselves in humanitarian crises by taking sides in conflicts or through other foreign policy interventions. The success of such interventions has been at best mixed, but the historical record suggests that states are most likely to intervene when their own perceived national interests seem threatened. The example of the Federal Republic's recognition in December 1991 of the two (then) breakaway Yugoslav republics, Slovenia and Croatia, illustrates how poorly planned intervention can compound an internal problem that is creating a refugee burden for other states. Although the disintegration of the former Yugoslavia was well advanced before Germany recognized the independence of Slovenia and Croatia, this action further aggravated the situation.

In taking this step, Germany acted on its own and against the initial opposition of both its EU partners and the United States. The sudden recognition of Croatia, as Heinz-Jürgen Axt has observed, automatically made the Serbian inhabitants there into a minority, which made them exceedingly vulnerable to predation from rising Croatian nationalism. It had other repercussions as well (Axt 1997). Recognition encouraged the Bosnians and the Macedonians to press for independence, which in turn provoked further Serbian aggression. The EU quickly followed Germany's lead in extending recognition, but this hardly confirmed the wisdom of the German initiative. As Axt points out about the "tactical aspect" in timing the recognition of Croatian independence, "it was a card that could only be played once. By recognizing Croatia, the European Union could no longer put pressure on the republic to tone down its nationalist tendencies and improve the situation of ethnic nationalism" (Axt 1997: 14). Germany may have acted from a desire to do something to stem a conflict that had already produced so many waves of refugees as well as from a certain feeling of affinity with the Croatians as Catholics and former allies, but its initiative ensured that many more waves would come. Such consequences, Axt concludes, were foreseeable and possibly avoidable had policymakers not acted in haste and considered different policy alternatives before they acted.

In weighing the burden of refugees on advanced industrial states, the fact that the heaviest burden is usually borne by neighboring (and poorer) countries needs to be kept in mind. Hania Zlotnik, Director of the UN Population Division, points out, for example, that though the total number of refugees in

Western Europe had by early 1993 "more than doubled" over a decade to "1.7 million, that number represented only 9 percent of the 19 million refugees in the world at the time." Of that total, she observes, "71 percent of the world's refugees … [were] living in developing countries" and "four million refugees (30 percent of the total) had found asylum in the world's least developed countries and were therefore exacerbating the many strains on those very poor countries" (Zlotnik 1994: 376; see also Schmeidl 2001: 65). In short, most refugee movement has remained confined to these regions. Nevertheless, fear over the migration pressures that might ensue from this high population growth among the world's poorest has long alarmed policymakers and their publics in the developed world, but these fears have considerably outdistanced the reality of actual migration patterns from south to north (Bade 2003: 324; Zolberg 2001: 1–8). In fact, political factors, most particularly civil war, appear to be the key engine that drives refugee movement (Schmeidl 2001: 82–85).

Although advanced industrial states have remained for the most part reluctant to host large numbers of refugees, the international community made significant strides after World War II toward creating a global refugee system. As a matter of international norms, Article 14 of the 1948 Declaration of Human Rights recognized the principle that "Everyone has the right to seek and to enjoy in other countries asylum from persecution." More concretely, the UN Convention Relating to the Status of Refugees established the international basis of the legal rights of refugees. It was adopted in 1951 and took effect in 1954. The Convention, as modified by a 1967 Protocol, stipulates that a person is a refugee, and therefore protected against return to a country where life or liberty would be threatened, if he or she has "a well founded fear of being persecuted for reasons of race, religion, nationality, membership of a particular social group or political opinion, is outside the country of his nationality and is unable or, owing to such fear, is unwilling to avail himself of the protection of that country; or who, not having a nationality and being outside the country of his former habitual residence … is unable or, owing to such fear, is unwilling to return to it" (Article 1A[2].)

This statement constitutes by far the most influential definition of "refugee" in international law. These criteria are open to expansive interpretation, but the term "persecution" (in practice) has been construed most commonly to refer to acts by state agents against deliberately targeted individuals. The narrowness of this construction has been subject to considerable criticism because it does not adequately take into account the complex causes and circumstances usually responsible for refugee flight. In addition, the vagueness of the definition's formulation permits state parties to the 1951/1967 Convention a wide degree of latitude in determining its application. Thus, for example, states have been able to invoke it to grant asylum to prominent artists and athletes while denying it to many more unheralded victims of civil strife. Terms such as "well-founded fear" leave unsettled the question regarding how this basis of fear should be measured. Finally, the focus on individual persecution misses the collective dimension when whole groups are targeted by virtue of their shared characteristics (Fitzpatrick 1997: 205–226; Hofmann 1997: 227–254).

The example of the Sri Lankan Tamil minority during the 1980s illustrates how difficult the application of such criteria to distinguish legitimate asylum claimants from broader classes of migrants can be. Some Tamils were fleeing the direct threat of violence; others were seeking to use established migration routes to improve their economic opportunities in the face of a deteriorating economic and political situation. Drawing any clear lines between the two for asylum purposes was highly difficult. Zolberg, Suhrke, and Aguayo observed, "It was not merely that the two groups traveled along similar routes and used the same networks. The migration experience itself had elements of deprivation that resembled the concept of persecution in Anglo-American jurisprudence. More restrictive access for Tamils to education and employment was the result of deliberate policies, and as the conflict wore on, the Tamils could claim that their economic difficulties derived from a deliberate punitive act" (1989: 149). Nevertheless, some sort of distinctions must be drawn. It is likely, however, that the application of the refugee category in such circumstances will depend on how the need for protection is understood.

Whatever its shortcomings, the 1951/67 Convention and Protocol established for the first time in international law a universal definition of "refugee" independent of any particular geographical context. The key principle that the Conventions established is the requirement of *non-refoulement*, namely, that no signatory state may expel a refugee from its territory or compel a refugee to return to a territory "where his life or freedom would be threatened on account of his race, religion, nationality, membership of a particular social group or political opinion." The Convention also obliged state signatories to "facilitate the assimilation and naturalization of refugees," and "in particular make every effort to expedite naturalization proceedings" (Article 34). More broadly, the Convention mandated that signatory states protect and promote the rights of refugees with respect to employment, welfare, education, and other core areas of civic life.

The international refugee regime established between 1951 and 1967 begins from the premise that each state bears primary responsibility for protecting the rights and welfare of its members, but recognizes that states do not always meet this responsibility. When there is a serious breakdown in national protection, other states must step into the breach to provide international protection to persons fleeing violence and persecution. Internal conflicts within states emerged during the 1980s as one of the primary catalysts behind the surging refugee population. As Kathleen Newland has argued, states have a "self-interest" in assuming the protective responsibility from failed ones in such circumstances. Maintaining the functionality of the international system is not ultimately a matter of altruism, but of enlightened self-interest. "Each failure of national protection," Newland observes, "is a failure of that system and undermines its stability" (Newland 1995: 45; 2003: 52). Moreover, for modern liberal-democratic states, refugee protection is a primary means through which the universalistic dimensions of their own norms obtain effect. By protecting the rights of individuals with no prior nexus to them, states reaffirm the universal status of those rights irrespective of citizenship or nationality. This universal status is explicitly recognized not only in modern liberal-democratic constitutions, such as the Federal Republic's Basic Law, the US Declaration of Independence, and the French Declaration of the Rights of Man, but it is also foundational to both modern international human rights and refugee law.

For Western states, the legal and policy framework that developed after World War II for handling international refugees proved manageable during the 1950s and 1960s (Zolberg, Suhrke, and Aguayo 1989: 27). However, the regime had some serious structural shortcomings that would prove crippling as the number of refugees rose. International refugee law, for example, provides no mechanism to enforce state compliance with its requirements. In addition, no international mechanism exists to allocate responsibility for supporting refugees among signatory states in order to promote a more equitable sharing of the resulting obligations. In the absence of such mechanisms, states, like Germany, that became magnets for refugees during the early and late 1980s, and in the 1990s, found themselves having to cope with these challenges largely on their own.

As long as the number of refugees seeking asylum remains relatively low, policies surrounding their admission typically will not provoke much public controversy within their host societies. Such was the case in the FRG until the early 1970s. Between 1953 and 1973, the total number of persons seeking asylum was 100,374. Of these, most came from "Eastern Bloc" states and they were received positively on humanitarian and political grounds. During this period, the numbers of asylum seekers admitted averaged approximately 4,780 per year, though there were occasional spikes in these numbers, such as those that followed the 1956 uprisings in Poland and Hungary and the 1968 Prague Spring. After guestworker recruitment stopped in 1973, the number of asylum petitions rose from 5,595 in 1973 to 11,123 in 1976. During the late 1970s, these numbers jumped markedly: from 33,136 in 1978, they grew to 107,818 in 1980. At the same time, the share of refugees coming from the Third World came to predominate over that coming from the "Eastern Bloc."

Germany's response to this situation is part of a much broader story during this period in which the international refugee regime established after World War II fell apart (Newland 2001: 508–510, 517, 529; Bade 2003: 265). The functioning of this regime had always depended on the commitment of state actors, especially the largest and wealthiest ones who set the standard for others. However, this commitment had been based on the assumption that the numbers of refugees would remain low. The threat of large influxes of refugees from the developing world undermined this commitment and produced public backlashes against their admission. In this climate, states shifted their policy focus from providing legal protection for refugees to finding ways to prevent them from coming into their territories in the first place. Furthermore, the refugee challenge became increasingly conflated with the problem of controlling illegal migration. The policy innovation of designating "safe third countries" to which refugees could be returned during the 1990s exemplified this trend. The breakdown of the old paradigm for refugee protection is also reflected in the growing importance of security concerns as the guiding motive for addressing refugee challenges. As B.S. Chimni has observed of this trend, "the language of burden-sharing has today been replaced by the language of threats against the security of states" (Chimni 2000: 11). One of the dangers of such a one-sided emphasis, Newland has pointed out, is that "it fosters an image of the refugee as a threat instead of portraying them as they are: a target of persecution" (Newland 1995: 45; see also Milner 2000).

Because of the Federal Republic's uniquely generous asylum policy anchored in its constitution, Germany became a major destination for asylum seekers during the 1980s and early 1990s. Article 16(2) of the Basic Law promised persons being persecuted on political grounds anywhere in the world a right to political asylum. Article 16(2) is consistent with the FRG's ratification of the 1951 Refugee Convention and German courts have interpreted this provision to include persecution on the grounds of race, religion, nationality, or membership in a social group (Fullerton 1990: 389). Coupled with Article 1, which guarantees respect for human dignity, and Article 19(4), which guarantees individuals recourse to the courts to uphold their constitutionally recognized rights, this provision gave asylum seekers a strong basis for securing temporary admission and the subsequent resistance of deportation through lengthy administrative and judicial hearings processes. Accordingly, the FRG's ability to expedite the handling of asylum claims as the number of such claims climbed was sharply constrained (Joppke 1999: 85–86). As these numbers soared, Germany's EU partners did nothing to share the Federal Republic's burden. If anything, they learned from the German case how politically costly the issue of asylum can be. This would be an unfortunate lesson to draw, because the German example offers a compelling argument for why burden sharing is necessary for an effective international refugee regime (Schuck 1997). The partisan political gamesmanship and the public debate that surrounded the German asylum controversy also brought to the surface cultural and social attitudes that had long influenced, more generally, the Federal Republic's membership policies. These attitudes reflected a deep discomfort with the cultural pluralism that is a byproduct of all migration.

In the face of the rising numbers of asylum seekers, the German federal government moved to tighten asylum procedures and to expedite the application review process. For example, a 1978 law expanded the staff at the Federal Office for the Recognition of Foreign Refugees and narrowed the right of appeals by asylum seekers against adverse decisions (Steiner 2000: 61). In 1980, the government introduced visa requirements to discourage travel into the FRG by potential applicants from Afghanistan, Bangladesh, India, Sri Lanka, and Turkey. It also introduced a ban on work permits for asylum seekers from non-East European countries for two years after their admission. For East Europeans, the ban was limited to one year (Aleinikoff 1984: 201–203).

In 1982, the government enacted an Asylum Procedure Law, which became the cornerstone of its asylum policy. The law introduced procedures to assign asylum seekers on a percentage basis to different *Länder* irrespective of any preferences an asylum seeker may have. To make asylum less attractive and to reduce expenses in upkeep, the law also provided for the housing of asylum seekers in mandatory group quarters. In 1987, the government passed a new asylum law that extended the prohibition of employment for non-East European asylum applicants to five years—a ban that was lifted in 1991 (Kanstroom 1993a: 194–197; Thränhardt 1999: 49). While Article 16's broad guarantee of asylum for those suffering "political persecution" remained unchallenged in principle during this period, the government adopted an increasingly aggressive policy of active deterrence. Nevertheless, these deterrence measures ultimately proved ineffective.

From 1981 to 1991, the FRG accepted more refugees than all of the other Western European countries combined. Beginning in the mid 1980s, the number of total asylum seekers entering the Federal Republic each year grew rapidly from a low point of approximately 19,737 in 1983 to 256,112 in 1991, and then reached a high in 1992 of 438,191. From 1988 to 1992, the proportion of asylum seekers per one thousand FRG residents grew from 1.31 to its high of 5.41. During these same years, this ratio rose from only .07 to .43 in the United Kingdom. In France, the ratio increased from .61 in 1988 to its height of just less than 1 percent in 1990 before declining to .43 in 1992. However, when compared on this basis, the FRG actually admitted fewer asylum seekers per capita than Sweden. From 1988 to 1992, the proportion of asylum seekers per thousand Swedes rose from 2.31 to 9.64, falling to 4.29 in 1993.

The Federal Republic gained popularity as a refugee haven for several reasons. As noted, until 1993, the FRG had one of the most "liberal" asylum laws anywhere. Moreover, during the late 1980s and early 1990s, the largest segment of the asylum seekers entering the FRG came from former Yugoslavia, a major source of workers for the Federal Republic before the Balkan wars in the 1990s. Proximity would also play a role. Many refugees were also attracted to the FRG because they viewed it as the richest country in Europe and as the natural

Table 13.1. Number of Asylum Applications and Acceptance Rate in the FRG, 1953–2003

Year	Number of Asylum Applications*	Number Granted Asylum	Acceptance Rate (%)
1953	1,906		
1954	2,174		
1955	1,926		
1956	16,284		
1957	3,112		
1958	2,785		
1959	2,267		
1960	2,980		
1961	2,722		
1962	2,550		
1963	3,238		
1964	4,542		
1965	4,337		
1966	4,370	501	11.46
1967	2,992	536	17.91
1968	5,608	846	15.09
1969	11,664	6,097	52.27
1970	8,645	3,488	40.35
1971	5,388	5,530	102.64
1972	5,289	2,464	46.59
1973	5,595	1,862	33.28
1974	9,424	3,961	42.03
1975	9,627	2,764	28.71
1976	11,123	2,530	22.75
1977	16,410	1,689	10.29
1978	33,136	1,838	5.55
1979	51,493	5,899	11.46
1980	107,818	12,488	11.58
1981	49,391	7,824	15.84
1982	37,423	5,027	13.43
1983	19,737	5,195	26.32
1984	35,278	6,563	18.60
1985	73,832	11,224	15.20
1986	99,650	8,853	8.88
1987	57,379	8,231	14.34
1988	103,076	7,621	7.39
1989	121,315	5,991	4.94
1990	193,063	6,518	3.38
1991	256,112	11,597	4.53
1992	438,191	9,189	2.10
1993	322,599	16,396	5.08
1994	127,210	25,578	20.11
1995	127,937	27,099	21.18
1996	116,367	26,182	22.50
1997	104,353	20,990	20.11
1998	98,644	12,797	12.97
1999	95,113	11,529	12.12
2000	78,564	12,257	15.60
2001	88,287	19,942	22.59
2002	71,127	7,050	9.91
2003	50,563	4,028	7.97

*First/new applications only.
Source: BAFL and UNHCR, Population Data Unit.

Table 13.2. Number of Asylum Seekers per 1,000 in Select European States, 1988–2003

Year	Number of Asylum Seekers per 1,000	Number of Asylum Seekers	Population
Germany			
1988	1.31	103,076	78,390,000
1989	1.53	121,315	79,113,000
1990	2.42	193,063	79,753,000
1991	3.19	256,112	80,275,000
1992	5.41	438,191	80,975,000
1993	3.97	322,599	81,338,000
Austria			
1988	2.08	15,790	7,599,791
1989	2.87	21,882	7,627,861
1990	2.95	22,789	7,722,953
1991	3.49	27,306	7,818,423
1992	2.05	16,238	7,914,969
1993	0.59	4,745	7,988,599
Sweden			
1988	2.31	19,595	8,469,339
1989	3.56	30,335	8,526,276
1990	3.42	29,420	8,600,815
1991	3.16	27,351	8,668,112
1992	9.64	84,018	8,718,867
1993	4.29	37,583	8,769,284
United Kingdom			
1988	0.07	3,998	57,159,603
1989	0.20	11,640	57,324,472
1990	0.46	26,205	57,493,307
1991	0.78	44,840	57,665,646
1992	0.43	24,605	57,866,349
1993	0.39	22,370	58,026,920
France			
1988	0.61	34,352	55,873,463
1989	1.09	61,422	56,416,625
1990	0.97	54,813	56,735,161
1991	0.83	47,380	57,055,448
1992	0.50	28,872	57,374,179
1993	0.48	27,654	57,658,289
Netherlands			
1988	0.51	7,486	14,761,339
1989	0.94	13,900	14,848,907
1990	1.42	21,208	14,951,510
1991	1.43	21,615	15,066,220
1992	1.34	20,346	15,174,244
1993	2.32	35,399	15,274,942

Source: The source for Germany's population figures is the Federal Statistical Office of Germany. The source for all other countries is the US Census Bureau, Population Division, International Programs Center (IDB Data Access).

Table 13.3. Total Number of Asylum Seekers Admitted, 1982–2001 (*in thousands*)
(*Convention Refugee Status and Persons Admitted for Humanitarian Reasons*)

Country of Asylum	1982–86	1987–91	1992–96	1997–2001	Total
Germany	36.9	40.0	104.4	86.4	267.6
United Kingdom	12.1	24.1	69.8	158.0	263.9
France	68.5	64.2	43.1	33.2	209.0
United States	27.3	22.8	43.0	103.6	196.8
Austria	25.4	9.1	5.9	6.7	47.1
European Union*	207.0	252.5	449.0	428.9	1,337.3

*1995–2003 data does not include new members

Source: UNHCR Statistical Yearbook 2001.

gateway between East and West (Ronge 1993: 16–17, 20). The fact that since the 1973 recruitment stop, the FRG has had no broad based immigration law to provide an alternative route and to regulate the admission of aliens across all categories in a balanced manner also raised the incentives to exploit the paths of admission that did exist. Finally, the FRG's services for supporting asylum seekers had been, comparatively speaking, rather attractive (Thränhardt 1999: 48–49). Along with these general factors that contributed to make the FRG a prime destination for asylum seekers, there were also specific political factors that shaped the timing and country of origin of different refugee flows. For example, the fall of the Shah of Iran in 1979, the rising tensions that resulted in the 1980 military coup in Turkey, the war in Afghanistan, and the crackdown on Poland's Solidarity movement in 1981 triggered spikes in numbers from these countries. Likewise, during the late 1980s and early 1990s, the civil war in Sri Lanka, ethnic cleansing in the former Yugoslavia, and the repression of the Kurdish minority population in Turkey and its neighbors sparked similar flows (Münz, Seifert, and Ulrich 1999: 54).

The rising influx of asylum seekers inevitably made the issue of asylum a mounting source of public controversy. Both the high percentage of rejected asylum petitions in the first instance and the lengthy, multilevel appeal processes that followed fed the perception that the FRG's asylum system was being overwhelmed and subverted by fraudulent asylum claims. During the appeal process that often took several years, most asylum seekers remained in the FRG. The associated financial costs mounted in proportion with the asylum seekers' number. By 1989 to 1990, the annual cost had reached DM 4 billion (Bade 2003: 265–266). Moreover, as a share of the total number of migrants entering the FRG, the number of asylum seekers had risen from under 1 percent at the beginning of the 1970s to more than 30 percent in the early 1990s (Münz, Seifert, and Ulrich 1999: 54–55). This trend deepened suspicions that

Table 13.4. New Asylum Applications Submitted in Industrialized Countries, 1982–1991 (*absolute numbers*)

Country of Asylum	1982	1983	1984	1985	1986	1987	1988	1989	1990	1991	Total
Germany	37,423	19,737	35,278	73,832	99,650	57,379	103,076	121,315	193,063	256,112	996,865
United Kingdom	4,223	4,296	4,171	6,156	5,714	5,863	5,739	16,775	38,195	73,400	164,532
France	22,505	22,350	21,714	28,925	26,290	27,672	34,352	61,422	54,813	47,380	347,423
Italy	2,520	1,993	2,766	4,093	5,429	10,115	—		4,827	23,317	55,060
Austria	6,314	5,898	7,208	6,724	8,639	11,406	15,790	21,882	22,789	27,306	133,956
United States	33,296	26,091	24,295	16,622	18,889	26,107	60,736	101,679	73,637	56,310	437,662
European Union	92,410	69,535	96,044	157,717	189,938	162,613	209,114	285,741	400,315	509,493	2,172,920

Source: UNHCR Statistical Yearbook, 2001.

Table 13.5. Total First Instance Recognition Rates, 1982–1991 (*percentage*) (*Convention and Humanitarian Refugees*)

Country of Asylum	1982	1983	1984	1985	1986	1987	1988	1989	1990	1991	Total
Germany	15.9	18.4	36.5	39.7	21.7	11.7	10.8	6.2	5.3	8.3	11.9
United Kingdom	69.3	72.0	74.1	80.8	83.0	77.4	84.0	89.3	85.9	50.3	77.1
France	73.9	70.0	65.3	43.3	39.0	32.7	34.6	28.1	15.4	19.7	33.2
Italy	19.6	24.1	20.4	8.7	6.1	7.3	3.5	55.7	59.5	4.5	9.2
Austria	84.5	64.6	45.6	45.2	35.8	31.4	26.6	19.2	6.8	12.5	36.3
United States	35.0	30.0	20.4	24.4	29.9	54.0	39.2	18.0	14.7	33.6	25.0
European Union	55.0	46.5	54.6	49.6	42.6	29.4	29.3	29.1	15.5	17.4	29.6

Source: UNHCR Statistical Yearbook, 2001.

many were using the asylum route to circumvent the migration restrictions that had been introduced with the 1973 recruitment stop. Since that time, asylum remained the sole channel open for non-family members or non-Germans to acquire permanent residency.

Unquestionably, the rising numbers of refugees posed a significant burden on the FRG that had to be addressed. The asylum issue also provided political leaders with a handy vehicle for partisan exploitation and with a potent source of symbolism to manipulate more generally the debate over migration. "The tactical use of the asylum question in inter-party conflicts," Thomas Faist observed, "is obvious in a phrase coined by CDU general secretary Volker Rühe: 'Every additional *Asylant* is a SPD-*Asylant*'" (Faist 1994: 61). This sort of partisanship inevitably contributed to the coarsening of the public debate, while blunting any effort of grappling with the FRG's migration and citizenship policies in broad or systematic terms.

However, the partisan use of the asylum issue emerged long before the influx of asylum seekers had grown significantly. The CDU/CSU first raised the accusations about the abuses of the asylum system in 1973 when the SPD-led coalition government announced a decision to accept left-wing refugees from Chile after a military coup had occurred there (Bade 2003: 270; Schönwälder 1999: 78). Charges of abuse of a lax and overly generous asylum system became a dominant motif in public debates over this issue thereafter. Critics of the system increasingly emphasized the economic motives of many of the asylum seekers. This kind of suspicion about the "true" motives of asylum seekers was hardly new in the FRG (or elsewhere), nor restricted to non-German refugees. Looking at a massive influx of refugees, one German official expressed the sort of skepticism that often accompanies their arrival: "Only 10 percent are real political refugees. Maybe 60 percent or more simply come because they are not happy there" (quoted in Levy 1999: 73). This official was referring to the post–World War II devastation in Europe and the subsequent flow of German refugees in the late 1940s. If the genuine protection needs claimed by these refugees under these circumstances were open to such suspicion, then it is not difficult to imagine the kind of suspicion that would greet later refugees when the causes of flight were more remote and the ethnicity was increasingly non-European.

The issue of asylum abuse came to the fore as a major public crisis and as a symbol of a more general threat than that posed by the "invasion" of foreigners. After a respite in the public's fears of the perceived negative consequences of immigration in the 1980s, by the early 1990s the German public once again turned against foreigners (Legge 2003: 33, 45). This time, however, they focused much of their agitation toward asylum seekers (Fetzer 2000: 72). In a September 1991 poll, for example, 76 percent of the people surveyed supported changing the asylum law to curb abuses by those who were not fleeing

Table 13.6. Germany, Inflows of Asylum Seekers by Nationality, 1992–2004 (*in thousands*)

	1992	1993	1994	1995	1996	1997	1998	1999	2000	2001	2002	2003	2004
Iraq	–	1.2	2.1	6.9	10.9	14.2	7.4	8.7	11.6	17.2	10.2	3.9	1.3
Turkey	28.3	19.1	19.1	33.8	31.7	25.9	11.8	9.1	9.0	10.9	9.6	6.3	4.1
Serbia and Montenegro	–	–	–	34.5	24.8	31.0	35.0	31.5	11.1	7.8	6.7	4.9	3.9
Fed. Rep. of Yugoslavia	115.4	95.6	39.3	32.7	20.9	17.7	35.0	33.7	11.1	7.8	6.7	–	–
Afghanistan	6.4	5.5	5.6	7.7	6.2	6.0	3.8	4.5	5.4	5.8	2.8	1.5	0.9
Russian Federation	–	–	–	–	–	–	–	2.1	2.8	4.5	4.1	–	–
Vietnam	12.3	11.0	3.4	3.0	1.9	2.9	3.0	2.4	2.3	3.7	2.3	2.1	1.7
Iran	3.8	2.7	3.4	4.3	5.3	4.5	3.0	3.4	4.9	3.5	2.6	2.1	1.4
India	–	–	1.8	4.6	4.1	3.0	1.5	1.5	1.8	2.7	2.2	1.7	1.1
Pakistan	–	–	–	4.6	3.8	3.8	1.5	1.7	1.5	1.2	1.1	1.1	1.1
Bulgaria	–	–	–	2.2	1.7	1.2	0.2	0.1	0.1	0.1	0.8	0.5	0.5
Syria	–	–	–	–	–	–	–	2.2	2.7	2.3	1.8	–	–
Bosnia Herzegovina	6.2	21.2	7.3	5.2	2.2	2.3	1.5	1.8	1.6	2.3	1.0	0.6	0.4
Ghana	–	–	–	0.8	0.7	0.7	0.3	0.3	0.3	0.3	0.3	0.4	0.4
Lebanon	–	–	–	2.0	1.7	1.5	0.6	0.6	0.8	0.7	0.8	0.6	0.3
Sri Lanka	–	–	–	6.7	5.6	5.1	2.0	1.3	1.2	0.6	0.4	0.3	0.2
Romania	–	–	–	5.5	2.1	1.2	0.3	0.2	0.2	0.2	0.1	0.1	0.1
Algeria	–	–	–	–	–	–	–	1.5	1.4	2.0	1.7	–	–
Azerbaijan	–	–	–	–	–	–	–	2.8	1.6	1.7	–	–	–
China	–	–	–	–	–	–	–	1.2	2.1	1.5	–	–	–
Sierra Leone	–	–	–	–	–	–	–	1.5	1.2	1.5	–	–	–
Georgia	–	–	–	–	–	–	–	1.1	0.8	1.2	1.5	–	–
Other countries*	265.8	166.3	32.2	44.9	46.1	48.2	26.8	28.2	26.7	31.4	30.0	24.5	18.3
Total	438.2	322.6	127.2	167.0	149.2	151.7	98.6	95.1	78.6	88.3	71.1	50.6	35.6

*SOPEMI data lists selected countries for each year; Data is updated through 2006 edition.

Source: Trends in International Migration: SOPEMI 2002, 2003, 2004 and 2006 editions.

political persecution. An almost unanimous 96 percent opposed accepting foreigners coming for economic motives, and 69 percent advocated curtailing the granting of asylum altogether. More disturbing, 36 percent voiced sympathies for right-wing groups whose programs emphasized "action against foreigners" (Marshall 1992: 262). The emergence of this crisis did not occur in a vacuum driven by numbers alone, but rather compounded the FRG's own troubled history in grappling with its so-called "foreigner problem." In this context, the issue of asylum seekers became a lightening rod at a time when the FRG was still officially declaring itself to be "not-an-immigration-land," against all the evidence to the contrary.

Not surprisingly then, from the 1970s through the early 1990s, the public debate over the asylum issue in the FRG strongly reflected the ethnocultural idiom of the German understanding of membership as well as the administrative categories through which the FRG had sought to channel migrants. The influence of both is evident in the fact that the very term "refugee" (*Flüchtling*) was reserved for ethnic Germans. All non-German refugees were designated *Asylbewerber* (asylum seekers), *Asylberechtigte* (asylum entitled), or most commonly *Asylant*.

The latter is not a legal term, and its usage is relatively new. It did not appear in the German dictionary *Duden* before 1978. In German, the word has a clearly pejorative meaning. As Jürgen Link (among others) has observed, the compound *Asyl-ant* conveys the same negative associations as similarly formed compounds such as *Ignorant* (ignoramus), *Simulant* (malingerer), *Querulant* (trouble maker), *Bumelant* (sluggard), and *Spekulant* (speculator) (Link 1988: 50–51; Wong 1992: 410–411). In the FRG, the use of *Asylant* originated in juristic commentaries of the 1960s, was picked up by the media during the 1970s, and its usage became common by the early 1980s. As Klaus Bade has observed of this period, "refugees and asylum seekers were disparaged systematically and polemically through the pejorative and defamatory" use of this term, and the media "turned it into a xenophobic leitmotif running through the political debate" (Bade 2003: 270).

At its crux, the term *Asylant* conveys not only a negative stereotype, but also underscores the dividing line between Germans and all foreigners. Like any stereotype, it conveys an artificial image based on an abstract generalization that obscures all of the concrete differences among the persons and groups lumped together under this symbolic category. In this sense, it conveys a collective image of an undifferentiated foreign "other," but it also facilitates the blending of an assortment of negative associations connected with migrants into a single compound stereotype. It was most closely associated with the asylum abuser, and this association made the stereotype a convenient lightening rod for all of the general resentments and dissatisfactions with the "foreigner problem" in the FRG. As Gerald Neuman has observed: "The criminal asylum-abuser becomes the symbolic representative for a concentric set of categories of foreigners: all rejected asylum applicants; all foreigners awaiting asylum decisions, including those whose claims have been granted; all foreigners coming to live in Germany; and all non-citizens, even those who were born in Germany" (1993: 515; see also Link 1988: 52–53; Gerhard 1993: 246).

In the public debates and media reports, the term *Asylant* was conjoined with a host of other words that expressed German anxieties about the potential threats that migration posed, such as *Asylantenflut* (asylum flood), *Asylantenstrom* (asylum stream), *Scheinasyl* (bogus asylum seeker), and *Asylantenkatastrophe* (asylum catastrophe) (Wong 1992: 410; Schönwälder 1999: 82–83). These compounds further deepened the ominous meaning that the root word conveyed by connecting it with a whole series of negative equivalences. In addition to the frequent associations drawn between asylum seekers and floods, military metaphors were also used to express the dangers that they represented in terms of an invasion, such as "Refugees gather at the borders of Western Europe" (Gerhard 1993: 245). Although this threat turned out to be highly exaggerated, the collapse of the Soviet Eastern Bloc seemed to create another vast potential pool of refugees and other migrants. Contemporary media reports encouraged public anxieties over migration pressures from the East. In the summer of 1992, an opinion survey of Russians suggested that as many as 13,000,000 people from the former Soviet Union were considering migrating to the West (Mühlum 1993: 9; Dornis 1997: 77–116; Dietz and Segbers 1997: 141–164).

In light of the preponderant share of asylum seekers it received in the 1980s and the 1990s, the Federal Republic has had one of the strongest interests among Western European states in developing new, regionally based solutions to managing the refugee challenge. Before the mid 1980s, there was no common EC policy toward asylum seekers (or immigration), and policies differed widely among EC Member States. With the Single European Act of 1987, the first hesitant steps were taken toward harmonizing policies, but it took the Maastricht Treaty of 1992 to provide a legal framework for the development of a common EU refugee policy (Papademetriou 1996: 22–24, 29–30, 59–63; Joly 1996: 44; Kanstroom 1993b: 213).

From an individual state-centered perspective, the FRG had good reason to believe it was doing more than its fair share and that the refugee burden should be distributed more evenly across EU Member States. The dominance of the state-centered perspective emerged early as the FRG moved to restrict the exercise of its own constitutionally guaranteed right of asylum to meet the perceived threat at its borders. From the perspective of the global refugee problem, however, in comparison with the frontline states neighboring those producing major refugee outflows, the EU and other wealthy Western states could not legitimately claim to be disproportionately over-burdened. During the 1990s, it was within this context that the FRG assumed a leading role in promoting the development of bilateral and multilateral arrangements to enhance the effectiveness of border controls, to streamline the administration of asylum claims, and to allocate responsibility for asylum claims among EU Member States. The core of these efforts were aimed at preventing and deterring the arrival of refugees and expediting the processing of asylum applications by those who did manage to enter, which seemed to be the only common denominator on which EU Member States could agree. While during the 1990s several EU Member States amended their asylum laws, Germany had to amend Article 16 of the Basic Law in order to restrict the constitutionally guaranteed right to asylum because of political persecution. In doing so, and so as to overcome the objections of the Social Democrats, the ruling conservative coalition had to agree to a modest easing of the German nationality law. Thus, the first major step toward a fundamental tightening of the conditions for admission of asylum seekers to Germany came to be known as the *Asylkompromiss* (asylum compromise) in 1993.

Chapter 14

Reunification

Triumph and Tragedy

The issue of reunification had long been invoked as a policy rationale to justify restricting immigrant access to citizenship in the FRG. Christian Joppke has succinctly explained this rationale: "As long as Germany was divided, and the free western part defined itself as the homeland of all Germans who were not free to determine their own fate—a definition enshrined in the Preamble of the Basic Law—Germany could tolerate immigrants only as 'guest workers,' who were expected to stay out of the nation's own unfinished business" (Joppke 1999: 261). In interpreting the Preamble to the Basic Law, the Federal Constitutional Court had emphasized that seeking reunification was not simply a desirable political goal, but a constitutional obligation that would be binding on the political organs of the FRG.[1] At the same time, however, the Court recognized that the FRG government had broad latitude to decide whether any particular measure would hinder the achievement of this goal. More specifically, the Constitutional Court, in its 1990 Schleswig-Holstein decision rejecting the provision for local alien suffrage, had recommended reducing restrictions on naturalization as an alternative remedy.[2] There is no reason to assume that the Court would have struck down earlier legislative efforts to facilitate naturalization. The constitutional argument would have a good deal more force if the legislative attempt had actually been made and was then subsequently rebuffed by the Court.

As a policy argument, this rationale also does not bear much scrutiny. The sudden collapse of the GDR and the immediate prospect of reunification caught the FRG leadership by complete surprise, because even the overwhelming

---

1. See judgment from 31 July 1973, BVerfGE 36, 1; see also judgment from 21 October 1987, BVerfGE 77, 137.
2. See judgment from 31 October 1990, BVerfGE 83, 37.

majority of Germans had long since reconciled themselves to the enduring existence of the two German states.[3] By the logic of the rationale, even if reunification were not to have occurred for another century or more, immigrants and their descendants should remain a perpetual subclass in German society until this national destiny is fulfilled. Other membership criteria, such as work, residence, birth, and taxation, would remain strictly subordinated to this single overarching consideration as factors used to determine eligibility for citizenship. It was pure supposition that providing broader citizenship access to a diverse population of immigrants would interfere with this national project. The concern among some that immigrant minorities, if given the means (e.g., voting rights), would inevitably obstruct efforts to reach this collective goal reinforced the notion of a fundamental boundary between insiders and outsiders. It is therefore not surprising that the authors of the 1982 Heidelberg Manifesto invoked the FRG's constitutional obligation to achieve reunification in advancing their argument against the integration of the resident foreigner population. However much weight one attaches to this kind of constitutional argument, reunification removed it as a consideration.

To conceive of German reunification as a singular event in which a divided people come together can obscure the multidimensional integration challenges that this process brought to the fore. The reunification of Germany in 1990 fulfilled a fundamental constitutional mandate of the Basic Law, but this mandate had two interrelated aspects. As one constitutional law scholar has observed, "the Basic Law contemplated two forms of unification: the 'inner' unification of Germany itself and the 'outer' unification of (at least Western) Europe, in which Germany was to play a central role" (Quint 1997: 248).[4] These two forms of unification had been inextricably linked both through a series of international treaties and through provisions of the Basic Law. The link between the recovery of German sovereignty and European integration had been established even earlier at a London summit in 1948 held by the three Western Allies and the Benelux countries. At this conference, the six governments present approved the creation of the West German state, in concert with measures advancing European economic integration (United States Department of State 1950: 75–84).[5] Later, in the 1955 "General

3. According to public opinion surveys, the percentage of West Germans who thought unification was likely within their lifetimes dropped steadily from the mid 1960s to only 3 percent by 1987 (Kuechler 1993: 31; Merkl 1993: 119, 122).

4. For a similar view, see Kirchner (1996: 156).

5. In a Communiqué from a three-power meeting of 8 April 1949 in Washington, DC, the governments of the United States, the United Kingdom, and France "agreed that a major objective of the three Allied Governments was to encourage and facilitate the closest integration, on a mutually beneficial basis, of the German people under a democratic federal state within the framework of a European association" (United States Department of State 1950: 89; Merkl 1993: 19).

Treaty"[6] between the Western Allies and the FRG, all of the signatories agreed to the goal of a "reunified Germany enjoying a liberal-democratic constitution like that of the Federal Republic, and integrated within the European Community" (Quint 1997: 253–254).[7] Consistent with the "General Treaty," German policymakers had realized that German reunification could only take place within the project of European integration and Germany must take a clear lead in this project to rehabilitate its national reputation. In pursuing their foreign policy, FRG leaders were much more comfortable casting their agenda in terms of broader European interests than narrower ones of national interest (Ash 1993: 357–362).

The rapidity of the GDR's collapse in late 1989 came as much as a shock to West Germans as it did to the FRG's fellow EC Member States.[8] When the Berlin Wall was breached on 9 November 1989, both East and West Germans celebrated the end of the division, but soon the realities concerning how much reunification would cost were to be felt.[9] These costs alone would have made the transition difficult, but they were compounded by additional burdens, such as the soaring numbers of refugees and *Aussiedler* that the FRG had been admitting since the late 1980s. In the face of these circumstances, the triumph of reunification was accompanied by severe economic hardships for East Germans and the tragedy of growing right-wing violence against foreigners.

One key issue that divided supporters of reunification was the problem of allocating the social and economic costs that any arrangement would entail. Throughout 1990, polls showed that West Germans and East Germans stood fundamentally opposed on this issue (Merkl 1993: 129–130). The vast majority of West Germans expressed a clear aversion to paying higher taxes and servicing a larger public debt, which would prove necessary in order to modernize

---

6. As Quint explains in an accompanying footnote to his text, "this agreement was originally signed in 1952, but its ratification was delayed when a companion treaty on the European Defense Community was rejected by the French National Assembly. After modification, the treaty was signed again in 1954 and came into effect after ratification by the signatory parties" (1997: 434).

7. The General Treaty had been the decisive step in the FRG's obtainment of sovereignty as an autonomous state. The treaty removed the Occupation Statute under which the Basic Law had been adopted, but the treaty also reserved important rights to the Western Allies. These rights most directly concerned the legal status of Berlin, the future boundaries of a reunified Germany, and a final peace settlement (Quint 1997: 253–254). Together with the Soviet Union, the Western Allies would relinquish most of these remaining rights in the Treaty on Final Settlement with Respect to Germany signed on 12 September 1990.

8. As Desmond Dinan observes, "It is impossible to exaggerate the shock that probable unification caused the EC and its Member States (including Germany)" (1999: 130).

9. The percentage of West Germans supporting reunification declined from 78 percent in March 1989 to 56 percent in December 1989, though it rose again to 80 percent by February 1990. Among East Germans, the percentage supporting reunification rose from approximately 50 percent in November 1989 to 80 percent in February and March 1990 (Kuechler 1993: 32–33).

the East German economy and to subsidize its social services. At the same time, most East Germans believed that the West Germans should share some of their wealth to offset the deep social and economic disparities between East and West. Many East Germans felt that they had borne an unfair share of the post-war burden, having lived for 40 years under communist oppression, while their western neighbors had grown rich.

From the beginning, the issue of allocating costs was subordinated to the issue of defining the form and pace of reunification. When, for example, on 28 November 1989, Helmut Kohl outlined his original ten-point plan for German reunification, the subject of costs was discussed only in passing.[10] At this time, Kohl was much more concerned with reassuring his nervous Western Allies that the Federal Republic remained faithful to its commitments within the European Community and the NATO alliance than with the problem of costs.[11] Moreover, no one then had any way of predicting how high these costs would be. Few realized how enfeebled the East German economy was and how near the East German government was to economic collapse.

Under his ten-point plan, Kohl envisioned a gradual process of reunification leading to some form of confederation between the two states. But this plan was quickly outdistanced by events. Massive out-migrations of East Germans heading west crippled the GDR economy and government even further, while overwhelming the FRG's ability to absorb the newcomers (Jarausch 1994: 62). The formal day of accession occurred on 3 October 1990. In assessing East German support for reunification during this period, the historian Konrad Jarausch has concluded, that it "did not arise from old-style Pan-Germanism, but a realization that the quickest path to a better life led through Bonn" (1994: 200). Despite Kohl's aspiration for a slow reunification process through confederation, it soon became clear that East Germany would be incorporated into the FRG's established constitutional order.

The newly united Germany held its first nationwide parliamentary elections on 2 December 1990. Kohl's victory in these elections seemed to vindicate his strategy of emphasizing the priority of rapid reunification and deflecting consideration of its social and economic costs. In seeking to minimize the issue over how the social and economic burdens accompanying reunification would be distributed, Kohl's team made the task of building a coalition of East German and West German supporters behind their policies easier, but he left

10. A translated text of this plan is available as "Document 10" in the appendix of Glaessner (1992: 160–163).

11. Thus, he declared, "The future structure of Germany must fit into the future architecture of Europe as a whole ... We understand the process leading to the recovery of the German unity to be of European concern. It must, therefore, be considered together with European integration" (Glaessner 1992: 162).

the German public unprepared for the sacrifices to come. These hardships fell most heavily on the East Germans. "The severity of the depression in East Germany," two economists have observed, "is without parallel in modern economic history. Not even the Great Depression of 1928–1933 was as bad" (Sinn and Sinn 1992: 29; Jarausch 1994: 155).

The political reception of the East Germans into the FRG stands in sharp contrast to the experience of the German expellees and refugees during the 1950s. Whereas the party elites in the 1950s had incorporated representatives of the latter at all levels of government, which facilitated their integration, East Germans found their representatives largely excluded from important government posts and systematically ousted from positions in the civil service.[12] Whereas the All-German Bloc (*Gesamtdeutscher Block/Bund der Heimatvertriebenen und Entrechteten*, GB/BHE) had entered a Bonn coalition government as early as 1953, the East German Party of Democratic Socialism (*Partei Demokratischer Sozialismus*, PDS) and its successor party, the Left Party,[13] its closest counterpart,[14] has never been able to develop an effective partnership with any of the established West German parties.[15] As David Patton has observed, "the western [political] establishment … deepened the regional divide by failing to bridge the under representation of East Germans among the leading political institutions of the Federal Republic … Westerners dominate within the parties, the ministries, the courts, the bureaucracies and in the interest groups" (1998: 27).[16] The success of the GB/BHE as a coalition partner spelled its demise, and it began to flounder within eight years of its founding.

12. David Patton has emphasized the contrast in these experiences. Aided by a federal law guaranteeing that refugees who had formerly belonged to the civil service would obtain new positions, by 1952 refugees and expellees made up 20 percent of the FRG civil service. By contrast, roughly 200,000 East German civil servants would lose their jobs by the fall of 1992 (Patton 1998: 23, 27; see also Patton 1996: 1–22; Schoenberg 1970: 46).

13. The PDS was the reformed successor party to the East German communist party, the Socialist Unity Party (Sozialistische Einheitspartei Deutschlands, SED). The PDS abandoned the Leninist principles of democratic centralism, and became a regionally based party that spoke largely for those East Germans who felt they had benefited the least from unification. In 2005, the PDS joined with a small West German Party, the WASG, to form the Left Party (*die Linke*). The Left Party won 8.7 percent of the vote in 2005, gaining 54 seats in the Bundestag, but no other German party will form a coalition with them on the national level.

14. Describing one party as the "counterpart" of the other is not intended to imply they shared similar ideologies. The BHE supporters tended to be conservative, often ultranationalistic. The Left Party, as the name reflects, remains a leftist party. The similarities between the PDS and the BHE are explored in Neugebauer and Stöss (1996).

15. This continues to be the case. Even after the PDS unified with the WASG, led by Oskar LaFontaine, a renegade former SPD senior political leader, to form the Left Party, all of the other parties in the Bundestag refused to negotiate a coalition government with them.

16. Jennifer A. Yoder reaches similar conclusions in her study. As she observes, "The initial preoccupation with institutional harmonization had the effect of extinguishing indigenous elite

By contrast, the PDS and its successor party, the Left Party, has maintained a strong following among East Germans to the present day.

Confronted with a collapsing economy and marginalized in their new political system, East Germans were ill-prepared to act generously toward foreigners living in their midst. However, the 1990 Reunification Treaty required the new eastern *Länder* to accept their quota of the asylum seekers admitted by the FRG. These admissions did not begin until December of 1990, and the full quotas were not reached until 1992. Even with the delay, the eastern *Länder* lacked the administrative infrastructure to handle its share of the quota as well as any tradition of receiving large numbers of asylum seekers of this type. The GDR had not been a signatory to the 1951 Geneva Convention Relating to the Status of Refugees, and did not have a corresponding asylum law, much less a constitutional guarantee of a right to asylum as the FRG's Basic Law provided at the time. The GDR had admitted individuals for asylum on a more ad hoc basis. It depicted these special cases as political "martyrs" of the Cold War and propaganda trophies. At a time when East Germans faced wrenching changes in their society, which threatened their own employment prospects and social security, the growing presence of asylum seekers would unleash the latent xenophobic tensions that had developed in the GDR (Kolinsky 2000: 152–158). Like the Federal Republic, the GDR had employed guestworkers, though in much smaller numbers, to fill labor shortages since the 1950s. Beginning in 1966, the terms of their employment became subject to intergovernmental agreements between the GDR and the sending states. The GDR preferred recruiting its contract workers from Eastern European states, but the growing popularity of democratic ideas in these states made their workers less attractive by the late 1980s. In 1989, for example, the GDR enlisted 60,000 Vietnamese workers, and had entered contracts with Mozambique to obtain another 100,000 workers.

While officially promoting a policy of friendship among peoples (*Volksfreundschaft*), the GDR never encouraged any kind of cosmopolitan appreciation for cultural differences or communication between East German natives and their foreign guests. Indeed, it had made every effort to deny these contract workers any prospect of integration into East German society by segregating their housing and employment (at the lowest ranks with below standard wages) and by limiting their contacts with East German natives. The latter tended to see the contract workers as "unwelcome competitors for consumer products and a danger to the economic equilibrium in the GDR" (Kolinsky 2000: 149–150; see also Kolinsky 2004: 153–157). When the East German economic, social, and

---

input in the determination of the pace, form, and content of political reconstruction in the east" (Yoder 1999: 155).

political system began to implode, the contract workers were most vulnerable to suffering its effects. "The social vacuum," Klaus Bade has observed, "brought by official isolation of foreigners and taboos surrounding their existence, caused rumors and suspicions and mistrust; fear, and hatred grew rampant" (Bade 1994b: 92). Unification of East and West Germany, then, created conditions ripe for a strong anti-foreigner backlash within the Federal Republic.

As the East Germans struggled to find a place for themselves in the FRG, West Germans had distinct grievances of their own. By July 1991, Kohl had introduced a 7.5 percent income tax surcharge on West Germans, which he described as a "solidarity tax increase." He also raised the value-added tax. His party's popularity quickly plummeted and his party lost subsequent *Länder* elections, even in his home state of Rheinland-Pfalz. After parties such as the *Republikaner* had suffered sharp reversals after November 1989, this decline in popularity created a further opening for more extreme right-wing parties to draw fresh support from disaffected conservative voters. Thus, for example, in April 1992, the *Republikaner* party won 10.9 percent of the vote in Baden-Württemberg state elections and 8.5 percent in Hessian municipal elections a year later. In April 1992, the DVU attracted 6.3 percent of the vote in Schleswig-Holstein state elections (Dalton and Bürklin 1993: 240–241; Conradt 1993: 71–72; Ritter and Niehuss 1995: 27, 29, 30).

As the extreme right grew, the number of violent criminal acts committed by right-wing radicals also rose rapidly, from an average of 200 per year in the late 1980s to 1,489 in 1991. The overwhelming majority of these acts were against foreigners. From 1991 to 1992, the total number of right-wing criminal acts, including non-violent acts, almost doubled from 3,884 to 7,121. That number rose again in 1993 to 10,561. During this same period, the number of murders committed by right-wing extremists jumped from 3 to 17, while the number of physical assaults rose from 449 to 725. The worst and most frequent outbreaks of violence against foreigners occurred in the eastern *Länder*, whose understaffed and poorly trained police forces were least equipped to handle such problems. From 1990 to 1991, the total number of extreme right-wing groups, including neo-Nazis and skinheads, increased from 39,800 to 41,900, and remained at roughly that number in 1992 (Human Rights Watch 1994: 7–8, 12; 1995: 17–27). In the September poll of that year, more than three-quarters of the respondents supported changing the asylum law to curb abuses, and 96 percent opposed allowing openings for foreigners coming for economic motives. More importantly for this discussion, one-third of the respondents expressed sympathies for right-wing groups with action-oriented, anti-foreigner agendas (*Der Spiegel* 1991a; also discussed in Marshall 1992: 262).

Meanwhile, the federal government continued to dither. "Instead of perceiving the attacked as *ausländische Mitbürger* (foreign fellow citizens) who were entitled to legal protection," Rita Chin has observed, "politicians like

[Federal Interior Minister Wolfgang] Schäuble viewed them as mere 'foreigners' whose presence understandably provoked neo-Nazi violence" (Chin 2007: 260). In a memorandum published in September of 1991, Eckart Schiffer, the director of the Constitutional Department of the Interior Ministry and Schäuble's top advisor on aliens policy, expressed his alarm at the threat posed to the preservation of German national "identity" by unassimilated foreign cultural elements. While acknowledging that foreign minorities had made life in the Federal Republic "more colorful" through their introduction of exotic new cuisines and music, he warned advocates of multiculturalism that they were sowing the seeds for an anti-foreigner backlash (*Der Spiegel* 1991b; also discussed in Marshall 1992: 262). Rather than speaking out strongly against xenophobia, government leaders focused almost exclusively on tightening asylum procedures and border controls. The Kohl government may have believed that this approach was the most effective means to undermine support for right-wing extremist groups by depriving them of their issues, but its failure to condemn strongly the growing anti-foreigner rhetoric and actions against them provoked outrage around the world. During July 1991, Liselotte Funke resigned in frustration from her position as Federal Commissioner of Foreigners, complaining of a lack of support from the government. Her departure left the federal government's foreigner policy rudderless and adrift (Bade 1994c: 77–78).

The problem of right-wing extremist violence in the FRG began to attract worldwide attention after a firebomb was thrown into a foreigners' hostel on 17 September 1991, in Hoyerswerda, Saxony. In October of that same year, a firebomb attack killed two Lebanese girls in the village of Hünxe near Düsseldorf. This cycle of violence continued into the next year. On 22 August 1992, right-wing extremists attacked a housing complex for asylum seekers in the port city of Rostock. As crowds of cheering residents watched, gangs of young assailants carried swastikas and shouted Nazi slogans. The attacks occurred over several days, leaving many to wonder why it took the police so long to restore order. A week later, extremists attacked refugee hostels in Cottbus and in two other Brandenburg towns.

The violence continued to grow. In 1992, there were a total of 2,584 attacks on foreigners in the Federal Republic, compared with twenty-eight in France, nineteen in Sweden, and eight in Spain.[17] The number of organized right-wing extremists rose to 65,000 in 1992 (*Der Spiegel* 1993, citing estimates from the Bundesamt für Verfassungsschutz). In the early morning hours of 23 November 1992, arsonist(s) set ablaze a three story, half-timbered house in Solingen, North Rhine-Westphalia. Five persons died in the fire. All were members of a

---

17. Comparative data on this issue are problematic, because the criteria and methods by which attacks against foreigners are counted and reported differ among states. The major source of these data are official government agencies.

family from a village in central Anatolia, Turkey, who had settled in Solingen twenty-three years earlier. Among the dead, Hatice Genc, eighteen, and her sisters Hulya, nine, and Sayime, four, had been born in Solingen. Gulsun Ince, twenty-seven, a relative, and Gulictan Yuksei, thirteen, a guest visiting on vacation, also died. A fifteen-year-old boy, a three-month-old baby, and a three-year-old child were injured. The attack on a Turkish family shocked the German public by puncturing the widely held conception that the anti-foreigner hostility and violence was limited to asylum seekers (Bade 1994c: 84).

Millions of Germans in cities across the FRG protested against the violence in silent vigils. Speaking at memorial services for the Solingen victims in Cologne on 3 June 1993, President Richard von Weizsäcker declared that the firebombings in Mölln and Solingen "are not unrelated, isolated atrocities. Rather they spring from a climate generated by the extreme right. Even criminals acting alone do not emerge from nothing" (Weizsäcker 1994: 253). As von Weizsäcker frankly acknowledged, the German public's rising hostility toward foreigners was symptomatic of the FRG's failure over three decades to facilitate the inclusion of immigrants into their host society (Weizsäcker 1994). In posing this issue to his fellow Germans, he asked, "[D]o we not speak too easily of 'the Turks?' ... Would it not be more honest and more human to say: 'German citizens of Turkish heritage?' They live by the rules of the German state, but without the ability to influence it that other citizens have. Should this remain so forever?" (Weizsäcker 1994: 255). This question cut to the heart of the integration challenge facing the FRG.

Likewise, FRG policymakers did not apply the lessons they had learned from the integration success of the refugees and expellees to the incorporation of the new East German *Länder*. Whereas the German refugees and expellees had been given significant institutional channels to represent their own interests at nearly every level of policymaking, the East Germans were treated largely as the passive objects of well-intended policies. The immediate process of internal reunification was largely directed (and funded) by the West Germans. The marginalization of East German participation in this process may have been the inevitable result of the speed at which reunification occurred, and the rapid pace was largely supported by East German voters. The abrupt and sweeping transplantation of the West German legal-political model to the east was the fastest path to formal reunification, but it did not leave much room for the East Germans to engage in the effective management of the new institutions and laws that would govern them.[18] In its implementation, integration was defined largely on West German terms. Jennifer A. Yoder has observed that "with the

---

18. Thomas A. Baylis reports that "only 11.6 per cent of the German elites surveyed in a nationwide study carried out by researchers from the University of Potsdam came from Eastern Germany—a little over half of the East German proportion of the population; East Germans were

accession of East Germany to the FRG, only the eastern society was expected to change" (1999: 204). Integration on these terms left many East Germans without a sense that their particular interests and views had adequate channels of representation. By the mid 1990s, Yoder reports that "only 21 percent of easterners believe the slogan 'We are one people' to be true. Instead 70 percent are of the opinion that they are treated as 'second-class Germans'" (Yoder 1999: 204). The substantive challenge of internal integration then did not end with the formal restoration of political unity; it only began a new chapter.[19]

But this internal experience is itself only one narrative side of the integration story of this period. Reunification was accompanied by (and in certain ways conditioned upon) the deepening of the integration of the FRG into the supranational framework of the European Community (EC). From late 1989 onward, the course of German reunification was clearly situated in the context of a stronger European integration. At a European Council summit in Strasbourg on 8 and 9 December 1989, Chancellor Kohl and his fellow EC leaders had made this external integration context explicit (Dinan 1999: 130–132). The Presidency Conclusions claimed, "All community policies in the economic and social spheres contribute directly and indirectly to consolidating a common sense of belonging. This movement must be broadened and accelerated" (European Council 1989). Likewise, US President George H. W. Bush speaking at a NATO meeting in Brussels on 4 December 1989, and his Secretary of State, James Baker, speaking at the Berlin Press Club on 12 December 1989, had tied US approval of reunification to (among other grounds) the FRG's deeper integration into the EC (Merkl 1993: 316–317; Ackermann and Kelleher 1993: 416–417).

Reflecting this basis of approval, the preamble of the reunification treaty of 31 August 1990 between the FRG and the GDR describes reunification as "a contribution to the unification of Europe and to the construction of a European peace order, in which borders no longer divide, and guarantees all European peoples a life together [based on] trust."[20] Likewise, President von

---

almost entirely absent from the administrative, business, judicial, and other key subsamples … Almost invariably at the federal level, and much of the time in the *Länder*, the most important positions are held by West Germans" (1999: 136).

19. As Thomas A. Baylis observes, "It is becoming apparent that the cultural, social and economic divide between Western and Eastern Germany is not just a temporary consequence of the years of political division and will disappear as the new states become the 'flowering landscape' of Kohl's rhetoric … If the idea of democratic representation is to mean anything, regional distinctiveness cannot be maintained at the cost of political voice. If the larger, wealthier region is able to ignore the interests and views of the smaller, poorer region, the latter will continue to feel more like a colony than an equal if somewhat different partner, with all the attendant consequences for its sense of regional pride and identity" (1999: 144).

20. "Vertrag zwischen der Bundesrepublik Deutschland und der Deutschen Demokratischen Republik über die Herstellung der Einheit Deutschlands vom 31. August 1990."

Weizsäcker, in a speech on 5 October 1990 marking the formal accession of East Germany into the FRG, observed that the old model of the sovereign nation-state as an independent actor was no longer viable. He declared, "The most important responsibilities today no nation can solve alone. This applies to security and ecology, the economy and energy, commerce and telecommunications. Sovereignty in our era signifies participation in the community of states ... For the peoples of Europe begins a fundamentally new chapter in their history. Its goal is pan-European unification" (Weizsäcker 1994: 194). This external integration process for the FRG would involve not only the adoption of the future Treaty on European Union, but also significant amendments of the Basic Law to permit the broader transfer of national authority to the supranational level. The same moment then that restored political unity to Germany heightened the FRG's interdependence within Europe and tightened the linkages of its people with those of the European Community generally.

German reunification, Joppke has contended, helped bring about a fundamental change in the FRG's approach to issues of immigration and membership. By making Germany whole again, it undercut the old rationale for restricting access to citizenship and favoring particular streams of migrants on ethnic grounds. At the same time, the growing challenge of integrating the second-generation immigrants and a declining public receptivity toward the *Aussiedler* were forcing German policymakers to grapple with the undeniable fact that the existing system was unsustainable. By this view, reunification proved pivotal in hastening the FRG's transition "from an ethnic toward a civic-territorial citizenship regime" (Joppke 1999: 144). During the 1990s, Germany did begin to effect this transition, but change came haltingly and met protracted resistance at various stages. In explaining the slow pace of reform, Rita Chin points out that the focus on reunification as part of a much longer narrative of national history and the new problems of integration that followed obscured attention to the challenges of promoting inclusion for Germany's immigrant communities (Chin 2007: 252, 264). Immigrants were not only treated as distant onlookers in the reunification process, but became more deeply identified with the so-called "foreigner problem" that the rising number of asylum seekers had dramatized. The violence against foreigners during this period did not awaken the Kohl government to any fresh appreciation of the dangers that the continued marginalization of these communities posed. Rather, the crisis atmosphere provided a useful public rationale to justify restricting the FRG's generous asylum law.

Casting German reunification as merely a step toward the broader unification of European peoples did not translate into audacious new commitments of making German society more accommodating toward diversity. Thus, for example, the Joint Constitutional Committee's proposal to add an amendment to the Basic Law's Article 20, which would have guaranteed that "The State respects the identity of the identity of ethnic, cultural, and linguistic minorities," was abandoned in the face of CDU/CSU opposition.[21] This new requirement was explicitly designed to apply to immigrants as well as traditional national minorities, but whether such a vaguely formulated provision would have promoted inclusion, deepened the stigmatization of cultural difference, or had little effect in substantive terms remains an open question. [22] It was certainly no substitute for addressing more concrete problems of integration, such as higher unemployment among immigrant workers and continuing barriers to the acquisition of citizenship. Nevertheless, the defeat of this provision highlighted symbolically the idea of Germany as a homogeneous nation. Reunification had been predicated on the premise that "we are one people," and the violence against foreign residents that accompanied reunification underscored the boundary lines between who belonged and who did not.

There was not only precedent for recognition of minority rights in the German constitutional tradition, but it also would have been consistent with emerging post–Cold War international norms aimed at the protection of minorities. These norms have their own precedent in the inter-war Minority Treaties and in the 1966 International Covenant on Civil and Political Rights.[23] However, the issue did not receive major attention before the collapse of communism across the Eastern Bloc thrust it back to the fore as a matter of international security. In response to the specter of growing ethnonational conflicts, both the Organization for Security and Cooperation in Europe (OECD) and the Council of Europe (COE) began devising codes of conduct for their Member States with respect to minority protection.[24] In December 1992, the OECD established the High Commissioner for National Minorities in order to "assist Member States' implementation of national minority standards and to help resolve national minority/majority conflicts" (Jackson Preece 1998: 49, 43–52, 123–139). In 1997, Germany ratified the COE Convention for the Protection of National Minorities, which came into force the next year.[25] In 1998,

---

21. Berichte der Gemeinsamen Verfassungskommission, Drucksache 12/6000 (05.11.93), Deutscher Bundestag 12.Wahlperiode, pp. 71–75.

22. Rainer Bauböck (1996, 2001) has developed a cogent case for recognizing the cultural rights for immigrants while distinguishing the rights of immigrants from those of national minorities (see also Habermas 2005).

23. Article 27 of this Covenant provides: "In those states in which ethnic, religious or linguistic minorities exist, persons belonging to such minorities shall not be denied the right, in community with other members of their group, to enjoy their own culture, to profess and practice their own religion, or to use their own language."

24. In 1992, the United Nations' General Assembly also adopted a resolution, entitled: "UN Declaration on the Rights of Persons Belonging to National or Ethnic, Religious and Linguistic Minorities." http://www.unhchr.ch/html/menu3/b/d_minori.htm (accessed 16 April 2009).

25. In ratifying this convention, the FRG was careful to note that it did not contain any definition of national minorities, so that it was left to the discretion of the State-Parties to define them. The FRG construed the definition to apply to Danes, Sorbs, Frisians, Roma, and Sinti of German

Germany also ratified the COE European Charter for Regional and Minority Languages.[26] In contrast to the inter-war Minority Treaties, these conventions were predicated on the principle of sovereign equality and applied universally to Member States (Jackson Preece 1998: 170). For the FRG, this emerging framework for the protection of minorities provided new instruments for improving conditions for German minorities in Central and Eastern Europe. After reunification, the FRG negotiated agreements with Czechoslovakia/the Czech Republic, Hungary, Poland, Romania, and Russia to provide material and cultural assistance for German minorities residing there as part of a more general effort to support the transition to democracy (Wolff 2000: 191–203; Heintze 2000: 208–217). In contrast to the Weimar Republic, the FRG's external minorities policy during the 1990s was not driven by any irredentist ambitions, but rather was aimed at promoting regional stability. It reflected not only a humanitarian concern for the welfare of German minorities, but also a self-interest to improve their local conditions so that they would be less inclined to seek resettlement in the FRG.

---

citizenship. Of course, this definition excluded immigrants. http://conventions.coe.int/Treaty/Commun/ListeDeclarations.asp?NT=157&CM=8&DF=4/18/2009&CL=ENG&VL=1 (accessed 16 April 2009).

26. In ratifying the convention, the FRG stipulated that protected minority languages would include Danish, Upper Sorbian, Lower Sorbian, North Frisian, and Sater Frisian languages, and the Romany language of the German Sinti and Roma. It designated Low German as the regional language within the meaning of the Charter in the Federal Republic. http://conventions.coe.int/treaty/Commun/ListeDeclarations.asp?NT=148&CM=&DF=&CL=ENG&VL=1 (accessed 16 April 2009).

Part 3

Germany inside the European Union

German reunification, Peter Katzenstein has observed, "was a central factor pushing the member states of the EU to commit themselves in Maastricht to further integration in the interest of binding a united Germany to Europe" (1997a: 259–261; see also Anderson 1997: 85–86). While hardly the only important factor, it provided a catalyst for accelerating a process already underway. In the mid 1980s, a new drive had emerged to promote greater economic integration and political cooperation among the then twelve Member States of the European Community. The Single European Act (SEA, 1986) set forth the goal of creating a single market without internal frontiers by the end of 1992. Achieving this goal meant eliminating restrictions on the movement of persons, capital, and services across the Member States. The cornerstone in the border reform effort was the Schengen Agreement that was concluded by the Benelux countries, France, and the FRG on 14 June 1985. At that time, the agreement had been largely a declaration of intent to abolish border controls by 1 January 1990 in advance of reaching an EC-wide single border system. The challenges in meeting this deadline proved insurmountable, but the original signatory parties (now joined by Italy) pressed forward with a Supplementary Convention entered on 19 June 1990 (Plender 1997: 810–862). The Supplementary Convention arranged for the removal of internal border controls on the movement of goods and persons, the coordination of common external borders, the implementation of a common visa policy for third-country nationals, and the development of tighter internal border control mechanisms for aliens, including greater interstate police cooperation and a pooled data processing system. Implementation of this Convention depended on ratification by the national parliaments of the signatory countries. Work toward implementing these reforms evolved into a plan for full economic and monetary union.

Chapter 15

Reforming the Frameworks
The Maastricht Treaty and the Basic Law

In April 1990, French President François Mitterand and German Chancellor Helmut Kohl threw their combined support behind a further goal of reform aimed at promoting European integration. They sent a letter to the President of Ireland, who at that time held the rotating presidency position of the European Council, proposing that plans for political union should be discussed alongside those for economic and monetary union. From these discussions, the Member States' heads of government, meeting in Maastricht, reached an agreement on a union treaty in December 1991.[1] The so-called Maastricht Treaty or Treaty on European Union (TEU) took effect on 1 November 1993. While the treaty introduced no radical changes, it further embedded Member States within an increasingly dense set of institutional relationships, bargaining frameworks, and policy networks.

Although the Maastricht Treaty formally established the European Union (EU) as such, the institutional and policy framework it provided was an interim arrangement reflecting the continuing divisions between those favoring closer integration and those intent on preserving key prerogatives of individual Member States (Moravcsik 1998: 467–471). The complex "three pillar" design of the EU framework seemingly satisfied both. The former were able to incorporate broader policy domains into the EU's ambit, while the latter were able to keep certain domains they considered "key" within the intergovernmental sphere of the Member States (Papademetriou 1996: 61). The first pillar encompasses the existing treaties through which the European Community had been organized and comprises those policy domains over which the Commission has competence. The second and third pillars pertain to those policy domains that remain subject to intergovernmental decision-making. They specify areas of cooperation toward

---

1. The letter's text is republished in Laursen and Vanhoonacker (1992: 313–314).

agreed goals and require unanimity in the decision-making process. The second pillar pertains specifically to Common Foreign and Security Policy (CFSP) and the third pillar concerns the Justice and Home Affairs (JHA) domains and includes issues relating to immigration and asylum matters.

For the first time in the evolution of the European Community, Article 8 of the Maastricht Treaty formally provided that "Citizenship of the Union is hereby established. Every person holding the nationality of a Member State shall be a citizen of the Union" (Rudden and Wyatt 1993: 30). The article stipulates five explicit rights of EU citizens:

8a)   the right to move and reside freely within the territory of the Member States;
8b)   the right to vote and to stand for election as a candidate at municipal elections and in elections of the European Parliament in the Member State of residence, under the same conditions as nationals of that state;
8c)   the entitlement to protection in third countries by diplomatic or consular authorities of any Member State;
8di) the right to petition the European Parliament;
8dii) the right to apply to the Ombudsman of the European Union.
(Rudden and Wyatt 1993: 30–32; see also Papademetriou 1996: 59–80)

By any measure of substantive citizenship as that provided under the Basic Law, this is a minimalist catalogue of rights, and does little more than collect, under the heading of "citizenship" rights, those rights already enjoyed by nationals of Member States. Even this interpretation is probably too generous. As critics have observed, this form of EU citizenship "is nothing more than a *functional* semicitizenship," designed primarily from a market perspective to facilitate transnational labor mobility (Martiniello 2000: 351–353). It conferred little of consequence to the vast majority of its recipients, especially since the vast majority live in their country of nationality. A key question then that only time can answer is whether this original formulation of EU citizenship will prove to be the floor upon which a fuller form of citizenship is built or will remain essentially a public relations ploy as some have charged (Beyme 2001: 78–83; Weiler 1999: 348).

Clearly, EU citizenship is designed to be subsidiary to the national citizenships of the Member States and to reinforces the importance of nationality as a criterion of full civic belonging in the EU. Not only does the acquisition of EU citizenship derive from the possession of a Member State nationality, but also the EU imposes few common standards that might harmonize the nationality rules of Member States or might limit their discretion in defining these rules.[2] As an alternative to nationality, the drafters of this formulation might have

2. Thus, a Declaration of the Interconference that led to the TEU provides, "The Conference declares that, wherever in the Treaty establishing the European Community reference is made to nationals of the Member States, the question whether an individual possesses the nationality

used some criterion of lawful residence to provide a non-nationality basis for EU citizenship or introduced an avenue through which third-country nationals could acquire it.

The effect of Article 8, as Martiniello has observed, was to create a "triangular citizenship structure" in the EU (2000: 371). On the top rung of this structure are those citizens of Member States who reside in their states of nationality. They enjoy the fullest bundle of civic, political, and social rights. At the intermediate level are those citizens of Member States who reside in the EU, but are outside their state of nationality. The bottom comprises all those without EU citizenship. Among those persons in the bottom level, two distinct classes are distinguishable. The first refers to those third-country nationals who have acquired legal residence in a Member State. "To a certain extent," Martiniello notes, they have "become integrated into the civil and socioeconomic life of European society ... and enjoy fundamental civil and socioeconomic rights" (Martiniello 2000: 371–372). Below this class of persons are those that have entered illegally, and hold few effective rights of any kind.

Germany, the Reform of the Basic Law, and the Maastricht Treaty

In December 1992, the German Bundestag voted to ratify the Maastricht Treaty by a vote of 543 to 17, with 8 abstentions (Quint 1997: 301–306). The Bundesrat then approved the Treaty as well. To accommodate the Treaty and the new reality of reunification, significant provisions of the Basic Law were amended. For example, the Preamble, Article 23, and Article 146 were revised to reflect that the goal of national reunification had been accomplished, that territorially the Federal Republic was complete, and that the Basic Law applies to the "entire German people" residing within the existing *Länder*. This achievement had been predicated upon the successful integration of the Federal Republic into a broader European institutional framework.

The amendments to the Basic Law not only reaffirmed the Federal Republic's place within this framework, but also authorized the further transfer of German sovereignty to the institutions of the EU. The revised Article 88, for example, provides for the transfer of national monetary authority to a European central bank. An amendment to Article 28(1) permits citizens of EU

---

of a Member State shall be settled solely by reference to the national law of the Member State concerned." Article F of the TEU further provides, "The Union shall respect the national identities of its Member States, whose systems of government are founded on principles of democracy" (Rudden and Wyatt 1993: 215, 226).

Member States to vote and to be candidates in elections for county and municipal elections. A new clause inserted in Article 24(1) authorizes the *Länder*, consistent with their jurisdictional competences, to transfer sovereign powers to transnational institutions with the approval of the federal government.

The linchpin intended to anchor the Federal Republic inside the EU, however, is the amended Article 23. It expressly prescribes that the FRG "shall participate in the development of the European Union," and authorizes the "transfer [of] sovereign powers by a law with the consent of the Bundesrat."[3] It conditions this participation and transfer on the EU's adherence to "democratic, social, and federal principles, to the rule of law ... to principles of subsidiarity, and to guarantees ... of fundamental rights essentially comparable to that afforded by this Basic Law." According to some scholars, these conditions reflect the degree of compatibility German policymakers see in the structure of the EU. As Peter Katzenstein has observed, "the similarity between European and German institutions and practices ... creates a milieu in which German political actors can feel at home" (Katzenstein 1997c: 40–41; more recently, see Haas, Roever, and Schmidt 2002). From their own domestic context in a decentralized state, German policymakers have considerably more experience than most of their European counterparts at the kind of bargaining process entailed by multi-tier systems of governance. By the 1990s, they had also become confident in their ability to further national objectives through multilateral frameworks.

The new Article 23 also enhances the potential influence and participation of the *Länder* in the decision-making processes of the EU, as prescribed through German federal structures, most notably the Bundesrat. Article 23 had to account for the *Länder*'s role in the EU, because the *Länder* in Germany's federal system enjoy substantial autonomy and play central roles as the implementers not only of their own laws, but those of the federal government as well (Leonardy 1996: 79–80). In assessing the significance of this constitutional change, Hans-Peter Schneider, Director of the German Institute for Federal Studies, has described the new *Länder* powers of EU participation as "extraordinarily far-reaching" (Schneider 1999: 75). Thus, for example, Article 23(6) provides, "when legislative powers exclusive to the *Länder* are primarily affected, the exercise of the rights belonging to the Federal Republic of Germany as a Member State of the European Union shall be delegated to a representative of the *Länder* designated by the Bundesrat." Revisions to Article 50 further enhance the role of the *Länder*. The amended version prescribes, "the *Länder* shall participate through the Bundesrat in the legislation and administration of the Federation and in matters concerning the European Union." Irrespective of the ambiguities these revisions left in the Basic Law, the new provisions established a broad

---

3. GG 23 at paragraph 1.

basis for the continuing development of a multi-level, extensively intra-penetrating governmental relationship between the FRG and the EU.[4]

Despite these constitutional amendments, the FRG's ratification of the Maastricht Treaty still had to overcome challenges submitted to the German Federal Constitutional Court. In this regard, some scholars caution about overestimating the extent the FRG's national experience coincides with and supports the development of a European legal system. Lars Hoffman and Jo Shaw have suggested that the FRG's adherence to the Basic Law's guarantee of a decentralized state (the so-called 'eternity clause') and protection of fundamental rights has at times slowed the process of juridical socialization within the EU (Hoffman and Shaw 2004: 628). They observed that the *Brunner* decision of 12 October 1993, in which the Constitutional Court addressed the constitutionality of the Maastricht Treaty, demonstrates the German court's insistence on its sovereignty over national legal norms, particularly as they pertain to fundamental rights (Hoffman and Shaw 2004: 628–629). Likewise, Bill Davies has argued that the Court's position vis-à-vis the EU on questions about fundamental rights reflects a longstanding tension between legal structures in Germany and the EU (Davies 2007: 43–89). In its decision on the *Brunner* case, the Court determined that the Maastricht Treaty is compatible with the Basic Law by relying on earlier precedence established in the *Solange I* (1974) and *Solange II* (1986) cases.[5] *Solange I* and *Solange II* clarified that the Federal Constitutional Court retained its authority to make final decisions in cases concerning German citizens' fundamental rights regardless of EU legal standards.[6] The Court would retain this position "so long as the [European] integration process has not proceeded far enough to allow a [European] Parliament to formulate and establish a set of basic rights commensurate with those set forth in the Basic Law."[7] As the *Brunner* case demonstrates, the Court has used the *Solange I* and *Solange II* decisions to reassert its independence to interpret cases according to the Basic Law when EU law proves insufficient.

Using the precedence set by the *Solange* cases, the Court dismissed arguments that granting voting rights to non-German EU citizens in local German elections violated any fundamental rights under the Basic Law.[8] At the same time, it cautioned that deeper European integration not accompanied by measures to reduce the democratic deficit within EU institutions may violate the German people's constitutionally protected right to democratic

---

4. On the new opportunities for the *Länder* to participate in European policymaking and their influence on the Maastricht treaty ratification process see Hrbek (1997: 12–21).

5. See judgment of 12 October 1993, BVerfGE 89, 155, §61.

6. See judgment of 29 May 1974, BVerfGE 37, 271, §1, and judgment of 22 October 1986, BVerfGE 73, 339, §3.

7. See judgment of 29 May 1974, BVerfGE, 37, 271, §1.

8. See judgment of 12 October 1993, BVerfGE 89, 155, §61.

representation in their lawmaking bodies. Until such measures are taken, the Bundestag then must retain substantial competences over lawmaking in order to uphold this right.[9]

Questions arose about the Court's independent authority in the *Brunner* case in ways also unrelated to fundamental rights (Hoffman and Shaw 2004: 629). In reaching its judgment, the Court treated the EU as an "integrated association of states" (*Staatsverbund*), within which Member States maintain their own separate attributes of independent sovereignty. The states need, the Court explained in its opinion, sufficiently meaningful areas of operation of their own that stand apart from EU institutions. These areas of state action enable the respective people of a state (*Staatsvolk*) to "unfold" (*entfalten*) and "articulate" themselves in a process, legitimated and controlled by the people, through which political demands and objectives (*Willensbildung*) are formulated. In so doing, "the [people]—relatively homogeneous—can give legal expression to the spiritual, social, and political bonds which hold them together."[10]

This understanding of the *Staatsvolk* as a "relativity homogeneous" body inevitably raises questions about the Court's debt to the jurisprudence of Carl Schmitt and, more generally, the jurisprudential tradition associated with him. Critics of the Court's opinion, such as J. H. H. Weiler, have argued persuasively that the Court must have been aware of the organic nationalist implications this kind of terminology radiated, despite the Court's efforts to give it a more neutral spin. At best, it would be odd for the FRG's highest court to seek to rehabilitate terminology that carried such notorious associations if it was not sympathetic to the ethnocultural assumptions underlying it. These same assumptions are reflected in the Court's conclusion that the peoples of the EU lack the necessary unity to be regarded as one people (as measured by the standard of a *Staatsvolk*), but may yet coalesce into one. Following this line of reasoning, until this unity is achieved, the EU will remain no more than an intergovernmental association of states. Since, as Weiler points out, the first of these alternatives is highly unlikely ever to be achieved and cannot be without sacrificing the distinctive national identities of its state members, it raises almost insurmountable barriers to the prospect of further integration. The two alternatives that the Court considers, thus, assume a sharp dichotomy in possible outcomes: either the EU grows into a unitary nation-state or it remains an intergovernmental association. The Court did not consider a third alternative, namely, that the EU can constitute a distinct supranational realm in its own right, guaranteeing adherents of minority cultures protected space alongside the dominant majority cultures of the Member States, and acting as a counterbalance against the narrow self-interest perspectives of Member State

9. See judgment of 12 October 1993, BVerfGE 89, 155, §§187–191.
10. See judgment of 12 October 1993, BVerfG 89, 155, §186.

governments. The EU could serve as a standard bearer for transnational civic values and interests that transcend the exclusivist, particular ones of Member States (Weiler 1995: 265–294; see also Gusy and Ziegler 1999: 222–247).

In contrast to Weiler's critique of the Constitutional Court's response to the Maastricht Treaty, Dieter Grimm offered what appeared to be a defense of the Court's position. Grimm argued that the path toward a European constitution and deepening Europeanization offered by Maastricht was untenable as long as Europe lacked a 'people' premised on a common political identity (Grimm 1995: 297; see also Habermas 2005: 305). For Grimm, such a people can exist only if there is an overarching communicative structure under which people realize their unity. Since, according to him, there was not and probably never would be a shared means of communication (i.e., a vernacular European language), there will be no European unity, no European people, and no basis for a constitutional European State. While Grimm did distance his argument from understanding unity only in ethnocultural terms, as Habermas points out in his response to Grimm, we must entertain and explain alternative means for discovering a European people if we are to avoid a particularistic European self-understanding (Habermas 1995: 305). Here, Habermas colludes with Weiler's argument that creating a sense of belonging in Europe should be premised on a democratic citizenship, or what Weiler called 'critical citizenship' (Habermas 1995: 305–306; Weiler 1995: 256). Both Habermas and Weiler find the possibility of a unified European people in this type of citizenship, which emphasizes civic values that reach beyond the boundaries of the nation-state. In this regard, the Maastricht Treaty was only a small step in this direction.

Nevertheless, critics of the Court, such as Weiler, have tended to neglect the importance the Constitutional Court attaches to its role as the supreme protector of fundamental rights guaranteed under the Basic Law (Mayer 2006: 295–296). As we have sought to show, in its 1993 Maastricht opinion, the Court took pains to describe its relationship with the European Court of Justice as "cooperative" rather than subordinate to preserve the Constitutional Court's role as the ultimate judiciary of German citizens' basic rights (Goetz and Cullen 1995: 21–24; Geiger 2005). Despite the expressed cooperative relationship between the German and European legal systems, the Court has yet to invalidate any Community law on the grounds of incompatibility. Since the enactment of the Maastricht Treaty and the subsequent criticisms of the Court's opinion on the Maastricht case, the Constitutional Court has been reluctant to question the supremacy of EC law. It has, however, refrained from formally relinquishing its independent authority to the European Court of Justice.

Two more recent cases illustrate that the Constitutional Court's position on matters of Community law and fundamental rights remains ambiguous. In the decision of 22 March 1995, the Court found that the federal government's acceptance of EC guidelines for opening national television broadcasts to the

European community did not in principle encroach on the *Länder* rights, even though regulation of television broadcasting was considered a *Länder* competency.[11] The judges explained that the federal government represents Germany's regional, state, and national interests within the European Union, and, therefore, *Länder* must abide by the EC guidelines for television broadcasting. However, in its final decision, the Constitutional Court did find the federal government in violation of the *Länder's* rights in so far as they did not consult directly with *Länder* governments regarding television broadcasting. This case strengthened the position of Germany's *Länder* vis-à-vis the federal government in matters of Community law, but it also demonstrated the Court's support for Community law when weighing it against the Basic Law.

The well-known banana case of 2000 marked another instance when the Constitutional Court found the European treaties in accordance with Germany's fundamental rights. The complainants, a group of banana importers in Germany, lodged the case because they felt that the EC Regulation, specifically the higher tariff placed on 'third-country' banana imports,[12] impinged on fundamental rights of fair treatment. The lower court sent the case to the European Court of Justice (ECJ) for review. After the ECJ's validation of the original Banana Regulation (Aziz 2001: 8), the lower court in Germany turned the case over to the Constitutional Court. In its final decision, the Court found the Banana Regulation compliant with the banana importers' fundamental rights as guaranteed by the Basic Law.[13] To justify its position, the Court relied specifically on the *Solange II* case, which required the Court to accept supremacy of EC law in areas of financial and business regulation when it does not infringe on fundamental rights (Aziz 2001: 9).[14]

The Constitutional Court's reluctance to question the constitutionality of regulatory laws in the EU reflects the broader pattern of widening and deepening European integration. The EU has remained very much a work-in-progress, involving expansion and structural reform, both in terms of its legal framework and its political competences. In a communication of 23 February 1994, the European Commission proposed a set of objectives for Community action with regard to immigration and asylum policy that drew upon earlier communications but also sought to explore the new possibilities for coordination

11. See judgment of 22 March 1995, BVerfGE 92, 203.
12. The EC Regulation spells out three categories of bananas for sale in the common market. "Third-country" bananas refer to those which are imported from countries outside of the EU ('community' bananas) and not originating from African, Caribbean or Pacific states (known as 'ACP' bananas). The latter category derives from the many Member States' colonial ties to ACP states. For a closer discussion of these categories of bananas, see the court decision of 7 June 2000, BVerfGE 102, 147, §§4–5.
13. See judgment of 7 June 2000, BVerfGE 102, 147.
14. Ibid., §§33–39.

that the TEU created. "The deepening of the European integration process," the Commission observed, "calls for an integrated and coherent response, which combines realism with solidarity, to the challenges which migration pressures and the integration of legal immigrants pose for the Union." It emphasized "the need for a comprehensive approach which addresses the key components of an effective immigration policy."[15] At the intergovernmental level, the TEU framework has allowed national politicians to escape the confines of their national constituency and find autonomy in the "escape to Europe" to arrive at "their preferred policy agenda" (Lavenex 2006: 331; see also Bulmer 1997: 52). In the case of immigration policy during the 1990s, the preferred policy agenda was to externalize control mechanisms and to export border management responsibilities to third countries (Lavenex 2006), such as by holding air carriers responsible for allowing the entry of illegal or irregular migrants into the respective European country. Throughout the 1990s, the FRG, in particular, pursued a variety of policy schemes, including policy externalization via the EU, to stem the flow of asylum seekers and other categories of immigrants into its territory (e.g., see Koslowski 1998: 738–739). In the next three sections, we will trace how the FRG redefined its migration control mechanisms in relation to asylum seekers, the *Aussiedler*, and Jewish emigrants from the former Soviet Union.

15. "Foreword." *Communication from the Commission to the Council and the European Parliament*, COM(94)23Final.

Chapter 16

The Restriction of Asylum

In confronting the continuing influx of asylum seekers during the early 1990s, the FRG clearly recognized that it could not control the admission of asylum seekers to its territory without the committed cooperation of its fellow Member States. Such cooperation became increasingly important in light of the agreed upon goal to abolish internal barriers among them. To develop a framework for this cooperation, eleven of the then twelve Member States signed the Dublin Convention on 15 June 1990.[1] It was designed in the largest part to prevent the submission of serial applications by the same individual to different Member States. However, the Convention did not come into effect until September 1997. This delay was emblematic of the difficulties that afflict all intergovernmental attempts to harmonize migration policies among the Member States.

By 1991, Kohl's coalition government was forced to walk a policy tightrope. On the one hand, there was acknowledgment that integration efforts aimed at Germany's foreign population had to be reinvigorated, if not created outright. On the other hand, the government was concerned that such moves would further alienate the increasingly vocal far right movement. Similarly, the government was struggling to develop a viable strategy to alter Article 16 of the Basic Law in order to limit asylum and to control the influx of the *Aussiedler*. By displaying toughness toward asylum seekers, German conservative parties felt they could reabsorb right-wing voters from the extreme right parties. At the same time, the achievement of reunification and the end of the Cold War created political space for cutting back the generous asylum provisions that had originally been justified as an obligation from the legacy of the Third Reich and the devastation caused by World War II. The reform of German

1. Denmark signed a year later. The text of the Dublin Treaty is excerpted in Plender (1997: 455–465). See generally Papademetriou (1996: 39–43).

asylum law could also be justified as part of broader efforts to strengthen the coordination of asylum policy among EU Member States.[2]

In the face of ever-rising numbers of asylum applications, the issue of asylum became a lightening rod for the "foreigner problem" in the FRG during the early 1990s. "Reform of immigration and refugee policy," observed Hollifield, "was given a new urgency in 1992 and 1993 by a series of much-publicized racist attacks against foreigners" (Hollifield 1994: 68). Eventually, in December of 1992, the center-right coalition government of the FDP and CDU/CSU reached an agreement with the SPD—which had opposed changing the Basic Law—to amend Article 16 of the Constitution.[3] The amendments went into force in July 1993. The compromise added a new clause to Article 16a, the constitutional basis for seeking asylum in Germany, which severely restricted the right of asylum. Paragraph 1 of Article 16a initially read that the "politically persecuted enjoy the right of asylum." The addition of Paragraph 2 states: "Paragraph one cannot be invoked by those who travel from a Member State of the European Community or from a third country where application of the Geneva Convention and the European Human Rights Convention is secured. Countries outside the European Community, to which sentence 1 above applies to, shall be determined by statute subject to the approval of the Bundesrat. In such cases deportation measures can be carried out during the pendency of an appeal."[4] The language of Article 16a, which still states that "those politically persecuted enjoy the right to asylum," remains consistent with the 1951 UN Convention on Refugees.[5] However, the additions to the article allowed the

---

2. As Kohl argued, "The new regulation of the right to asylum of 1 July was an important precondition for the fact that Germany can fully participate in a common European asylum policy" (Koslowski 2000: 162).

3. Amendment of the German Constitution requires a two-thirds vote of both the Bundestag and the Bundesrat, necessitating the consent of the SPD. The political agreement was reached on 6 December 1992, the legislation was adopted in May 1993, and the amendment of the asylum law went into effect on 1 July 1993. Neuman writes that the SPD feared it would be saddled with public responsibility for failure to "solve the asylum problem," even if the blocked amendment would have had only symbolic effect (1993: 517). Initially, the FDP was also very reluctant to amend the constitution. In fact, there are reports that during the entire discussion period, the FDP contemplated abandoning the coalition government with the CDU, especially during the phase when Kohl threatened to declare a state of emergency to cope with the "overload" of asylum seekers (*Der Spiegel* 1992a: 25). Even after the amendment to the asylum law, the FDP showed its discomfort with the new law, as demonstrated by FDP party leader Klaus Kinkel's statement that "the asylum compromise of December 1992 has essentially excluded the question of a legal arrangement for the regulation of immigration … This concludes that the essential problem, the immigration problem, does not find a solution in this law" (*Freie Demokratische Korrespondenz* 1993).

4. Article 16A, amended, effective 1 July 1993.

5. The Foreigners Law (*Ausländergesetz*) also has provisions, such as §51 (2), forbidding certain categories of persons from being deported.

German government to participate in the newest trend among states—that is, returning asylum seekers who arrive in Germany through a "safe third country" to that country. This "safe third country" principle, as will be seen, plays a key role in the development of a European asylum policy.

Individuals who arrive from a safe third country and request asylum are not entitled to a hearing by the German Federal Asylum Office.[6] In addition, a new section was added to the Asylum Law (*Asylverfahrensgesetz*) to deal with repeated applications (Section 71a), whose purpose is to prevent the duplication of asylum requests. For example, if a foreigner applies for asylum in Germany after having been denied asylum in a safe third country, Germany will only process the application if it is responsible for the application according to an international treaty with the safe third country.

The new Article 16a paragraph 3 of the German Basic Law, which introduced the concept of "non-persecuting states" (Bosswick 2000: 49), also led to the addition of Section 29a in the Asylum Law, which provided for "safe countries of origin"—a concept that differs substantially from the "safe third country" concept. Countries may be deemed "safe countries of origin" by the government on the assumption that neither political persecution nor human rights violations nor degrading punishment or treatment are practiced.[7] Unless the applicant can show proof that—despite the general situation in the safe country of origin—he or she is in danger of political persecution, according to Section 29a, applications of asylum seekers from these countries will be considered "manifestly unfounded" and, consequently, declined.[8] Another new clause, section 30, set out all of the categories of manifestly unfounded applications (these are in addition to the existing clause that states that applications not based on political persecution manifestly are unfounded), which may be rejected under a shortened and accelerated asylum procedure.[9]

6. *Asylverfahrensgesetz* (AsylVfG), Section 26a of amended version, effective 1 July 1993.

7. This is according to the Law Amending Asylum Procedures, Alien and Nationality Provisions in Germany, effective 1 July 1993. The list of safe countries of origin—determined by legislation requiring the consent of the Bundesrat—was originally composed of Bulgaria, Gambia, Ghana, Poland, Romania, Senegal, the Slovak Republic, the Czech Republic, and Hungary. As of May 1996, however, all of the African countries on the list have been removed. The German Parliament removed Gambia from the list in 1994, followed by Ghana and Senegal in 1996.

8. If the government determines through a decree—without the approval of the Bundesrat—that because of political and legal changes, a safe third country is no longer safe as stipulated by the conditions of Article 16a, this decree will remain in effect for up to 6 months (*Asylverfahrensgesetz* [AsylVfG], Section 29a, amended version, effective 1 July 1993). After the six months, the Parliament will have to formally approve the removal of the country from the list of safe countries of origin.

9. The categories were as follows: unsubstantiated statements; contradictory claims; forged or false documents; an applicant's refusal to give information to the authorities about his or her identity of nationality or lying about this information; filing for asylum to avert an impending

FDP Deputy Burkhard Hirsch scornfully referred to the safe third country concept as a "sanitary condom" that the German government wanted to put around itself (*Der Spiegel* 1992b: 30). Other commentators criticized the disparate treatment of asylum seekers from safe third countries and those from safe countries of origin. While asylum seekers who have transited through safe third countries are immediately deported back to the safe third country, those from safe countries of origin have the option of rebutting the presumption of safety from persecution in the course of an accelerated asylum procedure.[10] A related concern expressed by critics at the time of the law's creation, which has proven true over time, is that the incorporation of the safe third country and safe country of origin concepts encourages would-be refugees to lie about their travel routes, or their country of origin, or lead them to "lose" their passports, thus preventing deportation. This has remained possible since illegal "refugees" who enter Germany unnoticed and who decline to give their travel route can still obtain a short court process.

Indeed, as Hailbronner observed early on in its development, the safe third country rule has not always functioned as it originally was envisaged. In a considerable number of cases, Germany has not applied the clause because safe third states refuse to take back asylum seekers, either due to a lack of proof that the applicant has entered German territory from the safe country or because the applicant has not been able to meet formal requirements, such as time limits for filing a readmission request (Hailbronner 1994: 167). Since all of Germany's neighbors are considered "safe third countries," the major eligible category of asylum seekers remaining consists of individuals who proceed to Germany by air (or, as others have sarcastically noted, who parachute in).[11] With the reformed asylum regulation, Germany, like many other countries,

expiration of the applicant's residence authorization, despite ample opportunity to apply for asylum before; and flagrant failure to comply with obligations to cooperate in asylum procedures (*Asylverfahrensgesetz* [AsylVfG], Section 30, amended version, effective 1 July 1993).

10. However, if a safe third country does not receive the alien, the alien may still seek protection against return to the home country as the 1951 UN Convention on Refugees requires.

11. Even in such cases, if a foreigner arrives in a German airport from a safe country of origin and applies for asylum, under Section 18 of the amended AsylVfG, the asylum proceedings will be carried out before the applicant enters the country, provided he or she can be accommodated on airport territory during the proceedings. The same applies to applicants who request asylum at an airport, but are unable to prove their identity. While the asylum proceedings are in progress, the alien cannot leave the transit area. The procedures previously permitted the applicant to seek provisional legal protection within three days of a decision being taken by the Federal Office for the Recognition of Foreign Refugees. If no decision was made on this appeal within 14 days, the applicant was allowed to enter the country (*Asylverfahrensgesetz* [AsylVfG], Section 18, amended version, effective 1 July 1993). With the Constitutional Court's 14 May 1996 decision, in which the accelerated airport procedures were upheld, some small changes were made to the procedures. For example, the period for preparing an appeal in the airport procedure has been extended from

attempted to limit that category by imposing visa requirements[12] and imposing sanctions on carriers that transport passengers without proper documents.

The German high courts have generally shown deference to the legislative branch of the German government and have upheld the restrictive laws and policy decisions implemented by the government (Bosswick 2000: 52). The amendment of Article 16 in 1993 demonstrates this judicial deference, which led to numerous appeals and ultimately a ruling in 1996 by the Federal Constitutional Court that the new asylum policy was constitutional. The three cases decided by the Constitutional Court[13] held that the changes in Article 16 of the Basic Law were not unconstitutional and that they did not violate the provision of Article 79(3),[14] which forbids any amendments to the basic principles laid down in Article 1. The Court interpreted the right to asylum as not falling under the human dignity concept of Article 1 of the Basic Law, which the state has a duty to respect and protect.[15] Moreover, the Court explained that the changes in the asylum policy had laid the basis for a uniform European policy for political asylum, including the safe third country concept, a concept that indeed has, since the Court's decision, been enshrined in EU law. These three cases led to the Court's conclusion that Article 16a, paragraphs 3 and 4 were constitutional, as was the law establishing safe third countries and safe countries of origin.[16]

---

three to seven days. In addition, the government is obligated to provide applicants in the airport procedure with legal advice if they request it, whereas before legal advice was not guaranteed. Furthermore, the Court ruled that final appeals from the airport procedure to the Constitutional Court will not guarantee suspension of deportation pending the Court's decision (US Committee for Refugees 1996; Judgment of 14 May 1996, BVerfGE, vol. 94; starts at page 166).

12. As stipulated by the Schengen Agreement, the EU now has a common list of countries whose citizens do not require a visa to travel to Schengen countries.

13. Judgment of 14 May 1996, BVerfG 94, BVerfGE 115 (addressing Article 16a, paragraphs 3 and 4 and the concept of a safe country of origin) and Judgment of 14 May 1996, BVerfG 94 BVerfGE 49 (determining that the right to asylum does not belong to the guarantees contained in Article 1, section 1 of the Basic Law and that as long as the boundaries of Article 79, section 3 of the Basic Law were not disturbed, the legislation was free to change basic rights); 94 BVerfGE 166 (regarding airport procedures).

14. Article 79(3) of the Basic Law bars any amendment that would limit or infringe "the basic principles laid down in Articles 1 and 20" (Kommers 1989b: 139).

15. Judgment of 14 May 1996, BVerfG 94, BVerfGE 49.

16. Judgment of 14 May 1996, BVerfG 94, BVerfGE 115. The Court's decision was unanimous in sustaining the constitutionality of the safe third country concept embodied in the amended Article 16, as long as the country in question was found to apply the Geneva Convention on the Status of Refugees and the European Convention on Human Rights. The Court also ruled that a person coming to Germany through a safe third country could be denied asylum and summarily deported unless the asylum seeker was able to overcome the presumption that political persecution or degrading treatment does not occur in the third country (Kommers 1999b: 110).

The Constitutional Court not only decided that the concept of safe third countries was constitutional in principle, but the manner in which the German legislature drew up its list of safe third countries was also appropriate. Indeed, the Constitutional Court showed deference to the legislative branch in this area as well. The Court ruled that German legislators had taken sufficient consideration of the 1951 Refugee Convention's principle of *non-refoulement* when drawing up the list of safe third countries. For those being deported to a safe third country, the Court added that it is not a requirement that the asylum seeker, who is deported to a safe third country that is not their country of origin, be guaranteed access to a fair and comprehensive asylum determination procedure in that country. Rather, the Court found it only necessary that legal means to prevent deportation existed in such safe third countries. The Court also rejected the argument that applicants affected by the safe third country rule should have the chance in an individual hearing to rebut the presumption that the third country to which they are about to be sent back to, would, in fact, be safe for them (US Committee for Refugees 1996: 7).[17]

Furthermore, for those from safe third countries, in its May 1996 final decision, the Constitutional Court rejected the argument that if an applicant merely claimed that, despite the designation of his or her country of origin as "safe," he or she, as an individual, was subjected to persecution, the applicant would be allowed to enter the normal asylum procedure. That is, for a country designated as safe, all citizens were presumed to be safe, thereby disregarding the individual nature of the 1951 Geneva Convention. The Court, however, did leave a small amount of room for individuals from safe countries of origin to seek asylum. The Court ruled that an applicant must demonstrate "serious doubt" that the presumption of his or her country being free of persecution does not apply to him or her as an individual (US Committee for Refugees 1996: 8).[18]

Finally, the constitutionality of the imposition of visas for almost all refugee sending countries was challenged in Germany on the grounds that blocking refugee access to German territory renders meaningless any expressed intent to provide the right to asylum (Neuman 1993: 521). In other words, critics argued that Article 16, in addition to guaranteeing the principle of *non-refoulement*, should also prohibit excessive barriers to entry (Neuman 1993: 521).[19]

17. Judgment of 14 May 1996 BVerfG 94, BVerfGE 49 82, 83. Prior to this ruling, the safe country of origin clause of Article 16a had been difficult to implement because of cases where administrative courts requested that authorities thoroughly examine the assertions of individual persecution, in spite of the general presumption of safety of a country of origin.

18. Judgment of 14 May 1996 BVerfG 94, BVerfGE 49 85, 86.

19. The Convention Relating to the Status of Refugees and its 1967 Protocol prohibit the return of refugees to countries where their life or freedom would be threatened (*refoulement*), but they do not prohibit the return of refugees to other countries where they would be safe.

This German law, however, has remained in place, and, as we shall see, promoted the Europeanization of visa regimes.

Beyond changing the content of the German asylum law, the asylum compromise also streamlined and restricted the appeals process. For example, Section 36 stated that if an asylum application is rejected as manifestly unfounded, the Bundesamt will issue an expulsion warning, giving the applicant one week for voluntary departure. The applicant may, within one week, apply to the administrative court for provisional legal protection. The court then decides within one week (of the expiration of the expulsion warning) whether such protection is to be granted.[20] The court may only suspend the expulsion if there are serious doubts as to the legality of the ruling.[21] German judges themselves have lambasted this stipulation because they consider the time frame unworkable (Bosswick 2000: 51).

The asylum compromise did create important new legal mechanisms to deal with the changing nature of the post–Cold War era. As a result of the Social Democrats' negotiations during the debates, the asylum compromise created a temporary status for de facto refugees in Section 32 of the Foreigners Law (AuslG) to deal with individuals fleeing from war.[22] The recipients of this status, however, were not permitted to apply for asylum during the duration of the status. Until 1999, this temporary status could not be implemented because of a disagreement between the federal and state governments over how the status would be financed (Bosswick 2000: 49).[23] However, the status was implemented in 1999 for refugees from Kosovo.

The negative publicity over the asylum law change led to the development of an informal network of about 200 churches, both Protestant and Catholic, across Germany who coordinate to provide rejected asylum seekers shelter. Fearing worse publicity, the police were unwilling to apprehend those under protection of the churches, and, at times, refugee families stayed in this legally non-binding protected status for years. In 1995, the Interior Minister of

20. In circumstances where the court has an unusually heavy load of cases, the decision on the appeal may be postponed for an additional week, that is, for a total of two weeks from the initial date of the expulsion warning.

21. The previous asylum law simply stated that the applicant must appeal within a week to have his/her expulsion order suspended.

22. According to Hailbronner, when a democratic government shows that it has not lost control of the situation, the public is much more receptive to taking refugees. For example, he says that the public did not object to the new clause of the asylum law admitting civil war refugees, even though Germany has already admitted the most refugees from the former Yugoslavia (Hailbronner 1995).

23. Bosnian refugees have become victims of this impasse between the Federal government and the state governments. The majority of Bosnians (80 percent) stayed in Germany by obtaining the *Duldung* status (which simply defers deportation), rather than obtaining the civil war status, based on §32 of the Foreigners Law (AuslG) (Bosswick 2000: 52).

Bavaria, Günther Beckstein (who had been against the provision of shelter for rejected asylum seekers by churches), proposed that rejected asylum seekers in his state be allowed to turn to the churches for protection. The churches would thus in effect be able to "rent a refugee," if they agree to sponsor the refugee and support him or her financially (*Der Spiegel* 1995). However, at a March 1996 meeting of the Conference of Federal and Regional Interior Ministers, Beckstein withdrew his proposal to grant the Catholic and Protestant Church in Germany a "quota" of rejected asylum seekers who would be allowed to remain in Germany. This was a result of the decision by the interior ministers to implement a joint directive on the regularization of asylum seekers who had applied more than five years ago, the so-called *Altfälle* (*Migration News Sheet* 1996). While this regulation was supposed to be a more liberal aspect of the new asylum policy, only 7,800 of the estimated 20,000 who were eligible to take advantage of the status did so due to spurious bureaucratic regulations (Bosswick 2000: 52).

Social benefits for asylum seekers were also affected by the Asylum Seekers Benefit Law (*Asylbewerberleistungsgesetz*), which became effective on 1 November 1993. Whereas before 1993, asylum seekers partook in the same welfare system as the general population, the *Asylbewerberleistungsgesetz* created an independent public assistance system for asylum seekers for the duration of the asylum process. The new system curtailed welfare received by asylum seekers. During the first twelve months after the initial application, asylum seekers received benefits based on the guidelines of the Federal Social Assistance Law (BSHG) (corresponding to the reductions in benefits designated in §120 of the BSHG), which provided almost exclusively for benefits in kind. Foreigners with deferred deportation orders or a 'tolerated' status (*Duldung*) received assistance based on the *Asylbewerberleistungsgesetz*, but benefits were also curtailed according to §120 of BSHG (as long as their delayed departure or deportation from Germany was caused by obstacles beyond their control). If those with a *Duldung* created obstacles to their deportation, according to a 1998 amendment, they only received the "bare necessities" (Bosswick 2000: 52).[24]

Newly arrived asylum seekers were required to live in collective centers for durations anywhere between one and three months. The *Länder* would bear the costs for keeping asylum seekers in these centers. In addition, asylum seekers were allocated a monthly allowance of DM 40 (€ 20.45) for children

---

24. The *Duldung* or 'tolerated' status for asylum seekers was removed from the asylum law in the 2005 Immigration Act, which incorporated the *Asylverfahrensgesetz* into the new, comprehensive immigration and integration law (discussed in Part 4). Despite the removal of this provision from the law and authorities' attempts to decrease numbers of 'tolerated' asylum seekers, in 2007, some 50,000 'tolerated' asylum seekers lived in Germany (see Leise 2007).

under fifteen-years-old and DM 80 (€ 40.90) for those over the age of fifteen (Hägle 1995: 31). After their mandatory stay in the collective centers, asylum seekers would receive vouchers for their monthly expenses. There was also emergency medical and dental care coverage for the asylum seekers. While asylum seekers are living in the collective centers, they are forbidden from accepting employment. The exception is working in the centers for a modest hourly wage. After leaving the centers, they are allowed to obtain work permits based on the circumstances of the labor market. Also, the work permit is only given to asylum seekers after preference is given to German and EU nationals living in Germany who are also unemployed. The permit is usually limited to a particular employer and a specific position.

Those given asylum receive a special work permit that is not dependent on the labor market situation and does not restrict one to a particular employer. The same holds for convention refugees. Civil war refugees, however, can obtain a work permit that is subject to labor market conditions, which often restricts work to a particular area of the labor market (Hägle 1995: 32–34).

The policies leading to the restriction of asylum in Germany resulted in an immediate 60 percent reduction from the 322,599 figure of asylum applications in 1993 to 127,210 in 1994 and 127,937 in 1995, and a nearly continuous drop since then to 21,029 applications in 2006 (Federal Statistics Office).

The parameters laid down in 1993, and found constitutional by the Constitutional Court in 1996, provided a new framework for the judicial review of asylum cases. In some areas, the courts have continued to allow the legislature significant leeway. For instance, the courts have given state authorities more discretion in cases dealing with regulations regarding asylum seekers residing in Germany. In a 1997 case,[25] the Constitutional Court justified the restriction on the freedom of movement of asylum seekers and punishment of repeated offenders of the law, interpreting the freedom granted by Article 2, section 1 of the Basic Law as freedom to develop one's personality, not the right to go freely everywhere.[26]

While the courts generally upheld the government's new policy direction with regard to asylum, they expressed wariness at some of the ways the new legislation had been interpreted. For example, in a decision a few months after its May 1996 decision,[27] the Constitutional Court remanded the case of a Kurdish asylum seeker to the administrative court, questioning the validity of the lower court's finding that the asylum application manifestly was unfounded and the lower court's refusal to hear new information on the

25. Judgment of 10 April 1997, BVerfG 2 BvL 45/92.
26. Judgment of 10 April 1997, BVerfG 2 BvL 45/92.
27. Judgment of 7 November 1996, BVerfG 2 BvR 1318/95.

Table 16.1. New Asylum Applications Submitted in Industrialized Countries, 1992–2005 (absolute numbers)

Country of Asylum	1992	1993	1994	1995	1996	1997	1998	1999
Germany	438,191	322,599	127,210	127,937	116,367	104,353	98,644	95,113
United Kingdom	32,300	28,000	42,200	55,000	37,000	41,500	58,487	91,200
France	28,872	27,564	25,964	20,415	17,405	21,416	22,375	30,907
Italy	6,042	1,647	1,786	1,732	675	1,858	11,122	33,364
Austria	16,238	4,745	5,082	5,919	6,991	6,719	13,805	20,096
United States	103,964	143,118	144,577	149,065	107,130	52,200	35,903	32,711
European Union*	675,455	516,398	309,722	274,951	233,460	251,762	311,408	396,737

Country of Asylum	2000	2001	2002	2003	2004	2005	2006	Total
Germany	78,564	88,287	71,127	50,563	35,610	28,910	21,030	1,804,505
United Kingdom	98,900	92,000	103,080	60,050	40,620	30,840	27,850	839,027
France	38,747	47,291	58,971	59,768	58,550	49,730	30,690	538,665
Italy	15,564	9,620	16,015	13,455	9,720	9,500	10,110	142,210
Austria	18,284	30,135	39,354	32,359	24,630	22,460	13,350	260,167
United States	40,867	59,432	58,439	43,338	52,360	48,770	51,510	1,123,384
European Union*	391,275	388,372	393,441	309,329	241,000	239,770	198,900	5,131,980

*1995-2004 data does not include new members; 2005 and 2006 data include all 25 EU members.

Note: All figures rounded to nearest 10.

Source: UNHCR Statistical Yearbook 2001 and 2003, Asylum Trends 2005.

applicant's political activities in Germany.[28] In other similar cases,[29] the Constitutional Court determined that the lower courts had not adequately inquired into the asylum seekers' cases or had reasoned incorrectly, thereby giving the individual asylum seekers another chance to have their cases heard.

In addition, prior to the 1996 decision, the Court had continued to review asylum cases that arose as a consequence of the 1993 change in the asylum law. Some of these decisions show the Court's concern with the presumption that all EU countries and countries designated as safe third countries are actually safe. For example, in September 1993, the Court considered the new safe country law in a case related to a female asylum applicant from Iraq, who had traveled through Turkey to Greece and then on to Germany.[30] According to the asylum law as amended in 1992, the woman's passage through Greece—which, as an EU Member State, was now a de facto safe third country—disqualified her from seeking asylum in Germany.[31] The Constitutional Court, however, overruled the lower court's decision to deport this Iraqi woman back to Greece because of the restrictiveness of Greece's asylum procedures. Under these procedures, it granted asylum only if the applicant arrived in Greece directly from the country of persecution, which would prohibit this woman from seeking asylum in Greece.[32]

In the same year, the Court delivered a similar judgment with respect to the new safe country of origin law by ordering a stay in the deportation of an asylum applicant from Ghana, which at the time was listed as a safe country. The Court reasoned that an asylum seeker cannot be denied asylum based simply on the fact that the applicant arrived from a safe country of origin. Instead, it held that the asylum procedures in Germany still required that the authorities examine each applicant's case to determine whether the home country was unsafe for the applicant based on individual circumstances.[33]

The courts have also expanded protection to those from failed states. Until 2000, Germany did not consider asylum seekers fleeing a state incapable of

28. Judgment of 7 November 1996, BVerfG 2 BvR 1318/95.

29. Judgment of 22 July 1996, BVerfG 2 BvR 1416/94 (finding the Administrative Court's reasoning for denying the asylum seeker's application incorrect); Judgment of 24 March 1997, BVerfG, 2 BvR 1024/95 (reversing the Hamburg Administrative Court's decision that a Kurdish boy's asylum claim manifestly is unfounded because of the lower court's lack of investigation into the boy's claims).

30. Judgment of 13 September 1993. BVerfG 2 BvQ 1938/93 (cited in Blay and Zimmermann 1994: 376).

31. Judgment of 13 September 1993. BVerfG 2 BvQ 1938/93 (cited in Blay and Zimmermann 1994: 376–377).

32. Judgment of 13 September 1993. BVerfG 2 BvQ 1938/93 (cited in Blay and Zimmermann 1994: 377).

33. Judgment of 22 July 1993. BVferfG 2 BvR 1507, 1508/93, BVerfG 11 NVwZ 1 (Supp. 1, 1993) (cited in Blay and Zimmerman 1994: 377).

providing effective protection to its civilians, such as Afghanistan, as refugees. The German Constitutional Court, however, reviewed a judgment of the Federal Administrative Court concerning political asylum to refugees who came from Afghanistan. It ruled that persons fleeing the Taliban regime would have the right to obtain political asylum in Germany since the term "political persecution," interpreted to imply that the state or quasi state was the originator of the persecution, as interpreted by the Federal Administrative Court, was too narrow. In the Constitutional Court's view, the right of asylum could be granted since the Taliban regime, in fact, had stable control over large parts of the country for an extended amount of time. Hence, the Taliban could be regarded as a "quasi state" actor.[34] As a result, applications from those arriving from Afghanistan were suspended until the Federal Administrative Court reexamined the situation in the country to determine who was likely to be subjected to direct control of the Taliban and who was not. Asylum seekers, for example, coming from regions that were not subjected to Taliban control could be denied asylum, whereas others coming from regions directly controlled by the Taliban could have access to refugee status.

A new challenge to the courts has arisen with regards to the repatriation of many refugees from countries where a democratic regime is now in power. Since the defeat of the Taliban in Afghanistan in late 2001, the German Government slowly started revoking the refugee status of many Afghans and has tried to arrange for their repatriation. Starting in 2003, interior ministers of the federal and state governments in Germany decided that refugees coming from Iraq, Afghanistan, and Kosovo, for example, should be returned to their native countries as the situations in those countries that had led to the fleeing of the refugees had changed. (The deterioration of circumstances in Iraq since then shows how flexible the implementation of such decisions must be.) This is to be accomplished through "voluntary" means and then later through deportations, and, in fact, there have been reports of forcible deportations of Afghans residing in Germany.[35]

Some German courts do appear to recognize that not all persons are free from persecution in democracies such as Iraq, Afghanistan, or Russia. For instance, in February 2005, an administrative court in Kassel decided that members of the Northern Alliance of Afghanistan no longer could count on asylum in Germany "since they no longer have anything to fear in Afghanistan." However, the court ruled that members of the Communist Party, which supported the Soviet occupation of Afghanistan in the 1980s, would still be in danger if they returned to Afghanistan.[36] An administrative court in Lower

34. Judgment of 10 August 2000, BVerfG 2 BvR 260/98 and 1353/98.
35. See National Public Radio, "Deportations from Germany Rattle Afghans," by Rachel Martin, 28 November 2005.
36. See Deutsche Welle (2005).

Saxony found in June of 2005 that an Iraqi woman with a "Western" lifestyle could not be deported to Iraq for fear of persecution.[37] In another case involving Chechnya, a Hessen court reaffirmed that if people would be returned to certain areas of the country, they cannot be deported back to Chechnya. The court found that Chechens cannot be returned if it can be proven that they will be sent back to Chechnya (*Migration und Bevölkerung* 2006).

Given the drastically reduced asylum numbers in Germany since 1993, legislators may be happy to allow the courts to decide cases that do not have wide ranging precedent and may only affect a circumscribed number of individuals. This does not take away from the fact that Germany, like most Western states, has adapted its concept of asylum to the changing climate of the post–Cold War era and set the pace for more restrictive policies toward asylum seekers. In Germany's case, the achievement of reunification, as well as harmonization of immigration and refugee policies at the EU level, have led to a push by German politicians to restrict Germany's previously generous asylum policies. While Germany has maintained the foundation of asylum in Article 16 of the Basic Law, the amendment of Article 16 in 1993 resulted in a more watered-down version of asylum policy with high barriers to entry instituted through adoption of the concepts of safe third countries and safe countries of origin.

The courts, like politicians, have demonstrated an ambiguous attitude toward the regulation of asylum. Although the Constitutional Court ruled in 1996 that the amendment to Article 16 of the Basic Law was constitutional, it has required more rigorous legal protection for asylum seekers in some cases. The courts have done so by taking into account the political and individual context of the asylum seekers, even of those who have clearly passed through safe third countries. This strategy, while beneficial to individual asylum seekers who can demonstrate that their cases require exceptional treatment, has also made it difficult to predict how the courts will decide cases in the future and leaves policymakers and asylum advocates alike unsure of Germany's commitment to refugees.

37. Judgment of 9 June 2005, Verwaltungsgericht Göttingen 2 A 90/05.

Chapter 17

Rethinking Legacies

The New *Aussiedler* Policy

Throughout the Cold War era, the federal government had emphasized the status of the *Aussiedler* as returning Germans—a posture intended in part to keep policy debates over their reception separate from other migration issues. By the first half of the 1990s, this strategy had begun to fragment. The rapidly growing influx of the *Aussiedler* that had started in the late 1980s made the financial costs of their reception a continuing source of public debate and controversy. The all too obvious cultural differences that marked the ethnic Germans from Russia from those from Eastern Europe undermined the effectiveness of ethnocultural appeals to common German ancestry as a rationale for privileged admission and integration assistance. Recognizing this, the federal government tried to bolster support for its policies by stressing the *Aussiedler* contribution to the FRG's economic and demographic welfare. Such arguments, however, further eroded distinctions between the *Aussiedler* and other groups of migrants in the public's perception.[1]

Moreover, the use of this sort of utilitarian calculus invited comparisons of the contributions by the *Aussiedler* to those of other groups. If a good case

---

1. Throughout the 1990s, Klaus J. Bade took the lead in trying to persuade the German public to recognize that the *Aussiedler* should be considered as an inseparable part of a more general immigration policy framework. By conjoining the three main subjects of this policy into one heading, the title of his 1994 work, *Ausländer, Aussiedler, Asyl*, reflects this ambition. In this work, he emphasized that the *Aussiedler* should be understood as "immigrants par excellence," as opposed to returning settlers or whatever other euphemism had been used to distinguish them. He pointed out that the *Aussiedler* experienced fundamentally the same cultural, social, and psychological problems that immigrants commonly have experienced when adjusting to a new host society, and that the rules governing their admission and settlement in the FRG are simply a form of immigration policy (Bade 1994c: 27).

could be made for the prospective contribution of the *Aussiedler* to the FRG's future, an even stronger and more immediate case could be advanced for the contributions that the guestworkers and their families had already made over nearly four decades of actual residence. Given the sheer number of *Aussiedler* that began arriving in the late 1980s and the special costs associated with their settlement, the most obvious point of comparison was with the asylum seekers who were also coming in large numbers during this period and also required special forms of assistance (Levy 1999: 137–146).

As the number of *Aussiedler* entering the Federal Republic rose, their expressed reasons for coming also changed. Among a range of different motives, the *Aussiedler* typically had ranked a desire for family reunification and an opportunity to live as "Germans among Germans" (Fetzer 2000: 71) as their foremost reasons. They had not been blind to the economic and social advantages of living in the FRG, but these sources of attraction had not been paramount in their own ranking of motivating factors. In the early 1990s, however, this ranking changed. Previous patterns of settlement in the FRG had established local bases and long distant networks that now induced new arrivals to come. For these new arrivals, social and economic motives were paramount. Together with these reasons, they also cited a desire to escape the nationality conflicts in their homelands as a major factor (Oberpenning 1999: 283).

The growing influx of *Aussiedler* seeking to enter the FRG put pressure on the federal government in the early 1990s to find a means to restrict their admission without wholly abandoning its commitment to ethnic Germans in Eastern Europe and the former Soviet Union. The end of communist rule across these regions changed the presumption in federal government policy that the *Aussiedler* were by definition legitimate asylum seekers fleeing politically motivated discrimination and persecution. Because, in part, the *Aussiedler* had come to vote strongly in favor of the CDU/CSU, the Kohl government initially opposed any changes to the interpretation of Basic Law Article 116, which permitted unrestricted immigration of the *Aussiedler*.[2] By contrast, the SPD advocated a war settlement law that would restrict their admission.

Beginning in 1989, the federal government implemented a series of measures to defuse growing public disenchantment with the *Aussiedler*. The 1989 "Law for Establishing a Provisional Place of Residence for *Spätaussiedler*" (*Gesetz über die Festlegung eines vorläufigen Wohnortes für Spätaussiedler*) recognized the distance in time that had elapsed since the original policy toward

---

2. In the 1990s, 74 percent of the *Aussiedler* expressed a preference for the CDU/CSU. This political preference is not surprising, because most of the *Aussiedler* tend to have a far more religious and traditional outlook than typical native West Germans. Non-ethnic immigrants who came as workers in the 1960s and 1970s and their descendants tend to support the SPD (Münz, Seifert, and Ulrich 1997: 126, 129).

the *Aussiedler* had been formulated during the 1950s by reclassifying new admittees as *Spätaussiedler* (Groenendijk 1997: 465). The 1989 law provided for the assignment of the *Aussiedler* to temporary public housing for up to two years as a condition for receiving public assistance. Levy argues that the law was "mostly guided by administrative concerns over the controlled distribution of the *Aussiedler*," and was designed to spread the costs for their support across different localities (Levy 1999: 166). In imposing these new controls over their distribution, the law was intended to prevent the concentration of the *Aussiedler* into isolated communities of their own, which kept them segregated from mainstream social life and made them more visible as minorities.

Through its Integration Adjustment Law (*Eingliederungsanpassungsgesetz*) of 1 January 1990, the federal government went a step further in order to reduce the economic costs associated with the settlement and integration of the *Aussiedler*.[3] This law curtailed the financial privileges of the *Aussiedler*, which had provided for unemployment assistance, language instruction, etc. Reducing these costs was also intended to diminish the financial incentives believed to be drawing the *Aussiedler* to the FRG, but the *Aussiedler* were still drawn to the FRG.

To curtail their admission, the federal government enacted a law in June 1990. The Resettlers' Admittance Act (*Aussiedleraufnahmegesetz*) stipulated that prospective admittees must apply for consideration from their country of origin (rather than as visitors within the FRG), that their application must demonstrate a working knowledge of German, and that they must prove their German origin. (*Aussiedler* intending to immigrate were also required to complete a fifty-page questionnaire in German and pass a German language test.) Acceptance of these applications became far from automatic, which led to a lengthy backlog of pending applications and long delays in processing.[4] In 1991, the federal government began reducing the entitlement claims of the *Aussiedler* retirees to the FRG pension system.[5] Whether the reduction of such benefits had much deterrent effect on the desire of ethnic Germans to settle in the FRG remains an open question. Nevertheless, the number of arriving *Aussiedler* declined markedly—from approximately 400,000 in 1990 to 220,000 in 1991.

---

3. "Gesetz zur Anpassung von Eingleiderungsleistungen für Aussiedler und Übersiedler," BGBl. I, p. 2398 (see also Groenendijk 1997: 466).

4. Aspiring immigrants apply for a reception certificate (*Aufnahmebescheid*) from a German consulate in their country of residence.

5. As Rainer Münz and Rainer Ohliger explain, "the law on foreign pensions (*Fremdrentengesetz*) ma[d]e retired Aussiedler eligible for pensions in Germany even if they ha[d] not contributed to the public pension system.... Pensions of newly immigrating ethnic Germans who had acquired a legal claim for pensions in their countries of origin [were] reduced 30 percent in 1991. In spring 1996 the law on foreign pensions ... was again modified, and in October of that year the reduction was increased to 40 percent" (1998: 171). However, in contrast to other admitted asylum seekers, registered *Aussiedler* have also had an unrestricted right to work.

The linkage of the *Aussiedler* issue to those of asylum and citizenship acquisition was underscored in the asylum compromise reached by the four major parties in December 1992. In exchange for the amendment to the constitutional guarantee for asylum, the Kohl government agreed to a liberalization of the naturalization rules and a quota restricting the admission of *Aussiedler*. Under this compromise, the parties agreed to limit the admission of ethnic Germans, now classified as *Spätaussiedler*, to the annual average that had been admitted in 1991 and 1992. This figure amounted to roughly 225,000, but the actual allotment for future years was left open to adjustment by (plus or minus) 10 percent according to administrative discretion.

With this compromise, restrictive qualifying criteria were also accepted that were intended to restrict admission to ethnic Germans primarily from the successor states of the former Soviet Union. These criteria were grounded on the assumption that the basis for admission should be due to mistreatment as a consequence of World War II. For the *Aussiedler* in the successor states of the former Soviet Union this mistreatment would remain presumed, but for the *Aussiedler* in other parts of Eastern and Central Europe the allegations of mistreatment would have to be proved in each individual case. At the same time, *Aussiedler* born after 1992 would no longer be eligible for admission on this basis. Finally, integration assistance to those admitted was reduced still further.[6]

These changes meant that the preferential treatment for the admission of the *Aussiedler* would now be gradually phased out by eliminating the sanctioned claims of ethnic Germans living outside of the FRG to admission and settlement on the basis of their German ethnicity. The end of the Cold War and the dissolution of the Soviet Bloc had undermined the argument that the *Aussiedler* were entitled to special consideration due to the oppressive character of communist rule. The sheer number of new arrivals accompanying the Cold War's end applied immediate pressure on the government to restrict the flow.

During this same period, the federal government also aggressively moved to provide inducements for the *Aussiedler* not to seek admission into the FRG by ameliorating conditions in their countries and areas of origin. The federal government concluded treaties with a number of Eastern European states and with Russia to improve the protection of the rights of German minorities (Bade and Oltmer 1999: 25). In addition, it invested in these same regions a great deal of financial capital in promoting German schools, cultural centers, newspapers, and new business initiatives. This combination of measures to deter the influx of *Aussiedler* into the FRG may or may not have reduced their desire to emigrate to Germany, but it did curtail the numbers that would be admitted. As Kees

6. The terms of the compromise were enacted into law on 21 December 1992 as *Gesetz zur Bereinigung von Kriegsfolgengesetzen, Bundesgesetzblatt* I, Nr. 58 (1992): 2094–2107. See also Groenendijk (1997: 467).

Table 17.1. Intake of Ethnic German Returnees (*Aussiedler*) by Countries and Regions of Origin, 1968–2005

Region/Country of Origin	1968–1984	1985	West Germany 1986	1987	1988	1989	1990	1991	Germany 1992	1993	1994
Poland	365,234	22,075	27,188	48,423	140,226	250,340	133,872	40,129	17,742	5,431	2,440
Former USSR	72,664	460	753	14,488	47,572	98,134	147,950	147,320	195,576	207,347	213,214
Romania	147,528	14,924	13,130	13,994	12,902	23,387	111,150	32,178	16,146	5,811	6,615
Former Czechoslovakia	47,011	757	—	—	—	—	1,324	927	460	134	97
Hungary	7,065	485	—	—	—	—	1,038	952	354	37	40
Other countries	3,218	69	1,717	1,618	1,973	5,194	4,101	489	287	128	185
Total	653,092	38,975	42,788	78,523	20,673	377,055	397,082	221,995	230,565	218,888	222,591

Region/Country of Origin	1995	1996	1997	1998	Germany 1999	2000	2001	2002	2003	2004	2005
Poland	1,677	1,175	687	488	428	484	623	553	444	278	80
Former USSR	209,409	172,181	131,895	101,550	103,599	94,558	97,434	90,587	72,289	58,728	35,396
Romania	6,519	4,284	1,777	1,005	855	547	380	256	137	76	39
Former Czechoslovakia	62	14	10	16	11	16	22	13	0	0	0
Hungary	43	14	16	4	4	2	2	3	0	0	3
Other countries	188	83	34	17	19	8	23	4	15	11	4
Total	217,898	177,751	134,419	103,080	104,916	95,615	98,484	91,416	72,885	59,093	35,522

Source: *Asylum Seekers and Refugees: A Statistical Report, Vol 1: EC Member States. EUROSTAT, 1994, Migration, Integration und Asyl in Zahlen,* BAMF 2004.

Groenendijk reports, "the number of applications for reception certificates filed in the ex-USSR declined from 445,000 in 1991 to 223,000 in 1993" (1997: 472). These measures also seem to have defused somewhat the public debate over the reception of the *Aussiedler*, but public attitudes toward the *Aussiedler* have remained largely negative and skeptical toward the claim of their shared German identity.[7] Disappointed with their new lives in the FRG, some *Aussiedler* have undergone a "reethnicization process," shifting their personal identification back toward their countries of origin. As Klaus Bade and Jochen Oltmer have observed, *Aussiedler* from Russia, who found themselves treated in the FRG as more Russian than German, have replaced their new Germanized family names with Russified ones, reapplied for Russian passports (while retaining their German ones), and renewed connections with their Russian homelands (Bade and Oltmer 1999: 31).

The *Aussiedler* have also encountered understandable tensions with other immigrant minorities in Germany, especially Turks, who have not enjoyed the privileged access to the same rights and benefits as have the *Aussiedler*. The near automatic conferral of German citizenship has entitled the *Aussiedler* to vote, even when their knowledge of German has been too poor to read the ballot. Furthermore, the longstanding official disapproval of dual citizenship as a self-evident indicator of unacceptably divided loyalties notwithstanding, the *Aussiedler* have been permitted to retain their homeland passports alongside their new German ones. By contrast, acquisition of German citizenship for Turks has required surrendering their foreign citizenship, except in special circumstances. Turks raised in the FRG typically become fluent in German, and have even been employed as German teachers in language courses for the *Aussiedler*, but acquired a right to German citizenship only in the early 1990s after many years of residence in the FRG (Bade and Oltmer 1999: 35).

The federal government continued to tighten its control over the settlement arrangements of the *Aussiedler*. In early 1996, for example, it implemented a new law to regulate the distribution of the *Aussiedler* among the *Länder* to equalize the burdens in assisting them and to prevent their concentration in certain locations. This law required the arriving *Aussiedler* to remain for two years in their assigned residences unless they could demonstrate that they had a secure means of livelihood and access to their own housing (Groenendijk 1997: 467–468).

The reception of the *Aussiedler* invites comparisons with Germany's earlier experience with expellees and refugees after World War II. Although like the

---

7. As Rainer Münz and Rainer Ohliger have observed: "[T]he Aussiedler quickly recognize that mainstream German society perceives them as being different. In the best case, they are viewed as hyphenated Germans (Romanian-Germans, Russian-Germans, Polish-Germans)" (1998: 168).

latter, the *Aussiedler* have had the advantage of full formal citizenship in the FRG, observers, and the record so far, caution against any expectation that the FRG may readily duplicate the integration success it had with the refugees and expellees who settled in the late 1940s and 1950s. As many observers emphasize, the climate of reception has been entirely different (Bade 1994c: 164; Münz and Ohliger 1998: 179–180). The common hardships suffered after World War II, for example, gave natives and newcomers a basis for forging a shared understanding and collective bond that is missing today. Furthermore, the economic boom that began in the 1950s created many new opportunities for the refugees and expellees and native Germans that the economic uncertainties of the 1980s and 1990s did not.

But if the climate of reception has been very different, so too has been the commitment of the governing elites to give the *Aussiedler* an effective voice in the institutions that govern them. As FRG citizens, the *Aussiedler*, like the refugees and the expellees in the 1950s, have enjoyed the right to vote and to organize politically, but here the stories diverge dramatically for "there are no *Aussiedler* spokespersons in any of the German political parties" (Münz and Ohliger 1998: 180). The *Aussiedler* have remained largely passive members of the political process, focusing their energies in their own private domains.[8] The contrasting experiences of the refugees/expellees, on the one hand, and the *Aussiedler*, on the other, suggests that the FRG government needs to consider new, more activist integrationist strategies, especially in light of the altered climate of reception. Viewed together with the post-unification experiences of the East Germans,[9] these three cases make it clear that shared ties of "ethnicity" (as applied to peoples of markedly different historical backgrounds, cultural understandings, and socioeconomic orientations) is not the decisive ingredient in determining the conditions for the successful inclusion of newcomers.

8. As Daniel Levy observes, "Aussiedler have no institutional power and lack the cultural capital to influence public discourse. The Aussiedler who have come to Germany in the last decade have little command of the German language and their cultural and social habits differ from West Germans. Instead of shaping their policies they are merely subjects of decisions that are made in response to social and economic considerations rather than with respect to 'national priorities'" (1999: 135).

9. Thus, for example, Jennifer Yoder notes that from 1990 to 1995, the percentage of East Germans who identified with being "German" (as opposed to "East German") declined from 66 percent to 34 percent. In explaining the integration challenges that the FRG faced with unification, she observes that the "elite must encourage identification with the system by giving citizens a stake in the changes—by remobilizing them to be active rather than passive supporters of the new system" (Yoder 1999: 204–205, 207).

Chapter 18

Jewish Immigration
Contesting and Confirming Germany's
Policies toward Immigrants

Two of the most striking aspects of German reunification have been the remarkable expansion of the Jewish community in Germany and the lack of political backlash caused by this immigration. The fall of the Berlin wall in 1989 marked the beginning of a wave of Jewish migration into Germany from Russia. Although the number of Soviet Jews entering the FRG remained tiny compared to that of the *Aussiedler* and asylum seekers, the issue of controlling the admissions of Jewish refugees posed a delicate problem for the Kohl administration. On the one hand, it was making every effort to sharply reduce the flow of asylum seekers generally, and it did not wish to offend Israel, which strongly preferred itself as the destination for Soviet Jews. On the other hand, in light of Germany's Nazi past, it did not want to suggest even the appearance of anti-Semitism in refusing admission, and doubtlessly felt a genuine sense of moral obligation as well. In crafting a policy response to the growing demand of Soviet Jews seeking to enter the FRG, the Kohl administration also had to take into the account the views of the *Länder* governments who would play a major role in implementing any policy. Between 1991 and 2006, approximately 226,000 persons from the former Soviet Union immigrated to Germany under special provisions for Jewish immigration (Haug 2007: 8).

The history of post-war Jewish immigration, in many ways like the FRG's policy toward the *Aussiedler*, is based on a mixture of historical, moral, and political considerations. The Jewish community in Germany after World War II was only a remnant of its former size before 1933. Many who had survived the Holocaust emigrated to Israel, the United States, and elsewhere. In 1950, the number of Jews living in West Germany was estimated at 15,000, while

Table 18.1. Immigration of Jewish Persons from the Former Soviet Union, 1991–2004

Year	Immigration of Jews According to Acceptance Guarantees	Number of Acceptances by the *Länder*	Number of Applications
1991	—	12,583	19,288
1992	—	15,879	19,232
1993	16,597	15,785	14,299
1994	8,811	16,466	27,704
1995	15,184	22,777	29,824
1996	15,959	13,211	17,302
1997	19,437	12,931	21,098
1998	17,788	12,233	11,251
1999	18,205	15,549	24,854
2000	16,538	20,280	27,030
2001	16,711	23,300	19,899
2002	19,262	14,426	12,603
2003	15,442	13,098	8,009
2004	11,208	9,640	2,790

Source: *Migration, Integration und Asyl in Zahlen*, BAMF 2004.

estimates of the numbers in East Germany for this period have varied from 3,800 to 8,000. In 1950, the Central Council of Jews (ZDJ) (*Zentralrat der Juden*) was established as the main Jewish organization in the FRG. While the Jewish population continued to decline thereafter in the GDR, it rose in the FRG on account of immigration from Eastern Europe and, to a lesser extent, the Soviet Union. From the mid 1950s to the mid 1980s, 40,000 Jews immigrated to West Germany. However, many of these immigrants did not become formal members of the Jewish community. By 1989, the size of the Jewish community in the FRG has been estimated at 27,552 members, while it had shrunk to miniscule numbers in the GDR (Dietz, Lebok, and Polian 2002: 38–39; Weiss 2004: 182–183).

After World War II, the FRG sought to rectify its treatment of Jews as an integral part of its reintegration into the Western world (Mendel 2004). Article 116(2) of the Basic Law provides for German citizens and their descendants who were stripped of their citizenship on political, racial, or religious grounds during the Nazi era to recover their German citizenship. Jews that were former German citizens are clearly covered under this article. Beyond the Basic Law, specific legislation pertaining to Jews, mainly regarding reparations, was passed in 1953, 1956, and 1957. As part of the legislation passed in 1956, for example, the West German government agreed to allocate DM 6,000 for each Jew remigrating to Germany (Krauss 2004). At the urging of the ZDJ, the German government provided money to German Jews wishing to return. Since the late 1980s, the FRG policy toward Jewish refugees has been guided by two goals: to repay a historic debt and to rejuvenate dying Jewish communities (Remennick 2005: 31). Between 1989 and 2001, the size of the Jewish population in the FRG more than tripled from 27,552 to 87,756, according to the ZDJ's estimate. However, because the German government applies a broader definition of Jewishness in counting immigrants, its own estimate of the number of Jews is "roughly twice as large as the number registered by the Central Jewish Council." On account of the Jewish population's low fertility rate in Germany, all of the increase in its size is attributable to immigration (Remennick: 31; Dietz, Lebok, and Polian 1997: 39, 43).

Starting in the 1970s, Jews began to trickle out from the Soviet Union and a small number of them made their way to Germany (Legge 2003: 14; Dietz 2000: 639). The situation began to change drastically in the late 1980s under Gorbachev's perestroika reforms. Starting in 1989, the Soviet Union began removing restrictions on Jewish emigration. Soviet Jews seized the opportunity to leave for a variety of motives from religious to economic. Many were worried about deteriorating political, economic, and ecological conditions in the former Soviet Union. Some also expressed fears about signs of rising anti-Semitism and ethnic conflicts in the regions as motivating factors (Doomernik 1997: 19–27; Schoeps, Jasper, and Vogt 1999: 31–54). In the fall of 1989, the US government terminated its blanket asylum policy toward Soviet Jews in order to establish greater control on admissions and limit the flow (Harris 1998: 114). Henceforth, Soviet Jews wishing to come to the United States would have to apply through the regular immigration channels. On 20 May 1991, the Soviet Union enacted a new emigration law granting the right of individuals to exit and enter freely. The law became effective on 1 January 1993 (Chandler 1998: 94–96). During 1990, the Soviet Union's liberalization of travel restrictions since 1989 coupled with the reduced prospects for admissions into the US helped to spur Jewish immigration into Germany (Harris 1998: 115). Nevertheless, more Soviet Jews continued to emigrate to Israel and the United States than to Germany. In 1988, the United States admitted 11,225 Soviet Jews, while Israel admitted 2,166, and Germany admitted 568. In 1989, the United States admitted 38,395 Soviet Jews, while Israel admitted 12,172, and Germany admitted 546. In 1990, Israel admitted 181,759 Soviet Jews, while the United States admitted 32,714, and Germany admitted 8,513. In 1991, Israel admitted 145,005, while the United States admitted 35,568, and Germany admitted 8,000. In 1992, Israel admitted 65,100, while the United States admitted 46,083, and Germany 4,000 (Tress 1997: 23).

The impetus behind admitting the large scale Jewish immigration originated in the German Democratic Republic. The Communist East German regime had always refused to acknowledge any moral obligations connected with the Nazi past. Casting itself as the representative of German anti-fascism, it depicted the FRG as the successor state of the Third Reich. Accordingly, the GDR had never paid any reparations to Israel as compensation for the Holocaust. Seeking to drawing a sharp moral line between itself and its predecessor, the first freely elected East German parliament (*Volkskammer*) issued a declaration in April 1990 acknowledging, for its part, collective German responsibility for Nazi crimes and apologizing for them (Documents 20, Jarausch and Grasnow 1994: 138–139). On 11 July 1990, the GDR enacted a law that "granted asylum to foreigners who left their country based on fear of persecution because of race, religion, nationality, affiliation to certain social group or political conviction." The law further "guaranteed that upon approval of the asylum application the foreigner would receive a residency permit valid for five years" (Harris 1998: 122). In passing this law, Soviet Jews were a particular object of concern because of a rise of anti-Semitic incidents in the Soviet Union. Since late 1989, the East Berlin Jewish Cultural Association had been pressing the East German government to extend permanent residence rights to Soviet Jews. Soviet Jews were able to come to the East Berlin on tourist visas, and their numbers now dramatically increased. In order to receive special status, Jews only had to register with the authorities in Berlin[1] and demonstrate some form of Jewish identity (Tress 1997: 41; Dietz 2000: 639; Doomernik 1997: 53; Weiss 2004: 176–177).

Alarmed by these developments, the Kohl government asked the GDR to stop granting tourist visas and instructed its consulates in the Soviet Union not to process them as well. In response, during 1990, approximately 10,000 Jews submitted applications in Moscow for admissions as *Aussiedler* (Tress 1995: 41). The Kohl government rejected these applications, but the Office for Multicultural Affairs in Frankfurt took up the cause. Together with the mayor's office and the city council, it sought to develop the case for admitting the Soviet Jews as *Aussiedler* under the Federal Expellee and Refugee Law of 1953 on the grounds that they should be treated as German Jews. The rationale behind this argument was that many German Jews had fled the Nazis to the eastern territories that came under Soviet control, but there was no way for Soviet Jews to prove this situation applied to them. Moreover, as Frankfurt authorities pointed out, Soviet Jews would not be able to support their claims by use of Nazi records, such as the *Deutsche Volksliste* (German Peoples List),[2] that the FRG used to ascertain the Germanness of ethnic German applicants. The

1. The authority that traditionally registered foreigners in the GDR was the police. However, as Irene Runge notes, there was mass confusion at the time of Jewish immigration, and there were no official forms or process to take in the Jewish refugees. Furthermore, many Jews were confused as to with which authorities they were supposed to register (Runge 1995: 84).

2. The *Deutsche Volksliste* were a classification schema that the Nazis instituted during their occupation of Poland to rank individuals according to their degree of Germanness and their capacity for becoming Germanized. For a discussion of the history of this schema, see Majer (2003: 238–246).

Frankfurt city government's effort on behalf of the admission of Soviet Jews attracted increasing public attention to this issue. The *Länder* officials in Hesse and Lower Saxony also began indicating their willingness to take in Soviet Jewish refugees (Harris 1998: 123–131). It is hard to imagine that the Kohl government welcomed a debate over the kinds of issues this matter raised.

At the unification of the two German states on 3 October 1990, the Kohl government sought to have all foreigners in the former GDR return to their home countries. The ZDJ lobbied to have the several thousand Soviet Jews in the GDR exempted from this policy. On October 24, the Alliance/Green[3] faction in the Bundestag put forward a legislative proposal to establish a formal admissions policy for Soviet Jews similar to the policy applied to ethnic Germans. Despite this initiative, all of the parliamentary officials agreed that any debates over the issue should be conducted behind closed doors as much as possible, and the issue received little attention from the press (Tress 1997: 26; Harris 1998: 133, 138). By doing so, the ZDJ hoped to revitalize the waning strength of the Jewish community in Germany. This position again put the ZDJ at odds with the Israeli government, which had successfully convinced other European countries not to grant Soviet Jews refugee status (Tress 1995: 39; Harris 1998: 139; Dietz 2000: 639; Doomernik 1997: 162).

At a conference of *Länder* Minister Presidents in January 1991, Chancellor Kohl and Federal Interior Minister Schäuble hammered out an agreement on administrative procedural guidelines to govern the admission of Jewish refugees. Under this agreement, the FRG legalized the status of all Soviet Jews who had entered Germany between 1 June 1990 and 1 January 1991. On humanitarian grounds, they were classified retroactively as "quota refugees" based on a 1980 law known as the *Kontingentflüchtlingsgesetz* (Refugee Quota Law). The Quota Law had provided for the resettlement of refugees from Vietnam (the boat people). Now it would be used to incorporate the ad hoc GDR procedures into FRG regulations, with no specific numerical cap, for Jewish "refugee" immigration to the Federal Republic (Harris 1998: 140). Similar to the policy applied to the *Aussiedler*, this law provided for the distribution of Jewish immigrants throughout the *Länder*. While the majority of these Jews probably did not meet the conditions of "refugee" as stipulated under the Geneva Refugee Convention, the German government applied its provisions to them, including granting the right to work. Against objections from the Israeli government over its refugee policy toward Soviet Jews, the German government "explained that because of its historic past it simply could not close its borders to Soviet Jews" (Harris 1998: 139). Nevertheless, after 10 November 1991, Jews from the former Soviet Union, like the *Spätaussiedler*,

3. Alliance 90 (Bündnis 90) was a political coalition formed in February 1990 by the East German civic movements New Forum, Democracy Now, and the Initiative for Peace and Human Rights.

could no longer apply for refugee status in Germany, but had to do so from their country of origin. Upon being granted refugee status, Jews were granted permanent residence status, work permission, initial housing support, and access to the welfare system. This help was augmented by assistance provided by the Jewish community. Before the adoption of the new citizenship law in 1999, those who had refugee status as Jews could apply for naturalization after seven years of residence (Dietz 2000: 639, 644).

Problems beset the Jewish refugee policy from the outset. All applicants had to wait between two and five years for their claims to be processed. Jewish immigrants also faced high levels of unemployment; half of Jewish immigrants of working age were unemployed as of 2005 (Remennick 2005: 35). For those Jews from the Soviet Union who wished to join a particular Jewish community in Germany, the redistribution throughout the *Länder* caused problems. Most *Länder* did not take into consideration where Jewish communities existed, and many Jews were sent to small towns where they could expect no help from the Jewish community (Independent Commission on Immigration 2001: 183). Moreover, the issue of Jewish identity for many of the Soviet Jews who were immigrating to Germany came into conflict with the ZDJ's reason for supporting Jewish immigration to Germany. The anti-religious policies actively promoted by the Soviet Union had made practicing Judaism very difficult. As a result, the majority of former Soviet Jews understand their Jewishness in highly secular terms as more a form of ethnicity or nationality than a religious bond (Gitelman 2003: 58; Chervyakov, Gitelman, and Shapiro 2003: 71). As with the *Spätaussiedler*, there had also been high rates of intermarriage in the Soviet Union between Jews and non-Jews, and, because immigration regulations allowed for the accompaniment of spouses, many of those who immigrated to Germany were not Jewish. In an early study of the Jewish community in Berlin, it was found that 20 percent of those who had emigrated from the Soviet Union under Jewish refugee status were non-Jewish spouses (Doomernik 1997: 83). Of the remaining 80 percent who had immigrated as Jewish refugees,[4] some were not Jewish according to Jewish law, which requires that a child's mother be Jewish in order for the child to be Jewish.

During the 1990s, former Soviet Jews came to outnumber German Jews. This demographic change has had a strong impact on local Jewish community life. In some communities, Russian has replaced German as the dominant language, and the communities themselves have often splintered into subgroups organized around different interests and goals. Despite making active efforts,

---

4. The German decisions were based on Soviet nationality documents. Under Soviet law (the so-called fifth point), every Soviet citizen had to declare a nationality, of which Jewish was an option. In the case where parents were of different nationalities, parents could choose the nationality of their children.

the native Jewish communities have not had much success in helping new Jewish immigrants integrate into German society or assimilating them into the established order of their own organizations (Kessler 1999: 154; Weiss 2004: 188–191; Remennick 2005: 36–37). As a result of high rates of intermarriage, cultural alienation, and lack of religious interest, Jewish organizations in Germany estimate that only half of Soviet Jewish immigrants are members of a Jewish community.[5] Nevertheless, the Jewish community has been much more welcoming than the general public, and much more social integration has occurred between German and Soviet Jews than between Jews and ethnic Germans (including Russian-speaking *Spätaussiedler*) (Dietz 2000: 647). Even though many Soviet Jews have joined the Jewish community, their perceived lack of participation has led to disenchantment among many in the ZDJ and other Jewish community organizations. The latter have been critical of Jewish immigrants, especially the younger generation, for being more interested in social benefits than in religious observance (Remennick 2005: 48; Weiss 2004: 191). Since the ZDJ was the main force behind lobbying for Jewish immigration, they have moved toward promoting the immigration of only those Jews demonstrating interest in the Jewish community. Meanwhile, the ZDJ has also confronted the reality that many Jewish immigrants need extra resources to facilitate their adaptation to life in Germany, which has in some instances put a significant financial strain on the resources of local Jewish communities.

With respect to the German labor market, Jews from the former Soviet Union have faced their own distinctive challenges. As a group, they have typically been much older and more highly educated than the *Aussiedler*. Where Soviet Jews had highly urbanized backgrounds, the *Aussiedler* generally came from more rural or small town environments. Since the end of World War II, low fertility rates among Soviet Jews had raised the median age of their population. Most Soviet Jews acquired post-secondary school degrees and had worked in professional occupations in the former Soviet Union, but their credentials have proven not to be transferable due to differences in educational standards between Germany and the former Soviet Union. By contrast, as Larissa Remennick has observed, "Aussiedler with academic degrees from Soviet universities and colleges are entitled by law to have them regarded as comparable to German degrees when applying for jobs or in regard to wage levels" (Remennick 2005: 50; see also Remennick 2005: 35–36). In addition, the *Aussiedler* were entitled to automatic citizenship upon arrival, while the Soviet Jews were not. Further handicapped by low competency in German (as has also been the case for the younger generation of *Aussiedler*), Soviet Jews have found it difficult to obtain jobs commensurate with their qualifications,

5. Involvement in a Jewish community does not necessitate religious practice, as there are many cultural venues for participation as well.

and have thereby experienced considerable downward mobility. They have had to contend with chronic unemployment and long-term dependency on social welfare benefits. However, the younger generation of Soviet Jews, who have grown up in Germany, have demonstrated a much higher degree of educational achievement and economic upward mobility than the younger generation of the *Aussiedler* (Remennick 2005: 36; Weiss 2004: 179–180).

Former Soviet Jews typically have little close personal contact with Germans and have concentrated their social activities within their own networks. In part, this lack of contact has been due to poor language skills, and most have settled into their own enclaves in German towns and cities. The outreach efforts of local Jewish communities then have often provided the most important point of contact with their host society. For their part, most Germans have difficulty distinguishing Russian-speaking *Aussiedler* from Russian-speaking Jews, so they tend to conflate the two groups under the general moniker of "Russian immigrant" (Dietz 2003: 13–16; Remennick 2005: 35–37, 41–42, 52–53). Although former Soviet Jews have expressed fears about German anti-Semitism, it appears that these fears are not well-founded except for the extreme right-wing fringe. Cognizant of the Nazi past, most Germans seem to regard anti-Semitism as beyond the pale, and the public incitement of hatred or violence on the grounds of race, religion, and ethnicity is punishable by law. "Public awareness about antisemitism," Hermann Kurthen has observed, "is high, and anti-Jewish resentment is neither politically nor intellectually respectable, nor is it officially embedded in the political culture" (Kurthen 1997: 60). The results of different public opinion surveys show some variance, but tend to support this conclusion. A 2003 EMNID Institute poll, for example, reported that 85 percent of the German interviewees are completely indifferent to whether one of their neighbors is Jewish, and 79 percent believe that at most only a small minority of Germans hold anti-Jewish attitudes (EUMC 2004: 260–262).

Upon considering the problems with Jewish immigration to Germany, in 2001, the Independent Commission on Immigration concurred with the ZDJ's recommendation that further Jewish immigration to Germany should serve to strengthen Jewish communities by only allowing those who were Jewish—according to Jewish law—to immigrate (Independent Commission on Immigration 2001: 183). While the exact language of the Commission was not adopted, in 2005, the laws regarding Jewish immigration were changed. In an attempt to curtail welfare payments to Jewish refugees, Germany now requires that Jews be under forty-five years of age, have a good working knowledge of German, and be financially self-sufficient if they wish to immigrate. Under the newest immigration law from 2005, these guidelines are similar to those applied to persons wishing to enter the FRG for reasons of family reunification and family-forming migration. Additionally, potential immigrants must show an invitation from a Jewish community.

In the FRG, the immigration of former Soviet Jews has been depicted as a symbolic means to restore a strong Jewish community in Germany and thereby to normalize relations between Germans and Jews. However, the reality of the Jewish immigration has not conformed to these simplistic expectations. The secularity and mixed heritage of many former Soviet Jews as well as visible tensions within the Jewish community itself has raised doubts about the authenticity of their Jewish identity. The German public has begun to question the continued social spending that supporting Jewish immigrants has involved (Remennick 2005: 38; Weiss 2004: 184–185, 192). Similar to policies with regard to *Aussiedler*, Jewish immigration has been curtailed purportedly to winnow out not only those who are not true Jews or Germans, but also those who cannot contribute to the economy. In fact, policies toward Jews and ethnic Germans now appear much more similar to active recruitment schemes for economic immigrants. Both flows of migration have merit and historical logic. They enhance the diversity of German society, and are examples of the myriad of ways that Germany has been rebuilding itself through immigration since the end of World War II. However, because the FRG has treated both groups as special categories, which set them apart from its general policies toward immigrants and refugees, it has not sufficiently thought through how its different membership policies affect the overall integration of society. Furthermore, by segregating different categories of migrants into separate policy domains, the FRG thwarted the creation of a comprehensive framework for migration through which competing priorities and considerations could be weighed and apportioned.

Chapter 19

Reforming German Citizenship Law

By codifying the idea of a "European citizenship," the Maastricht Treaty opened the door to a broader public debate over the rights, obligations, and conditions that should be attached to it. One glaring feature of the Treaty's definition of this idea was its exclusion of third-country nationals. To rectify this problem, the European Parliament, the Council of Europe, and various organizations, including the Anti-racist Network for Equality in Europe, the Churches' Commission for Migrants in Europe, and the European Union Migrants' Forum, have advocated the introduction of residence-based measures for the acquisition of European citizenship independent of Member State nationality (Wiener 1998: 410). Such measures have not been adopted, and, in fact, run directly counter to the Treaty's definition of EU citizenship as deriving from Member State nationality. In the face of this barrier, the main path to expanding access to European citizenship for third-country nationals would have to be through liberalizing the nationality rules of individual Member States.[1] During the 1990s, Germany moved slowly along this path.

Decades of resistance to grappling with the reality of immigration could not be easily overcome. "For issues of immigration," Klaus Bade observed, "the Federal government [of Chancellor Kohl] wanted to see only European solutions, not national ones" (Bade 1996: 135). Despite this preference, the task of reforming German citizenship law could not be transferred to the European level. The violence that had erupted against foreigners during the reunification process had tied earlier failures to assume this task to deeper questions of the German national character. Much of the German public, as well as their political leaders, were

1. For discussion of the reform options, see Hansen (1998: 751–768).

shocked by these episodes of violence. At the same time, it had become simply untenable to maintain the fiction that the immigrants who had settled in Germany from the 1950s onward could be still treated as temporary residents. Against this background, the issue of citizenship law reform would now be addressed.

Throughout the 1990s, the Christian Democratic Union (CDU) and Christian Social Union (CSU) continued to prefer a naturalization policy that required a high degree of cultural assimilation. Both parties further rejected the view that asylum abuse could be managed through either an immigration law or quotas for particular groups of migrants.[2] Instead, they supported a two-prong policy aimed at integrating foreigners who already lived in Germany[3] and at preventing further abuse of the asylum law. The Kohl government favored small, incremental changes in the citizenship law. Although the CDU/CSU coalition supported reforming the discretionary naturalization policy by conferring a legal right to citizenship upon application after ten years of legal residence, it continued to reject proposals for dual citizenship. The CDU, and particularly its sister party, the CSU, believed that requiring those who naturalized in Germany to relinquish their previous citizenship was the only way to ensure that newly naturalized Germans would integrate into German society (Green 2005: 200).

Differences over an *Ausländerpolitik* (foreigners' policy) were the focal point of a dispute between the CDU/CSU and its coalition partner, the Free Democrats (FDP). On the one hand, the FDP consistently perceived liberalizing access to citizenship as a political and legal measure that would enhance the integration of foreigners. The party saw the best way for meeting Germany's future labor needs and international legal obligations as a narrowly conceived and

2. In a November 1996 *Frankfurter Allgemeine Zeitung* article, Interior Minister Kanther strongly criticized the SPD and Green Party proposals for an immigration law with annual quotas. Kanther has repeatedly denied that Germany is an immigration country (in fact, the title of the article is "*Deutschland ist kein Einwanderungsland*"). He believed that Germany did not have any need for an active immigration policy. In the article, he gave a number of reasons, such as the four million unemployed Germans, integration problems for the existing foreigner population, the burden on the social welfare system, and the already large numbers of foreigners accepted by Germany in various categories (asylum seekers, family reunification, war refugees, etc.). Kanther criticized both the SPD's and Green Party's proposals as being unrealistic and as hurting Germany. He also argued that quotas would be problematic with respect to Germany's constitutional commitment toward asylum seekers. "What would happen to the first asylum seeker who applies once the quota has been filled?" he asks (Kanther 1996). Other opponents of an immigration law saw no need for quotas because the current migrant groups coming to Germany are all in political categories, such as the *Aussiedler*, migrants from EU Member States, family reunification categories, and asylum seekers (Bernt 1996).

3. During this period, the federal government, the *Länder* and municipalities, and the Federal Institute for Employment allocated more than DM 1 billion for integration measures each year (OECD 1995: 5).

well-managed immigration regime, as well as for reducing some of the social tensions surrounding these issues. On the other hand, the FDP did not want to risk a breach with its coalition partners and lose its place in government. Thus, though it was closer to the Social Democrats (SPD) in its argument for changing the country's citizenship policy and for instituting a German immigration law with quotas, the FDP never forced a show down with its governing partners over such issues.

In the early 1990s, the SPD continued to push for more liberal citizenship and immigration policies, consistently citing a responsibility of the German government to foster the integration of migrant workers and their descendants. In an effort to bolster its profile as an asylum and immigration advocate, the SPD issued a press release in March 1993, indicating that the change of the Basic Law had not satisfied the SPD's requirements regarding a comprehensive immigration law.[4] However, SPD leaders also recognized the difficulty of instituting a comprehensive immigration law in Germany while unemployment remained high.

After retreating somewhat from their advocacy in the early 1990s for an open borders policy, the Greens continued to advocate generous asylum and immigration principles for Germany. Their advocacy was often stronger in staking out principles than in working out the details of actual programs (Thränhardt 1999: 35; Markovits and Gorski 1993: 183). In the Green Party's 1989 citizenship proposal (*Die Grünen* 1989: 4), they cautioned that Germany must not encourage the most educated people to leave developing countries and migrate to Germany, because these migrants would be the very people developing countries need most. The Greens and the FDP also advocated for the formation of a commission that would establish annual quotas for immigrants to Germany (*Der Spiegel* 1996).

The trend toward the liberalization of the naturalization policy would ultimately prove irresistible, but only after protracted debate and failed attempts to find feasible alternatives. As part of the December 1992 "asylum compromise," the federal government made permanent the provisional naturalization rule that had been adopted in the 1990 Aliens Law. This provided generally for naturalization after fifteen years of residence, but had been scheduled to expire in December 1995 (Rubio-Marin 2000: 217). In 1993, the federal government amended the 1990 Aliens Law to confer for the first time an individual right of naturalization on foreigners who satisfied the necessary requirements. The number of naturalizations among non-ethnic German foreigners nearly doubled that same year from 37,042 in 1992 to 74,058 in 1993. Under the new regulations, Münz and Ulrich report that "more than 29,000 foreigners were

---

4. "Bundestagsfraktion will Ausländern Einbürgerung erleichtern und die Hinahme der Doppelstaatsangehörigkeit ermöglichen," Pressemitteilung der SPD Bundestagsfraktion, 10 March 1993, 606.

naturalized ... in addition [to] 44,900 naturalizations of foreigners on a discretionary decision of German authorities" (Münz and Ulrich 1997: 100–101).

During the October 1994 elections, there was very little discussion of immigration issues.[5] Both the CDU and the SPD made the fight against rising unemployment the mainstay of their campaigns. While immigration remained a preoccupation, polls showed that Germans were more concerned about the economy and crime than about the issue of "foreigners" or right-wing extremism.[6] It appears that the major parties had struck a tacit bargain to avoid debating the immigration issue until after the elections, in order to avoid playing into the hands of the right-wing parties.

In October 1994, the CDU/CSU/FDP coalition won reelection, while support for extreme right-wing parties declined. With a slim parliamentary majority, the coalition proposed reforming the citizenship law, but remained staunchly opposed to dual nationality. In January 1995, the SPD countered with its own proposal that went well beyond anything the CDU/CSU leadership would accept. Because the SPD's proposal was similar to the FDP's, conservatives worried that FDP members might defect. In fact, the SPD acknowledged that they used a previous bill drafted by FDP member Cornelia Schmalz-Jacobsen, the commissioner for foreigner's affairs, as a model. The SPD proposed legislation that would have conferred automatic citizenship upon third-generation foreigners who were born in Germany, that is, on the basis of *jus soli*. The proposal further provided for reducing the residency requirement for naturalization to eight years and permitting greater toleration of dual citizenship for new citizens. Finally, the bill permitted discretionary naturalizations after five years and eliminated prohibitions against dual citizenship as a bar to naturalization (Neuman 1998: 276).

In February 1995, the Greens put forth their own proposal to reform the citizenship law in Germany, which went farther than the SPD proposal. Specifically, citizenship would be granted to second-generation immigrants if they were born in Germany. Dual citizenship would also be permitted. The initiative was declared dead on 8 February, however, when the sponsors of the bill, spokesperson Kerstin Muller and Representative Cem Özdemir, could not garner enough signatures to bring about a vote in the Bundestag on the measure (Hailbronner 2002: 126–127; Cooper 2002).

---

5. From 13 March 1994 to 16 October 1994, Germany had a total of nineteen elections (including the European elections in June).

6. However, some polls showed immigration issues as still ranking near the top on the electorate's priority list. For example, the *Financial Times* (Peel 1994) reported that unemployment was the greatest concern of the electorate beyond law and order, immigration, social welfare, housing or education.

In June 1996, the FDP renewed its call for reforming the immigration and naturalization policy. Klaus Kinkel, the FDP party leader and foreign minister, announced that "Germany needs an overall concept for immigration and integration" (*Migration News* 1996). Kinkel specifically mentioned establishing an annual level of immigration, which would be dependent on the housing and labor market. The FDP's goal was to make it easier for new immigrants to move to Germany. Kinkel went on to say that if there should be reform of the citizenship law, "it must be easier for foreigners whose lives center on Germany in the long term to have access to German citizenship" (*Migration News* 1996).[7] The FDP proposed that foreigners who are born in Germany be granted citizenship at birth; they would be allowed dual citizenship until the age of eighteen, when they would be forced to choose (hence the name *Optionsmodell*, or options model). Both the CDU and the CSU opposed the FDP's proposals. Bernard Protzner, the secretary general of the CSU, stated that "Germany is not a land of immigration, and we will not make it into one. There will be no such law (annual immigration levels) as long as the CSU can help it" (*Migration News* 1996).[8]

On 26 October 1997, Kohl gave a speech to the CDU youth movement, where he publicly opposed granting dual citizenship to children of foreigners born in Germany, as advocated by the FDP and parts of Kohl's own CDU. Such a change in citizenship law, Kohl claimed, would lead to a flood of Turkish immigration. He said that while Turks should be allowed to apply for citizenship, caution should be exercised, particularly in light of the cultural differences between Germans and Turks, which could lead to social fragmentation (*Süddeutsche Zeitung* 1997a). The loudest protests over Kohl's comments came from Turkish groups, although the FDP and some members of his own party who supported dual citizenship also protested. Guido Westerwelle, general secretary of the FDP, criticized Kohl for using a floodgate argument that employed "misleading and factually inaccurate statements" (*Süddeutsche Zeitung* 1997b). Westerwelle also said that "the Free Democrats believe that integrating foreigners into German society is one of the country's biggest challenges and must become a top priority of the government" (Drozdiak 1997). The younger members of the CDU also challenged their party's leadership on the issue.[9]

During these years, all of the FDP, Green, and SPD reform initiatives failed in parliament. Throughout the period preceding the next national elections,

---

7. For a complete discussion about the party platforms for citizenship reform, see Green (2004: 92–95).

8. Cooper (2002) and Green (2004) discuss the CDU and CSU opposition to the FDP proposals.

9. On 29 October 1997, for example, four CDU members of the Bundestag publicly criticized Kohl's comments and endorsed the model of granting temporary dual citizenship to foreign children born in Germany until their eighteenth birthday (when they will have to choose) (*Süddeutsche Zeitung* 1997c).

parties continued to debate reform proposals, but none were successful. Still, the balance was clearly shifting in favor of reform, even as the CDU/CSU leadership fought the change. A new Social-Democratic/Green party coalition entered office after federal elections on 27 September 1998, with a strong determination to "modernize" Germany's citizenship law by adopting the birth-based principle of *jus soli* and a tolerant attitude toward dual citizenship (Green 2001b: 97).[10] In May 1999, the new ruling coalition pushed through legislation that supplemented the traditional principle of citizenship acquisition by descent (*jus sanguinis*) with provisions for acquisition by birth (*jus soli*).

The intention of the new coalition government to abolish the ban on dual citizenship was widely attacked by the CDU. With the Turkish minority uppermost in mind, CDU and CSU leaders raised the specter of immigrants using their new German citizenship to establish political parties that would work to promote the interests of foreign states (Nathans 2004: 256). In a hotly contested election in the state of Hesse in 1999, the CDU started a petition campaign against dual citizenship (Cooper 2002; Minkenberg 2001: 7). The success of the CDU in the Hesse elections shook the resolve of the coalition government, and it retreated from its original proposal to abolish the ban on dual citizenship (Cooper 2002; Green 2001b: 97). The CDU/CSU had long feared that enfranchising many of the new immigrants groups would most immediately benefit the SPD, which had long been the favored party of German residents of Turkish descent. The SPD's concessions to the CDU/CSU "disappointed Turkish voters' hope for dual citizenship," but the degree to which these concessions may have cost the SPD support from Turkish voters remains an open question (Østergaard-Nielsen 2003: 90, 92–93).

As pushed through by the coalition government, the new law granted automatic acquisition of citizenship for children born in Germany of foreign parents who meet prescribed residency requirements. This legislation, as Chancellor Gerhard Schröder's accompanying policy statement observed, was predicated on the recognition "that the immigration to Germany that has taken place over past decades is irreversible."[11] Equally striking, in explaining the rationale of the new citizenship law to the Bundestag, Interior Minister Otto Schily observed: "We must understand that in a Europe that is slowly growing together, different

---

10. During the election campaign, even members of the ruling CDU/CSU coalition argued over whether their joint platform should continue to not characterize Germany as an immigration land, but in the end the CDU, under Kohl's leadership, agreed to omit the phrase. The FDP, their partners in the federal government, had advocated a more inclusive citizenship policy as part of a more general reconsideration of FRG migration policy, but did not want to rupture the governing alliance over this issue (Cooper 2002: 96–97).

11. Policy statement by Gerhard Schröder, Chancellor of the Federal Republic of Germany, in the Bundestag on 1 November 1998. See http://www.germany-info.org/relaunch/politics/speeches/111098.html.

nations, cultures, ethnic and language groups will come together in different forms than taken in the homogeneous national-state, which was an error of the previous century" (quoted in Nathans 2004: 257). The amendment of the 1990 *Ausländergesetz*, with respect to the acquisition of German citizenship at birth and by naturalization, came into force in January 2000. The most important changes involve the granting of citizenship to long-term immigrants and their descendants born in Germany.

Under the new provisions, German citizenship is acquired at birth either by descent (*jus sanguinis*) or birth in the country (*jus soli*). However, children born in Germany to parents with foreign citizenship acquire German citizenship only if one of the parents fulfills certain conditions of residency, i.e., the relevant parent must have been living in Germany for at least eight years and must have acquired the status of a permanent resident before the birth of the child. According to a transitional provision, children born in Germany before the enactment of the new *jus soli* regulation are entitled to acquire German citizenship if one of the parents fulfills the above-mentioned conditions. In this case, an application had to be made before 31 December 2000.

Children who acquire German citizenship after January 2000, according to the new *jus soli* rules, and who already possess the "foreign" citizenship of their parents by descent have to declare before the age of twenty-three whether they wish to keep their German citizenship. If such a declaration is not made, the person in question automatically will lose his/her German citizenship, unless the authorities agree to the retention of the German citizenship. If a declaration is made in favor of the German citizenship, the person in question has to prove the renunciation of his/her "foreign" citizenship before reaching the age of twenty-three.

The new law provided one possible exception to these general requirements. An individual may apply before reaching the age of twenty-one for the grant of an official permission to retain the "foreign" citizenship. The permission is to be granted if renunciation or loss of the foreign citizenship is not possible or if certain conditions are fulfilled, as specified in §87 *Ausländergesetz* 1990 (as amended in 1999), with respect to "toleration" (*Hinnahme*) of dual citizenship. Dual citizenship may be tolerated, for example, if the renunciation of the original citizenship requires high fees or creates considerable economic disadvantages, or the applicant is an elderly person and denial of naturalization would cause a hardship, or the applicant has been recognized as a refugee according to the Geneva Convention or admitted to Germany within the framework of humanitarian relief action.

Under the new law, foreign citizens born abroad, that is, first generation immigrants, have an entitlement to naturalization after eight years of legal residence (instead of fifteen years). This entitlement is conditioned on knowledge of the German language, the absence of criminal convictions, and sufficient income to support themselves and their family members (if the candidate has reached the age of twenty-three). In addition, naturalization applicants are required to make a declaration that expresses their belief in and loyalty to the liberal-democratic constitutional order of Germany. Family members (spouse and children under the age of sixteen) of foreign citizens who acquire German citizenship can naturalize at the same time regardless if they have fulfilled the eight-year requirement. According to the Administrative Guidelines approved by the Bundesrat in April 2000, spouses must have been lawfully resident in Germany for four years and be married to the naturalization applicant for at least two years; for minor children to be naturalized together with their parent(s), the residence requirement is three years if the child has reached the age of six (*Allgemeine Verwaltungsvorschrift zum Staatsangehörigkeitsrecht* [Administrative Guidelines], §85.2.1.2.1 and §85.2.1.2.2).[12]

The reform of the legal provisions concerning German citizenship by the SPD/Green government includes further changes with respect to foreign-born children of German citizens and foreign citizens recognized as *Spätaussiedler*. Children born abroad to a parent with German citizenship who has (after January 2000) also been born abroad may acquire German citizenship by descent, but only if they would otherwise become stateless or if the German parent registers the child as a German citizen within one year after the child's birth. Finally, ethnic Germans with foreign citizenship acquire German citizenship automatically upon their recognition as *Spätaussiedler*.

The new law, however, has done apparently little to encourage most immigrants in Germany to naturalize and become more active in the German polity. Naturalization rates increased to 2.6 percent in 2000 compared to 2.0 percent in 1999, primarily due to family reunification policies enacted in the new 1999 citizenship law, but they dropped in 2001 and 2002 (respectively, 2.4 and 2.1 percent) (Green 2004: 145). The naturalization rate among Turks shows a significant decrease from 1999 to 2002 (from 5.0 percent compared to 3.4 percent), despite the citizenship reform in 1999. Naturalization numbers in the Turkish community have in fact declined from 103,900 in 1999 to 32,661 in 2005 (Federal Statistics Office). The rejection of dual citizenship policies coupled with Turkey's objection to citizenship renunciation (despite the amendment of its nationality law in 1995 allowing dual citizenship), have contributed to low naturalization rates among this immigrant group. Kaya and Kentel also argue that the "expectations [of immigrant groups] diminished, and they did not see any further benefit in acquiring German citizenship" (Kaya and Kentel 2004: 12).

The politics of immigrant exclusion that were long practiced in Germany thus continues to have the detrimental effect of impeding self-identification

12. A complete list of the guidelines is found at the Interior Ministry's Web site, http://vwvbund. juris.de/bsvwvbund_13122000_V612400513.htm#ivz10.

Table 19.1. Naturalized Persons by Selected Former Citizenship, 1980–2005*

Year[1]	Greece	Italy	Yugo-slavia[2]	Croatia[3]	Poland	Former Soviet Union[4]	Spain	Turkey	Hungary	Bulgaria	Total
1980	376	1,010	3,475	—	3,303	4,138	217	399	1,868	—	37,003
1981	281	972	3,131	—	4,206	3,583	181	534	1,895	151	35,878
1982	235	1,084	3,201	—	7,807	3,243	211	580	1,669	241	39,280
1983	350	1,134	3,117	—	7,182	2,446	261	853	1,570	208	39,485
1984	264	946	3,334	—	5,988	1,704	323	1,053	1,432	161	38,046
1985	246	797	2,815	—	5,925	1,146	191	1,310	1,200	143	34,913
1986	173	597	2,721	—	7,251	945	171	1,492	1,105	108	36,646
1987	199	551	2,364	—	9,439	1,111	135	1,184	1,203	71	37,810
1988	191	618	2,119	—	13,958	4,810	155	1,243	1,157	92	46,783
1989	179	548	2,076	—	24,882	13,557	108	1,713	1,556	122	68,526
1990	158	437	2,082	—	32,340	33,339	103	2,034	1,532	212	101,377
1991	194	679	2,832	—	27,646	55,620	107	3,529	1,178	309	141,630
1992	285	1,947	1,947	269	20,248	84,660	168	7,377	1,425	283	179,904
1993	301	1,154	1,988	2,196	15,435	105,801	224	12,915	1,663	529	199,443
1994	341	1,417	4,374	3,695	11,943	164,296	185	19,590	1,902	783	251,600
1995	428	1,281	3,623	2,637	10,174	214,927	189	31,578	1,305	513	300,316
1996	493	1,297	2,967	2,391	7,872	194,849	152	46,294	1,027	332	302,830
1997	418	1,187	2,341	1,914	5,763	179,601	172	42,240	911	369	278,662
1998	427	1,156	2,881	2,373	5,151	170,381	141	59,664	652	389	291,331
1999	375	1,185	3,608	1,648	2,865	89,372	152	103,900	537	303	248,206
2000	1,413	1,036	9,776	3,316	1,604	11,358	190	82,861	561	614	186,688
2001	1,402	1,048	12,000	3,931	1,774	12,254	183	76,573	593	615	178,098
2002	1,105	847	8,375	2,974	2,646	11,523	137	64,631	516	649	154,547
2003	1,114	1,180	5,504	2,048	2,990	11,839	114	56,244	454	579	140,731
2004	1,507	1,656	3,539	1,689	7,499	—	100	44,465	465	404	127,153
2005	1,346	1,629	8,824	1,287	6,896	5,055	85	32,661	395	400	117,241

*Including Aussiedler until July 31,1999. [1]From 1980 to 1990 former West Germany; from 1991 in Deutschland. [2]From 1980 to 1991 Yugoslavia; from 1992 Serbien and Montenegro. [3]From 1992. [4]From 1980 until 1991 USSR; from 1992 including all successor states.

Source: © Statistisches Bundesamt, Wiesbaden 2005. Für nichtgewerbliche Zwecke sind Vervielfältigung und unentgeltliche Verbreitung, auch auszugsweise, mit Quellenangabe gestattet. Die Verbreitung, auch auszugsweise, über elektronische Systeme/Datenträger bedarf der vorherigen Zustimmung. Alle übrigen Rechte bleiben vorbehalten.

with the German political culture. In fact, in many ways, the lack of citizenship rights led to the development of a second class of permanent residents, for whom the absence of political representation and "agency" has also had negative repercussions on access to "rights such as welfare services, political suffrage, and protection from expulsion from the country," including equal access to economic opportunities (Wasmer and Koch 2003: 95). Substantial economic and social marginalization of immigrant communities from the fabric of German society, combined with an exclusionary approach to immigrant political integration, has also contributed to physical segregation. This segregation is reflected in patterns of community formation, political mobilization, and transnational political association networks, which will be discussed further in the penultimate chapter.

Chapter 20

Bilateral Agreements

With the Constitutional Court's broad, though ambiguous, approval of its new asylum policy, the FRG had to ensure that the government remained in control of their borders. Germany's government realized that the EU offered new opportunities to relieve the financial costs of doing so. As a result, the German government became a staunch supporter of increased cooperation within the EU to manage its borders. One reason for their activism for deeper cooperation was Germany's geographic position at the easternmost buffer zone between the EU and non-EU Central and Eastern European countries. Another, more important, reason relates to a compromise reached between Germany and the EU during the process of German reunification. In the agreement, the FRG pledged to increase control of the border between unified Germany and Poland and the Czech Republic, if the EU would forego accession requirements and ease the integration of the former GDR into the EU (Marshall 2000: 119–124).

Beginning with a conference of ministers convened in Berlin on 30 and 31 October 1991, the FRG initiated efforts to promote broader (East-West) European cooperation in controlling unchecked migration. For this conference, the German Federal Interior Minister had invited his counterparts from the other EU Member States and those from more than a dozen states in Central and Eastern Europe. The conclusions reached at this conference reflected a growing concern that European states were losing their ability to manage their own borders and the channels of entry into their countries. The group endorsed a set of initiatives for improving the coordination of policies designed to curb illegal immigration, such as the introduction of stiff new penalties for traffickers of clandestine migrants and tighter border controls.

The emergence of this group is indicative of the fear driving immigration policy in these years. It illustrates, one commentator has observed, that the "focus of attention [had] made a clear shift away from the question of human rights and international solidarity to an emphasis on prevention and control" (Lavenex 1999: 102). Building on this meeting, a larger Ministerial Conference on Uncontrolled Migration was held in Budapest on 15 and 16 February 1993 to develop further policy proposals for cooperation, with a particular focus on clandestine immigration. These proposals included greater coordination in the criminal prosecution of traffickers, sharing of information on clandestine immigration, and upgrading of border control mechanisms. One of the key subjects considered at the conference was readmission agreements (Reermann 1997: 124; Rotte 2000: 378–379; Lavenex 1999: 102–103).

During this same period, the FRG was promoting the use of new bilateral and multilateral approaches to issues of border and immigration controls in the intergovernmental discussions surrounding the drafting and ratification of the Maastricht Treaty. In a 1991 work program prepared at Germany's request and adopted by the Maastricht European Council, the "Ministers Responsible for Immigration"[1] endorsed using bilateral and multilateral agreements (Guild 1996: 467), an endorsement reiterated the following year at the European Council in Edinburgh (Niessen 1996: 46–47).

Meanwhile, the Dublin agreement addressed the problem of "asylum shopping" and the allocation of state responsibility for individual asylum applications, but did not answer the FRG's most pressing refugee concern, "namely, how to reduce the sheer volume of applications" (Piotrowicz 1998: 427). The FRG's incorporation of "safe third country" principles, under which asylum seekers must lodge a claim in the first safe country they get to, into its 1993 asylum reform was designed to meet this challenge, but the implementation of this principle required concluding readmission agreements with its eastern neighbors. Accordingly, both Poland and the Czech Republic were classified as not only "safe" countries of origin, but also safe third countries for foreign nationals fleeing persecution in other countries.[2]

The first readmission treaty had been concluded between Poland and the Schengen states on 29 March 1991. Under this treaty, Poland agreed to accept repatriation of its citizens who were deemed to have unlawfully entered or remained in any of the (then six) Schengen states. The duty of a state to admit its own nationals into its territory is now a settled principle of international law, but this treaty provided for expedited means for handling the readmission process consistent with Schengen procedures.

In 1992, Germany signed a similar agreement with Romania. The agreement, under which Romania agreed not to resist the return of rejected asylum seekers

1. This intergovernmental body of Justice and Interior Ministers from the Member States first met as the "Ministers Responsible for Immigration" in London 1986 (Papademetriou 1996: 25).
2. Asylum Procedure Law 26 June 1992, as amended by the Law of 30 June 1993. Paragraphs 21, 29a, 26.

(among which many were Roma and Sinti) in exchange for small amounts of financial assistance (DM 30 million for a five-year integration program for repatriation, job training and employment assistance, and housing), attracted much world attention (Neuman 1993: 514).

Since about 80 percent of asylum seekers in the early 1990s entered Germany through Poland and the Czech Republic, the Kohl government's priority was to reach an agreement with these two countries.[3] In return for promises of large amounts of financial and technical assistance, as well as support for eventual entry into the EU, the countries of Eastern Europe agreed to contain refugee flows to the extent possible.[4] Germany and Poland signed another agreement on 29 July 1994, which obligated the latter to accept third-country nationals who had entered the FRG via Poland but were subsequently denied residence in Germany.[5] Under the guidelines of the agreement, Germany committed to pay Poland the equivalent of $76.4 million (DM 120 million) in 1993 and 1994 to provide shelter for such immigrants and to improve surveillance of its borders with German technical equipment (Marshall 2000: 124). While no migrants admitted before the agreement were to be perfunctorily deported, the agreement allowed the Germans, as a general matter, to return unlimited numbers of rejected applicants within six months of their arrival from Poland (Devine 1993: 806).[6]

3. At the time, domestic critics questioned the fairness of such bilateral agreements. Many SPD critics of the new asylum law and a small group of FDP asylum supporters did not want to permit a wealthy Germany to "export" its asylum dilemma to its two eastern neighbors, especially since these countries had severe economic problems (*Der Spiegel* 1992b).

4. According to *Der Spiegel* (1994), the German government was using economic assistance and the promise of EU entry to keep the Eastern European countries "well-behaved" with respect to the containment of refugees. Between 1989 and 1993, Germany contributed $25 billion in aid to Central and Eastern European countries. More than half of the Eastern European trade with the EU is with Germany (Smyser 1994–1995: 146). Germany's bilateral official net aid disbursements to Poland alone were $219.4 million in 1991 and $849.6 million in 1992. Its disbursements to Czechoslovakia were $12 million in 1991 and $29.9 million in 1992 (OECD 1993). Although Germany continues to contribute to EU, World Bank, and IMF economic assistance programs, bilateral assistance to Poland was phased out in 2002 in preparation for EU accession. However, according to the German Foreign Ministry, "237 German enterprises invested USD 8 billion in Poland as of 30 June 2003. As of 30 June 2003, aggregate German direct investments in Poland amounted to USD 68.3 billion." See http://www.auswaertiges-amt.de/www/en/laenderinfos/laender/laender_ausgabe_html?type_id=14&land_id=136#2.

5. During these years, the number of persons arrested for entering the FRG illegally from Poland had risen from 200 in 1990 to 30,390 in 1992. Such data can be used only to guess at the much larger total number of persons who probably entered illegally from Poland during this period (Czapliński 1994: 641).

6. However, the agreement adds that in the event of exceptional circumstances resulting in sudden or massive influxes of immigrants into the territory of Poland, Germany will authorize entry for certain categories of such persons in order to prevent Poland from being placed under excessive strain.

Germany negotiated a similar agreement with the Czech Republic in 1994. Prior to that agreement, the Czech Republic only took back refugees who were caught in Germany within forty-eight hours after they left the Czech Republic (Buchsteiner and Klingst 1994). According to the agreement, Germany gave the Czech Republic DM 60 million (spread out over three years) to improve the border police's technical equipment, set up central data systems for the foreigners' police, and create an asylum department (Marshall 2000: 124). At the same time, the designation of Poland and the Czech Republic as "safe" countries of origin along with the efforts to externalize controls of refugees to these governments complemented the new short-term labor migration schemes (discussed in detail in part 4) that were incorporated into the 1992 reforms to the foreigners law and which relied to a great extent on labor migrants from these same countries (Martin 2004: 239–241).

The number of asylum applications by Poles had already dramatically declined from 26,092 in 1989 to 3,448 in 1991. In 1992, the number went below 100 (Larrabee 1993: 24). This decrease was partly the result of the increased freedom of travel for Poles, especially the decision by the FRG to drop visa requirements for Polish citizens (for travel not exceeding ninety days) as of April 1991, and democratization and economic growth within Poland. The drop of visa requirements fueled a new form of "commuter" migration, whereby many Poles traveled to Germany, engaged in temporary (and mostly illegal) work and then returned to Poland. Some literally "commuted" on a regular basis, engaging in black market trade (Larrabee 1993: 24). Border crossings between the two countries rose from 7.2 million in 1990 to about 60 million in 1994 (Lindemann and Bobinski 1995). The same phenomenon of circular illegal migration occurred with other countries set to join the EU, such as Romania, where visas had been also abolished (Heckmann 2004).

While asylum applications from the former Warsaw pact countries decreased substantially, these countries became important transit countries for illegal immigrants and asylum seekers from the former Soviet Union and Asia. However, these countries' accession to the EU in 2004 required them to comply with Dublin Convention regulations, which forced them to take back asylum seekers who had traveled through their territory and to develop modern border control regimes.

While flows of asylum seekers continued from the former Soviet Union, many of the flows shifted to Southern Europe and Northern Africa. Like Poland, countries such as Morocco served both as a source of asylum seekers and as a transit country through which those from sub-Saharan Africa passed in order to claim asylum in Europe. The success of the earlier bilateral agreements with Eastern European countries spurred Germany to seek similar agreements with Mediterranean countries, both on its own and through the EU.

Chapter 21

Temporary Labor Migration
Programs

While the FRG was restricting its asylum policies and fortifying the border, the government continued to rely on temporary labor migration programs to fill persistent labor gaps. After the halt to guestworker recruitment in 1973, the FRG renewed temporary labor programs during the early 1990s as a response to the increasing numbers of Eastern Europeans who were seeking short-term work in the FRG in such areas as construction, hotels and resorts, and agriculture (Hönekopp 1997: 168–169). Many German employers found these workers very appealing as a low cost and flexible labor source. By providing jobs, training, and income to be returned home, such programs could be held out as forms of developmental aid to Eastern European states and as steps toward integrating them into the wider EU economy (Hönekopp 1997: 176–177).

As part of the reforms to the foreigners law in 1990 and 1992, the German government created four exceptions to the 1973 foreign labor recruitment ban, which were implemented through bilateral labor treaties previously established with Eastern European countries. Subsequently, the government created two more programs enshrined in the new immigration law, which will be discussed later. For the original four programs, Germany signed bilateral treaties primarily with countries that have since joined the European Union. However, several countries, such as Albania, remain quite far from membership, and Russia, included in several programs, is perceived as not being a potential EU Member State. These programs are still used by workers from the new EU Member States, whose movement to Germany will be restricted until at least 2009.[1]

---

1. The current labor market restrictions are the result of transitional arrangements between the EU-15 and the European Commission. Under these agreements, access to EU-15 welfare

Each program prescribes strict limits on the work and residence periods permitted; sets quotas on the number of workers eligible on an annual basis; observes, where practical, prevailing wage standards; and requires that prospective employers first show that no qualified German or EU citizen is available for hire.

The project-tied work program is tailored to the construction industry. The program permits German companies to employ foreign firms as subcontractors to perform part of a contract. These firms then supply the employees to do the work on that part of the project. The *seasonal work program* allows German employers to hire foreign workers[2] for ninety-day periods in such areas as agriculture, food processing, and the hotel and restaurant trade. The *cross-border commuters program* permits Polish or Czech nationals within thirty miles to work in Germany on condition that they return home every day or spend no more than two days a week at the place of employment. Germany perceives this program as increasing "neighborly" relations and building up the border economy (Liebig 2003). In 2004, 4,822 Czech or Polish nationals were employed as cross-border workers. The *guestworker program* is treated as a vehicle for training and educational purposes and as a very limited form of developmental assistance. Based on bilateral agreements with the sending country, the program permits qualifying Eastern Europeans the opportunity to live and work in Germany for as long as eighteen months in order to better their language or occupational skills.[3] The workers, according to the German government, are expected to use their skills acquired in Germany to further their own employability at home and develop their respective economies. The guestworker program contained a yearly quota of 10,250 workers, but these quotas were never reached. As of 2003, no more than 6,000 workers entered Germany in any given year under this program (Liebig 2003).

Of these four short-term work vehicles, the project-tied work program and the seasonal work program have been by far the largest in terms of the number of participants. During most of the 1990s, the number of workers per year under the first ranged from 40,000 to 94,000, while those under the second fluctuated from 90,000 to 212,000 (Rotte 2000: 374–375; see also Hönekopp 1997: 169). In recent years, the numbers have continued to grow,

---

systems and labor markets for citizens of the new EU Member States can be regulated for a maximum of seven years.

2. For this program, Germany currently has treaty agreements with Poland, the Czech Republic, Bulgaria, the Slovak Republic, Bulgaria, Romania, Hungary, Croatia, and Slovenia.

3. For this program, Germany currently has treaties with Hungary, Poland, the Czech Republic, the Slovak Republic, Albania, Bulgaria, Latvia, Estonia, Romania, the Russian Federation, Lithuania, and Slovenia (Liebig 2003).

averaging over 300,000 per year between 2000 and 2005. An assessment of the success of these programs cannot be attempted here. Some economic studies assessing the impact of the selective importation of foreign workers in Germany during the early 1990s have found a positive effect on national income and advocated its continuation (Bauer and Zimmermann 1997: 269–306). Others have pointed to the beneficial investment effects of the significant income transfers that foreign workers have made to their home countries. Between 1991 and 1995, Elmar Hönekopp reports that "program workers transferred an estimated DM 6 billion to their countries of origin" (Hönekopp 1997: 175).

Table 21.1. Employment of Seasonal Labor, 1994–2005

1994	137,819
1995	176,590
1996	197,924
1997	205,866
1998	207,927
1999	230,347
2000	263,805
2001	286,940
2002	307,182
2003	318,549
2004	333,690
2005	329,789

Note: Seasonal labor includes show and carnival workers.
Source: © Statistisches Bundesamt, Wiesbaden, 2005.

The effects of these programs on reducing illegal immigration are less certain. The numbers of illegal migrants almost surely rose during the first half of the 1990s, but since then have leveled off (Heckmann 2004: 1107–1108; 2006: 204). In addition, illegal stays in Germany are much more difficult and people tend not to stay long term. Data by the border police, such as arrest statistics, from which inferences about illegal immigration may be drawn are problematic and make precise estimates difficult.[4]

Since 1994, the federal government has worked to correct problems with unauthorized employment by expanding labor importation control mechanisms, promoting coordination among responsible administrative agencies, increasing penalties against employers who violate the rules regulating the usage of foreign labor, and increasing efforts to enforce prohibitions against

4. The problems with using such data to estimate the total number of illegal migrants is discussed in Lederer and Nickel (2000) and Heckmann (2004).

Table 21.2. Inflows of Seasonal Workers in Selected OECD Countries, 1991–2004 (thousands)

	1991	1992	1993	1994	1995	1996	1997	1998	1999	2000	2001	2002	2003	2004
France	54.2	13.6	11.3	10.3	9.4	8.8	8.2	7.5	7.6	7.9	10.8	13.5	14.6	15.7
Germany	—	212.4	181.7	155.8	192.8	220.9	226	201.6	223.4	219	277.9	298.1	309.5	324
Italy	—	1.7	2.8	5.8	7.6	8.9	8.4	16.5	20.4	30.9	30.3	—	68	77
United Kingdom*	—	3.6	4.2	4.4	4.7	5.5	9.3	9.4	9.8	10.1	14.9	19.4	—	19.8
United States	—	16.4	16.3	13.2	11.4	9.6	—	27.3	32.4	33.3	27.7	31.5	29.9	31.8

*UK data only includes seasonal agricultural workers.
Source: Trends in International Migration: SOPEMI 2002, 2003, 2004, and 2006 editions.

Table 21.3. Stocks of Foreign and Foreign-Born Labor Force in Selected OECD Countries, 1991–2004 (thousands and percentages)

	1991	1992	1993	1994	1995	1996	1997	1998	1999	2000	2001	2002	2003	2004
Stocks of foreign labor force														
Austria	277.2	295.9	304.6	316.5	325.2	328.0	326.3	327.1	333.6	345.6	359.9	370.6	388.6	402.7
% of total labor force	8.7	9.1	9.3	9.7	9.9	10.0	9.9	9.9	10.0	10.5	11.0	10.9	11.8	11.9
France	1506.0	1517.8	1541.5	1593.9	1573.3	1604.7	1569.8	1586.7	1593.8	1577.6	1617.6	1623.8	1515.9	1537.6
% of total labor force	6.0	6.0	6.1	6.3	6.2	6.3	6.1	6.1	5.8	6.0	6.2	6.2	5.6	5.6
Germany	—	—	—	—	—	—	3575.0	—	3545.0	3546.0	3616.0	3634.0	3703.0	3701.0
% of total labor force	—	—	—	—	—	—	8.9	—	8.8	8.8	9.1	9.2	9.4	9.1
Italy	285.3	296.8	304.8	307.1	332.2	580.6	539.6	614.6	747.6	850.7	800.7	840.8	1479.4	—
% of total employment	1.3	1.4	1.5	1.5	1.7	2.6	2.4	2.7	3.6	3.6	3.8	3.8	6.0	—
Spain	171.0	139.4	117.4	121.8	139.0	166.5	178.7	197.1	199.8	454.6	607.1	831.7	982.4	1076.7
% of total labor force	1.1	0.9	0.8	0.8	0.9	1.0	1.1	1.2	1.2	2.7	3.4	4.5	5.2	6.3
United Kingdom	828.0	902.0	862.0	864.0	862.0	865.0	949.0	1039.0	1005.0	1107.0	1229.0	1251.0	1322.0	1445.0
% of total employment	3.0	3.6	3.4	3.4	3.4	3.3	3.6	3.9	3.7	4.0	4.4	4.6	4.8	5.2
Stocks of foreign-born labor force														
Canada	2681.0	—	—	—	—	2839.1	—	—	—	—	3150.8	—	—	—
% of total labor force	18.5	—	—	—	—	19.2	—	—	—	—	19.9	—	—	—
United States	—	—	—	12900	13492	15314	16712	17373	17068	18055	19020	20964	21564	21985
% of total labor force	—	—	—	9.8	10.3	11.6	12.3	12.7	12.3	12.9	13.4	14.6	14.8	15.1

Note: Data include the unemployed in the United Kingdom. Cross-border workers and seasonal workers are excluded.
Source: Trends in International Migration: SOPEMI 2002, 2003, 2004, and 2006 editions.

the use of illegal foreign labor.[5] In its most recent effort to combat illegal economic migration, the federal government has made the Federal Ministry for Finance, instead of the Ministry for Employment, responsible for illegal work, while the work of customs officials and workplace inspectors have become integrated (Sinn, Kreienbrink, and Loeffelholz 2006). Currently, the law allows a penalty, in normal cases, of up to three years in jail or a fine of €500,000 for employing unauthorized foreign labor. In extreme cases, a six-month to five-year prison sentence is mandated.

Nonetheless, critics have argued that greater governmental efforts to monitor the unauthorized employment of foreign labor have been matched, if not exceeded, by the innovations of private employers to conceal their usage of such workers. The high cost of German labor and difficulties in recruiting German workers in industries such as construction and *Altersfürsorge* (elderly care) have created incentives for employers to evade governmental regulations (Federal Council for Immigration and Integration 2004). Additionally, the savings accrued to the employer from using low cost foreign labor often more than offset the potential costs of any penalties imposed for violations of the law (Rudolph 1998).

While the contractual worker programs proved useful during the 1990s, after the accession of most Central and Eastern European countries to the EU in 2004, they became less important as a tool for border control and economic development. Furthermore, as the pressures on the FRG to maintain its commitment to controlling westward migration became increasingly burdensome, the German government began emphasizing the need for a harmonized approach to controlling Europe's perimeter.

---

5. See, for example, the new 1995 law against the employment of illegal workers. "Gesetz zur Bekämpfung der Schwarzarbeit," *Bundesgesetzblatt* 1995 Teil I. Art 166, and "Gesetz zur Bekämpfung der Schwarzarbeit und illegalen Beschäftigung," *Bundesgesetzblatt* I 2004, 1842.

Chapter 22

The Amsterdam Treaty and the Emergent EU Migration Policy

Differences among Member States over the pace and scale of integration continue to divide the European Union. Following the accession of three new Member States in 1995,[1] the prospect of further enlargement magnified the stakes involved over these differences.[2] The Maastricht Treaty had provided for an intergovernmental conference to be convened in 1996.[3] This conference provided the occasion for reviewing the foundational treaties of the EU.[4] From this reform effort, the heads of the fifteen EU Member States signed the Amsterdam Treaty on 2 October 1997. After relatively rapid ratification by national parliaments, the Treaty came into force on 1 May 1999. In contrast to the Maastricht Treaty, the Amsterdam Treaty was designed to revise existing structures and practices rather than to introduce bold new changes (Nugent 1999: 80–82). Among its more symbolic reforms, the Amsterdam Treaty reinforced the fundamental normative guidelines governing the EU by incorporating an explicit statement of commitment to the principles of liberty, democracy, the rule of law, and the respect for basic rights. Member States found in violation of these principles may temporarily forfeit their voting rights.[5] The treaty also strengthened the legal basis for combating discrimination. Article 13 of the

1. Austria, Finland, and Sweden became members on 1 January 1995.
2. Estonia, Cyprus, the Czech Republic, Hungary, Latvia, Malta, Lithuania, Poland, Slovenia, and the Slovak Republic joined on 1 May 2004. Bulgaria and Romania were admitted in 2007.
3. Treaty on European Union, Article N (Rudden and Wyatt 1993: 225). (This volume contains both the EC Treaty and the TEU Treaty as amended through 1993.)
4. Its opening summit was held in Turin on 24 March 1996. On the course leading to the Amsterdam Treaty, see Dinan (1999: 159–184).
5. Treaty on European Union, Article 7 (ex. Article F) (Rudden and Wyatt 1993: 224–226).

treaty empowers the Council to implement "appropriate" measures to deter discrimination on the grounds of gender, race, ethnic origin, religion, age, sexual preference, and disability.[6] Although this provision applies to both EU and non-EU citizens, it does not include nationality among its grounds.[7] At the same time, the treaty also clarified the supplementary character of EU citizenship by inserting the following: "Citizenship of the Union shall complement and not replace national citizenship." As Martiniello pointed out, this clarification "closes the door for now to the conferral of EU citizenship to third-country nationals residing on the territory of the EU" (Martiniello 2000: 349). National citizenship would thus remain the only basis for acquiring EU citizenship for the foreseeable future.

The Amsterdam Treaty's most significant reform for the purpose of this discussion, however, is the shifting of many matters dealing with immigration, asylum, border controls, and the rights of third-country nationals from the intergovernmental third pillar to the supranational first pillar under a new Title IV of the EC Treaty.[8] The expressed objective of Title IV is "to establish progressively an area of freedom, security and justice" anchored within the first pillar. This shift was intended to allow for policy development relating to immigration control and asylum. With respect to immigration, the treaty encouraged new policy measures concerning conditions of entry and residence as well as setting standards on procedures for the issue of long-term visas and residence permits by Member States. Other measures are to be directed against illegal immigration, including the repatriation of illegal residents.[9] With respect to asylum, any new policy measures were to be consistent with the 1951 and 1967 Geneva Convention, as well as other relevant treaties, and involved the prescription both of minimum standards for handling asylum cases and of criteria for assigning Member State responsibility for these cases.[10] These changes reflect the fact that Member States had generally agreed on extending the harmonization of the EU's border control and asylum policies (Juss 2005).

6. Treaty establishing the European [Economic] Community as Amended by Subsequent Treaties (EC), Article 13 (ex Article 6a) (Rudden and Wyatt 1993).
7. Some basis for legal and political action against discrimination on this ground is provided under a provision introduced at Maastricht, in EC Article 17 (ex Article 8) (Rudden and Wyatt 1993).
8. The treaty leaves matters involving police and judicial cooperation under the third pillar. As set forth under title VI, these matters include combating racism, xenophobia, and trafficking in persons.
9. This discussion summarizes leading provisions under Article 63. This article also addresses measures concerning refugees and displaced persons as well as the rights and conditions governing the settlement of third-country nationals, other than those who are lawful residents, in Member States. Article 62 authorizes the Council to adopt measures with respect to border controls and visas during this same period.
10. The establishment of criteria and mechanisms for this purpose are exempted from the five year requirement.

Table 22.1. EU Pillar Structures Regarding Immigration, Visa, and Border Control Policies after the Amsterdam Treaty

	Treaty on European Union (TEU, or Maastricht Treaty) (1992)*	Treaty of Amsterdam (1997)**
First Pillar [European Community] Decisions made at supranational level by qualified majority voting		*Title IV of TEU: Visas, Asylum, Immigration and Other Policies Related to Free Movement of Persons* • Free movement of persons across internal borders • External border controls • Asylum • Immigration • Safeguarding the rights of third-country nationals • Judicial cooperation in civil matters
Second Pillar [Common Foreign and Security Policy] Decisions made at intergovernmental level by unanimity		
Third Pillar [Justice and Home Affairs] Decisions made at intergovernmental level by unanimity	*Title VI of TEU: Provisions on Cooperation in the Fields of* *Justice and Home Affairs* • Asylum policy • Rules on external border controls of Member States • Immigration policy and policy regarding third-country nationals (a) Conditions of entry and movement of third-country nationals in Member States (b) Conditions of residence for third-country nationals, including family reunion and access to employment (c) Combating unauthorized immigration residence and work by third-country nationals in Member States • Combating drug addiction • Combating fraud on an international scale • Judicial cooperation in civil matters • Judicial cooperation in criminal matters • Customs cooperation • Police cooperation to prevent and combat terrorism, unlawful drug trafficking, and other serious forms of international crime	*Title VI of TEU: Provisions on Cooperation in the Fields of* *Justice and Home Affairs* • Police and judicial cooperation

*Treaty on European Union (TEU, or Maastricht Treaty) is available at http://eur-lex.europa.eu/en/ treaties/dat/11992M/htm/11992M.html#0001000001.

**Treaty of Amsterdam is available at http://eur-lex.europa.eu/en/treaties/dat/11997D/htm/11997D. html#0001010001.

The Treaty of Amsterdam may have marked a more general turning point in the EU's approach to matters of immigration and asylum as well (Geddes 2007: 54–55). Instead of developing policies on EC migrant workers' rights and protections and consolidating the single market as it did throughout the 1970s and 1980s (e.g., Mancini 1992), the EU increasingly turned its attention to its external borders. The emergent European migration policy would be based on the economic benefits of controlled immigration and increasing cooperation along the external border, what some have described as building a 'Fortress Europe' (Favell and Hansen 2002: 582).[11] Part of this shift also reflected a growing interest on the part of many Member State politicians in more high-skilled labor migration and tighter controls on 'unwanted' migrants, including asylum seekers (Geddes 2007: 53, 56–57). This became especially evident under Commission Vice President and the Justice, Freedom, and Security Commissioner Franco Frattini, who served in these capacities from late 2004 until mid 2008. The tilt toward this more pragmatic approach, however, had already become evident during the later years of his predecessor, Antonio Vitorino. In this regard, the Treaty of Amsterdam reflected increasing synergy between the EU and the Member States in an emergent European migration policy based upon the economic benefits of managed immigration.

Shifting migration policy from the third to the first pillar and encouraging deeper harmonization required a compromise in which Germany figured prominently. As a long-time advocate of deeper integration, Germany helped lay down many of the seeds of a Europeanized migration policy (Prümm and Alscher 2007: 73). But during the negotiations of the Treaty of Amsterdam, a new German demeanor toward the EU emerged (Marshall 2000: 118–137). To protect its veto power in the Commission, Germany insisted that matters of migration policy be determined by unanimity instead of qualified majority voting (QMV), as required by decision-making rules for policy areas in the first pillar. Since QMV would encourage deeper policy harmonization, Germany's position marked a reversal of its traditional pro-integrationist stance (Marshall 2000: 128; Prümm and Alscher 2007: 73–74). To reach consensus in the treaty negotiations, a five-year transitional period from unanimity to QMV was introduced.

At the same time, the treaty's reach into the area of asylum and immigration controls remained limited due in large part to Germany's developing reluctance to continue supporting a comprehensive European immigration policy leading up to and following Amsterdam. This reluctance emerged for two reasons. First, after a long battle with the Member States during the early and mid 1990s over sharing the burden of asylum seekers and streamlining the

11. In their article, Favell and Hansen are questioning, not supporting, the idea of a 'Fortress Europe.'

asylum application process, Germany became wary about further harmonization and feared adverse domestic policy effects. Kathrin Prümm and Stefan Alscher (2007), for instance, have argued that Europe's evolving policy on asylum since Amsterdam threatened to loosen Germany's comparatively strict policy established with the 1993 "asylum compromise." One way to safeguard its policy was to insist on the extension of unanimity voting, which would preserve Germany's veto power. As a second point, Prümm and Alscher have also noted that the increasing power of the *Länder* to weigh in on decisions taken at the European level weakened Germany's pro-integration demeanor during and after the negotiations of the Treaty of Amsterdam (2007: 73–74). As a result, by 1997 the FRG had shifted its focus and support away from deeper harmonization and instead pursued an agenda to extend intergovernmental cooperation (Marshall 2000: 128; Lavenex 2006: 331).

Germany's shifting of support away from deeper harmonization did not preclude the possibility of closer cooperation at the European level after Amsterdam. The EU's 'pillarized' institutional structure insured that even though some states, like Germany, tried to "keep the EU out of the immigration policy area" (Favell and Hansen 2002: 595), the EU would be able to realize some level of success in developing a harmonized migration policy. After the Amsterdam Treaty took effect, the European Council held a special meeting on 15 and 16 October 1999 in Tampere, Finland, to focus on the creation of an area of freedom, security, and justice, as envisioned under the treaty.

Migration policy was central to the meeting's agenda. As reported in the meeting's official Presidency Conclusions, the Council reaffirmed the goal of developing a common policy toward immigration and asylum, and, in particular, of establishing a "Common European Asylum System" consistent with the Geneva Convention. The Tampere meeting also represents a turning point in that the Council recognized the need to promote a "more vigorous integration policy" for all immigrants and that the rights of lawfully settled, third-country nationals should be made as equivalent as possible with the rights of Member State nationals. The Council further endorsed the "objective that long-term legally resident third-country nationals be offered the opportunity to obtain the nationality of the Member State in which they are resident" (European Council 1999b: §21). The Council noted that the "challenge of the Amsterdam Treaty" is to ensure "that freedom, which includes the right to move freely throughout the Union, can be enjoyed in the conditions of security and justice accessible to all" (European Council 1999b: §2). Strikingly, the application of "all" was pointedly not limited to EU citizens, but included in principle all lawful residents. As the Council explained, "this freedom should not … be regarded as the exclusive preserve of the Union's own citizens. Its very existence acts as a draw to many others world-wide who cannot enjoy the freedom that Union citizens take for granted" (European Council 1999b: §3).

Despite this more positive, proactive approach to immigration, a central focus of the Presidency's Conclusions remained preventing unwanted migration through curbing abuse of asylum procedures, stopping criminal networks, strengthening border controls, and using development aid to lessen incentives to migrate. Although this focus was consistent with the objectives set forth in the Amsterdam Treaty,[12] its defensive posture only reinforced negative public perceptions of migration as a threat to security, as a source of criminality, and as an administrative burden (Guild 2003: 94). Nowhere did the Presidency Conclusions speak of the positive contributions immigrants have made in their host societies or of the important role immigration may play in societies with low birth rates and aging populations. Nowhere did they suggest how the consideration of economic and demographic factors arguing for more immigration might inform the development of a common migration policy for EU Member States.[13] The European Council also called "for the fight against racism and xenophobia to be stepped up" (1999b, §19), but nowhere did it address the need for Member States to educate their citizenry about the benefits of immigration.

Managing Borders

In consolidating the legal and political basis for harmonizing the migration policies of Member States and increasing cooperation on controlling the EU's external border, the Treaty of Amsterdam incorporated the Schengen *acquis* into the EU institutional framework.[14] The Schengen *acquis* encompasses rules

12. NGO critics of post-Amsterdam EU migration policy have called attention to the one-sided nature of this focus. In their joint assessment of this policy, the European Council on Refugees and Exiles (ECRE), the European Network Against Racism (ENAR), and the Migration Policy Group (MPG) have written the following: "That the European Union seeks to manage migration is entirely justified. The establishment of a more effective migration and refugee regime is in the interest of receiving and sending countries as well as the migrants and refugees themselves. However, the European Union has narrowed considerably the meaning and scope of 'management.' It has come to mean restricting immigration and most of the measures taken aim only to limit the number of immigrants and refugees, facilitate the return of rejected asylum-seekers and undocumented or irregular migrants, strengthen control mechanisms, and assist neighboring States with putting similar controls in place" (ECRE, ENAR, and MPG 1999: 3).

13. At best, the Presidency Conclusions hint in this direction with respect to harmonizing Member State policies, declaring, "The European Council acknowledges the need for approximation of national legislations on the conditions for admission and residence of third-country nationals, based on a shared assessment of the economic and demographic developments within the Union, as well as the situation in the countries of origin" (European Council 1999b: §20).

14. The *acquis* has four main components: the Schengen Agreement of 14 June 1985 between France, Germany, and the Benelux countries; the Convention of 19 June 1990 that implemented

to regulate (among others) the crossing of external borders, the designation of the state responsible for processing asylum claims, the coordination of visa policies, and the transborder movement of third-country nationals. With the exception of the United Kingdom and Denmark, all of the EU-15 Member States formally acceded to the Schengen Convention by 1997. The 2004 accession Member States were required to meet all Schengen criteria by 2007, a goal that was met with sufficient time for controls to be lifted on 21 December 2007 for land and sea borders and on 31 March 2008 for air borders.[15]

With the Schengen *acquis*, the Member States have shifted border control away from the internal EU borders to a "common external frontier" (Guild 2003: 91). Using a mixture of levers that include developmental aid, technical assistance, and possible accession as incentives, the EU has sought to use states along its external border to deter migration from the East (Hailbronner 2000b: 173–174). "For central and eastern European countries," one observer has recently concluded, "this has meant a change in status from being countries of transit for international migrants to being countries of destination" (Grabbe 2000: 527). The FRG was the key party behind the Schengen process, but, as discussed above, this process was only one of a variety of bilateral and multilateral approaches to migration control and border management issues that Germany pursued during the 1990s. The combination of bilateral and multilateral migration control schemes reflected the recognition that replacing the old East-West divide in Cold War Europe with an increasingly fortified EU perimeter was tainted by historical divisions and that any effective system of migration controls required a multifaceted, regionally coordinated effort.

Implementing Schengen across all Member States would prove to be a complex task that demanded more cooperation and coordination between national governments and the European Union's institutions. For the Member States, this form of cooperation meant that they would have to gradually cede part of their sovereignty over border controls to the European Union (Monar 2006; Lavenex 2006). At the 2001 Laeken Council, Member States signaled willingness to move forward with a more comprehensive approach to managing Europe's expanding external borders. Italy and Germany became important players in stepping up efforts to devise a plan for a European Border Patrol (EBP). In order to create the EBP, the two countries drafted a feasibility report in 2001, which presented Europe's leaders with two border management

---

the agreement and was signed by the five states named above in addition to Luxembourg and the Netherlands; the Accession Protocols to the 1985 Agreement; and the Implementation Convention signed with Austria, Denmark, Finland, Greece, Italy, Portugal, Spain, and Sweden.

15. Switzerland and Lichtenstein are slated to join Schengen in 2008 (see Gelatt 2005), while Cyprus remains outside of the system due to the unresolved issues about the island nation's divided status.

options. The first proposal, known in some quarters as the 'integrated-force model,'[16] aimed to establish a fully integrated EBP that would take over all responsibility for air, land, and sea borders from the national governments. Building EBP would require Member States to cede all sovereignty over their borders to the EU, which was a highly implausible proposal (Monar 2006: 178). Nevertheless, Germany and Italy supported an integrated border management system because they found this to be the most efficient system over the long run. However, the proposal would find little support from the Member State governments.

The feasibility report presented a second option for Member States to consider. Instead of a fully integrated border system, Member States could rely on the existing national border guard agencies and the European Union's institutions to pool national resources into a cooperative European border agency. This model, dubbed the 'network model,'[17] would not require the Member States to surrender any control over their national borders. Instead, they would continue to patrol their own land, air, and sea borders, but they could also rely on the competencies and resources of the other Member States' agencies to enhance security at their borders when necessary. Member States might have been expected to find this model more appealing since it would increase their border management resources without challenging national borderlands (Monar 2006: 179). The obstacles to devising a network model would be numerous, however. Since a single EU agency would not exist, the persistence of the national agencies' cultures, management structures, and political constraints would make achieving standardization across Europe costly, timely, and nearly impossible (Monar 2006: 179). In fact, under the network model, many of the same obstacles to effectively implementing the Schengen standards that existed in the mid 1990s would continue to plague any effort to create a standardized European border management system.

After the institutionalization of Schengen with the Treaty of Amsterdam, and against mounting pressure to control migration flows along the Eastern-land and Southern-maritime borders, Member States agreed to advance plans for a European border agency. While Member States continued to reject a fully integrated agency, the impetus for high-level cooperation through an EU institution gave way to a new border control agency in 2005. This agency assumed the title of the European Agency for the Management of Operational Control at the External Borders of the Member States of the European Union, also known as Frontex.

16. Jörg Monar named this first option the 'integrated-force model' and provides a detailed description of what the model entails and the barriers to implementing this model in the EU (2006: 177–179).
17. This is Jörg Monar's term to describe this model (2006: 177–179).

224 | Immigration Policy in the Federal Republic of Germany

Frontex began operations in May 2005 from its headquarters in Warsaw, Poland. The agency's primary mandate is to coordinate the flow of information between Member States, data analysis, and plans of action at the border.[18] Frontex would be best known for its Rapid Border Intervention Teams (RABITs).[19] For instance, at the 2006 World Cup in Germany, Frontex launched Operation FIFA2006. Under this action plan, Frontex enlisted the human and technological resources of a number of Member States in order to assist in data gathering and analysis at Germany's overwhelmed land and air borders. Similarly, Frontex was enlisted to assist Spain patrol the waters between the Canary Islands and the coast of Africa in order to reduce the flows of immigrants seeking to reach the Spanish islands. In 2007, Frontex would reprise that role, while adding the Mediterranean to its repertory.

Executing these projects requires a number of other institutional mechanisms, however. The National Frontex Points of Contact (NFPoCs), which exist in every Member State, provide a pathway through which information can be shared between Frontex and the Member States. The Frontex Joint Support Team (FJST) is comprised of Frontex-dedicated personnel from each national border guard. The team aims to increase the cooperative environment by working through their national agencies to provide Frontex with the necessary information, equipment, technology, and other resources that allow it to operate. These avenues of supranational cooperation would secure Frontex's mandate to control Europe's borders.

While Schengen and Frontex represent major steps toward the abolition of internal border controls and restrictions on the movement of EU citizens, the movement of lawfully settled third-country nationals remains subject to restriction. As Elspeth Guild has explained, "third-country nationals who are resident and participating in the labour market are ... entitled to move [for a three month period], but not to exercise economic activities in another Member State" (Guild 1999: 73). Guild's observation points to the persisting inequity between European nationals and non-European nationals within the legal frameworks of Europe's area of "freedom, security and justice." This should not be surprising, however, since European citizenship rests on citizenship at the Member State level, where naturalization regulations have yet to be harmonized and often times are restrictive. In this regard, the period following the Treaty of Amsterdam has been one of fits and starts in the building of a coherent European migration policy.

---

18. See Council Regulation (EC) 2007/2004, 26 October 2004.

19. For instance, Ilkka Laitinen drafted a report about the myths and facts of Frontex, in which she discusses the role of RABITs in Frontex. The report is found on Frontex's Web site: http://www.frontex.europa.eu/newsroom/news_releases/art26.html.

A more clearly demarcated European border has helped to define where the EU begins and ends and who does and does not belong inside it, but Member States have clung to immigration policies crafted according to their own perceived political, economic, and social interests. Germany has struggled, for instance, to overcome the historical legacy of importing labor while not recognizing itself as a country of immigration. As a result, Germany today faces the increasingly urgent and complicated task of reforming its policies vis-à-vis immigrants, particularly those relating to the integration of these immigrants and their progeny. The reform process, however, has been a balancing act for policymakers, who must be careful to address the needs of immigrants and to realize the economic and social benefits of controlled immigration while not isolating or ignoring their constituents' concerns. In light of these challenges, in the chapters that follow we will turn to a more detailed discussion about Germany's latest efforts to reform its immigration and integration policies.

Part 4

Germany Faces the Future
New Initiatives, Old Habits

During the next quarter century, the German economy will have to rely on immigrants even more than it has had to at any time since the 1960s. Unless Germany learns to adjust to the country's large and growing ethnic diversity, it can expect to continue facing problems of social and cultural integration (and particularly ones involving religious integration) and, under certain scenarios, adverse economic consequences. Making these adjustments, however, has proven to be a difficult task if we consider the political discourse surrounding many of the government's recent efforts to rethink its immigration and integration policies. In his study of German political debates over citizenship and immigration reform from 1998 to 2002, Matthias Hell has observed, for example, that "the definition of integration, which is frequently connected to questions of immigration, takes little inspiration from the possibility of [immigrants'] participation in the structuring of society, and instead prefers to demand immigrants' willingness to assimilate into German culture" (2005: 87). From this observation, Hell explains that the economic imperative to restructure immigration controls in favor of skilled labor has not trumped the currency of conservative and often anti-immigrant politics, which are based on a narrative of protecting a homogeneous German culture. This part opens by examining the continuing conflicts between culturally focused approaches and more pragmatic approaches attentive to economic as well as demographic needs. The latter has increasingly come to dominate in public discourse. This change suggests a "paradigm shift at the discursive level away from the closed, ethnic conception of German nationhood toward an identity that emphasizes economic achievement and welfare to which immigration can contribute" (Bauder 2008: 109). Nevertheless, as the chapters on the 2005 Migration Law will demonstrate, the extent to which this still emerging shift has fundamentally changed policy making remains open to question.

Chapter 23

Green Cards and *Leitkultur*

By 2000, the ominous demographic trends and their consequences were well known in Germany, but the politics of immigration seldom turn on findings of social science research. Germany's struggle to develop a new and more positive approach to immigration was reflected in the 2000 controversy over the so-called "Green Card" initiative. After the adoption of the 1999 Citizenship Law reform, the issue of immigration receded again from the forefront of public discourse in the Federal Republic of Germany (FRG). It reemerged again, however, in the debate over the introduction of a "Green Card" program. Using the start of the CeBIT information and electronics show on 23 February 2000 as the occasion, the industry's association, *Bundesverband Informationswirtschaft, Telekommunikation und neue Medien e.V* (BITKOM), called publicly on the German government to permit the recruitment of 30,000 foreign professionals to help fill an estimated 75,000 vacant positions for computer programmers, technicians, and engineers. BITKOM argued that this action was necessary because of the shortage of domestic workers qualified to perform these jobs. After BITKOM issued this call, other German industry associations, notably in the biotech and health fields, asked the government for similar help (*Migration News* 2000a).

In response, Chancellor Gerhard Schröder proposed on 13 March 2000 a plan to provide for the expedited issuance of as many as 20,000 temporary work permits valid for five years. To address the concerns of domestic workers over job competition with foreigners, he announced that the government would spend an additional DM 200 million on domestic training and retraining programs. This amount raised the total government expenditure in this endeavor annually to DM 1.2 billion. At the same time, the Chancellor reported that by 2003, German industrial groups were pledging to double the number of apprenticeships available for young Germans joining the workforce. Despite these provisions, German labor leaders were not mollified. Both Dieter Schulte, the chairman of the *Deutscher Gewerkschaftsbund* (German Federation of Labor, or DGB), and Federal Labor Minister Walter Riester (SPD), criticized opening the domestic labor market to more international competition during a period of high unemployment. They also questioned the resolve of past efforts to find German workers to fill the jobs. The German public also expressed wariness toward the proposal. According to a March opinion poll, 56 percent of Germans opposed it, while only 37 percent supported it (*Migration News* 2000a).

Seeing an opportunity to drive a wedge between the Social Democrats (SPD) and its traditional core constituencies, Jürgen Rüttgers, the Christian Democrat (CDU) candidate for premier during the 2000 state elections of North Rhine-Westphalia, made the Green Card issue a focal point of his campaign in this customary SPD stronghold. Since India had established a worldwide reputation for producing computer specialists available for the global market, he used as one of his early campaign slogans the phrase, *Kinder statt Inder* (Children instead of Indians). The phrase pitched in crude anti-foreigner sentiment the argument that Germany should put the long-term interests of its youth before the short-term advantages of its employers. In the face of criticism for the phrase's explicit anti-foreigner appeal, Rüttgers subsequently adopted the more neutral slogan, *Mehr Ausbildung statt mehr Einwanderung* (More training instead of immigration). The appeal failed to sway enough minds, as the CDU received only 37 percent of the vote in the May 14 elections (*Migration News* 2000b).

Meanwhile, plans for the German Green Card program moved ahead. On May 31, Schröder's Cabinet approved new regulations to facilitate the recruitment of the foreign computer specialists. These Green Cards allowed workers to work for five years with the ability of one extension for up to another five years. On 1 August 2000, the Green Card Law went into effect for a period of three years; it was further extended in 2003 through 31 December 2004. Overall, the program was considered a failure. In the five years of its existence, a mere 17,831 people came to the country through the program (BMI 2006a: 23). Many of the restrictions placed on the German Green Card program frustrated both employees and employers. For example, workers' partners were not allowed to work for the first two years of the five-year period, while employees had to pay a minimum annual wage of €51,000 if the candidate did not have a degree in a specific IT field (Bauer, Larsen, and Matthiessen 2004). Most important, though, was the duration of the Green Card. In an interview with the Confederation of German Workers, Dr. Reiner Klingholz, Director of the Berlin Institute for Population and Development, claimed that IT workers see themselves as having no future in Germany and would rather immigrate to a country where they can have a long-term future.[1] Nevertheless, as will be seen below, the new immigration law made high tech workers a permanent exception to the labor recruitment ban and made it a fifth category of temporary labor recruitment.

The opposition parties, the CDU/CSU and the Free Democrats (FDP), criticized the ad hoc character of the plan, noting that it had not been considered within a broader immigration policy framework, a remarkable recognition by them that Germany must have something called an *immigration* policy. As Angela Merkel, the CDU's Secretary-General at the time and now chancellor, observed, "a society that is growing older naturally needs immigration, an orderly immigration." The FDP went a step farther by reintroducing a proposal for a general immigration law with quotas set according to unemployment rates and integrative capacity (*Migration News* 2000b).

Although the proposal failed to draw support from the leadership of the other parties, it put more pressure on the government to address directly the immigration question. On June 25, Federal Interior Minister Otto Schily announced plans to create a national commission on immigration to conduct a comprehensive review of Germany's policy and to put forward recommendations. In an attempt to build broad bipartisan consensus, Schily appointed former Bundestag President Rita Süssmuth (CDU) to serve as the commission's chair. Among other commission members, he also appointed Hans-Jochen Vogel, a former national SPD leader, and Cornelia Schmalz-Jacobsen (FDP), the former commissioner for foreigners under Helmut Kohl's government (*Süddeutsche Zeitung* 2000a). The SPD and Green parliamentary caucuses announced that they would defer action on immigration until after they reviewed the commission's findings. The commission published its report in July 2001.

As German officials began rethinking immigration and integration policy, the main opposition party, the CDU, aroused controversy by putting forward the notion of a *Leitkultur* (guiding culture)[2] as the basis for the integration of immigrants. According to its position statement released on 6 November 2000,[3] the elements comprising this notion involved learning the German language, professing loyalty to the German nation, and accepting Germany's legal and political institutions.[4] Had the statement focused only on these elements, and not used the term *Leitkultur*, the CDU's announcement might not

---

1. For a transcript of the interview, see http://www.arbeitgeber.de/www/bdaonline.nsf/id/ArbHef8-2_DE/$file/Arbeitgeber_Heft_08-04.pdf (accessed 16 April 2009).

2. The term, *Leit*, translated here as "guiding" has also been translated as "defining."

3. "Arbeitsgrundlage für die Zuwanderungs-Kommission der CDU Deutschlands" (Berlin, 6 November 2000).

4. The concept of a "guided culture" was similarly endorsed in the *Thesen zur Zuwanderungspolitik* by the Bavarian Interior Minister, Dr. Günther Beckstein (13 November 2000).

have garnered much public attention. Some observers argued that the CDU adopted this nationalistic stance toward immigrants out of partisan, tactical considerations. Fearful that the national commission, created by the SPD/Green coalition, but headed by a senior member of the CDU, would defuse immigration as an effective campaign issue,[5] the CDU leadership established its own party's commission to develop and promote its own distinct approach.[6] The adoption of the *Leitkultur* idea certainly offered the party at least a symbolic means to highlight the distinctiveness of its approach and, perhaps, to prevent the defection of supporters on the far right. However, the concept immediately became the target of considerable criticism from representatives of Jewish and Islamic groups inside Germany, and from the SPD/Green spokespersons (Cohen 2000a; 2000b).

The CDU's position statement set forth the cultural issues raised by immigration at the forefront of its concerns. The statement thus began with the declaration that "an immigration policy and integration policy can only succeed if we are certain of our national and cultural identity … We Germans have developed our national identity and culture on the foundation of European civilization in the course of history, which finds expression in our language and in arts, in our morals and customs, and in our understanding of law and democracy, of freedom and civic duty." At first glance, the most striking feature of this formulation of a collective identity is its amorphousness. It did not specify a particular constellation of beliefs and values that constitute this identity, much less offer any rationale for a criterion to select and prioritize among different cultural elements. Rather, it reflected the traditional Romantic understanding of the "inner unity," which gives every nation its own distinctive character as expressed most visibly in a people's language, arts, and customs (Greenfield 1992: 364, 367–369). This holistic vision neatly obscured the deep divisions in religious loyalties, regional orientation, political ideology, and class (among others) that have marked both German and European history for centuries.

Instead of addressing what this legacy of division and conflict may mean for understanding a common culture or for accommodating pluralist differences, the CDU's statement pointed to the more immediate event of German reunification to highlight "the commonality of our cultural and historical inheritance" (*Zuwanderungs-Kommission der CDU Deutschlands,* 2000). This inheritance demonstrates that "our common will to freedom and unity are an expression of national identity and the foundation for the growing together

---

5. CDU leaders opposed Rita Süssmuth's appointment to chair the commission, and her authority to speak on behalf of the joint (CDU/CSU) parliamentary committee was rescinded when she accepted the assignment (*Süddeutsche Zeitung* 2000b; Schlötzer 2000).

6. Sharpening the party's stance on immigration may also have reflected a struggle for influence inside the CDU. Friedrich Merz, who led the CDU/CSU parliamentary group, first came out advocating for a more aggressive position on this issue under the *Leitkultur* banner, over the initial reservations of CDU chairperson, Angela Merkel (*Süddeutsche Zeitung* 2000b).

of persons in our reunited people and state" (*Zuwanderungs-Kommission der CDU Deutschlands*, 2000). The reference to "growing together" aptly invokes the traditional organic idiom of German Romantic nationalism. Indeed, as the philosopher and historian of ideas, Isaiah Berlin, has observed, "the conception of the political life of the nation as an expression of this collective will is the essence of political romanticism" (1998: 598).

The CDU tried to position its concept of *Leitkultur* as a middle way between an integration model of "one-sided assimilation," on the one hand, and a model of multicultural segregation, on the other. The CDU distinguished its approach from the former by highlighting its commitment to fostering a "culture of toleration" based on the principle that "the free unfolding of personhood corresponds to multiplicity of opinions, needs, and interests of citizens." However, this idea of "multiplicity" did not extend to embracing differences in culture. The CDU's portrayal of the multicultural model emphasized the potentially fragmenting effect of such differences, whereby individuals or groups live "unconnectedly aside one another" in "parallel societies" (*Zuwanderungs-Kommission der CDU Deutschlands*, 2000).[7]

At the center of the CDU's depiction of a guiding culture was the proposition that "Germany belongs to the value community of the Christian West (or Occident, *Abendland*)" (*Zuwanderungs-Kommission der CDU Deutschlands*, 2000). In describing this community of values, the CDU offered a brief list of broadly drawn cultural components. This community comprises the "value-order of our Christian-Occidental culture, which has been formed by Christianity, Judaism, ancient philosophy, humanism, Roman law, and the Enlightenment" (*Zuwanderungs-Kommission der CDU Deutschlands*, 2000). Beyond the self-evident fact that all of these elements (among many others not included) exercised influence to one degree or another across the millennia, the logic that joins them into a cohesive whole is never explained. The CDU simply may have found it prudent not to try. As Agnes Heller has pointed out, the idea of a unitary European culture is itself inevitably an artifice, as it would be assembled by abstracting different elements from a variety of particular contexts and repackaging them together under the more general label "European" (Heller 1992: 15–16; Stråth 2002). It is possible to think of such disparate thinkers as Aristotle, Augustine, Machiavelli, Bentham, and Nietzsche as belonging in some broad sense to the same tradition, but much harder to imagine them as representatives of a cohesive body of thought or a shared community of values. Given the diffusion of their influence around the globe, it is also unclear how they can now be claimed as uniquely constitutive of a

7. As Slaughter has observed, some conceptions of multiculturalism have favored some form of separatism among different groups, but others simply "recognize the existence of difference and want to incorporate it into existing structures" (1994: 370).

distinctly European and/or German culture. In the end, the CDU's portrayal of this common culture was not only too bland to inspire much popular enthusiasm, but also ignored the deep tensions and sometimes violent conflicts that had sharply divided cultural partisans throughout European history.

For a party that has long advocated "European solidarity" (Kohl 1984: 208), the CDU's identification of German culture with a broader European one in its concept of *Leitkultur* did not mark a new departure from the party's basic orientation. Moreover, the appeal to a shared European culture has long been central to efforts to promote the legitimacy of European integration. In April 1990, for example, the European Council, at its Dublin summit meeting, had applauded the end of the Cold War as another important step toward this end. Expressing its support for recent developments in Central and Eastern Europe, the Council had saluted the "continuing process of change in those countries with whose peoples we share a common heritage and culture" (European Council 1990). Looking back on the wars that had devastated the continent during the first half of the twentieth century, the Council observed how this step "brings ever closer a Europe, which, having overcome the unnatural divisions imposed on it by ideology and confrontation, stands united in its commitment to democracy, pluralism, the rule of law, full respect for human rights, and the principles of the market economy" (European Council 1990). The notion that Europeans were merely passive subjects upon whom extremist ideologies preyed was indicative of the continuing difficulty involved in coming to terms with that past (Judt 2000: 296–307).

The reference to "unnatural divisions" spoke most immediately to the postwar division between East and West. It also reflected a desire to portray European integration as a natural destiny that could be achieved on the premise that closer unity is compatible with increasing diversity. These same themes have been often reiterated in various forms over the years. For example, the preamble to the Draft Treaty that proposed a Constitution for Europe, adopted by consensus by the European Convention on 13 June and 10 July 2003, echoed these themes as follows:

> Convinced that, while remaining proud of their own national identities and history, the peoples of Europe are determined to transcend their ancient divisions and, united ever more closely, to forge a common destiny,

> Convinced that, thus "United in its diversity," Europe offers them the best chance of pursuing, with due regard for the rights of each individual and in awareness of their responsibilities towards future generations and the Earth, the great venture which makes of it a special area of human hope.[8]

---

8. Available from http://eur-lex.europa.eu/LexUriServ/LexUriServ.do?uri=OJ:C:2004:310:0003:0010:EN:PDF (accessed 16 April 2009).

This vision, however, glosses over the hardest questions that fulfilling this destiny poses, particularly concerning how different nation-states, with their own distinctive traditions, historical memories, specific interests, and practical problems, would be accommodated within the framework of a united Europe. The notion of "unnatural divisions" raised the issue of how the status of nation-states themselves should be conceptualized, as well as how the relationship between nationality, statehood, and European identity should be understood. It suggests that some fundamental divisions separating the peoples of Europe are artificial and should be overcome, but it is left unclear which specific divisions are meant or what removing or bridging them might entail. The expressed commitment to a respect for pluralism and human rights did not offer any concrete answers. The meaning of terms such as pluralism is open to a wide range of interpretation, and, as a result, this kind of commitment is not particularly informative about the specific type of policies it entails. Moreover, the idea of the common European heritage and culture standing behind this vision remained highly schematic. Since at least 1973, Western European policymakers have been promoting the notion of some sort of generic "European identity" without ever being able to flesh out its actual substance. As one might expect, the history of these efforts reveals that the content of the various identity constructs being promoted have changed over time according to new circumstances and policymaking objectives (Passerini 2002: 191–200; Stråth 2000: 401–405).

The CDU's concept of *Leitkultur* brought no new clarity to these issues, but its focus was not addressed to promote a closer union of European states. Rather, it invoked the idea of a common culture as a domestic basis for fostering the integration of immigrants. By emphasizing the broader European character of the values and loyalties the proposal championed, its authors probably intended to blunt criticisms of the ethnonational flavor of their *Leitkultur* concept. Applying the idea of common culture to a migration context brings to the fore the issue of minorities and membership in ways that focusing on the state level can obscure. When applied in this context, it becomes clear that this type of concept blurs critical distinctions without coming to grips with the underlying issues at stake. For example, it takes no account of any distinction between ethnic and civic understandings of belonging or between national and transnational levels of membership. It also simply ignores differences in perspective on collective identity between and among adherents of majority and minority cultures within states. More broadly, the CDU's concept conflated a normative claim about the desirability of an idealized set of cultural values with a descriptive claim about the actual character of a particular culture. This conflation obscures the gaps between the two claims, making the ideal the lens through which the real is perceived.

In blurring such distinctions, the concept of *Leitkultur* also sharpened boundary lines between natives and immigrants who do not share the CDU's understanding of the common German-European heritage. For example, the

CDU's express identification of this heritage with the Judeo-Christian tradition stigmatized—whether intentionally or not—adherents of Islam as conspicuous outsiders. Such an approach seems likely to discourage minorities with Muslim backgrounds from identifying with *Leitkultur* as defined by the CDU, and to encourage them to define their own local identities against it. The problem of extending equitable recognition to minority identities within a majority culture is not limited to Germany or other nation-states. Rather, it is rooted in the inevitable "asymmetrical" structure shaping the relationships between minorities and majorities. Constructing categories by which to classify similarities and differences is fundamental to the demarcation of any group's boundaries, that is, to distinguishing members from nonmembers. In other words, the definition of any group depends as much on whom it excludes as whom it includes. Designating a subordinate class of persons as the "alien other," the historian Reinhart Koselleck has observed, provides a powerful conceptual means through which a dominant group defines its own collective identity to itself, justifies its advantages over others, and inculcates a shared consciousness of group solidarity. "In such cases," he explains, "a given group makes an exclusive claim to generality, applying a linguistically universal concept to itself alone and rejecting all comparison. This kind of self-definition provokes counter concepts which discriminate against those who have been defined as the 'other'" (Koselleck 1985: 160). Such practices have a long history. In his examination of this history, Koselleck begins with the classical distinction drawn originally by the ancient Greeks between the *Civilized* (*Hellene*) and the *Barbarian*. As the ancient world came to a close, Koselleck observes, this distinction was ultimately superseded by the distinction between *Christian* and *Heathen*.

It is not difficult to find the imprint of both of these older dualisms in the CDU's concept of *Leitkultur*. In explaining this concept, its authors spoke in exclusionary terms of "We Germans," "our cultural and historical inheritance," "our common will," and "our national identity"; all of this culminated "in our reunited people and state." Immigrants and other minorities simply have no positive role to play in this storyline, especially when it is recalled that the constitutional mandate to seek reunification was often invoked to justify the restrictiveness of the German Citizenship Law prior to 1990 (Hailbronner 1989: 57). More broadly, it presupposed a highly insular understanding of both German and European culture and their historical development. This understanding minimized any contributions and influences from outside of itself. It ignored the long complex interactions that have occurred between Islamic and Christian groups in this development (see Goody 2004). If the goal was to foster the inclusion of immigrants with many different heritages and cultural attachments, it would seem especially important to have emphasized the hybrid, porous, and capacious character of their host society's culture. In the case of Islam, this would have involved recognizing its place in the history of Europe, rather than writing it out (Asad 2002: 211–220). Recognizing that all so-called national cultures comprise a diverse mix of elements deriving from many different sources also seems more consistent with the global character of cultural interactions today.

In promoting the deepening of European integration and the expansion of Member States, the argument that cultural variety is positive, enriching, and a source of strength has often been made.[9] There is a clear aspirational quality to this argument, reflecting both a desire not to repeat mistakes of the past as well as the recognition that closer unity cannot be achieved without a continued respect for diversity. By contrast, the CDU's *Leitkultur* proposal seemed predicated on the view that the cultural diversity engendered by immigration is a threat to national solidarity and the preservation of a common culture. It too had a clear aspirational quality, but one that took no account of either the legacy of past policies in foster-ing the marginalization of immigrant groups or the multidimensional character of membership in any modern, pluralistic state. It emphasized the cultural aspects of integration while it glossed over the structural ones that involve expanding opportunities for participation in economic, social, and political life. Moreover, its treatment of integration as primarily a cultural issue focused one-sidedly on how immigrants should adapt while offering little room for the accommodation of different cultural standpoints and minority identities.

In grappling with issues of membership, Europe's "burgeoning multiplicity," defying any effort to "distill" some sort of common "essence," clearly poses both significant challenges as well as opportunities (Judt 2005: 752, 777). The EU's mul-tipolar, institutional structure is not equipped to homogenize a common culture in the manner of a nation-state, even if this were determined to be desirable. At the EU level, closer union will depend upon finding new ways to accommodate diversity. However, this effort cannot succeed if Member States base their own approaches to integration on models of cultural homogeneity, because Member States remain the primary units within the EU's organizational structure. As a case in point, the CDU's *Leitkultur* proposal seemed indicative of a party still trapped by its past. Despite the manifest failures of the CDU's policies when mea-sured even on their own terms, the advocates of *Leitkultur* showed that they could not bring themselves to break with the basic assumptions of the party's old policy thinking. As a result, they could not critically look back at the FRG's policy record or look forward with fresh eyes to the challenges ahead. But the newly created Independent Migration Commission would take up these tasks.

9. In its 1973 "Declaration on European Identity," for example, the European Council at its Copen-hagen summit expressed their goal "to preserve the rich variety of their national cultures," adding, "The diversity of cultures within the framework of a common European civilization, the attachment to common values and principles, the increasing convergence of attitudes to life, the awareness of having specific interests in common and the determination of take part in the construction of Europe, all give European Identity its originality and its own dynamism" (European Council 1973).

Chapter 24

Germany's and Europe's Demographic Dilemmas

No serious contemporary analytical or policy conversation about Germany, its immigrants, and the country's unavoidable opening to further immigration can occur without a deep understanding of the country's demographic predicament.[1] Although the political connection between demographics and future immigration flows were made explicit only rather recently,[2] recognition of the existence of a problem is not new.[3] In 1995, for instance, Max Wingen from the Federal German Ministry for Family and Senior Citizen Affairs examined the interconnectedness between an aging German population, low fertility rate, and immigration. He concluded that "the demographic deficits of an aging population can only be corrected to a limited extent through immigration" (Wingen 1995: 710). As Wingen and others have observed,[4] the economic fallout from a shrinking labor supply will necessitate increasing the levels of younger, skilled immigrants. However, increased immigration will also pose difficult social policy challenges relating to welfare systems and the integration of new immigrants. As will be seen, the overlap between these economic and social challenges has tested Germany's, and many of its fellow EU Member States', ability to navigate the politically treacherous immigration waters.

Even though the troubling demographic trends in Europe were becoming more apparent throughout the 1990s, it was the United Nations' publication

1. This chapter draws on Papademetriou (2006: xiv–lxiii).
2. The 2001 Süssmuth Commission's report introduced the demographic argument into the policy discussion about immigration policy (e.g., see Anil 2006: 448).
3. For example, see Münz and Ulrich (1997: 103–109); Johnson and Zimmermann (1993); Klauder (1992); and Felderer (1989).
4. See, for example, Herbert (2001: 333–334).

in 2000 on "Replacement Migration" (United Nations 2000) that brought this challenge to the fore of public policy concerns. Mainstream demographers have criticized the report for "working back from the future" and complained that the UN chose an arbitrary goal and then simply calculated how much immigration would be needed to keep each state's population and work force at 2005 levels by 2050 (Lutz and Scherbov 2006). Nevertheless, whatever its methodological shortcomings, the sense of urgency the UN publication created was palpable. It spotlighted two alarming dimensions of the demographic challenge facing Germany and much of the rest of Europe: national populations that are both shrinking and aging.

The facts are straightforward. Low rates of native population growth across most of Europe have meant that migration is already a large demographic force. In fact, immigrants now account for most of the EU's population growth[5] and provide net gains in the number of workers in many EU Member States. Although Italy and the other Southern European Member States, as well as most Eastern European ones, are faring particularly poorly in these regards, Germany's data are also bleak. Since 2003, the German population has declined due to the birth deficit no longer being compensated by migration flows.[6] With a net migration rate of 1.2 people per 1,000 people in 2005, immigration to Germany has dampened nevertheless the effect of the country's population decline for that year from 1.7 people per 1,000 to 0.5 people per 1,000.[7]

The facts behind this phenomenon are not in dispute. Chronically low fertility for almost a generation now is at the root of the problem. The "average" woman in Germany bears about 1.4 children during her lifetime, a number that has fallen to below 1.3 since 2005.[8] While the timing and severity of the

5. The Czech Republic, Italy, and Slovenia experienced population growth solely because of migration. In Germany, the population decline would have been much larger were it not for its strongly positive migration balance (Münz 2007).

6. Even if we assumed that Germany's life expectancy rose by 7.6 years for men and 6.5 years for women and that annual immigration levels were maintained at 100,000 medium-aged people, the population would decline to 69 million by 2050. Even if annual immigration levels were at 200,000 people, the population would still only be 74 million people (from the current level of 82 million) by 2050. In either case, the population would decrease anywhere between 10 and 17 percent from 2005 to 2050 unless dramatic changes occur in German demographics (Federal Statistical Office, "Germany's Population by 2050—Results of the 11th Coordinated Population Project," November 2006).

7. Rainer Münz, "Ageing and Demographic Change in European Societies: Main Trends and Alternative Policy Options," the World Bank, Special Protection, March 2007. See http://siteresources.worldbank.org/SOCIALPROTECTION/Resources/SP-Discussion-papers/Labor-Market-DP/0703.pdf (accessed 16 April 2009).

8. Statistisches Bundesamt Deutschland, "Germany's Population by 2050—Results of the 11th Coordinated Population Project," November 2006. For a country to be able to "replace itself," that number needs to be closer to 2.1 children.

Table 24.1. EU 25 Old-Age Dependency Ratio Projections, 2000–2050

Sample of the EU 25	2000	2005	2025	2050
Austria	22.9	23.6	34.5	53.2
Denmark	22.2	22.6	33.8	40.0
France	24.6	25.3	36.9	47.9
Germany	23.9	27.8	39.3	55.8
Greece	24.2	26.8	35.5	58.8
Ireland	16.8	16.5	25.2	45.3
Italy	26.8	29.4	39.7	66.0
Latvia	22.1	24.1	30.7	44.1
Netherlands	20.0	20.7	32.5	38.6
Poland	17.6	18.7	32.8	51.0
Spain	24.5	24.5	33.6	67.5
Sweden	26.9	26.4	36.5	40.9
UK	23.9	24.4	33.2	45.3
EU 25 average	23.4	24.9	35.7	52.8

Source: Münz (2007: 22).

demographic challenge will vary among developed states, the trend of low birth rates and late pregnancy is unmistakable and, for the next twenty years, the outcome is practically predetermined. The forces that drive it are powerful. They include continuing improvements in medical science, almost limitless access to state-supported or subsidized medical care, ever higher rates of female participation in the labor force, and affluence, which further depresses fertility and supports longer life spans by improving access to more advanced medical services. As the post–World War II baby boomers pass from the economic scene over the next decade or so, most EU Member States will experience substantial native working-age population shortages as well as the threat of deflationary pricing as the domestic consumer market shrinks while competition for foreign customers intensifies.

The bulge in the retirement age population is of equal interest to this analysis. The significant aging of their populations, one demographer has concluded, "make Germany, along with other European countries and Japan, likely victims of a pension time bomb" (Edmonston 2006: 542). The number of retirees across the advanced industrial world will reach absolute and relative sizes unlike anything we have witnessed in history. With people living much longer than ever before, the taxes of fewer and fewer workers will have to support ever larger numbers of retirees—a ratio known as old-age support (or dependency). Today, the total support ratio[9] in Germany is 65 people at non-working age to

---

9. The *total* support ratio is the ratio of the sum of those who are already retired and those who are too young to be working relative to the number of persons in the workforce.

100 people working and aged between 20 and 64, but that ratio is projected to reach between 91:100 and 98:100 by 2050, that is, roughly one worker's taxes will have to support one person who is not in the labor force.[10] Thus, the greatest policy challenge may be securing adequate living standards for pensioners without putting "crushing" tax burdens on workers (Papademetriou 2005). This challenge will get tougher every decade.[11]

Even if fertility were to increase dramatically and immediately, it would have little effect on old-age support ratios during the next two decades because of the time it takes most young persons to prepare for entering the labor force fulltime. If participation rates in the labor market among those above the age of fifty and among women increase, however, the projected decline in the labor force can be significantly slowed while easing pension costs in the near term. Nevertheless, even under the most optimistic scenarios envisioning significantly rising labor force participation rates, the absolute size of the labor force is projected to fall by 1.2 million by 2015. Since, as Klaus Zimmermann and his co-authors point out, a "positive growth trend in participation rates cannot continue forever," a shrinking population size will eventually have a dramatic negative effect on the available labor supply. Assuming that participation rates do rise considerably, they estimate that the supply will still drop "by six million workers during 2020–2030" (Zimmermann et al. 2007: 92).

Countries with significant migration inflows in the last several decades will also notice a much faster change in the racial and ethnic composition of their workforces, as much larger proportions of these workforces will be immigrants and their offspring. These trends will be most obvious initially in large cities where most immigrants concentrate and where there are already several examples of "majority-minority" situations. Cities such as Stuttgart, where individuals with an immigrant background comprise 40 percent of its population, Frankfurt on the Main (39.5 percent), and Nuremberg (37 percent), have been among the first to experience this ethnic compositional shift.[12] Successful adaptation to these shifts will require that all residents learn how to live together in new pluri-cultural and pluri-religious settings brought about by increased diversity.

Few analysts believe that immigration by itself can somehow solve the policy challenges arising from this demographic predicament. The numbers of immigrants it would take to do so would be massive, making the immigration option

10. Statistisches Bundesamt Deutschland, "Germany's Population by 2050—Results of the 11th Coordinated Population Project," November 2006.

11. By some estimates, the median age of Germany's population is projected to rise from 40 years in 2000 to 48 years in 2045 (Edmonston 2006: 542).

12. Statistisches Bundesamt Deutschland, "New Data Available on Migration in Germany," 5 April 2007. See http://www.destatis.de/jetspeed/portal/cms/Sites/destatis/Internet/EN/press/pr/2007/05/PE07__183__12521.psml (accessed 16 April 2009).

neither socially nor politically viable. "With 500,000 emigrants (the anticipated levels in Germany's population projections)," Barry Edmonston observes, "Germany requires about 1,255,000 immigrants annually to maintain the current SPE [Stationary Population Equivalent] of 81.3 million" (Edmonston 2006: 543). While large-scale immigration may have a significant positive impact on slowing demographic declines, it is questionable whether over the long term it will have much effect on trends toward a rising median age of the population (Zimmermann et al. 2007: 94–97). Moreover, any contemplation of utilizing large-scale immigration as a policy tool must contend with the already high rates of unemployment among workers with immigrant backgrounds. In Germany, the unemployment rate of 18.3 percent among the foreign-born—a rate that is 10 percent higher than that of the native-born—illustrates the magnitude of this problem.[13] As a result, policies aimed at attracting larger numbers of temporary workers as an alternative immigration option are likely to become very popular for many advanced industrial societies and will gain in significance relative to permanent immigration. As noted earlier in this volume, Germany is already well on the way to exploiting that option. Introducing age biases in permanent immigration formulas—as currently done in Canada and Australia—may also become more common.

This scenario suggests that societies addressing these demographically centered challenges sooner and more aggressively will enhance their prospects for economic stability and growth. Those that do not are likely to experience greater economic instability and, under certain extreme scenarios, economic decline. Both alternatives also imagine a spillover into social instability, which will require active policies that strive to maintain social cohesion. These demographic difficulties, however, should not be understood as a judgment that Germany and other European states have no ammunition with which to combat them. Nevertheless, every policy response entails significant pain for important segments of society, which suggests that governments likely will attempt to prolong the status quo and postpone more aggressive initiatives. This tactic will prove both inadequate and harmful in the long run.

Most EU Member States and other advanced industrial societies are already experimenting with several of these approaches and a list of innovative ideas and good practice is emerging. However, the political pushback for the most obvious routes is already strong and will only intensify. While all of the policy options delineated above will be in the mix, there are three truly salient long-term policy approaches that hold the greatest promise, if they are tried in concert. These approaches center on substantially pushing back the retirement age, inducing significant changes to fertility behavior, and accepting more immigration.

---

13. Organisation for Economic Co-operation and Development, *Jobs for Immigrants. Volume 1: Labour Market Integration in Australia, Denmark, Germany and Sweden*, 2007.

The problem is that none of these policy approaches seem to be politically viable anytime soon, and the prospect for their implementation is bleakest in Germany. The first policy will pit the government against retirees and those nearing retirement, two groups that typically hold disproportionate shares of a country's wealth and political power. The second one, changes in fertility, implies a reversal in long-term trends and will require a revolution in prevailing social norms and economic logic. The policy instrument of choice in this regard is robust economic incentives for having more children. The third and final option, far larger immigration intakes, will require even sharper attitudinal adjustments. This assessment implies that Germany must overcome the resistance to immigration and be willing to make the necessary social and cultural adjustments.

Chapter 25

Embracing Immigration
Laying the Foundation for a New Policy

In its 2001 report, the Independent Commission on Immigration to Germany created by the SPD/Green-led federal government took up the challenges that would be involved in defining a new policy framework for immigration. In developing this framework, the Commission emphasized the importance of both economic needs and humanitarian considerations. "Germany must fulfill its responsibility and obligation," the report declared, "Germany must also meet its responsibilities and obligations as an important and reliable member of the international community of states. This applies particularly to the scope of the Geneva Refugee Convention and the European Human Rights Convention." (Independent Commission on Immigration 2001: 11–12). Citing the UN demographic study (referred to earlier) for support, it built a case for Germany's continuing need for immigrants to offset a low birth rate, aging population, increasingly strained retirement system, and a shortage of highly skilled workers. "Immigration," the Commission observed, "can have a considerable long-term effect on long-term prosperity" (Independent Commission on Immigration 2001: 69). From this basis, the report called for a "paradigmatic change" in migration policy thinking—from the old law based on the 1973 recruitment stop to a new concept based on the principle of "managed immigration" (Independent Commission on Immigration 2001: 82). Fundamental to this change is a "new labor market orientation" aiming at implementing controlled immigration through policy initiatives that, subject to testing and evaluation, would remain open to revision and further experimentation.

Of course, through its admission of family members, *Aussiedler*, asylum seekers, and others, the FRG had been admitting immigrants throughout most of this period, but not in a systematic way calibrated to the labor market and from behind an official rhetoric denying the principle of immigration as any kind of organizing concept for policymakers. Likewise, from the late 1950s to the recruitment stop in 1973, the FRG had aggressively sought to attract foreign labor, but under the assumption that their stay would be temporary and with a view toward filling low-skilled labor shortages. Since that time, the fulcrum for economic growth and international competitiveness shifted from the industrial sectors to the high tech and information sectors of the FRG's economy. Attentive to this trend, the Commission tailored its proposals toward attracting highly skilled and educated workers. For the FRG to compete effectively on the global labor market for such workers, the Commission recognized that Germany would have to liberalize its rules governing entry, residence, and work to make them comparable with those of other advanced industrial, liberal-democratic receiving states. At the same time, as opposed to the rotational labor importation system of the guestworker era, devising an immigration policy brought issues of integration to the fore. In addressing these issues, the Commission repudiated the "guiding culture" approach of the conservatives. It also emphasized the importance of integration as a policy objective, partly with an eye toward addressing the public anxieties that the CDU/CSU leadership has proven so adept at exploiting over the years. Any effort to build a public case for immigration and, more generally, to develop a comprehensive migration policy required taking up the issues of asylum seekers and clandestine (or illegal) migration, which had long been the most controversial entry channels into the FRG. Such an effort also required situating German migration policy within the larger framework of the EU.

In calling for a new approach to migration, the Commission still found it necessary to reiterate the obvious point that Germany had become a "country of immigrants," and "that immigration has greatly influenced the development of German society" (Independent Commission on Immigration 2001: 13). Among these influences, the report highlighted the essential contributions that immigrants had made to the growth of the FRG economy during its first several decades (Independent Commission on Immigration 2001: 69). This long and extensive experience with immigration, the report observed, gives the FRG a vast knowledge base from which to develop a new migration policy framework—one which takes into account the policies that have proven most successful in the past and ignores those that have not. In seeking to emphasize the positive side of this legacy, the Commission pointed to the FRG's success in integrating the *Aussiedler* and the *Spätaussiedler* (ethnic returnees), as well as foreign workers (Independent Commission on Immigration 2001: 13), albeit in more limited social terms. By drawing all of these different groups of newcomers into a common migration tradition, the report broke with the old approach that had tried to keep them confined to separate administrative categories. As we have seen, this kind of conceptual segregation was first breached with the 1993 asylum compromise, and the Commission's own approach was in many ways simply reflecting changes that occurred in that decade. The report dealt with all these different categories in its attempt to define a comprehensive migration policy framework, by treating all aspects of migration, ranging from asylum to temporary workers, as interrelated elements of a common whole. At the same time, the report recognized that immigration alone was no panacea to these problems. It, therefore, also called for general reforms in the education system, workers' training, and family support.

The Commission proposed the introduction of an immigration law that would provide four main "doors" (avenues) for selective admission. The first door applied to the recruitment of well-educated young people based on a points system (similar to Canada's) to supply workers for the existing and anticipated employment niches in the high end of the labor market. For these immigrants, the Commission advocated granting immediate permanent residence linked to the clear prospect of eventual naturalization. The second door applied to the recruitment of temporary workers and aimed at filling existing gaps in the labor market by offering limited residence permits of up to five years. To determine and certify the need for such workers, the report recommended two reforms: upgrading the statistical diagnostic capabilities of the Federal Office for Employment and allowing German businesses to pay a levy for the foreign workers they recruit. The third door focused on attracting high-income executive personnel with proven managerial skills and top scientists or other academic researchers by simplifying admission and residence requirements for them. The fourth door aimed at attracting young persons to study in Germany by offering a range of educational and training opportunities. Altogether, the Commission proposed initial admissions of 50,000 persons per year, including 20,000 under the point system, 20,000 on a temporary basis, and 10,000 as trainees.

Although supporting measures to curb illegal migration, the report pointed out that their actual number is unknown. At best, there are highly speculative estimates ranging from 100,000 to 1,000,000. "There is, however, no doubt," the report observed, "that Germany is subject to considerable pressure from illegal immigration" (Independent Commission on Immigration 2001: 192). The perception of hundreds of thousands of clandestine migrants evading border controls, increasing burdens on social services, taking jobs from the native born, and generally flouting the law has long been a potent symbol of migrants abusing the system and of the inability of governments to control migration. Rather than attributing the problem to the motives of migrants, the Commission emphasized the incentives that local employers had in "exploiting" them by reducing wage costs and tax and social insurance payments, as well as giving themselves more flexibility in hiring and firing. The Commission also pointed out that the illegal migrants themselves bear the burden of lower wages, lack of access to healthcare, and insecurity in the workplace. In recognition of these disadvantages, the Commission recommended informing school authorities that they have no obligation to report on the status of children of parents without lawful residence. It also called for abolishing any penalties to civil groups, such as churches, that provide support to illegal migrants.

In developing its plan for managed immigration, the Commission identified an active promotion of integration as a "central" policy objective. Its approach began from the premise that immigration must be understood as not simply "an economic and demographic requirement, but also a cultural enrichment" for the host country (Independent Commission on Immigration 2001: 195). Forty years of immigration, the report observed, has made the FRG much more pluralistic. This change is evident in the classroom, the workplace, and the family. Moreover, through travel and education, native-born Germans have also become more cosmopolitan. As a result, the report concluded, "national borders are becoming less and less important in our everyday culture" (Independent Commission on Immigration 2001: 195). Such a conclusion clearly presupposes thinking of Germany within the broader context of the European Union.

In setting forth a new, more inclusive basis for integration, the Commission recognized that growing cultural diversity had generated tensions and anxieties within the majority culture, which for a long time manifested themselves most defensively in the denial of the FRG's character as an immigrant receiving state. The report sought to position its recommendations between two perceived extremes: on the one hand, the specter of increasing cultural fragmentation through the emergence of separatist, self-organized ethnic groups, and, on the other hand, the "one-sided," strongly assimilationist *Leitkultur* model of integration. To prevent the former, the report prescribes that all newcomers be expected and actively encouraged to learn German as the language for operating within their host society. It set as a minimum integration requirement that all newcomers and long-settled immigrants accept the fundamental liberal-democratic norms embodied in the Basic Law. To this end, it declared that certain cultural practices, such as female genital mutilation, should not be tolerated. Against the latter, extreme model of integration, the report argued that adaptation within a receiving state is a two-sided process of mutual adaptation, learning, and dialogue. Successful integration, the report observed, depends on a "will to integrate," but, it added, this applies as much to the adherents of the majority culture as to newcomers. The report concluded that a politically responsible integration policy should aim at "making [it] possible for migrants to be participants on equal terms in social, economic, cultural, and political life that respects cultural diversity" (Independent Commission on Immigration 2001: 196). Toward this end, the report recommended, for example, that Islamic religious instruction should be available in the schools for all children being raised in that religious faith. However, it only touched on the more general problem of discrimination in the most cursory way, and recommended merely the expeditious implementation of the new EU guidelines issued in June 2000.

A staple assumption behind the restrictiveness of German naturalization policy has long been the view that citizenship should only be conferred after an alien had abandoned any substantial identification with his or her country of origin and had become fully assimilated into the host society. The Commission repudiated this view, declaring, "Naturalization is a decisive step on the way to successful integration, since it provides immigration with numerous opportunities for social participation: from being involved in politics to gaining equal status before the law" (Independent Commission on Immigration 2001: 240) The report made clear that promoting integration was the driving consideration in its approach toward citizenship policy, and stressed that a policy aimed at this goal must be treated as part of any immigration strategy.

This was not just talk; the Commission had done the math. The report pointed out that any immigration strategy designed to offset "unfavorable demographic trends" in the host society must make integration, through a generous citizenship-acquisition policy, a priority or risk an ever-growing resident population of non-citizens. The report emphasized the importance of political rights in the integration process, recognizing that active participation is key not only in fostering a sense of belonging, but also in giving individuals and groups a stake in the political system. The Commission went so far as to advocate the extension of municipal (or local) voting rights to third-country nationals. It warned, however, that the latter was not a substitute for the acquisition of the full rights of membership through citizenship. It endorsed the 1999 citizenship reform that had introduced elements of *jus soli* and held out the hope that this change would start to break the identification in the public mind of citizenship with ethnic origin. After reviewing the current status of the law and noting that it was too soon to assess the effect of the recent changes, the Commission recommended the adoption of a more "generous" policy toward multiple nationalities. More specifically, it recommended allowing immigrants who entered the FRG prior to the 1973 recruitment ban the opportunity to maintain multiple nationalities, as well as exempting them from passing a German language test as a condition for naturalization.

In addition to immigration and integration, the report's third focus was asylum policy. The so-called "asylum crisis" of the late 1980s and early 1990s had brought to the fore major questions about the government's capacity to control its borders, to regulate admissions and conditions of residence, and, more generally, to manage migration policy. The immediate crisis had abated after the "asylum compromise" of 1993, but many basic questions remained. The Commission supported the amendments to the Basic Law, adopted as part of the asylum compromise, that restricted the exercise of a right to asylum. Against those who called for restoring the original provisions, it defended the amended version as a reasonable balance between Germany's humanitarian considerations, historical responsibilities incurred by National Socialism, and the legitimate self-interests of any host society. It also opposed any further weakening of the existing constitutional guarantees. At the same time, the Commission advocated reforming the application procedures and their administration in order to accelerate the handling of asylum claims, as well as to improve the inspection and verification of those claims.

The report, in fact, argued that delays in processing claims subverted both the purposes and legitimacy of the asylum system. First, the inefficiency encouraged asylum seekers to enter Germany without justifiable claims on the expectation that any final outcome would be subject to a long process during which they could remain living in Germany. The longer the delay, the report argued, the more attractive the asylum channel becomes as an entry route for those desiring the social and economic opportunities Germany offers its residents. In addition, the longer the delay, the more attenuated the links become that asylum seekers have with their country of origin. Second, the public perception that the system is being rampantly exploited and clogged by too many asylum seekers with bogus claims risks undermining the necessary domestic backing for it. Public support, the report argued, is essential not only for preserving the guarantees of asylum, but also for the social acceptance of asylum seekers into the FRG.

For the Commission, a key principle that should regulate asylum policy (and migration policy as whole) is that foreigners residing in Germany without permission must return to their home countries or to a third state. "The right to stay," the Commission declared, "is inseverably linked to the obligation to leave the country if a negative decision is taken. The entire procedure would be meaningless if foreigners failed to meet this obligation" (Independent Commission on Immigration 2001: 146). More broadly, the Commission argued that the inefficiencies in the asylum system limit the ability of the government to set priorities and meet goals in controlling migration. The idea that migration must be controlled in many ways permeates the report, but it emphasizes that this control is a shared responsibility between Member States, such as Germany, and the European Union. "German asylum and migration policy," the report observed, "is inseparably combined with European integration." In part, this emphasis reflected the legacy of decisions made during the asylum crisis of the early 1990s to use a European-wide strategy to deter unwanted asylum seekers from ever reaching Germany in the first place, but it was also indicative of attempts since then to promote policy coordination at the EU level. The Commission pointed out that the Amsterdam Treaty had given the EU competency in this policy domain, while the EU summit at Tampere established the mandate for the creation of a common EU asylum policy. The report called for the most expeditious implementation of the policies included in the Amsterdam Treaty concerning refugees and asylum seekers.

Tightening the administration and procedures of the asylum process at every level was a clear thrust of the report's recommendations, but the Commission also endorsed an expansive understanding of the recognition of refugee protection to include women suffering the threat of persecution on gender-specific grounds, such as rape. In addition, it further endorsed including those refugees fleeing from the threat of persecution in situations where state structures capable of providing protection have ceased to exist, such as in Somalia. The Commission acknowledged that its members could not agree whether current refugee law is adequate for these purposes, and, thus, it called for the adoption of a uniform interpretation of applicable law across the EU.

Consistent with the FRG's recognition of the need for continuing immigration as well as its new focus on integration policy, the European Council, at its meeting on 19 and 20 June 2003 in Thessaloniki under the Presidency of Greece, also called for new initiatives in these policy domains. Similar to the Independent Commission's approach with respect to Germany, the European Council recognized the reality of the "new demographic and economic challenges which the EU is now facing" (European Council 2003a: 9). To meet these new challenges, the Thessaloniki Council emphasized the need for promoting integration through a "comprehensive and multidimensional policy" and "for exploring legal means for third-country nationals to migrate to the Union" (European Council 2003a: 8).

In positing the guiding principles for the integration policy, the Thessaloniki Council returned to the position that the Council had taken in October 1999 at Tampere, prescribing that the rights and obligations granted to third-country nationals should be comparable to those of EU citizens in areas such as employment, education and language training, health and social services, housing and urban issues, as well as culture and participation in social life. Stopping short of calling for conferring municipal voting rights to resident third-country nationals, the Council, in its focus on social and economic rights, left the issue of political rights to be decided by the Member States. This deference was consistent with the Council's view that "primary responsibility" for the "elaboration and implementation" of integration policies belongs to the Member States. In prescribing guidelines, the Council also emphasized that "integration policies should be understood as a continuous, two-way process based on mutual rights and corresponding obligations of legally residing third-country nationals and the host societies" (European Council 2003a: 9). At the same time, the Council reiterated its resolve, expressed at Tampere and repeated in 2002 at its Seville summit, to establish a common European Asylum System and called for the consideration of new mechanisms to enhance the management of external borders and the Member States' cooperation in controlling illegal immigration.

Chapter 26

From Policy Vision to Legislative Reality

The Making of the 2005 Migration Law

After years of missed opportunities in immigration management, the SPD/ Green coalition had come to power in 1998 with the political agenda to reform and modernize Germany's citizenship, immigration, and integration policies. The objective of the coalition was to overturn fundamental assumptions that had governed earlier policy approaches to migration, which were anchored on the long-standing claim that Germany is not a country of immigration. Even before the coalition came to power, these assumptions had grown increasingly untenable. As Kruse, Orren and Angenendt observe, "there was a new acceptance ... that Germany needed immigration, particularly of highly skilled workers; that efforts at integration for and by long-term immigrants needed to be redoubled; and that a comprehensive political apparatus had to be developed to co-ordinate future immigration movements" (Kruse, Orren, and Angenendt 2003: 130). The mounting threat of substantial demographic decline reflected in the aging German population, labor shortages, and an increasingly strained pension system reinforced the drive to develop a new legal and policy framework.

This drive culminated in the reform of the Citizenship Law in 1999 and the creation in 2000 of the Independent Commission on Immigration. Following the Commission's report in 2001, the Federal Minister of the Interior, Otto Schily, introduced the first draft of the bill on immigration control and regulation on 3 August 2001, stating, "The aim [of the bill] is to have a modern immigration act that will safeguard Germany's competitiveness, create jobs, and help shape the future; at the same time limiting immigration, preventing illegal immigration and counteracting abuse of the right of asylum" (Federal Ministry of the Interior 2001). The promise of the economic competitive advantages associated with more flexible migration laws attracted the support of a great number of industrialists, associations, employers, trade unions, local authorities, and academics.

False Starts: The First Legislative Initiative

The Schily bill was intended to establish Germany's first-ever regulated immigration system. The bill contained many of the Commission's recommendations. The CDU/CSU leadership opposed the bill from its inception on the grounds that it would encourage immigration and that it did not impose enough measures to strictly limit immigration. To support their argument for the need of stringent controls, the CDU/CSU pointed to the 3.8 million persons unemployed in Germany. Calling attention to the financial burden of integration, they also criticized the law as too costly.[1] After long negotiations, the Bundestag passed a much-revised bill on 1 March 2002. Three weeks later, the Bundesrat also approved the bill in a procedurally contested vote. President Johannes Rau (SPD) signed the new legislation on 20 June 2002, preparing the ground for the law to come into force on 1 January 2003.

However, after Rau announced his decision to sign the legislation, conservative opposition leaders declared their intent to challenge the constitutionality of the Bundesrat voting procedures used to pass the law.[2] On 18 December 2002,

1. For a discussion about the CDU's position on Schily's proposal, see, for example, Ansgar Graw, "CDU weist Vorwürfe der Wirtschaft zurück," *Die Welt*, 25 August 2001; Nikolai Kreitl, "Schröder hat keine Vision," *Focus*, 9 August 2001; "Kritik aus der Koalition an Schilys Entwurf," *Frankfurter Allgemeine Zeitung*, 24 August 2001.

2. As explained earlier, the representatives of the Bundesrat are composed of officials from the various *Länder* governments. Each *Land* (a single state) has between three and six representatives who sit on the Bundesrat. According to the Article 51 (3) of the Basic Law, in the Bundesrat all representatives from each *Land* must vote unanimously (*nur einheitlich*). This means that in practice one representative is sent to the capital to vote by proxy for the rest of the *Land* representatives. Traditionally, the representative will abstain from voting, which constitutes a "nay" vote, if there are differences (as is often the case because many *Länder* have coalition governments) between *Land* representatives (Neunreither 1959: 715). In the 2002 vote for the immigration law, Brandenburg's four votes were needed in order for the legislation to pass. The government in Brandenburg, however, was composed of a SPD/CDU coalition in which the CDU representative, Jörg Schönbohm, refused to budge from his stance against the immigration law. When the immigration bill came up for a vote, the presiding officer, Klaus Wowerweit, the Social Democratic Mayor of Berlin, did not ask Brandenburg to vote unanimously, rather he called on the two representatives, one from each party, who voted "yes" and "no," respectively (Kommers 2002). Wowerweit then asked Brandenburg's Social Democratic Prime Minister, Manfred Stolpe, for his vote on behalf of the entire *Land*. Stolpe responded "yes," the chair accepted his vote, and the bill passed with a 35 to 34 majority. CDU and CSU representatives declared that the voting procedures violated Germany's constitutional law.

the Constitutional Court declared the 2002 *Gesetz zur Steuerung und Begrenzung der Zuwanderung* (Act on the Management and Limitation of Immigration) void because the act did not receive a valid majority vote in the Bundesrat.[3] The Court did not deal with any questions related to the content of the act and discussed only the constitutionality of the legislative procedure.[4] As a result of the Court's ruling, the act was returned to the government; in response, Federal Interior Minister Otto Schily once again made clear the government's determination to push through substantially the same immigration law. On 2 May 2003, the Bundestag passed the original legislation a second time, but the conservative opposition's now outright control of the Bundesrat stalled it.

At this stage, advocates of the legislation changed tactics and began to emphasize that the purpose of the new immigration law was one of "limiting" immigration to the FRG (Süssmuth 2006: 96). The insertion of the word "limitation" into the legislation's title was in fact intended to mollify conservative opponents, but it also reflected the continuing ambivalence that many Germans felt toward immigration—seeing it as much as a potential threat as an opportunity. The proposed legislation had made clear that it sought to permit and to channel immigration, subject to the ability to integrate newcomers, as well as to the FRG's economic and labor market needs. The law's emphasis was unmistakable: immigration would be regulated to serve the greater national interest and with a clear eye toward the potential disruptive effects that it could have on the social and cultural life of the host society. The law also promised more "control" than any immigration law can hope to achieve, because, as German policymakers had every reason to know from a long history of experience, the creation of migration networks and settlement patterns introduces its own dynamic into the process. The categorical distinction drawn between "Germans" and "foreigners" perpetuated the binary approach to national membership that has long characterized state policy on migration and citizenship in the FRG. This ambivalence, as well as a certain defensiveness on the part of immigration proponents, undermined the underlying spirit of an immigration law, which, consistent with the thrust of the findings of the Independent Commission, should admit most newcomers as prospective citizens—that is, as persons occupying a middle or transitional membership category somewhere between foreigner and citizen.

---

3. 2 BvF 1/02, Decision of 18 December 2002 on *Gesetz zur Steuerung und Begrenzung der Zuwanderung und zur Regelung des Aufenthalts und der Integration von Unionsbürgern und Ausländern vom 20. Juni 2002*. See http://www.bundesverfassungsgericht.de (accessed 5 January 2008).

4. The case was brought before the Court by six of the eight *Länder* who had voted against the new immigration law or had abstained from voting in the Bundesrat. They challenged the formal compatibility of the voting procedure in the Bundesrat with the Basic Law and sought a nullification of the act (see Arndt and Nickel 2003: 4).

The proposed law reasonably prescribed no absolute ceiling on the numbers of persons to be admitted for the purposes of work. Rather, the numbers would be determined each year, and the selection of applicants seeking employment would be based on a Canadian-style points system that would have relied on criteria such as age, education, work history, family status, language skills, and links with Germany. The Federal Ministry of the Interior projected that, initially, 20,000 work-related visas would be issued under this system, along with 5,000 for the most highly skilled workers. The proposed law also provided a separate entry category for entrepreneurs. This category applied to persons who pledged an investment of a minimum of one million Euros and to establish a new business enterprise in Germany that would employ at least ten persons, a provision borrowed directly from US law. The Federal Interior Ministry expected to admit roughly 500 persons under this category. To assess the need for immigrants in any given year and to recommend admission targets, a new "Migration Council" would be established as an advisory group with expertise in demography, labor economics, migration, and related disciplines. The Federal Interior Minister would appoint the Council's seven members to four-year terms. The Federal Labor Ministry would also be involved in evaluating labor market conditions and the need for immigrants.

The proposed law also intended to simplify the complex regulations of residence and employment permits. For example, it would have reduced the number of available residence permits to two types: temporary and unlimited. It would also have linked unlimited (or settlement) permits with work permits. Immigrants who qualified as highly skilled workers under the point system would automatically receive settlement permits. To promote the integration of immigrants, the law would have provided for supporting courses in the German language and for the study of the FRG's history, culture, and legal institutions. The immigrants would be expected to pay a portion of the instruction costs and the refusal to attend such courses would be grounds for the denial of an unlimited residence permit. The law did not indicate how much of the financial burden for these courses would be borne by the federal government and how much by the states and municipalities. A newly named *Bundesamt für Migration und Flüchtlinge* (Federal Office for Migration and Refugees, or BAMF) would have the responsibility for overseeing the integration courses for immigrants, along with the duties connected with administering asylum procedures it would inherit from the former *Bundesamt für die Anerkennung ausländischer Flüchtlinge* (Federal Office for the Recognition of Foreign Refugees, or BAFL).

The proposed law would also have tightened the rules governing asylum. Without this change, asylum seekers whose applications have been approved receive unlimited residence permits. The proposed change would have made them eligible initially for only temporary residence permits. If the criteria for asylum were still met after three years, asylum seekers would be granted an unlimited residence permit. At the same time, the proposed law would have expanded the coverage for refugee protection by conferring the recognition of "Convention-refugee status" on those threatened by non-governmental or gender-based persecution.

Slimming Down: Toward the Migration Law of 2005

The bill Minister Schily introduced in 2001 never became law, and the law that eventually passed in 2004 fell far short of the Independent Commission's recommendations. It failed to break with an exclusionary model of immigrant integration and to reconceptualize the German migration and integration policy framework. Most significantly, the new law did not create a system to facilitate the immigration of those wishing to work in Germany with skills that the German economy needs. Nor did the law create a system that would effectively integrate new immigrants or those already living in established immigrant communities.

The debate over the law that would replace the failed bill of 2001 occurred during a period of retrenchment in public opinion toward immigrants, particularly toward Muslims, who constitute the bulk of Germany's non-ethnic German immigrants. The International Helsinki Federation for Human Rights (IHF) reports that, according to a 2003 public opinion survey in Germany, "negative stereotypes against Muslims are on the rise among all groups of society. Among its findings, 46 percent of all those interviewed in the survey fully or partly agreed with the statement that 'Islam is a backward religion,' 34 percent with the statement that 'I am distrustful of people of Islamic religion,' and 27 percent with the statement that 'immigration to Germany should be forbidden for Muslims'" (IHF 2005: 76). This kind of negative reaction has been applied to immigrant communities as a whole, but primarily to Turkish immigrants, who represent the largest and most established group of immigrants in Germany.

A 2003 report initiated by the European Commission reiterated that German xenophobia, though worse than the EU average, is part of a larger European-wide phenomenon (Coenders, Lubbers, and Scheepers 2003). The report found that the number of Europeans who favored repatriation policies for legal immigrants and who believed that multicultural society had reached its limits increased significantly between 1997 and 2003. In 2003, more than 40 percent of both East and West Germans favored the repatriation of legal immigrants and over 80 percent believed multicultural society had reached its limits. Additionally, the report found high opposition to granting civil rights to legal immigrants across the EU, while an even higher proportion (approximately 40 percent) of Germans opposed granting immigrants such rights. Needless to say, the case for embracing immigration was a hard sell to the German public.

In Germany, as elsewhere, high unemployment rates reinforced xenophobic attitudes. Domestic unemployment hovered at around 10 percent of the labor force and the unemployment rate for Turkish citizens was more than twice the national average. The situation in the eastern part of the country was even worse, with unemployment rates for German citizens at twice the western level and comparable to the Turkish rates of unemployment (OECD 2004: 31). During the 2002 political campaign, CSU leader Edmund Stoiber, emphasized the rhetorical connection between high unemployment rates and openings to immigration by declaring that "with four million unemployed, we can't have more foreign workers coming to Germany" (Stoiber, quoted in Martin 2004: 222).

Table 26.1. Unemployment in Germany, 1975–2006

Year	Total Unemployed	Overall Unemployment Rate (%)	Unemployed Foreigners
1975	1,074,217	4.7	151, 493
1976	1,060,336	4.6	106,394
1977	1,029,995	4.5	97,692
1978	992,948	4.3	103,524
1979	876,137	3.8	93,499
1980	888,900	3.8	107,420
1981	1,271,574	5.5	168,492
1982	1,833,244	7.5	245,710
1983	2,258,235	9.1	292,140
1984	2,265,559	9.1	270,265
1985	2,304,014	9.3	253,195
1986	2,228,004	9.0	248,001
1987	2,228,788	8.9	262,097
1988	2,241,556	8.7	269,097
1989	2,037,781	7.9	232,512
1990	1,883,147	7.2	202,975
1991	2,602,203	6.3	221,884
1992	2,978,570	8.5	269,772
1993	3,419,141	9.8	359,449
1994	3,698,057	10.6	420,903
1995	3,611,921	10.4	436,261
1996	3,965,064	11.5	495,956
1997	4,384,456	12.7	547,816
1998	4,279,288	12.3	534,008
1999	4,099,209	11.7	508,181
2000	3,888,652	10.7	470,414
2001	3,852,564	10.3	464,528
2002	4,061,345	9.8	499,433
2003	4,376,795	10.5	542,966
2004	4,381,281	10.5	545,080
2005	4,860,685	11.7	672,903
2006	4,487,057	13.1	643,752

Source: Statistisches Bundesamt Jahrbuch (Federal Bureau of Statistics Yearbook), 1980, 1990, 2007.

Table 26.2. Unemployment Rates by Selected Nationalities, 1980–2005
(*percentage*)

Country	1980	1985	1990	1995	2000	2005
Greece	3.8	11.5	10.0	15.7	16.1	3.8
Italy	4.8	14.3	11.0	15.9	15.2	7.3
Portugal	2.0	7.4	5.8	11.9	11.5	1.2
Spain	3.0	8.8	7.2	10.7	11.7	—
Former Yugoslavia	2.6	10.0	6.3	9.2	11.2	12.4
Turkey	5.9	14.6	10.3	18.9	21.2	31.4
Germany (overall rate)	—	—	—	10.4	10.7	11.7

Source: "Structuring Immigation – Fostering Integration: Report by the Independent Commission on Migration to Germany," 2001; Federal Labor Agency, "Analyse des Arbeitsmarktes für Ausländer, November 2006."

Against this backdrop, the German government began negotiations over a new migration law that would take the place of the one found unconstitutional in 2002. Because the CDU/CSU now held an overwhelming majority in the Bundesrat, any legislation had to be agreed to by both the SPD/Green coalition as well as the CDU/CSU. This made the return to the 2002 migration law unrealistic. The CDU/CSU leadership opposed any measure that would establish a general system for legal immigration. The legislative focus also shifted increasingly more toward security measures as the need for domestic protection increased after the 2003 bombings in Madrid reinforced the notion that an event such as 11 September 2001 could also happen in Europe.[5] However, rifts also existed within the CDU/CSU coalition between those who were more culturally conservative and, hence, more exclusionist, and those who were more free-market oriented and therefore saw the need to take economic realities into consideration when debating immigration reform. The CDU/CSU was united in its view that the new migration law provided a way to enhance its reputation for toughness on security. The coalition demanded new security provisions to tighten the screening of immigrants by the German domestic intelligence service and to simplify deportation procedures.[6] The resulting compromise was enacted by the Bundestag on 1 July 2004, the Bundesrat approved it on 9 July 2004, and the new law took effect on 1 January 2005.

5. On the general impact of 9/11 on European policymakers and public opinion, see Faist (2006).
6. Annika Joeres, "CDU will Multi-Kulti beenden," *die tageszeitung*, 14 May 2004; "Union zweifelt Kompromiss an," *Frankfurter Rundschau*, 29 May 2004.

The Migration Law of 2005

The new law, as enacted in 2004, is comprehensive in nature in that it regulates not only the admission of third-country nationals, but ethnic Germans and EU citizens as well.[7] Institutionally, the law restructures the organization of migration and centers all migration-related policy in the Federal Office for Migration and Refugees (BAMF), as had been recommended by the Independent Commission. The law also adopted the Commission's recommendations with regards to a combined work and residence permit; an individual's work status is now stated on the combined permit. The consolidation of two permits into one has created what the German government calls its "one-stop government." Legally resident foreigners now only have to interact with their respective foreigners' office. In many instances, the Federal Employment Agency (*Bundesagentur für Arbeit*) has to approve the issuance of a work permit, but they remain in the background. The number of types of non-temporary residence permits is also reduced from five to two types. Now, every non-temporary resident either has a permanent (*Niederlassungserlaubnis*) or limited term (*Aufenthaltserlaubnis*) residence permit. The new law also simplifies the registration process for EU nationals, who no longer have to apply for a residence permit.

With regard to non-EU nationals, the legislation does not adopt a point system designed to attract and select highly skilled immigrants, which had been the centerpiece of the Independent Commission's legislative proposals. Instead, it preserves the recruitment ban that had been introduced in 1973. In an incisive critical appraisal of the new law from the standpoint of labor market policy, Klaus Zimmermann and his co-authors described the omission of the point system as "particularly deplorable." This kind of selection system, they argue, provides the most effective means to fill chronic labor shortages in the most technically advanced sectors of the German economy without compounding the unemployment problem among the immigrant population (Zimmermann et al. 2007: 30–35). However, the law did provide three new exceptions to the ban on immigration, in addition to the existing exceptions for nurses, information technology specialists, and seasonal agricultural workers.

The first exception allows highly qualified workers, such as distinguished scientists and upper level managers, to immigrate to Germany. These highly

---

7. The law's official title is *Gesetz zur Steuerung und Begrenzung der Zuwanderung und zur Regelung des Aufenthalts und der Integration von Unionsbürgern und Ausländern* (literally, the Law for Controlling and Limiting Immigration and for Regulating the Residency and Integration of EU Nationals and Foreigners). The law's colloquial name is *Zuwanderungsgesetz* (Immigration Law). For the full version of the law, see http://www.bmi.bund.de/Internet/Content/Common/Anlagen/Gesetze/Zuwanderungsgesetz,templateId=raw,property=publicationFile.pdf/Zuwanderungsgesetz.pdf (accessed 5 January 2008).

qualified workers are now eligible for permanent residence permits upon entry rather than limited-term permits, as was applied under the previous legislation. Highly qualified workers, however, must have concrete job offers and the foreigners' offices have to send the work permit application to the Federal Employment Agency in order to verify that no other EU citizen or other privileged worker could feasibly take the job offered. In some cases, the Federal Employment Agency must also verify whether the residence permit is justified with regards to integration.

A second exception to the ban on immigration grants foreign students, who successfully completed their university studies, the option to remain in Germany for up to one year to find employment. If a foreign student finds work, the job must be in the student's area of academic training. In the course of that year, graduates are entitled to a combined residence permit and work permit. However, no provisions exist to allow these students to remain in Germany after the year is over.

The third exception, taken directly from US legislation, applies to investors, who receive a limited residence permit if they invest at least one million Euros and create ten new jobs in Germany. In order to do so, however, potential investors must go through an extensive vetting process in which the proper professional bodies examine the potential investor's business plan and the benefit it may bring to the community. To date, the use of this program has been negligible.

The new law makes four other significant changes with regard to immigration. First, as recommended by the Independent Commission on Immigration and with respect to the designation of refugee status, the law provides that Germany will recognize persecution by non-state actors as well as gender-specific persecution, including both sexual orientation and genital mutilation, as a basis for asylum. Second, the law grants *Länder* the ability, if they so desire, to create *Härtefallkomission* (Hardship Commissions) to allow state parliaments to examine the cases of individuals whose applications for asylum were rejected, but who might encounter hardship if repatriated. Since the "tolerated" status or *Duldung* was removed from the asylum law in the 2005 legislation, this provision created a new means for rejected asylum seekers to seek deeper and more sensitive review of their application. Moreover, the law allows these commissions to recommend that state authorities grant applicants residence in Germany on the basis of such "hardship." Each state is allowed to devise its own procedures for its hardship commissions. In doing so, the law gives *Länder*, rather than the federal government, control over one avenue of possible immigration. By late 2006, all *Länder* either already had or had planned to set up hardship commissions.

Third, with respect to the security measures demanded by the CDU/CSU, the migration law streamlines the procedures for the expulsion of terrorist suspects while introducing new expulsion grounds for leaders of banned organizations and radical agitators advocating incendiary acts. The case of Metin

Kaplan, the Caliph of Cologne, highlights the difficulty that implementing these new security laws posed.[8] Metin Kaplan is a Turkish national, who had been granted political asylum in Germany in 1983 because he faced the death penalty in Turkey. Despite having DM 2 million in cash, Kaplan also illegally drew social assistance benefits from the German state. In Germany, Kaplan had succeeded his father as leader of a group named *Kalifatstaat* (Caliphate State). This group, which sought to overthrow the secular government in Turkey and establish an Islamist government, was one of the first groups banned under Germany's tough new terrorism laws. Under these laws, Kaplan was arrested and ordered deported for inciting terrorism. Kaplan resisted the deportation by claiming that he could not be returned to Turkey because he would face the death penalty. Kaplan was eventually deported after a year of litigation and after Turkey had banned the death penalty as part of its bid to join the EU.[9]

The fourth significant change that the 2005 law introduced was the abolishment of the residency permit requirements for EU citizens as mandated by Section 5 of the EU Act on the General Freedom of Movement for EU citizens. EU citizens now have their own registration office at foreigners' offices, and like all German citizens, must register their address. In recent years, nationals of the fifteen "old" European Union Member States have made up between 12 and 15 percent of all migration into Germany, equaling between 98,000 and 130,000 persons annually (Federal Statistics Office).

8. Mark Terkessidis and Yasemin Karakasoglu, "Gerechtigkeit für die Muslime!" *Die Zeit*, 1 February 2006; Jürgen Gottschlich, "Kölner Kalif verurteilt; Lebenslang für Metin Kaplan," *die tageszeitung*, 22 June 2005; Frank Dierung, "Stadt Köln kämpft weiter juristisch um schnelle Abschiebung Metin Kaplans," *Die Welt*, 4 June 2004.

9. Though fighting terrorism remains an important political goal, Germany's deportation laws make the assumption that all radical voices are foreign nationals. As the London bombings of July 2005 demonstrated, members of radical groups are now often citizens of the respective country. Thus, the focus on deportations only serves to increase anti-Muslim sentiment and conflate terrorism with foreigners who can be easily deported.

Chapter 27

Integration and the Migration Law

The new migration law was supposed to regulate immigration, and it does so, if only at the margins. Its greatest contribution, however, has been to bring integration to the center of federal policymaking. Integration gained prominence as an EU-wide issue in Tampere and a subsequent European Commission communication in 2000, which urged national governments to adopt more effective integration strategies.[1] The discussion about integration in German national politics was novel in many ways, however, because federal level immigrant integration policies until the late 1990 had to contend with the legacy of the 1960s mentality that immigrants would somehow return home.[2] However, some German cities, most notably Berlin and Frankfurt, have developed a thicket of integration policies over the course of many years.

The new migration law helped to reconceptualize Germany's exclusionary policies toward foreigners by introducing an explicit integration agenda. Of course, integration is always an ambiguous, value-laden term, a fact that helps explain why arriving at the best policy usually evades policymakers. Its meaning is always subject to change and remains open to competing interpretations (Stråth 2000; Favell 2001). Here, we are primarily concerned with examining the policy goals behind the migration law's integration agenda and the measures that have been taken to reach these goals. We argue that while considerable progress has been made, such progress falls short of the goals charted by the Independent Commission, which aim at promoting a more inclusive society.

---

1. The European Commission, Com (2000) 757 final: 19.
2. This is what Rinus Penninx (2006) labeled an "exclusionary definition" of integration. Under this definition, as was the case in Germany until very recently, "there are no logical grounds for inclusive policies that would incorporate these immigrants as full citizens or political actors" (Penninx 2006: 40).

The federal government has assumed a central role in the integration dialogue. As Bade (2005) also has observed, the Merkel government decided to
confront the fallout of social disintegration which its predecessor governments
had bequeathed it through decades of prolonged indifference by engaging
with immigrants as permanent members of society. The Independent Commission report had dealt extensively with the topic of integration, defining it
as "a process that depends on reciprocal contributions which both the host
and the immigrant society make" (Independent Commission on Immigration 2001: 196). The Commission thus recognized that integration involves a
two-way dynamic of adaptation and accommodation (Bade 2005; Papademetriou 2006: xiv–lxiii; Spencer 2006). This recognition, however, required that
Germans find a way to preserve diversity, or at least respect for peoples' differences, without affecting social unity (Davy 2005: 128). As such, the Independent Commission conceived of integration as a multi-dimensional process:
"[T]he objective of integration as a political responsibility is to facilitate the
equal participation of immigrants in social, economic, and political life, while
respecting cultural diversity at the same time" (Independent Commission on
Immigration 2001: 196). The Independent Commission rejected both liberal
multicultural models and notions of a *Parallelgesellschaft* (parallel society) as
desirable policy alternatives by emphasizing the need for reciprocal action
between the Germans and immigrants and a more open society that encourages full participation by immigrants.

In developing its approach to integration, the Independent Commission
concurred with a broad consensus among students of migration who had long
argued for greater participation in society by immigrants (Süssmuth 2006).
Effective participation presupposes that the immigrants acquire a basic knowledge of the host society's language, institutions, customs, and laws so that
they can avail themselves of new opportunities. A number of working groups
were assembled by the Carnegie Endowment for International Peace/Migra-
tion Policy Institute in 2001 and 2002. Composed of a wide range of leading
migration researchers from Europe, North America, Australia, and Japan,
these working groups reached similar conclusions with regard to the need to
integrate immigrants across all aspects of civic and public life (Aleinikoff and
Klusmeyer 2003). As the scholars in these working groups, among others, have
recognized, different areas of integration—political, social, and economic—are
mutually reinforcing. The more stakes immigrants perceive that they have in
the host society and the more opportunities immigrants have to acquire such
stakes, the more likely they will be to identify themselves over time with their
host country and seek to participate in a system that guarantees those stakes.

Ruud Koopmans and Paul Statham (1999) add theoretical rigor to this
insight. They develop a powerful argument that immigrants' willingness to
integrate and to be involved in national public life generally is shaped by what

they call the "opportunity structures"[3] of the receiving country. These structures are not limited to political measures such as the right to vote and to participate in elections. They are also embedded throughout the fabric of a receiving country's concrete laws and institutions, as well as less tangible variables such as those that target social exclusion and racism (Koopmans and Statham 1999). From their comparative research, Koopmans and Statham conclude that Germany has had weak opportunity structures, which generally do not facilitate non-ethnic German immigrants' integration. As a result, many immigrant communities have long been economically, politically, and socially disengaged and disadvantaged.

While the evolving insights on integration and the Independent Commission's recommendations have shaped the policy debates in Germany since 2001, policymakers applied such comprehensive approaches to integration in the new migration law very selectively (Süssmuth 2006: 104). The focus on incorporating immigrants into German society through rigorous German language and civics training in many ways reveals how much ground multiculturalism has lost in discussions about immigration and integration policy (Nielsen 2004: 154–159). The expressed policy goal is for everyone to be able to speak the same language and share similar cultural values. What we see happening in German integration policy is, thus, a turn toward an assimilationist-based discourse. Such a discourse was familiar to the integration policies in North America and parts of Western Europe, notably France, during the 1960s and 1970s and has regained favor once more throughout most immigrant receiving societies. Political discourses (perhaps "distractions" might be a better term) aside, however, it is clear that the current policy course in Germany is a proactive attempt to address the decades-long shortfall of German federal policy attention to immigrants' economic, political, and social incorporation, and, by extension, needs.

Economic Integration

Education has long been considered one of the main forces of economic integration in immigrant receiving countries because it has particularly strong effects on immigrants' upward mobility. The Independent Commission highlighted the need for policy that harvests the education system's ability to achieve early integration for children with immigrant backgrounds through proper language instruction. A key Commission recommendation called for instituting a curriculum for teaching German as a second language and hiring

---

3. Koopmans and Statham recognize that their concept of "opportunity structures" owes much to Patrick Ireland's earlier concept of "institutional channeling" (Ireland 1994).

teachers with immigrant backgrounds or higher qualifications for teaching in a diverse schoolroom environment. We have yet to see any wide-scale policy movement in this direction. While these recommendations are highly useful and should be taken seriously, the fact remains that both the Independent Commission and policymakers since then have failed to address directly the problem that Germany's educational system fails far too many immigrant and immigrant-origin children.

The system, which sets students far too early on tracks toward either vocational or professional job training, has long been criticized for leaving many immigrants unprepared for the transition into the labor market (Faist 1993; Crul and Vermeulen 2003; Worbs 2003; Süssmuth 2006; Crul 2007; Papademetriou and Weidenfeld 2007). As the largest immigrant group and one of the longest established,[4] the case of Turks in Germany best illustrates the education system's poor record as a facilitator of immigrant integration. A study carried out by the German government in 2001 encouragingly found that among younger Turks in Germany, German language ability had improved significantly compared to older generations (Beer-Kern 2001). This finding is consistent with more recent research, which has found that generational status, rather than length of stay, better determines language ability (Diehl and Schnell 2005). Nevertheless, only 66.4 percent of 15- to 29-year-old Turks in Germany could write well—a prerequisite for most vocational and skilled jobs in Germany. The situation was especially dire for those Turks in Germany who only have the lowest level secondary degree (*Hauptschulabschluss*), a group that comprises approximately 70 percent of all second-generation Turkish immigrants (Worbs 2003: 1020). Of all Turkish immigrants with a *Hauptschulabschluss,* only 63.1 percent spoke German well and only 41 percent wrote it well (Beer-Kern 2001). Language deficiencies are a considerable barrier to immigrants' entry into the labor market, and, thus, they exacerbate immigrants' unequal access to employment and mobility opportunities.

Language deficiencies also contribute to the greater problem of the employable-skills deficit for immigrant youth, who are mainly found in vocational training positions (Worbs 2003: 1020) but often in fields with dwindling job opportunities. Educational and training gaps between immigrant groups and natives exacerbate unemployment issues and sharpen inequitable access to the labor market. The OECD reports that, "On average, immigrants have a significantly lower qualification than the domestic population" (OECD 2004: 133). According to a study conducted in 1999, only 13 percent of second-generation Turks completed their education at the *Gymnasium* and received the *Abitur,* a prerequisite for attending university and entering the professional job market,

---

4. In 2001, 67 percent of Turkish nationals had been in the country for more than ten years and 37 percent of the Turkish population was born in Germany (Green 2003b: 234–235).

compared to 40 percent among native Germans (Worbs 2003: 1020). In 2000, 46.9 percent of Germans attended the upper educational track (*Gymnasium*) compared to 20.8 percent of non-Germans, while 45.2 percent of non-Germans attended the lower educational track (*Hauptschule* or *Gesamtschule*) compared to 19.8 percent of Germans (Doerschler 2004: 454). The situation has improved only marginally in more recent years.

Lack of educational qualifications impedes upward mobility among immigrants. More immediately, it is an obstacle to gaining and retaining employment in an economy that has fewer and fewer low-skilled industrial jobs suitable for those without the *Abitur* and higher educational experience. It is instructive that 64 percent of Turkish immigrants obtained lower or intermediate school degrees without occupational training during the period between 1980 and 1999, and 23 percent of Turks were unemployed in 1998 compared to 5.9 percent in 1980 (Bender and Seifert 2003: 61–62). Although highly skilled Turkish and other immigrant workers have probably benefited from policy efforts aimed at their integration into the German economy, highly skilled Turks still constitute only a small minority of all Turks in Germany.

The gaps in the educational attainment of native and immigrant youth in Germany nonetheless reflect broader issues of inequalities in the immigrants' access to the labor market as an effect of the German education system. In the 1980s, policymakers had attempted to address some of the immigrants' educational and job-preparedness deficits by instituting a dual system of apprenticeship and job-based education. Introduced during a time of heated debate about how to address the social and economic fallout of the guestworkers and their offsprings' permanence in Germany, the dual system granted all recipients of a *Hauptschule* diploma an apprenticeship as well as job-specific classroom education. This system was a major improvement in terms of inclusion, because prior to the dual system, such opportunities were reserved for German citizens (Worbs 2003; Faist 1993). More importantly, the reformed apprenticeship system allowed politicians to bypass the challenges of an extensive educational reform, which is practically impossible in Germany where the federal system reserves educational policy for the *Länder*.

While comprehensive reform of Germany's educational system may be necessary to address the more endemic causes of immigrants' economic disadvantage, the dual system has had some success in transitioning the second-generation immigrants from school to the labor market (Faist 1993). The reform may also partly be responsible for the fact that second-generation Turks in Germany experience higher rates of employment compared to second-generation Turkish immigrants in France and the Netherlands. Moreover, employment rates for immigrants tend to be higher in Germany than in any other country of large-scale immigration across continental Europe (Crul and Vermeulen 2003: 977). It appears, then, that Germany's dual system has improved economic security, if only at the margins. However, the system fails to induce upward mobility, which is generally achieved through higher education (Worbs 2003: 1031; Crul and Vermeulen 2003: 977).[5]

Political Integration

While barriers to economic integration and upward mobility remain unresolved, political integration has become the paramount topic of recent legislation. Despite the adoption of a more inclusive citizenship policy in 1999, Germany continues to have the largest population of resident non-citizens in Europe. At the turn of the twenty-first century, there were approximately 1.6 million non-nationals who were born in Germany (Green 2003b: 229), and a large portion of them, especially Turks, had lived in Germany for two generations. The Independent Commission's report attributed the deficit in naturalizations of immigrants in Germany to exclusive citizenship practices, particularly the ban on dual citizenship. As part of its recommendation to allow for dual citizenship, the report recognized that exclusion from the political process fails to provide immigrants with the leverage necessary to motivate politicians to act on their behalf. This leaves immigrants without a political stake in German society and, in effect, with few incentives to naturalize.

Their status as non-citizens does not mean that immigrants are absent from the political process. As Gökçe Yurdakul documents in Berlin, German political parties, including the CDU/CSU, have begun to take Turkish immigrant associations more seriously (Yurdakul 2006). "The immigrant associations," Yurdakul observes, "have strongly defended immigrant rights vis-à-vis German political parties, and occasionally vis-à-vis the local and the federal German authorities" (2006: 436). This representation, however, is not political representation in the sense of one-person-one-vote. Rather, it is channeled through Germany's corporatist political structure, which provides immigrants only a passive political voice through participation in their community organizations (Green 2003a). In Berlin, for example, the more conservative Turkish *Cemaat*, an organization that advocates for transnational politics, has aligned itself with the CDU despite its clash with the CDU's concept of integration. The Turkish communities' interest in preserving their neighborhoods encourages *Cemaat* to cooperate with local authorities in Berlin in matters of policing and security, which in turn provides a basis for the relationship between the CDU and *Cemaat* (Yurdakul 2006).

---

5. The trend of low social mobility rates among immigrant youth, particularly within the Turkish population, may be explained in part by the immigrants' dependence on social networks to receive apprenticeships (Faist 1993). Many young Turks, as a result of their networks, take jobs in the same blue-collar jobs as their parents because they have access to personal contacts in these sectors.

Unfortunately, when naturalized citizens from these immigrant populations do participate fully in the German political process, they have been often used as a wedge between political parties. For instance, in the 2005 federal elections, in which, for the first time, the 600,000 naturalized Turks made up a substantial enough voting block to have a potential impact on the election, some accused Gerhard Schröder of treason when he visited a Turkish language newspaper to court voters. The populist newspaper *Bild* printed a picture of Schröder in front of a Turkish flag with the caption: "Will Turks Decide the Election?"[6] Accusations of politicians betraying German voters by supporting or simply acknowledging the interests of German Turks reinforces political isolation among the Turkish voters and makes it difficult for them to form a relationship, political or otherwise, with the German state (Kastoryano 2002). An environment of immigrant distrust and alienation makes self-identification with the host country difficult and discourages participation in the social life of the country. In fostering a more favorable climate, political rhetoric matters a lot. The CDU/CSU's public advocacy of a 'guiding culture' model earlier in the decade had predictably polarizing effects, and, unfortunately, similar rhetoric appeared during the debates over the new immigration law. This kind of rhetoric provides little incentive for immigrants to integrate at all (Sollors 2004: 2).

Social Integration

One remedy for the social fragmentation that results from political isolation is an inclusive citizenship practice—a stance taken by the Independent Commission, as well as by the Carnegie Endowment for International Peace/Migration Policy Institute (Aleinikoff and Klusmeyer 2003). Comparisons here are illuminating. Ruud Koopmans's research, for example, demonstrates that in Britain, which has an inclusive citizenship policy, most migrants and minority communities mobilize in order to make claims for greater integration and inclusion. By contrast, political mobilization in Germany occurs predominantly around homeland politics (Koopmans 2004: 462–466). The integration challenges for Germany can also be compared to those in the Netherlands, where policymakers have continued to introduce far-reaching social integration policies despite recent national level political arguments about their effectiveness. In Germany, researchers "have found inward-oriented and even fundamentalist attitudes among Turkish youngsters on a large scale. In the Netherlands, in contrast, researchers found a much more positive attitude towards integration, involvement, and participation, particularly in local society" (Penninx 2006:

---

6. Petra Ahne, "Schröder fast ein Heimspiel," *Berliner Zeitung*, 15 September 2005.

35). When immigrants and, more generally, minorities, feel they will not be completely accepted as members of their host societies they are more inclined to remain invested in the politics and social life of their former homeland. The lack of institutional standing within the political system exacerbates that tendency. Yet, despite the apparent reemergence of the importance of homeland politics, only 10 percent of second-generation Turks claimed to feel "totally Turkish" in 2001, compared to 40 percent in 1989 (Diehl and Schnell 2005). The vector of such sentiments in the immigrant-weary, post–September 11 climate, however, has yet to be measured accurately.

Implementing inclusive national policies with regard to integration is particularly complicated because, unlike the granting of work permits, both naturalization and attitudes toward integration, while generally guided by federal policy, are strongly shaped by actions at the *Länder* and city government levels. Extensive research has pointed to the fact that in regions where more proactive integration policies have been implemented, integration has been much more successful.[7] But encouraging people to naturalize as German citizens is difficult if they do not feel that they are part of German society, especially since they are required to relinquish their original citizenship. We see the effects of effective local integration policies, for instance, in Frankfurt and Berlin, which have the highest naturalization rates in Germany. Immigrants in these cities also enjoy a general pro-immigrant sentiment by the general population (Koopmans 2004: 457–458). Bavaria, by comparison, which has done relatively little to integrate immigrants and where politicians have often employed anti-immigrant rhetoric, has the lowest levels of naturalization. These findings suggest that an immigrant's propensity to acquire German citizenship depends on a number of factors at the *Land* and local levels, but inclusive integration strategies play a determinative role.

In sum, immigrants' access to the labor market, engagement in the political process, and social inclusion and acquisition of citizenship in their country of residence are critical variables of economic, political, and social incorporation. The current legislation in Germany, however, falls woefully short in incorporating these areas systematically as core components of an overall integration *strategy*. Instead, the legislation focuses on language and civic-values education as the primary pathways into German society and treats naturalization as the last step of full integration into German society. Before the immigrant can gain full access to the benefits of living in Germany, he or she must first prove they are entitled to these benefits by passing language and civic tests and making vows of loyalty to the German state. While these measures are important governance

7. Koopmans discusses this research in more detail in his text. As examples of this kind of research, he names Lie (1995), Rex (1998), Shain and Sherman (1998), and Van Hear (1998) (Koopmans 2004: 450).

tools, the legislation misses an opportunity to take a decisive stance in favor of inclusiveness, which, in turn, could do more for social cohesion than any of the formal integration measures introduced thus far.

Integration and Language Training

Judged in comparison to the scope of the challenge, the new migration law does relatively little to change the status of immigrants and their offspring in Germany. However, the new law did adopt the Independent Commission's recommendation that long-term immigrants learn German, though it did not establish requirements for German-language learning for children. While a modest step in terms of full integration, rigorous language training will likely help immigrants integrate better into the labor market and will certainly facilitate their social interaction with Germans. How much of this occurs, of course, will be shaped, as pointed out earlier, by the opportunity structures in place for immigrant participation. The new law also falls short in promoting another means through which immigrants become imbedded in society and its component communities: their employment in the state bureaucracy and police force, a failure that Chancellor Merkel has also highlighted.[8] The Commission emphasized the importance of such measures because public service "must play a pioneering role in this area and set an example for other areas of employment" (Independent Commission on Immigration 2001: 13). The new law does take steps toward the harmonization of Germany's treatment of all immigrants, regardless of their ethnic origin. This move brings the rights of permanently resident foreign nationals closer to those enjoyed by *Aussiedler*, who have long been the beneficiaries of integration programs (Koopmans and Statham 1999). These policy revisions are very important, especially as they occur against a backdrop of policies that actually hindered integration for decades. Reversing such a trajectory is no easy task and the Merkel government's efforts must be seen also in this light.

Nonetheless, rather than addressing the core causes of the gaps in immigrant integration, the new migration law focused predominantly on the language skills of immigrants. While insufficient knowledge of the German language has undoubtedly played a significant role in terms of poor integration outcomes, it is often a sign of the failure of other policies. The law's underlying assumption, that once immigrants become more conversant in German they will be more involved in mainstream German society, is only partly correct. The new law introduced both an entitlement and obligation for immigrants to take German-language

---

8. Chancellor Merkel addressed the need to use civil service jobs as a means of integrating immigrants into German society ("German Poster Campaign Publicises Aid for Immigrants," *Expatica News*, 13 July 2007).

courses. Those who fail to comply with the new provisions are subject to sanctions, which can even affect secure residence rights and social benefits. The law provides for 600 hours of instruction to promote the learning of German, and 30 hours of civics education to familiarize participants with the fundamentals of German law and culture. Under the law, the federal government will publicly finance these courses, with a small part of the fees paid by financially able immigrants.[9] The projected cost of the integration program to the German government will increase by €14 million to €154 million for the 2008 fiscal year.[10]

In December 2006, the Interior Ministry released an in-depth analysis of the efficacy of the language and civics courses introduced in the 2005 law.[11] The report offered a generally positive evaluation, citing high quality teachers, consistent rates of participation in and completion of the courses, and fairly effective implementation of the language program. The report also recommended that the federal government raise the course fees from €2.05 to €2.20 per hour and decrease the federal government's subsidies to immigrants who cannot fully afford to pay the course fees. Nonetheless, the federal government's willingness to have the implementation and effectiveness of the integration courses evaluated independently is an encouraging sign.

The step toward a national integration policy has not displaced the state and local governments' concern with addressing the integration needs of their immigrants. For their part, the *Länder* have taken up specific policy recommendations by the Independent Commission. The governments of several important *Länder*, as well as many localities, have built on the Commission's recommendations and have instituted *Mama lernt Deutsch* (Mother Learns German) programs. These programs are designed specifically for women of immigrant origin, who often have the most limited language skills, to learn German along with their children.

The Controversy over Difference

The outsider status of immigrants makes them vulnerable to double standards, discrimination, and stereotyping. For example, after the Constitutional Court ruling in 2003, discussed earlier in this volume, several *Länder* enacted legislation that prohibits Muslim schoolteachers from wearing headscarves. In January 2006, the state of Baden-Württemberg imposed a set of requirements

---

9. From January 2005 until September 2006, of the 322,311 immigrants eligible for or required to enroll 219,973 did so, and approximately 80,700 finished the courses ("Integrationsbilanz für das Jahr 2006," BAMF, 31 March 2007).

10. "Reform des Zuwanderungsrechts fördert Integration in unserem Land," BMI, 6 July 2007.

11. "Evaluation der Integrationskurse nach dem Zuwanderungsgesetz," BMI, December 2006.

purportedly to ensure that Muslims who wished to immigrate to Baden-Würt-temberg agreed with the principles of the Basic Law—with questions ranging from attitudes toward homosexuality to the September 11 attacks—for any citizen from any of the 57 members of the Organization of the Islamic Conference (OIC),[12] or anyone else known to be Muslim and wishing to immigrate to the state. These requirements, which sparked controversy in German media and policy circles, precipitated more fundamental questions about how far Germans have gone and are willing to go to welcome all immigrants into their national community.

Widely covered media events inside and outside of Germany reflect public anxieties over the immigrants' place in German society. The murder in Amsterdam of filmmaker Theo van Gogh, who together with Dutch Parliamentarian Ayaan Hirsi Ali had produced the short film *Submission*, in November 2004 at the hands of Mohammed Bouyeri, was widely covered in Germany. Ali's book, *Ich klage an* (literally, *I Accuse*), a polemic against Islam's treatment of women in which she deals extensively with the practices of genital mutilation and honor killings, topped the nonfiction bestseller list in Germany for weeks. The German media has also increased its coverage of similar topics, such as honor killings and the mistreatment of Muslim wives and daughters. For instance, a case in Wiesbaden, in which a brother killed his sister for marrying an ethnic German in order to defend the honor of the family, was widely covered by the press (*Der Spiegel* 2005). German books have tackled the topic as well, including one written by Necla Kelek, a German sociologist of Turkish origin. In her book, *Die fremde Braut* (*The Foreign Bride*), Kelek exposes the social isolation and often-abusive living conditions of Turkish brides who are brought to Germany by socially estranged German-Turkish men. Kelek's book started a public debate between concerned politicians, immigrant associations, and academics. Many politicians involved in the debate hailed the book for demonstrating why Muslims, especially Turks, must be integrated into Germany society by highlighting the book's portrayal of Islam's oppression of women. However, many immigrants and academic scholars criticized the book as fictional and unrepresentative of the conditions facing Muslim women in Germany.[13] The effect of such controversies has been a public discussion about the compatibility between a Muslim

12. The OIC is an intergovernmental organization, which is now composed of fifty-seven Member States (including the Palestinian Authority) having a substantial Muslim population. Among the organization's goals are the strengthening of Muslim solidarity, the elimination of racial discrimination, and scientific and technological cooperation among Member States.

13. Yasemin Karakasoglu, for example, is a vociferous opponent of figures like Kelek. For a complete list of the 60 migration scholars who signed the 'Justice for Muslims' petition in response to Kelek's book, see Mark Terkessidis and Yasemin Karakasoglu, "Gerechtigkeit für die Muslime!" *Die Zeit*, 1 February 2006. For a discussion of the role played by Turkish brides as symbols of cultural difference in German debates over immigration, see Beck-Gernsheim (2006).

(particularly Turkish) and German *Weltanschauung*. This type of issue has become a central theme for the media, and it shows why progress is so difficult in such climates of opinion. The media's focus on the sensational has helped neither policymakers, including the German Chancellor and her aides, nor the Interior Minister nor some senior *Länder* politicians, seeking to emphasize the practical.

This kind of practical approach to integration offers some encouragement. For example, the *Land* of North Rhine-Westphalia has made enormous strides on integration since 2005, when the ruling CDU party created a Ministry for Intergenerational Affairs, Family, Women and Integration. Led very ably by Armin Laschet, the Ministry has followed a deeply pragmatic approach toward integration in part by articulating a vision of being "in this together" and taking every opportunity to explain to citizens and immigrants alike that they are bound to a common future in which all have an important role to play. Minister Laschet was elevated to the governing body of the CDU in 2008. In another high-profile case, Cem Özdemir, a second generation ethnic Turk who has served as a member of both the *Bundestag* and the EU Parliament, was elected in 2008 as a co-leader of his Green Party. While two examples do not a metamorphosis make, they do contribute mightily to the sense that something fundamental is changing in Germany, a theme that we take up again in the conclusion to this volume.

Considering such high-profile progress, one must at least allow the possibility that the ambiguities in the new law and its implementation may reflect the fact that policymakers are tackling those aspects most likely to be palatable to the German public first. And in fact, the drafters of the 2005 law did not see it as a final policy statement. Rather, they viewed this as a law-in-progress, by incorporating the basis for future revision into the law itself. The law's ambiguous outcomes, therefore, set the stage for future reform as part of the German government's search for an effective integration policy. Rita Süssmuth (2006) reminds us that changing the direction of policy requires time. The question now turns to how the FRG has exactly used this time to reform its integration policy thus far.

Conclusion

Negotiating Difference and Belonging
in Today's Germany

Few advanced democracies have absorbed more persons born in other countries than Germany has since the end of World War II, and few European countries have been as consistently "immigrant dense"[1] as Germany. Even more to the point, if one were to count foreign-born persons, rather than indulge the counting games that countries have devised for their own political and ideological ends, Germany is about as immigrant dense as the United States—and it has been so for more than a generation.[2] As this volume has demonstrated clearly, Germany has experience with successfully integrating very large numbers of foreign-born persons in its recent history. More than ten million post–World War II ethnic German refugees and expellees were incorporated in the 1950s into Germany's political, economic, and sociocultural corpus, in a process that was both remarkably swift and complete. Of course, the historical context and conditions in which this occurred were very different from circumstances today, but this earlier successful experience with integration nevertheless provides a useful precedent for rethinking Germany's approach to immigration.

---

1. Immigrant density refers to the proportion of foreign-born persons in a country's population.

2. If one were to account for the fact that the US, unlike any European country, includes estimates both of illegally resident foreign-born persons in its immigration statistics (they constitute nearly one-third of all US immigrants) as well as about 1.5 million foreigners on longer term temporary visas, the comparison would lean decidedly in favor of Germany as a much more "immigrant-dense" country than the United States. That statement holds true even after adjusting for such German counting anomalies as designating as foreigners those persons born in Germany to immigrant parents.

Until very recently, Germany's approach to immigration and integration decisions has clung stubbornly to a "that was then, and this is now" attitude that has not served anyone well, particularly not the German polity. As a result, German society has lost valuable time in trying to come to terms with its ever deepening diversity and ever growing numbers of newcomers, many of them ethnic Germans with moral and legal claims just as valid as those of the millions that returned to Germany in the 1950s. One is tempted to attribute the lost opportunities to a combination of miscalculations and political opportunism. This volume has introduced enough evidence to suggest that such claims are entirely plausible. Our principal contention, however, has been that the lion's share of the blame lies with the sins of omission and commission made by successive German governments almost regardless of which party held power.

The omissions were primarily due to a lack of imagination and political courage. Germany's stubborn refusal to accept its status as a country of immigrants until the very end of the last century and the consequent decades-long failure to engage in the difficult but essential task of crafting a comprehensive immigration and integration policy demonstrate both of these shortcomings. But even the occasional courageous politician probably felt hemmed in by a society that, after decades of misinformation and manipulation by the political and bureaucratic classes, had come to feel threatened by immigration. The 2007 PEW Global Attitudes Project, for example, found that 66 percent of those surveyed in Germany supported stricter immigration controls and 64 percent of those who responded in favor of more restrictions also felt that increased immigration posed a threat to German culture.[3] To be fair, Germans have had much company in these regards both in Europe and around the globe.[4]

The failures of commission, however, have been almost uniquely German and are, as a result, at the very heart of this volume's analysis. Foremost among them has been the remarkable stubbornness of viewing the complex issues of negotiating difference exclusively through the ethnocultural lens. Despite high levels of immigration to Germany since the late 1950s, Germany's policymakers created the first coherent immigrant integration policy only in 2005. And while these new policies represent great progress over the denials of the past, the basic narrative has remained emphatic that immigrants must accept Germany's cultural norms if they want to take part in German

3. *The PEW Global Attitudes Project* (Washington, DC: PEW Research Center, 2007), 26–27.

4. The same report found that 87 percent of Italian, 75 percent of British, and 76 percent of French respondents support tougher immigration controls. Similar attitudes were reported in Turkey (77 percent), Lebanon (67 percent), India (84 percent), Argentina (68 percent), and Venezuela (77 percent).

society. Such narratives are now almost commonplace in several European countries. However, no other country carries as much baggage from a fifty year history of denial, and in no other country does the tonality of the narrative sound so unyielding.

Nonetheless, the last fifteen or so years have seen a gradual loosening in the political stranglehold that a generation of influential conservative analysts and policymakers have had on policy toward foreigners. While the legal and constitutional changes of the early-to-mid 1990s still had a strong conservative hue to them, it was also becoming obvious that the political monopoly over the issue that the Kohl government had exercised for so long was beginning to weaken. As discussed earlier, the victory by Gerhard Schröder's SPD in 1998 did, indeed, bring about significant changes in the government's attitude toward immigration, initially on citizenship matters. Hopes that these changes would be followed by a new and comprehensive immigration and integration policy were dashed, however, when the government failed in its attempt to pass such legislation in 2002. That failure led to a pause in, if not a reversal of, the government's willingness to press for a carefully calibrated liberalization of immigration policy. A key consequence of this decision was that the Schröder government missed an opportunity to create a rational and modern immigration system based on Germany's long-term economic and social interests. The timid 2004 legislation reflected precisely that pause in momentum. Neither was the domestic dimension the only one in which Germany would show its renewed nervousness about immigration and the immigration-integration nexus.

New EU Policy Standards

This reemerging skepticism spilled over into Germany's posture toward migration related initiatives also at the EU level. The skepticism's most public expression came in a last-minute demand in 2003 by then Interior Minister Schily that the European Constitution grant Germany a veto right in matters of European immigration policy to protect its national interest (Schreiber 2003). While the EU's, and particularly the European Commission's, interest in "migration" arguably dates back to the Treaty of Rome, the interest in integration is quite recent. In the 2000 Lisbon Agenda, the EU realized the importance of integration as part of much broader EU policy concerns about competitiveness,[5] poverty reduction, and social inclusion. It is in this context that Europe's leaders set up the political foundation for moving toward targeting immigrant inclusion as

5. The 2000 "Lisbon Agenda" set the goal of making Europe's economy the most competitive one in the world by 2010 by creating a 'knowledge-based economy and society' and eradicating the causes of 'social exclusion' (European Council 2000b).

an EU-wide priority.[6] Indeed, the European Commission and many European Councils since 1999 have promoted more and more systematically the need for effective integration policies across Member States (see, inter alia, European Council 1999b, 2000b, 2003a, 2003b, 2004). It was the Thessaloniki European Council in June 2003, however, that legitimated European activism on integration by explaining that, "in order to intensify the development of such a [European] framework, the definition of common basic principles should be envisaged" (European Council 2003a: 9). The Council's call to action was answered by the Dutch Presidency of the EU during the second half of 2004. The Dutch Presidency engaged the services of the Athens Migration Policy Initiative (AMPI), a group of European experts convened and led by Washington's Migration Policy Institute, to flesh out the Thessaloniki Conclusions, which had been prepared with the hands on involvement of AMPI.[7] The resulting "common basic principles" (CBPs) of immigrant integration and the 2004 Hague Program's strong emphasis on integration, helped guarantee that the European Commission's work program for the 2004–2009 period would have a pronounced tilt toward integration and the funds to promote it.

The December 2004 European Council formalized Europe's commitment to work toward including immigrants into its social fabric through the incorporation of the CBPs into the Commission's work.[8] In recognition both of the

6. The Tampere Council in 1999 provided the first opportunity for beginning to focus on immigrant integration when it acknowledged the need to maximize the economic gains of immigration and secure the financial futures of national welfare systems (European Council 1999b: §20). In 2001, the Laeken Council called for "the first joint report on social inclusion and the establishment of a set of common indicators" to achieve the Lisbon Agenda's goal of eradicating poverty and promoting social inclusion (European Council 2001: §28). Finally, at the Brussels Council in 2003, the Council members identified "the importance of sharing best practice in the social inclusion field and of targeting help on under-represented and disadvantaged groups, including migrants" (European Council 2003b: §52).

7. Demetrios G. Papademetriou led both of these exercises.

8. The CBPs recognize that "(1) Integration is a dynamic, two-way process of mutual accommodation by all immigrants and residents of Member States.... (2) Integration implies respect for the basic values of the European Union.... (3) Employment is a key part of the integration process and is central to the participation of immigrants, to the contributions immigrants make to the host society, and to making such contributions visible.... (4) Basic knowledge of the host society's language, history, and institutions is indispensable to integration; enabling immigrants to acquire this basic knowledge is essential to successful integration.... (5) Efforts in education are critical to preparing immigrants, and particularly their descendants, to be more successful and more active participants in society.... (6) Access for immigrants to institutions, as well as to public goods and services, on a basis equal to national citizens and in a non-discriminatory way is a critical foundation for better integration.... (7) Frequent interaction between the immigrants and Member State citizens is a fundamental mechanism for integration. Shared forums, inter-cultural dialogue, education about immigrants and immigrant cultures, and stimulating living conditions in urban environments enhance the interactions between immigrants and Member State citizens.... (8) The practice of

sensitive nature of the issue (issues surrounding citizenship go to the very heart of sovereignty) and of the fact that Member State governments face different integration challenges, the principles were pitched in ways that would allow Member States to emphasize and interpret them according to their specific national, regional, and local needs.

An example might suffice to demonstrate the sensitivity of the issues. The ninth principle encourages including immigrants in political and other processes that affect them. The most direct way to approach this goal would be by granting voting rights at the local level across the EU and requiring Member States to liberalize naturalization policies. An unambiguous call for such liberalization, however, would have run counter to how many Member States view and wish to regulate naturalization, and would have risked the consensus that the adoption of the CBPs required.[9] As a result, the CBPs set out to facilitate the inclusion of immigrants while staying clear of any mandate to change Member State policies on naturalization. Instead, the CBPs were designed to provide a normative and practical framework for Member State integration policies. Accordingly, rather than aiming to establish legal standards and norms, or seeking to give new legal powers to the Commission, the CBPs set out evocative goals and emphasized the exchange of information and good practices.[10]

---

diverse cultures and religions is guaranteed under the Charter of Fundamental Rights and must be safeguarded, unless practices conflict with other inviolable European rights or national law.... (9) The participation of immigrants in the democratic process and in the formulation of integration policies and measures, especially at the local level, supports their integration.... (10) Mainstreaming integration policies and measures in all relevant policy portfolios and levels of government and public services is an important consideration in public policy formation and implementation.... (11) Developing clear goals, indicators, and evaluation mechanisms is necessary to adjust policy, evaluate progress on integration, and to make the exchange of information more effective" (Dutch Presidency's draft conclusions on the Common Basic Principles, European Council document 14776/04, 18 November 2004).

9. The naturalization issue is, indeed, a sensitive one. Rainer Bauböck and his colleagues surveyed the trends in naturalization and citizenship policies across Europe and found that these policies have become increasingly restrictive in places such as Austria, Denmark, France, and the Netherlands, among others. However, they do not conclude that such restrictive measures constitute a decisive shift or counter-trend toward restrictive naturalization practices in the Member States. Instead, their survey provides an argument for Europe to usher in a more standardized approach to naturalization to ensure that immigrants in Europe have equal access to the benefits of community membership (Bauböck et al. 2007).

10. See, for example, the two annual reports on migration and integration by the European Commission, COM(2004) 508 final and SEC(2006) 892, respectively; see also Council Conclusions of the Informal Meeting of EU Ministers in Potsdam, Germany, May 2007, "Strengthening of Integration Policies in the European Union," http://www.consilium.europa.eu/ueDocs/cms_Data/docs/pressData/en/jha/94682.pdf#page=23 (accessed 16 April 2009).

Beyond the 2005 Migration Law

As noted earlier, in drafting the 2005 law, German policymakers had clearly anticipated the need for ongoing reforms.[11] After she took office in late 2005, Chancellor Angela Merkel created expectations both within and outside of Germany by vowing to conduct a national-level dialogue on integration.[12] The national integration plan and the *Islamkonferenz* (Conference on Islam) that have been at the heart of this dialogue, as well as two government-sponsored evaluations of the law's provisions, became the means for Germany's government to advance its work on integration.

The first independent evaluation of the migration law's integration provisions, published in July 2006,[13] focused on how the government could improve on the integration law's transparency. The evaluators recommended that the government clarify the enrollment process and who must attend the integration courses, as well as the penalties for failing to complete the courses. In addition, the evaluators proposed extending the participation requirements so as to bring more immigrants who meet the minimum competency levels (*Leistungsempfänger*) into the classroom and making more space available to those immigrants who voluntarily choose to take the courses. As part of a secondary set of recommendations, the evaluators also proposed that the government consider making room available for German citizens to take integration courses, which alluded to the necessity to address the integration needs of the *Aussiedler*.[14]

The same report also tackled issues of family reunification. In addition to recommending that the government increase the waiting time for granting limited-term residency permits (*Aufenthaltserlaubnis*) to foreign spouses of German citizens and legal residents from two to three years, the report further advised policymakers to require German citizens who wish to bring their spouses from abroad to vouch for the financial security of the family. The rationale behind this latter recommendation was tied directly to the costs of integration: "The proof of financial security for spouse-related family reunification (*Ehegattennachzug*) is requested on the grounds of integration policy (*integrationspolitischen Gründen*). The requirement for proof of financial security is particularly applicable to those who have recently naturalized as German citizens and who wish to bring their foreign spouse to Germany, since both parties

11. Zuwanderungsgesetz §43(5), §93(8), and §94(2).
12. For examples of the Chancellor's avowal, see "Integration wird Chefsache," *Frankfurter Rundschau*, 23 November 2005; and "Merkel skeptisch gegenüber schärferen Sanktionen," *Süddeutsche Zeitung*, 15 July 2006.
13. The report did not evaluate the content of the integration courses.
14. The complete list of recommendations appear on pages 11–13 in the report, found here: http://www.bmi.bund.de/cln_028/nn_122688/Internet/Content/Themen/Auslaender__Fluechtlinge __Asyl__Zuwanderung/DatenundFakten/Evaluierungsbericht.html (accessed 5 January 2008).

may have to take part in integration courses" (BMI 2006a: 108). In other words, the report sought to reduce the likelihood that joining spouses might become dependent on the welfare state, which would make the government responsible for paying these newcomers' integration course fees. The report went even further, however, to recommend that when the person seeking to be joined by his or her spouse from abroad is a recently naturalized German citizen, he or she should also be required to participate in the integration courses.

The Interior Ministry found the first evaluation's overall analytical thrust and recommendations useful and sponsored a second report focusing on the implementation and efficacy of the integration courses themselves. The overall conclusion in this latter report, which the Interior Ministry released in December 2006, was that "the integration courses demonstrate a strong qualitative improvement in Germany's integration policy" (BMI 2006b: i). The report also pointed to the need for better oversight, standardization, and financing of the courses. With regard to financing, the report proposed that participants be allocated a certain amount of public money to complete the necessary courses. Specifically, the participants would receive incremental reimbursements as they enrolled in and completed the integration program.

Continuing the Dialogue on Integration: The National Integration Plan and the Islamkonferenz

The CBPs, the Interior Ministry's deep engagement with the National Contact Points on Integration—a mostly informal EU-wide group established to exchange ideas and good practice on integration issues—and the evaluation reports have in many ways served as a backdrop to the Merkel government's headline initiative that called for a national dialogue on integration. After Merkel became Chancellor in 2005, she appointed Maria Böhmer as her senior integration advisor, situated her in the Federal Chancellery, and asked her to develop a national integration plan. Böhmer responded by organizing a series of meetings in which various working groups developed recommendations about how to better integrate immigrants. The working groups consisted of national, state, and local leaders, representatives from the immigrant communities, educators, and experts. Their task was to identify ways for improving integration outcomes through interventions in education and athletics, inclusion in the workforce, improving school-to-work transitions, and meeting the needs of special immigrant groups. In March 2007, Böhmer presented the working groups' conclusions at an integration summit. Subsequently, the Federal Agency for Migration and Refugees (*Bundesamt für Migration und Flüchtlinge*, BAMF) developed a national integration plan that incorporates Böhmer's working-group conclusions.

In some cases, the working groups took their cue from the evaluation of the integration courses. For instance, the working groups identified youth, women, and those with limited literacy skills as groups requiring integration courses geared to their specific needs. Accordingly, and recognizing that many Muslim women felt most comfortable in female-only classrooms so as to remain separated from men in the public sphere, the working groups recommended offering female-only courses and access to free childcare during the hours of language instruction.[15] Although this recommendation seems to enable cultural traditions about which Germans have been uneasy, BAMF correctly anticipated that providing women with an environment in which they felt most comfortable would increase participation in, and hence the value of, the integration courses. And, indeed, it appears to be doing so, while also demonstrating a new respect for cultural diversity and the preservation of each individual's cultural sensibilities.

In sum, the goal of the national integration plan has been to provide a set of guidelines for officials at all levels of government and for those that offer the integration courses. In turn, these guidelines are to be responsive to ongoing evaluations of the integration program so as to more effectively meet the needs of immigrants. The national integration plan also sends a powerful message to immigrants that the German government takes seriously its responsibility toward them.

Chancellor Merkel unveiled the national integration plan at an integration summit in Berlin on 12 July 2007. The celebration, and the Chancellor's declaration that the development of a national integration plan was a "milestone in the history of integration" of Germany's immigrant communities, was met by a boycott by the four main Turkish organizations whose leaders attacked the reforms as discriminatory against Muslim Turks.[16] Specifically, the four groups threatened to sue the government if it did not reverse language requirements for those wishing to reunite with their family members living in Germany. The issue has not been resolved.

The *Islamkonferenz* has been the second way in which Germany is engaging directly with its immigrant, and particularly its religious, minorities. Concerns over Muslim radicalization and its security implications played a dominant role in the development of the conference. Accordingly, in September 2006, Interior Minister Wolfgang Schäuble invited a group of Muslim leaders to participate in the first of several roundtable discussions on Muslims in German society. The diversity and ecclesiastical decentralization of Muslim communities was

15. See the "Internetportal" on integration at BAMF's website: http://www.bamf.de (accessed 16 April 2009).

16. See "Meilenstein in der Geschichte der Integrationspolitik," *Deutsche Welle*, 13 July 2007. See also *Frankfurter Allgemeine Zeitung* (2007b).

making it difficult for the German government to 'fit' them into its hierarchical state-church model. As a result, one of the aims of the conference centered on how Muslims might organize under an umbrella organization, comparable to those that exist for Jews (Central Jewish Council of Germany) and Christians (Working Group of Christian Churches) in Germany. In fact, shortly before the second Conference on Islam convened in May 2007, the four main Muslim organizations in Germany agreed to create a *Koordinierungsrat* (Coordination Council), with a rotating presidency.

The conference has also instigated a constructive dialogue on the future of Muslims in Germany. For instance, in the weeks leading up to the May 2007 roundtable, a passionate debate emerged about whether a veiled Muslim woman should be included on the panel of participants. Those in favor of this proposal argued that since secular women, including the sociologist Necla Kelek, who had sparked a national debate about Islam's treatment of women with her best-selling novel *Die fremde Braut* (*The Foreign Bride*), sat on the panel, a more traditional Muslim woman should also be included. Opponents countered that this would send the wrong signal to the public, because the meetings were about integration and progress, values that a veiled Muslim woman, in their view, did not represent. In the end, Schäuble wisely refrained from taking sides and stood by his original decision to ask the original fifteen participants back to the table (see *Frankfurter Allgemeine Zeitung* 2007a; Zekri 2007).

Legal Reforms, June 2007

While Germany's government officials were engaging with immigrant and minority ethnic and religious communities in the national integration plan and *Islamkonferenz*, the German Parliament in June 2007 enacted substantial changes to the 2005 migration law. The amendments raise the age limit from 16 to 18 for prospective immigrants to join their spouse in Germany, require all new family unification immigrants to prove a minimum level of German language competency prior to entering Germany, and compel immigrants who receive social security to sign integration contracts and register for mandatory language courses. Furthermore, the applicant in Germany must have lived in Germany for at least two years, possess a valid residence permit, vouch for the financial independence of the entire family, and meet minimum German language requirements.[17] Schäuble argued that the reforms

---

17. For a complete list of the reforms, see the Bundestag's publication, "Entwurf eines Gesetzes zur Umsetzung aufenthalts- und asylrechtlicher Richtlinien der Europäischen Union," document 16/5065, 23 March 2007.

were needed in order to take a stand against forced marriage (*Zwangsheirat*), a measure directed at the Muslim communities, and specifically at the Turks, living in Germany.[18]

The legislation also increases the maximum language instruction hours from 600 to 900. In addition, it requires that in order to acquire German citizenship one must show adequate knowledge of the German language and culture, a prelude to introducing a uniform federal citizenship test which took effect in the fall of 2008. Finally, the law compels German citizens who cannot prove they meet the minimum level of required German language proficiency also to enroll in the integration courses.[19] Those who are required to enroll but fail to do so or fail to complete the courses will be subject to monetary fines and face the possibility of losing their residency permit. These rather stern measures, however, are accompanied by positive inducements. Those who successfully complete the courses are to be granted permanent residency, and the required number of years-in-residence for naturalization would be reduced from eight to seven.[20]

Once more, these changes derived in large part from the recommendations of the evaluation reports discussed earlier. At the same time, however, they are a clear attempt to bring Germany's policies in line both with EU directives and the tougher immigrant integration standards adopted by several other EU Member States, most notably the Netherlands, Denmark, and France.[21] In a manner reminiscent of the 1980s and much of the 1990s, the SPD, the CDU's coalition partner, offered only muted criticisms. And while the Greens rejected outright nearly all the changes based on humanitarian concerns and the unfair treatment of Muslims, the FDP focused its reservations on the financial obligations placed on legally resident foreigners who bring their spouses to Germany, which it found unreasonable.[22]

18. See the extract from the parliamentary session from 14 June 2007 where Schäuble spoke to the representatives about the latest reforms at the following website of the Interior Ministry: http://www.bmi.bund.de/nn_663020/Internet/Content/Nachrichten/Reden/2007/06/BM__BT__Sitzung__103.html (accessed 10 January 2008).

19. The number of hours each immigrant must complete depends on the results of his or her placement exam.

20. See "Entwurf eines Gesetzes zur Umsetzung aufenthalts- und asylrechtlicher Richtlinien der Europäischen Union."

21. BMI, "Minister Dr. Wolfgang Schäuble: "Reform des Zuwanderungsrechts fördert Integration in unserem Land," 6 July 2007, http://www.bmi.bund.de/nn_334158/Internet/Content/Nachrichten/Pressemitteilungen/2007/07/Zuwanderungsrecht.html (accessed 10 January 2008).

22. For a more detailed discussion about the party's response, see the official brief provided by the government: "Innenausschuss stimmt Neureglung des Ausländerrechts zu," document 161/2007, 13 June 2006.

Facing the Road Ahead

Germany's CDU/SPD governing coalition has been quite active on immigration and integration matters. Underlying that activism is the Chancellor's and the Interior Minister's deep appreciation of the importance of the issue for Germany's long-term social stability and domestic security. The resulting carrot-and-stick approaches detailed in the last two chapters also reflect the fact that Otto Schily's sharp move to the right on these issues after 2003 offered a government whose conservative credentials cannot be in dispute an opportunity to make substantial progress on a politically sensitive matter. Yet, the Merkel-Schäuble initiatives have not always moved in internally consistent directions. Concerns about a status quo that is thought to be enabling the incubation of Muslim radicalization, for instance, has given impetus to initiatives that both tighten rules for admission and promote greater integration—if with a somewhat heavy hand. Not surprisingly, the early results have been mixed. Most worrisome among them is evidence that some second- and third-generation Muslim immigrants have reverted back to their Muslim heritage to reidentify with an Islamic way of life (Fetzer and Soper 2005: 105; Süssmuth 2006).

Meanwhile, Germans continue simultaneously to exhibit ambivalence and anxiety about the permanence of immigrant communities and the growing presence of Muslims in their midst, as the following exchange over a grand mosque's construction in Cologne demonstrates. The city's mayor, Fritz Schramma (CDU), responded to the mosque's construction by explaining that for him "it is self-evident that the Muslims need to have a prestigious place of worship … But it bothers me when people have lived here for 35 years and they don't speak a single word of German" (Landler 2007). Bekir Alboga, a Turkish Imam who has lived in Germany for 26 years, explained that his Turkish organization, DiTiB,[23] which is funding the mosque, is a "bulwark against radicalism and terrorism" and points to the decision not to broadcast the daily calls to prayer as evidence of pragmatism (Landler 2007).

Anxieties about the presence of immigrants are no longer ubiquitous, however. During the campaign for the Hesse Landtag elections in January 2008, rhetoric focusing on immigrants as a problem reappeared in the CDU's bid

---

23. DiTiB, also known as Diyanet, is a Turkish umbrella organization that is funded and directed by the Turkish state. Its role as a Turkish organization is to advance the social, cultural, and religious interests of Turks. DiTiB consists of over 230 organizations and refers to itself as the "strongest migrant organization in Germany." In terms of immigrant integration, DiTiB fully supports the two-way process as defined by the German government, but also promotes Turkish language education for Germans and more inclusive social activities, including athletic events. See the DiTiB website at http://www.diyanet.org/de (accessed 16 April 2009).

for reelection. In the wake of the beating of a 76-year-old German man in the Munich subway station by two young men, one from Turkish background, the other from Greek, the incumbent state minister of Hesse, Roland Koch (CDU), vowed to introduce stricter sentences for youth criminality in his next term (*Frankfurter Allgemeine Zeitung* 2008b). Citing the event in Munich and highlighting the disproportionate number of young criminals with immigrant backgrounds, Koch proposed increasing the maximum sentence for adolescent criminals from 10 to 15 years and automatically deporting non-citizens under 18 years of age who receive prison sentences exceeding one year. Alongside Chancellor Merkel's support for the proposal, Koch's interior minister in Hesse, Volker Bouffier, exclaimed, "If a foreigner is repeatedly delinquent, then we should send him back to his home country. We do not need people living in Germany who make a career of criminality" (quoted in *Frankfurter Allgemeine Zeitung* 2008b). Contrasted with the SPD's promise to introduce a minimum wage and to lower taxes, the CDU's choice to focus on youth criminality and immigrants appeared oddly out of place and not in keeping with the times. The CDU lost nearly 12 percent of the vote compared to their 2003 election total, while the SPD retained its 2003 share of the electorate (*Hessisches Statistisches Landesamt*). While it may be difficult to draw firm conclusions from a single case, the CDU's severe loss suggests that there may now be limits to the appeal of politics seeking to exploit concerns about immigration.

It is too early to assess with any degree of confidence whether the future of Germany and its immigrant and ethnic communities will be one of greater understanding and accommodation—and the more natural symbiosis that is at the heart of better integration and social cohesion—or one of confirming mistrust and conflict. There are certainly enough reasons to hope. Most notably, the "body language" of the German government toward Germany's immigrants has been changing in the direction of greater tolerance and inclusion; yet it has some way to go before it fully embraces the mutuality of accommodations that are at the heart of true integration. To be sure, measurable progress is clearly being made. Germany now offers its immigrants multiple opportunities for dialogue and the possibility of naturalization after, at most, eight years of residency under conditions that are more transparent than at any time in the past. Transparency should lead to predictable outcomes, which could, in turn, entice more people to naturalize. At the same time, however, integration measures still tend to have a degree of heavy handedness to them that dilutes the intended message of "being in this together."

For the German government's many investments on integration to take root and succeed, the government must remain single-mindedly determined to uphold its end of the bargain by sending an unmistakable signal to Germany's immigrants and their families—and to the broader society—that immigrants are, indeed, both welcome in Germany and an undeniable part of Germany's future. For their part of this bargain, immigrants have an obligation to accept the authority of the laws of their new polity and to adapt themselves to its prevailing norms. The basis of political obligation in any liberal-democratic society rests on the principle of consent, and consent is seldom more explicit than when individuals elect to join a society through the act of immigrating (as opposed to mere birth on its territory). For this bargain to succeed, both sides need to recognize that they each share responsibility for making it work.

Selected Bibliography

Ackermann, Alice, and Catherine McArdle Kelleher. 1993. "The United States and the German Question: Building a New European Order." In *The Germans and Their Neighbors*, ed. Dirk Verheyen and Christian Søe, 401–426. San Francisco: Westview Press.

Ahne, Petra. 2005. "Schröder: Fast ein Heimspiel." *Berliner Zeitung*. September 15.

Ahonen, Pertti. 2003. *After the Expulsion: Germany and Eastern Europe 1945–1990*. New York: Oxford University Press.

Alba, Richard, Peter Schmidt, and Martina Wasmer. 2004. *Germans or Foreigners? Attitudes Towards Minorities in Post-Reunification Germany*. New York: Palgrave MacMillan.

Aleinikoff, T. Alexander. 1984. "Political Asylum in the Federal Republic of Germany and the Republic of France: Lessons for the United States." *Michigan Journal of Law Reform* 17: 183–241.

_____, and Douglas Klusmeyer, eds. 2000. *From Migrants to Citizens: Membership in a Changing World*. Washington, DC: Carnegie Endowment for International Peace.

_____. 2001. *Citizenship Today: Global Perspectives and Practices*. Washington, DC: Carnegie Endowment for International Peace.

_____. 2003. *Citizenship Policies for an Age of Migration*. Washington, DC: Carnegie Endowment for International Peace.

Alston, Philip, and J. H. H. Weiler. 1999 "An 'Ever Closer Union' in Need of a Human Rights Policy: The European Union and Human Rights." In *The EU and Human Rights*, ed. Philip Alston, 3–66. Oxford: Oxford University Press.

Amnesty International, IANSA (International Action Network on Small Arms), and Oxfam. 2005. "The G8: Global Arms Exporters Failing to Prevent Irresponsible Arms Transfers." Control Arms Briefing Paper (June). http://www.globalpolicy.org/socecon/bwi-wto/g7-8/2005/0622g8arms.pdf.

Anderson, Jeffrey J. 1997. "Hard Interests, Soft Power, and Germany's Changing Role in Europe." In Katzenstein 1997b, 80–107.

Anderson, Margaret Lavinia. 2000. *Practicing Democracy: Elections and Political Culture in Imperial Germany*. Princeton, NJ: Princeton University Press.

Anil, Merih. 2006. "The New German Citizenship Law and Its Impact on German Demographics: Research Notes." *Population Research Policy Review* 25: 443–446.

Ansay, Turgrul. 1994. "The New UN Convention in Light of the German and Turkish Experience." *International Migration Review* 25(4): 831–847.

Arendt, Hannah. 1979. *The Origins of Totalitarianism*. New York: Harcourt Brace & Co.

Arndt, Nina, and Rainer Nickel. 2003. "Federalism Revisited: Constitutional Court Strikes Down New Immigration Law." *German Law Journal* 4(2): 71–89.

Asad, Talal. 2002. "Muslims and European Identity: Can Europe Represent Islam?" In Padgen 2004, 209–227.

Ash, Timothy Garton. 1993. *In Europe's Name: Germany and the Divided Continent*. New York: Random House.

Axt, Heinz-Jürgen. 1997. "The Impact of German Policy on Refugee Flows from Former Yugoslavia." In Münz and Wiener 1997, 1–33.

Aziz, Miriam. 2001. "Sovereignty Lost, Sovereignty Regained? The European Integration Project and the *Bundesverfassungsgericht*." San Domenico, Italy: European University Institute.

Backes, Uwe. 1990. "The West German Republikaner: Profile of a Nationalist, Populist Party of Protest." *Patterns of Prejudice* 24: 3–18.

Bade, Klaus J. 1983. *Vom Auswanderungsland zum Einwanderungsland: Deutschland 1880–1980*. Berlin: Colloquium.

———. 1987. "Labour, Migration and the State: Germany from the late 19th Century to the Onset of the Great Depression." In *Population, Labour and Migration in 19th- and 20th-Century Germany*, ed. Klaus J. Bade, 59–85. New York: Berg.

———, ed. 1994a. *Manifesto der 60: Deutschland und die Einwanderung*. Munich: C.H. Beck.

———. 1994b. "Immigration and Social Peace in United Germany." *Daedalus* 123(1): 85–106.

———. 1994c. *Ausländer, Aussiedler, Asyl*. Munich: C.H. Beck.

———. 1995. "Germany: Migrations in Europe up to the End of the Weimar Republic." In *The Cambridge Survey of World Migration*, ed. Robert Cohen, 131–135. Cambridge: Cambridge University Press.

———. 1996. "Immigration and Social Peace in United Germany." In *In Search of Germany*, ed. Michael Mertes, Steven Muller, and Heinrich August Winkler, 123–146. New Brunswick: Transaction Publishers.

———. 2001. "Immigration, Naturalization, and Ethno-national Traditions in Germany: From the Citizenship Law of 1913 to the Law of 1999." In *Crossing Boundaries: The Exclusion and Inclusion of Minorities in Germany and the United States*, ed. Larry Eugene Jones, 29–49. New York: Berghahn Books.

———. 2003. *Migration in European History*. Translated by Allison Brown. Oxford: Blackwell Publishing.

———. 2005. "Nachholende Integrationspolitik." "Die neue Integrationspolitik des Zuwanderungsgesetzes—eine Zwischenbilanz." Roundtable Discussion on Migration and Integration, Friedrich-Ebert-Stiftung and the Arbeiterwohlfahrt Bundesverband e.V. Berlin. June 6.

———, and Jochen Oltmer. 1999. "Einführung: Aussiedlerzuwanderung und Aussiedlerintegration. Historische Entwicklung und aktuelle Probleme." In *Aussiedler: deutsche Einwanderer aus Osteuropa*, ed. Klaus J. Bade and Jochen Oltmer, 9–54. Osnabrück: Universitätsverlag Rasch.

Baring, Arnulf. 1969. *Aussenpolitik in Adenauers Kanzlerdemokratie*. Munich: R. Oldenbourg.

Bark, Dennis L., and David R. Gress. 1993. *A History of West Germany*. 2nd ed. 2 vols. Oxford: Blackwell Publishers.

Barth, Wolfgang. 2005. "Zuwanderungsgesetz verabschiedet: Wie geht es weiter mit der Integration." *Migration und Soziale Arbeit* 2: 107–115.

Bartlett, Roger P. 1979. *Human Capital: The Settlement of Foreigners in Russia, 1762–1804*. Cambridge: Cambridge University Press.

———, and Bruce Mitchell. 1999. "State-Sponsored Immigration into Eastern Europe in the Eighteenth and Nineteenth Centuries." In *The German Lands and Eastern Europe: Essays on the History of Their Social, Cultural and Political Relations*, ed. Roger Bartlett and Karen Schönwälder, 91–114. New York: St. Martin's Press.

Bartov, Omer. 1996. *Murder in Our Midst: The Holocaust, Industrial Killing, and Representation.* Oxford: Oxford University Press.

———. 2000. *Mirrors of Destruction: War, Genocide, and Modern Identity.* Oxford: Oxford University Press.

Bauböck, Rainer. 1994. *Transnational Citizenship: Membership and Rights in International Migration.* Brookfield, VT: E. Elgar.

———. 1996. "Cultural Rights for Immigrants." *International Migration Review* 30(1): 203–250.

———. 1999. "International Migration and Liberal Democracies: the Challenge of Integration." *Patterns of Prejudice* 35(4): 33–49.

———. 2001. "Cultural Citizenship, Minority Rights, and Self-Government." In *Citizenship Today: Global Perspectives and Practices*, ed. T. Alexander Aleinikoff and Douglas Klusmeyer, 319–348. Washington, DC: Carnegie Endowment for International Peace.

Bauböck, Rainer, Eva Ersboll, Kees Groenendijk, and Harald Waldrauch. 2007. *Acquisition and Loss of Nationality, Vols. 1 and 2: Policies and Trends in 15 European Countries: Country Analyses.* Amsterdam: Amsterdam University Press.

Bauder, Herald. 2008. "Media Discourse and the New German Immigration Law." *Journal of Ethnic and Migration Studies* 34(1): 95–112.

Bauer, Thomas, Claus Larsen, and Poul Chr. Matthiessen. 2004. "Immigration Policy and Danish and German Immigration." In *Migrants, Work and the Welfare State*, ed. Torben Tranaes and Klaus F. Zimmermann, 31–74. Odense: University Press of Southern Denmark.

Bauer, Thomas, and Klaus F. Zimmermann. 1997. "Integrating the East: Labor Market Effects of Immigration." In *Europe's Economy Looks East: Implications for Germany and the European Union*, ed. Stanley W. Black, 269–306. Cambridge: Cambridge University Press.

Bauman, Zygmunt. 1989. *Modernity and the Holocaust.* Ithaca, NY: Cornell University Press.

Baylis, Thomas. 1999. "East German Leadership after Unification: The Search for Voice." In *The Federal Republic of Germany at Fifty: The End of a Century of Turmoil*, ed. Peter H. Merkl, 135–146. New York: New York University Press.

Beauftragte der Bundesregierung für Ausländerfragen. 1999. *Daten und Fakten zur Ausländersituation.* Berlin.

Beck-Gernsheim, Elisabeth. 2006. "Turkish Brides: A Look at the Immigration Debate in Germany." In *Migration, Citizenship, Ethnos*, ed. Y. Michal Bodemann and Gökçe Yurdakul, 185–194. New York: Palgrave Macmillan.

Beer-Kern, Dagmar. 2001. "Sprachvermögen von Deutsch Türken." Beuaftragte der Bundesregierung für Migration, Flüchtlinge und Integration. May. http://www.integrationsbeauftragte.de/download/sprachvermoegen.pdf.

Bender, Stefan, and Wolfgang Seifert. 2003. "On the Economic and Social Situations of Immigrants Groups in Germany." In Alba, Schmidt, and Wasmer 2003, 45–68.

Bendix, John. 1985. "Rights of Foreign Workers." In *Turkish Workers in Europe*, ed. Ilhan Basgöz and Norman Furniss, 23–56. Bloomington: Indiana University.

Berger, Maria, Christian Galonska, and Ruud Koopmans. 2004. "Political Integration by a Detour? Ethnic Communities and Social Capital of Migrants in Berlin." *Journal of Ethnic and Migration Studies* 30(3): 491–507.

Berlin, Isaiah. 1990. *The Crooked Timber of Humanity*, ed. Henry Hardy. Princeton, NJ: Princeton University Press.

———. 1998. "Nationalism: Past Neglect and Present Power." In *The Proper Study of Mankind*, ed. Henry Hardy and Roger Hausheer, 581–604. New York: Farrar, Straus and Giroux.

Bernt, Conrad. 1996. "Staatsbürgerschaft meistbietend versteigern?" *Die Welt.* May 31.

Betts, Raymond F. 1998. *Decolonization.* 2nd ed. New York: Routledge.

Beyme, Klaus von. 2001. "Citizenship and the European Union." In *European Citizenship between National Legacies and Postnational Projects*, ed. Klaus Eder and Bernhard Giesen, 61–85. Oxford: Oxford University Press.

Blackbourn, David. 1987. "Progress and Piety: Liberals, Catholics and the State in Bismarck's Germany." In *Populists and Patricians: Essays in Modern German History*, ed. David Blackbourn, 143–167. London: Allen & Unwin.

_____. 1998. *The Long Nineteenth Century: A History of Germany, 1780–1918*. New York: Oxford University Press.

Blanke, Richard. 1975. "Upper Silesia, 1921: The Case for Subjective Nationality." *Canadian Review of Studies in Nationalism* 2: 241–260.

_____. 1981. *Prussian Poland in the German Empire (1871–1900)*. Boulder, CO: East European Monographs: New York: Distributed by Columbia University Press.

_____. 1993. *Orphans of Versailles: The Germans in Western Poland, 1918–1939*. Lexington: University of Kentucky Press.

Blay, Sam, and Andreas Zimmermann. 1994. "Recent Changes in German Refugee Law: A Critical Assessment." *American Journal of International Law* 88: 361–378.

BMI (Bundesministerium des Innern). 2006a. "Bericht zur Evaluierung des Gesetzes zur Steuerung und Begrenzung der Zunwaderung und zur Regelung des Aufenthalts und der Integration von Unionsbürgern und Ausländern (Zuwanderungsgesetz)." Berlin: BMI. July 1.

_____. 2006b. "Evaluation der Integrationskurse nach dem Zuwanderungsgesetz." Berlin: BMI. December 1.

Boehm, Max Hildebart. 1959. "Gruppenbildung und Organisationswesen." In *Die Vertriebenen in Westdeutschland*, Band 1, ed. Eugen Lemberg and Friedrich Edding, 521–605. Kiel: F. Hirt.

Bosswick, Wolfgang. 2000. "Development of Asylum Policy in Germany." *Journal of Refugee Studies* 13(1): 43–60.

_____. 2003. "Germany—Still a Reluctant Country of Immigration?" In *Immigration in Europe. Issues, Policies, and Case Studies*, ed. D. Turton and J. Gonzalez, 127–148. Bibao: Deusto University Press.

_____. 2008. "Immigration Policy in Germany." In *Migration and Globalization: Comparing Immigration Policy in Developed Countries*, ed. Astushi Kondo, 107–138. Tokyo: Akashi Shoten.

Bradley, Oliver. 2005. "Soviet Jews Flooding Germany." *European Jewish Press*. August. http://www.ejpress.org/article/1969.

Brandes, Detlaf. 1992."Die Deutschen in Russland und der Sowjetunion." In *Deutsche im Ausland—Fremde in Deutschland: Migration in Geschichte und Gegenwart*, ed. Klaus J. Bade, 85–134. Munich: C.H. Beck.

Breuilly, John. 1994. *Nationalism and the State*. 2nd ed. Chicago, IL: University of Chicago Press.

Bridenthal, Renate. 2005. "Germans from Russia: The Political Network of a Double Diaspora." In *The Heimat Abroad: The Boundaries of Germanness*, ed. Krista O'Donnell, Renate Bridenthal, and Nancy Reagin, 187–218. Ann Arbor: University of Michigan Press.

Brownlie, Ian, ed. 1992. "Universal Declaration of Human Rights, 1948." In *Basic Documents on Human Rights*. Oxford: Clarendon Press.

Brubaker, Rogers. 1992. *Citizenship and Nationhood in France and Germany*. Cambridge, MA: Harvard University Press.

_____. 1996. *Nationalism Reframed: Nationhood and the National Question in the New Europe*. New York: Cambridge University Press.

_____. 2001. "The Return of Assimilation? Changing Perspectives on Assimilation and Its Sequels in France, Germany, and the United States." *Ethnic and Racial Studies* 24(4): 531–548.

Buchsteiner, Jochen, and Marin Klingst. 1994. "Ein abschreckender Erfolg." *Die Zeit*. July 8.

Bulmer, Simon J. 1997. "Shaping the Rules? The Constitutive Politics of the European Union and German Power." In Katzenstein 1997b, 49–79.

Bultmann, Peter Friedrich. 2002. "Dual Nationality and Naturalisation Policies in the German Länder." In Hansen and Weil 2002, 136–157.

Bundesgesetzblatt (BGB1). 1983. Gesetz zur Förderung der Rückkehrbereitschaft von Ausländern vom 28. November 1983: 1377–1380.

Bundesminister für Arbeit und Sozialordnung. 1997. "Vorschläge der Bund-Länder-Kommission zur Fortentwicklung einer umfassenden Konzeption der Ausländerbeschäftigungspolitik." Bonn, Germany. February 28.

Buscher, Frank. 2003. "The Great Fear: The Catholic Church and the Anticipated Radicalization of Expellees and Refugees in Post-War Germany." *German History* 21(2): 204–224.

BverfGE. 1991. *Entscheidungen des Bundesverfassungsgerichts.* Tübingen: J.C.B. Mohr.

Carens, Joseph H. 1987. "Aliens and Citizens: The Case for Open Borders." *Review of Politics* 49(3): 251–273.

Casteel, James E. 2007. "The Russian Germans in the Interwar German National Imaginary." *Central European History* 40: 429–466.

Castles, Stephen. 1985. "The Guests Who Stayed: The Debate on 'Foreigners Policy' in the German Federal Republic." *International Migration Review* 19(5): 517–534.

———. 1989. "Immigrant Workers and Trade Unions in the German Federal Republic." In *Migrant Workers and the Transformation of Western Societies.* Occasional paper no. 22. Ithaca, NY: Cornell University.

———. 2002. "The International Politics of Forced Migration." In *Socialist Register 2003: Fighting Identities: Race, Religion and Ethno-Nationalism*, ed. Leo Panitch and Colin Leys, 172–192. London: Merlin Press.

———, Maja Korac, Ellie Vasta, and Steven Vertovec. 2002. *Integration: Mapping the Field.* Report of a Project carried out by the University of Oxford Centre for Migration and Policy Research and Refugee Studies Centre contracted by the Home Office Immigration Research and Statistics Service. December.

———, and Godula Kosack. 1973. *Immigrant Workers and Class Structure in Western Europe.* London: Oxford University Press.

———, and Mark J. Miller. 2003. *The Age of Migration: International Population Movements in the Modern World.* 3rd ed. New York: The Guilford Press.

Chandler, Andrea. 1998. *Institutions of Isolation: Border Controls in the Soviet Union and its Successor States, 1917–1993.* Montreal: McGill-Queen's University Press.

Chervyakov, Valeriy, Zvi Gitelman, and Vladimir Shapiro. 2003. "*E Pluribus Unum*? Post-Soviet Jewish Identities and Their Implications for Communal Reconstruction." In *Jewish Life after the USSR*, ed. Zvi Gitelman, with Musya Glants and Marshall Goldman, 61–75. Bloomington: Indiana University Press.

Chickering, Roger. 1984. *We Men Who Feel Most German: A Cultural Study of the Pan-German League, 1886–1914.* Boston: George Allen & Unwin.

Childs, David. 1991. "The Far Right in Germany since 1945." In *Neo-Fascism in Europe*, ed. Luciano Cheles, Ronnie Ferguson, and Michalina Vaughan, 290–307. London: Longman Group UK Limited.

Chimni, B. S. 2000. "Globalisation, Humanitarianism and Refugee Protection." Refugees Studies Centre Working Paper No. 3. Oxford University.

Chin, Rita. 2007. *The Guest Worker Question in Postwar Germany.* New York: Cambridge University Press.

Çinar, Dilek. 1994. "From Aliens to Citizens: A Comparative Analysis of Rules of Transition." In *From Aliens To Citizens: Redefining the Status of Immigrants in Europe*, ed. Rainer Bauböck, 49–72. Aldershot: Avebury.

Cobban, Alfred. 1951. *National Self-Determination*. Rev. ed. Chicago, IL: University of Chicago Press.

Coenders, Marcel, Marcel Lubbers, and Peer Scheepers. 2003. *Majorities' Attitudes Towards Minorities in European Union Member States: Results from the Standard Eurobarometers 1997–2000–2003*. Vienna: European Monitoring Centre on Racism and Xenophobia.

Cohen, Roger. 2000a. "Is Germany on the Road to Diversity? The Parties Clash." *New York Times*. December 4.

———. 2000b. "Sending Kosovars Home, an Awkward German Moment (and Don't Say Deport!)." *New York Times*. November 20.

Compact Edition of the Oxford English Dictionary, The, Vol. I. 1979. London: Oxford University Press.

Conradt, David. 1993. "The Christian Democrats in 1990: Saved by Unification?" In *The New Germany Votes: Unification and the Creation of a New Germany Party System*, ed. Russell J. Dalton, 59–75. Providence, RI: Berg Publishers.

———. 2005. *The German Polity*. 8th ed. New York: Longman.

Conze, Werner. 1992. *Ostmitteleuropa. Von der Spätantike bis zum 18. Jahrhundert*. Munich: C.H. Beck.

Cooper, Alice Holmes. 2002. "Party-Sponsored Protest and the Movement Society: the CDU/CSU Mobilises Against Citizenship Law Reform." *German Politics* 11: 88–104.

Cordell, Karl. 2000. *The Politics of Ethnicity in Central Europe*. New York: St. Martin's Press.

Craig, Gordon A. 1978. *Germany, 1866–1945*. New York: Oxford University Press.

Cremer, Hans-Joachim. 1997. "Internal Controls and Actual Removal of Deportable Aliens." In Hailbronner, Martin, and Motomura, 1997b, 45–116. Providence RI: Berghahn Books.

Crul, Maurice. 2007. "Pathways to Success for the Second Generation in Europe." *Migration Information Source*. Washington, DC: Migration Policy Institute. April 1. http://www.migrationinformation.org/Feature/display.cfm?ID=592.

———, and Hans Vermeulen. 2003. "The Second Generation in Europe." *International Migration Review* 37: 965–986.

Currie, David P. 1994. *The Constitution of the Federal Republic of Germany*. Chicago, IL: University of Chicago Press.

Cyrus, Norbert, and Dita Vogel. 2005. "Current Immigration Debates in Europe: Germany." In *Current Immigration Debates in Europe: A Publication of the European Migration Dialogue*. Brussels: Migration Policy Group. http://www.migpolgroup.com/multiattachments/2971/DocumentName/EMD_Germany_2005.pdf.

Czapliński, Władysław. 1994. "Aliens and Refugee Law in Poland: Recent Developments." *International Journal of Refugee Law* 6(4): 636–642.

Dahrendorf, Ralf. 1976. *Society and Democracy in Germany*. New York: W.W. Norton.

Dalton, Russel J., and Wilhelm Bürklin. 1993. "The German Party System and the Future." In *The New Germany Votes: Unification and the Creation of a New Germany Party System*, ed. Russell J. Dalton, 233–256. Providence, RI: Berg Publishers.

Davies, Bill. 2007. "The Constitutionalism of the European Community: West Germany between Legal Sovereignty and European Integration: 1949–1975." PhD diss. defended October 2007. London: King's College London (University of London).

Davy, Ulrike. 1999. "Rechtliche Instrumente der Integration: In welchem Kontext steht die Verleihung der Staatsangehörigkeit?" In *Politische Integration der ausländischen Wohnbevölkerung*, ed. Ulrike Davy, 58. Baden-Baden: Nomos Verlagsgesellschaft.

———. 2005. "Integration of Immigrants in Germany: A Slowly Evolving Concept." *European Journal of Migration and Law* 7: 123–144.

———, and Klaus Barwig, eds. 2004. *Auf dem Weg zur Rechtsgleichheit? Konzepte und Grenzen einer Politik der Integration von Einwanderern*. Baden-Baden: Nomos Verlagsgesellschaft.

de Zayas, Alfred M., ed. 1979. *Nemesis at Potsdam: The Anglo-Americans and the Expulsion of the Germans*. Rev. 2nd ed. Boston: Routledge & K. Paul.

Der Spiegel. 1989. "Gespräch mit dem Parteivorsitzenden Franz Schönhuber über die Zukunft der Republikaner."

———. 1991a. "Schwacher Aufwind für CDU/CSU." September 16.

———. 1991b. "Der neue Fremdhaß." September 30.

———. 1992a. "Tips zum Verfassungsbruch." November 9.

———. 1992b. "Asyl: Legal, illegal, rektal." December 14.

———. 1993. "Weder Heimat noch Freunde." June 7.

———. 1994. "Asylanten: Die Bronx von Europa." April 4.

———. 1995. "Flüchtlinge: Asyl vom Sponsor." July 17.

———. 1996. "Ausländer: Die Brauchen Wir." June 24.

———. 2005. "Türke erschießt seine Schwester." June 15.

Deutsche Welle. 2005. "Germany Reviews Afghan Refugees." February 11.

Devine, Michael W. 1993. "Germany Asylum Law Reform and the European Community: Crisis in Europe." *Georgetown Immigration Law Journal* 7(4): 795–815.

DeWind, J., C. Hirschman, and P. Kasinitz, eds. "Immigration Adaptation and Native-Born Responses in the Making of the Americans." *International Migration Review* 31(4): 797–1111.

Die Grünen. 1989. "Citizenship Proposal." Bundestagsdrucksache 11/4464. May 3.

Diehl, Claudia, and Rainer Schnell. 2005. "'Ethnic Revival' among Labor Migrants in Germany? Statements, Arguments, and First Empirical Evidence." Paper presented at the International Union for the Scientific Study of Population, XXV International Population Conference Tours. France. July 18–23.

Diering, Frank. 2004. "Stadt Köln kämpft weiter juristisch um schnelle Abschiebung Metin Kaplans." *Die Welt*. June 4.

Dietz, Barbara. 2000. "German and Jewish Migration from the Former Soviet Union to Germany: Background, Trends, and Implications." *Journal of Ethnic and Migration Studies* 26(4): 635–52.

———. 2003. "Jewish Immigrants from the Former Soviet Union in Germany: History, Politics and Social Integration." *East European Jewish Affairs* 33(2): 7–19.

———. 2006. "Aussiedler in Germany: From Smooth Adaption to Tough Integration." In *Paths of Integration: Migrants in Western Europe (1880–2004)*, ed. Leo Lucassen, David Feldman and Jochen Olter, 116–136. Amsterdam: Amsterdam University Press.

———, Uwe Lebok, and Pavel Polian. 2002. "The Jewish Emigration from the Former Soviet Union to Germany." *International Migration* 40(2): 29–48.

———, and Klaus Segbers. 1997. "Policies Toward Russia and Other Successor States." In Münz and Wiener 1997, 141–164.

Dinan, Desmond. 1999. *Ever Closer Union: An Introduction to European Integration*. 2nd ed. Boulder, CO: Lynne Rienner.

Dirke, Sabine von. 1994. "Multikulti: The German Debate on Multiculturalism." *German Studies Review* 17(3): 513–536.

Dittgen, Herbert. 1997. "The American Debate about Immigration in the 1990s: A New Nationalism after the End of the Cold War?" *Stanford Humanities Review* 5(2): 256–85.

———. 1998. "*Volk* Nation or Nation of Immigrants? The Current Debate About Immigration in Germany and the United States in Comparative Perspective." In *Immigration, Citizenship, and the Welfare State in Germany and the United States, Part B: Welfare Policies and Immigrants' Citizenship*, ed. Hermann Kurthen, Jürgen Fijalkowski, and Gert G. Wagner, 107–139. Stamford, CT: JAI Press.

Doerschler, Peter. 2004. "Education and the Development of Turkish and Yugoslav Migrants' Political Attitudes in Germany." *German Politics* 13(3): 449–480.

Doomernik, Jeroen. 1997. *Going West: Soviet Jewish Immigrants in Berlin since 1990*. Aldershot: Avebury.

Dornis, Christian. 1997. "Migration in the Russian Federation since the Mid-1980s: Refugees, Immigrants, and Emigrants." In Münz and Weiner 1997, 77–116.

Drozdiak, William. 1997. "Citizenship Debate Divides Germans; Dual Nationality Is Proposed for Offspring of Immigrants." *Washington Post*. November 5.

Düding, Dieter. 2002. *Heinz Kühn, 1912–1992: Eine politische Biographie*. Essen: Klartext-Verlag.

Economist, The. 1994. "Western Europe's Nationalists: The Rise of the Outside Right." October 15.

———. 2001. "How Restive Are Europe's Muslims?" October 18.

ECRE (European Council on Refugees and Exiles), ENAR (European Network Against Racism), and MPG (Migration Policy Group). 1999. *Guarding Standards—Shaping the Agenda*. Brussels.

Edmonston, Barry. 2006. "Population Dynamics in Germany: The Role of Immigration and Population Momentum." *Population Research and Policy Review* 25: 513–545.

EUMC (European Monitoring Centre on Racism and Xenophobia). 2004. *Manifestations of Antisemitism in the EU 2002–2003*. Vienna: EUMC.

European Commission. 1994. *Communication from the Commission to the Council and the European Parliament*, COM(94)23 final. Brussels. February 23.

———. 2000. *Communication from the Commission to the Council and European Parliament on a Community Immigration Policy*. COM(2000)757 final. Brussels. November 22.

———. 2004. *First Annual Report on Migration and Integration*. June 16.

———. 2005. *Second Annual Report on Migration and Integration*. June 30.

European Council. 1973. *Declaration on European Identity*. http://www.ena lu?lang=2&doc=6180.

———. 1989. *Conclusions of the Presidency Strasbourg Summer*. December 8, 9. http://aei.pitt.edu/1395/.

———. 1990. *Conclusions of the Presidency Dublin Summit*. April 28. http://aei.pitt.edu/1397/01/Dublin_april_1990.pdf.

———. 1999a. *Presidency Conclusions Cologne*. June 3–4. http://ue.eu.int/ueDocs/cms_Data/docs/pressData/en/ec/kolnen.htm.

———. 1999b. *Presidency Conclusions Tampere*. October 15–16. http://ue.eu.int/ueDocs/cms_Data/docs/pressData/en/ec/00200-r1.en9.htm.

———. 2000a. *Presidency Conclusions Nice*. December 7–9. http://ue.eu.int/ueDocs/cms_Data/docs/pressData/en/ec/00400-r1.%20ann.en0.htm.

———. 2000b. *Presidency Conclusions Lisbon*. March 23–24. http://www.bologna-berlin2003.de/pdf/PRESIDENCY_CONCLUSIONS_Lissabon.pdf.

———. 2001. *Presidency Conclusions Laeken*. December 14–15. http://ue.eu.int/ueDocs/cms_Data/docs/pressData/en/ec/68827.pdf.

———. 2003a. *Presidency Conclusions Thessaloniki*. June 19–20. http://ue.eu.int/ueDocs/cms_Data/docs/pressData/en/ec/76279.pdf.

———. 2003b. *Presidency Conclusions Brussels*. March 20–21. http://www.consilium.europa.eu/ueDocs/cms_Data/docs/pressData/en/ec/75136.pdf.

———. 2004. *Presidency Conclusions Brussels*. November 4–5. http://ue.eu.int/ueDocs/cms_Data/docs/pressData/en/ec/82534.pdf.

———. 2005a. *Council and Commission Action Plan Implementing the Hague Programme on Strengthening Freedom, Security and Justice in the European Union*. August 8. http://eur-lex.europa.eu/LexUriServ/site/en/oj/2005/c_198/c_19820050812en00010022.pdf.

———. 2005b. *Presidency Conclusions Brussels*. December 15–16. http://www.consilium.europa.eu/ueDocs/cms_Data/docs/pressData/en/ec/87642.pdf.

European Monitoring Centre on Racism and Xenophobia. 2004. "Manifestations of Antisemitism in the EU 2002–2003." http://fra.europa.eu/fra/material/pub/AS/AS-Main-report.pdf.

Fahrmeir, Andreas. 2000. *Citizens and Aliens: Foreigners and the Law in Britain and the German States 1789–1870*. Oxford: Berghahn Books.

Faist, Thomas. 1993. "From School to Work: Public Policy and Underclass Formation among Young Turks in Germany during the 1980s." *International Migration Review* 27: 306–331.

_____. 1994. "How to Define a Foreigner? The Symbolic Politics of Immigration in German Partisan Discourse, 1978–1992." *West European Politics* 17(2): 50–71.

_____. 2006. "The Migration-Security Nexus: International Migration and Security Before and After 9/11." In *Migration, Citizenship, Ethnos*, ed. Y. Michal Bodemann and Gökçe Yurdakul, 103–119. New York: Palgrave Macmillan.

Fassman, Heinz, and Rainier Münz. 1994. "European East-West Migration, 1945–1992." *International Migration Review* 28: 520–38.

Favell, Adrian. 2001. "Integration Policy and Integration Research in Europe: A Review and Critique." In *Citizenship Today: Global Perspectives and Practices*, ed. T. Alexander Aleinikoff and Douglas Klusmeyer, 349–399. Washington, DC: Carnegie Endowment for International Peace.

_____, and Randall Hansen. 2002. "Markets Against Politics: Migration, EU Enlargement and the Idea of Europe." *Journal of Ethnic and Migration Studies* 28(4): 581–602.

Federal Constitutional Court (Germany). 1996. Press release "Flughafenverfahren," no. 23. Karlsruhe. May 7.

Federal Council for Immigration and Integration. 2004. "Migration und Integration—Erfahrungen nutzen, Neues wagen. Jahresgutachten 2004." Berlin.

Federal Ministry of the Interior. 2001. "Schily Presents Draft of an Immigration Act." Press Releases, Fr 2001/08/03.

Feld, Werner. 1965. "The Association Agreements of the European Communities: A Comparative Analysis." *International Organization* 19(2): 223–249.

Felderer, Berhard. 1989. "Immigration, Geburtenentwicklung und Wirtschaft." *Politik und Zeitgeschichte* (supplement to *Das Parlament*). Bonn, B. 18/89: 16–22. April.

Fetzer, Joel. 2000. *Public Attitudes toward Immigration in the United States, France, and Germany*. Cambridge: Cambridge University Press.

_____, and Christopher Soper. 2005. *Muslims and the State in Britain, France and Germany*. Cambridge: Cambridge University Press.

Fink, Carol. 1972. "Defender of Minorities: Germany in the League of Nations, 1926–1933." *Central European History* 5(4): 330–357.

_____. 1979. "Stresemann's Minority Policies, 1924–29." *Journal of Contemporary History* 14(3): 403–422.

_____. 2004. *Defending the Rights of Others: The Great Powers, the Jews, and International Minority Protection, 1878–1938*. Cambridge: Cambridge University Press.

Fischer, Joschka. 2000a. "From Confederacy to Federation: Thoughts on the Finality of European Integration." Speech given at Humbolt University, Berlin. May 12. http://www.auswaertiges-amt.de/www/de/infoservice/download/pdf/reden/redene/r000512b-r1008e.pdf.

_____. 2000b. "Vom Staatenverbund zur Föderation—Gedanken über die Finalität der europäischen Integration" [From Confederacy to Federation—Thoughts on the Finality of European Integration]. In *What Kind of Constitution for What Kind of Polity*, ed. C. Joerges, Y. Mény and J. H. H. Weiler. http://www.jeanmonnetprogram.org/papers/00/symp.html.

Fitzpatrick, Joan. 1997. "Is the 1951 Convention Relating to the Status of Refugees Obsolete?" In Hailbronner, Martin, and Motomura 1997, 205–226.

Fleischhauer, Ingeborg. 1983. *Das Dritte Reich und die Deutschen in der Sowjetunion*. Stuttgart: Deutsche Verlags-Anstalt.

_____. 1986a. *Die Deutschen im Zarenreich*. Stuttgart: Deutsche Verlags-Anstalt.

_____. 1986b. "The Ethnic Germans under Nazi Rule." In Fleischhauer and Pinkus 1986, 92–102.

_____. 1986c. "'Operation Barbarossa' and the Deportation." In Fleischhauer and Pinkus 1986, 66–91.

_____. 1986d. "The Germans' Role in Tsarist Russia: A Reappraisal." In Fleischhauer and Pinkus 1986, 13–30.

_____, and Benjamin Pinkus. 1986. *The Soviet Germans: Past and Present*. New York: St. Martin's Press.

Foreign Broadcast Information Service, Western Europe. 1994. "Republikaner Discuss Leader's Possible Ouster." July 6.

Forsthoff, Ernst. 2000. "The Total State." In *Weimar: A Jurisprudence in Crisis*, ed. Arthur J. Jacobson and Bernhard Schlink. Translated by Belinda Cooper and Peter C. Caldwell, 320–322. Berkeley: University of California Press.

Foster, Nigel. 1993. *German Law & Legal System*. London: Blackstone Press.

Fourlanos, Gerassimos. 1986. *Sovereignty and the Ingress of Aliens*. Stockholm: Almqvist and Wiksell International.

Frankfurter Allgemeine Zeitung. 2000a. "Kann die CDU noch glaubwürdige Alternativen anbieten?" October 20.

_____. 2000b. "CDU will sich schnell entscheiden." November 2.

_____. 2001. "Kritik aus der Koalition an Schilys Entwurf." August 24.

_____. 2007a. "Islamkonferenz ohne Beschlüsse." May 3.

_____. 2007b. "Merkel: 'Der Regierung stellt man keine Ultimaten.'" July 12.

_____. 2007c. "Merkel weist 'Ultimaten' türkischer Verbände zurück." July 13.

_____. 2008a. "Im Bann der Härte." January 21.

_____. 2008b. "Bouffier plädiert für harte Hand; CDU legt in Debatte um kriminelle Ausländer nach." January 2.

Franz, Fritz. 1975. "The Legal Status of Foreign Workers in West Germany." In *Manpower Mobility across Cultural Boundaries: Social, Economic and Legal Aspects*, ed. R.E. Krane, 46–60. Leiden: E.J. Brill.

Freeman, Gary P. 1986. "Migration and the Political Economy of the Welfare State." *Annals of American Academy of Political and Social Sciences* 485: 51–63.

Freie Demokratische Korrespondenz. 1993. "Kinkel: FDP fordert gesetzliche Zuwanderungsregelung." July 30.

Frentz, Christian Raitz von. 1999. *A Lesson Forgotten: Minority Protection under the League of Nations: The Case of the German Minority in Poland, 1920–1934*. New York: St. Martin's Press.

Friedrich, Carl J. 1968. *Trends of Federalism in Theory and Practice*. New York: Frederick A. Praeger Publishers.

Fullerton, Mary Ellen. 1990. "Persecution Due to Membership in a Particular Social Group: Jurisprudence in the Federal Republic of Germany." *Georgetown Immigration Law Journal* 4: 381–444.

Geddes, Andrew. 2003. *The Politics of Migration and Immigration in Europe*. London: Sage Publications.

_____. 2007. "The Europeanization of What? Migration, Asylum and the Politics of European Integration." In *The Europeanization of National Immigration Policies: Between Autonomy and the European Union*, ed. Thomas Faist and Andreas Ette, 49–72. New York: Palgrave Macmillan.

Geertz, Clifford. 1973. "The Integrative Revolution: Primordial Sentiments and Civil Politics in New States." In *The Interpretation of Cultures: Selected Essays*, ed. Clifford Geertz, 255–310. New York: Basic Books.

Geiger, Rudolf. 2005. "EU Constitutionalism and the German Basic Law." Jean Monnet/Robert Schuman Paper Series 5(1A).

Gelatt, Julia. 2005. "Schengen and the Free Movement of People Across Europe." *Migration Information Source*. Washington, DC: Migration Policy Institute. October 1. http://www. migrationinformation.org/Feature/display.cfm?id=241.

Gerhard, Ute. 1993. "'Fluten,' 'Ströme,' 'Invasionen'—Mediendiskur und Rassismus." In *Zwischen Nationalstaat und Multikultureller Gesellschaft: Einwanderung und Fremdenfeindlichkeit in der Bundesrepublik Deutschland*, ed. Manfred Hessler, 239–254. Berlin: Hitit.

Gibney, Matthew J. 2004. *The Ethics and Politics of Asylum: Liberal Democracy and the Response to Refugees*. Cambridge: Cambridge University Press.

Gieseck, Arne, Ullrich Heilemann, and Hans Dietrich von Loeffelholz. 1993. "Wirtschafts- und sozialpolitische Aspekte der Zuwanderung in die Bundesrepublik." *Aus Politik und Zeitgeschichte* 7: 29–41.

Giesinger, Adam. 1988. *From Catherine to Khruschev: The Story of Russia's Germans*. Lincoln, NE: American Historical Society of Germans from Russia.

Gitelman, Zvi. 2003. "Thinking about Being Jewish in Russia and Ukraine." In *Jewish Life after the USSR*, ed. Zvi Gitelman, Musya Glants, and Marshall I. Goldman, 49–60. Bloomington: Indiana University Press.

Glaessner, Gert-Joachim. 1992. *The Unification Process in Germany: From Dictatorship to Democracy*. Trans. Colin B. Grant. New York: St. Martin's Press.

———. 1996. "Government and Political Order." In Smith, Paterson, and Padgett 1996, 14–34.

Goerlich, Helmut. 1988. "Fundamental Constitutional Rights: Content, Meaning and General Doctrines." In Karpen 1988, 45–66.

Goetz, Klaus, and Peter J. Cullen. 1995. "The Basic Law after Unification: Continued Centrality or Declining Force?" In *Constitutional Policy in Unified Germany*, ed. Klaus H. Goetz and Peter J. Cullen, 5–46. Portland, OR: Frank Cass.

Goody, Jack. 2004. *Islam in Europe*. Cambridge: PolityPress/Blackwell Publishing.

Gordenker, Leon. 1987. *Refugees in International Politics*. New York: Columbia University Press.

Gosewinkel, Dieter. 1998. "Citizenship and Nationhood: The Historical Development of the German Case." In *European Citizenship, Multiculturalism, and the State*, ed. Ulrich K. Preuss and Ferran Requejo, 125–136. Baden-Baden: Nomos Verlagsgesellschaft.

———. 2001a. *Einbürgern und Ausschließen: Die Nationalisierung der Staatsangehörigkeit vom Deutschen Bund bis zur Bundesrepublik Deutschland*. Göttingen: Vandenhoeck und Ruprecht.

———. 2001b. "Citizenship, Subjecthood, Nationality: Concepts of Belonging in the Age of Modern Nation States." In *European Citizenship: National Legacies and Transnational Projects*, ed. by Klaus Eder and Bernhard Giesen, 17–35. Oxford: Oxford University Press.

———. 2002. "Citizenship and Naturalization Politics in Germany in the Nineteenth and Twentieth Centuries." In *Challenging Ethnic Citizenship: German and Israeli Perspectives on Immigration*. New York: Berghahn Books.

Gottschlich, Jürgen. 2005. "Kölner Kalif verurteilt; Lebenslang für Metin Kaplan." *die tageszeitung*. June 22.

Grabbe, Heather. 2000. "The Sharp Edges of Europe: Extending Schengen Eastwards." *International Affairs* 6(3): 519–536.

Graw, Ansgar. 2001. "CDU weist Vorwürfe der Wirtschaft zurück." *Die Welt*. August 25.

Green, Simon. 2001a. "Immigration, Asylum and Citizenship in Germany: The Impact of Unification and the Berlin Republic." *West European Politics* 24(4): 82–104.

———. 2001b. "Citizenship Policy in Germany: The Case of Ethnicity over Residence." In *Towards a European Nationality: Citizenship, Immigration and Nationality Law in the EU*, ed. Randall Hansean and Patrick Weil, 24–51. New York: Palgrave.

———. 2003a. "Towards an Open Society? Citizenship and Immigration." In *Developments in German Politics 3*, ed. by Stephen Padgett, William Paterson, and Gordon Smith. Durham, NC: Duke University Press.

_____. 2003b. "The Legal Status of Turks in Germany." *Immigrants and Minorities* 22(2–3): 228–246.

_____. 2004. *The Politics of Exclusion: Institutions and Immigration Policy in Contemporary Germany*. Manchester: Manchester University Press.

_____. 2005. "Immigration and Integration Policy: Between Incrementalism and Non-Decision." In *Governance in Contemporary Germany: the Semisovereign State Revisited*, ed. Simon Green and William Paterson, 190–211. Cambridge: Cambridge University Press.

Greenfeld, Liah. 1992. *Nationalism: Five Roads to Modernity*. Cambridge, MA: Harvard University Press.

Grimm, Dieter. 1995. "Does Europe Need a Constitution?" *European Law Journal* 1(3): 282–302.

Groenendijk, Kees. 1997. "Regulating Ethnic Immigration: The Case of the *Aüssiedler.*" *Journal of Ethnic and Migration Studies* 23(4): 461–482.

Gross, Michael B. 2004. *The War Against Catholicism: Liberalism and the Anti-Catholic Imagination in Nineteenth-Century Germany*. Ann Arbor: University of Michigan Press.

Gugel, Günther. 1990. *Ausländer, Aussiedler, Übersiedler: Fremdenfeindlichkeit in der Bundesrepublik Deutschland*. Tübingen: Verein für Friedenspädagogik Tübingen.

Guild, Elspeth, ed. 1996. *The Developing Immigration and Asylum Policies of the European Union*. Boston: Kluwer Law International.

_____. 1999. "Discretion, Competence and Migration in the European Union." *European Journal of Migration and Law* 1(1): 61–87.

_____. 2003. "The Border Abroad—Visas and Border Controls." In *In Search of Europe's Borders*, ed. Kees Groenendijk, Elspeth Guild, and Paul Minderhoud. The Hague: Kluwer International.

Guiraudon, Virginie. 1998. "Citizenship Rights for Non-Citizens: France, Germany, and the Netherlands." In *Challenge to the Nation-State: Immigration in Western Europe and the United States*, ed. Christian Joppke, 109–152. Oxford: Oxford University Press.

Gusy, Christoph, and Katja Ziegler. 1999. "Der Volksbegriff des Grundgesetzes: Ist die Position des Bundesverfassungsgerichts alternativenlos?" In Davy 1999, 222–247.

Haas, Ernst B., Sally Roever, and Anna Schmidt. 2002. "German and the Norms of European Governance." *German Politics & Society*. 20(2): 1–48.

Habermas, Jürgen. 1992. "Citizenship and National Identity: Some Reflections on the Future of Europe." *Praxis International* 12(1): 1–19.

_____. 1995. "Remark on Dieter Grimm's 'Does Europe Need a Consitution?'" *European Law Journal* 1(3): 303–307.

_____. 2005. "Equal Treatment of Cultures and the Limits of Postmodern Liberalism." *Journal of Political Philosophy* 13(1): 1–28.

Hagen, William W. 1980. *Germans, Poles, and Jews: The Nationality Conflict in the Prussian East, 1772–1914*. Chicago, IL: University of Chicago Press.

Hägle, Helmut. 1995. *Staatliche Leistungen an Asylbewerber und andere Ausländer im innereuropäischen Vergleich*. Königswinter: Europäisches Forschungs Institute.

Hailbronner, Kay. 1989. "Citizenship and Nationhood in Germany." In *Immigration and the Politics of Citizenship in Europe and North America*, ed. Rogers Brubaker, 67–80. Latham, MD: University Press of America.

_____. 1994. "Asylum Law Reform in the German Constitution." In *Immigration Law: United States and International Perspectives on Asylum and Refugee Status*, joint issue of *The American University Journal of International Law and Policy* and *Loyola of Los Angeles International and Comparative Law Journal* 9(4): 159–179.

_____. 1995. "Recent Immigration Developments in Germany: Lessons and Implications for the U.S." Presentation at the workshop at the American Institute for Contemporary German Studies. Washington, DC. March 28.

_____. 1999. "The Treaty of Amsterdam and Migration Law." *European Journal of Migration and Law* 1(1): 9–27.

_____. 2000a. "Fifty Years of German Basic Law—Migration Citizenship and Asylum." *SMU Law Review* 53(2): 519–542.

_____. 2000b. *Immigration and Asylum Law Policy of the European Union.* The Hague: Kluwer Law International.

_____. 2002. "Germany's Citizenship Law under Immigration Pressure." In Hansen and Weil 2002, 121–135.

Hailbronner, Kay, David Martin, and Hiroshi Motumra. 1997a. *Immigration Admissions: The Search for Workable Policies in the United States and Germany.* Providence RI: Berghahn Books.

_____. 1997b. *Immigration Controls: The Search for Workable Policies in the United States and Germany.* Providence RI: Berghahn Books.

Hailbronner, Kay, and Guenter Renner. 1991. *Staatsangehörigkeitsgesetz.* Munich: C.H. Beck.

Haller, Michael, and Gerhard C. Dieters. 1991. "Alte Parolen, neue Parteien: Die Republikaner und die Deutsche Volksunion—Liste D." In *Rechtsextremismus in der Bundesrepublik*, ed. Wolfgang Benz, 248–272. Frankfurt am Main: Fischer Taschenbuch Verlag.

Hamburger Abendblatt. 2007. "Integrationsgipfel—Türken verteidigen Boykott." July 14.

Hamilton, Richard F. 1982. *Who Voted for Hitler?* Princeton, NJ: Princeton University Press.

Hannum, Hurst. 1992. *Guide to International Human Rights Practice.* 2nd ed. Philadelphia: University of Pennsylvania Press.

Hansen, Randall. 1998. "A European Citizenship or a Europe of Citizens? Third Country Nationals in the EU." *Journal of Ethnic and Migration Studies* 24: 751–768.

_____, and Partick Weil, eds. 2002. *Dual Nationality, Social Rights and Federal Citizenship in the U.S. and Europe.* New York: Berghahn Books.

Harris, Paul. 1998. "Jewish Migration to the New Germany: The Policy Making Process Leading to the Adoption of the 1991 Quota Refugee Law." In *Einwanderung und Einbürgerung in Deutschland, Jahrbuch Migration—Yearbook Migration 1997/98*, ed. Dietrich Thränhardt, 105–147. Münster: LIT Verlag.

Haug, Sonja. 2007. "Soziodemographische Merkmale, Berufsstruktur und Verwandtschaftsnetzwerke jüdischer Zuwanderer." Berlin: Federal Agency for Migrants and Refugees (BAMF).

Hechter, Michael. 2000. *Containing Nationalism.* New York: Oxford University Press.

Heckmann, Friedrich. 2003. "From Ethnic Nation to Universalistic Immigrant Integration: Germany." In *The Integration of Immigrants in European Societies: National Differences and Trends of Convergence*, ed. Friedrich Heckmann and Dominique Schnapper, 45–78. Stuttgart: Lucius & Lucius.

_____. 2004. "Illegal Migration: What Can We Know and What Can We Explain? The Case of Germany." *International Migration Review* 38(3): 1103–1125.

_____. 2006. "Illegal Migration: What Can We Know and What Can We Explain?" In *Migration, Citizenship, Ethnos*, ed. Y. Michal Bodemann and Gökçe Yurdakul, 197–217. New York: Palgrave Macmillan.

Heintze, Hans-Joachim. 2000. "The Status of German Minorities in Bilateral Agreements of the Federal Republic." In *German Minorities in Europe: Ethnic Identity and Cultural Belonging*, ed. Stefan Wolff, 205–217. New York: Berghahn Books.

Heitman, Sidney. 1980. *The Soviet Germans in the USSR Today.* Bonn: Bundesinstitut für Ostwissenschaftliche und Internationale Studien.

Hell, Matthias. 2005. *Einwanderungsland Deutschland? Die Zuwanderungsdiskussion 1998–2002.* Wiesbaden: VS Verlag für Sozialwissenschaften.

Heller, Agnes. 1992. "Europe: An Epilogue?" In *The Idea of Europe: Problems of National and Transnational Identity*, ed. Brian Nelson, David Roberts, and Walter Veit, 12–25. New York: Berg Press.

Herbert, Ulrich. 1990. *A History of Foreign Labor in Germany, 1880–1980.* Trans. William Templer. Ann Arbor: University of Michigan Press.

———. 1997. *Hitler's Foreign Workers: Enforced Foreign Labor in Germany under the Third Reich.* Trans. William Templer. Cambridge: Cambridge University Press.

———. 2001. *Geschichte der Ausländerpolitik in Deutschland: Saisonarbeiter, Zwangsarbeiter, Gastarbeiter, Flüchtlinge.* Munich: C.H. Beck.

Herdegen, Gerhard. 1989. "Aussiedler in der Bundesrepublik." *Deutschland Archiv* 22(8): 912–924.

Hobsbawm, E. J. 1994. *Nations and Nationalism since 1780.* Cambridge: Cambridge University Press.

Hoffman, Lars, and Jo Shaw. 2004. "Constitutionalism and Federalism in the 'Future of Europe' Debate: The German Dimension." *German Politics* 13(4): 625–644.

Hoffmann, Lutz. 1990. *Die Unvollendete Republik: Einwanderungsland oder deutscher Nationalstaat.* Cologne: Papy Rossa.

Hofmann, Rainer. 1997. "Refugee Definition." In Hailbronner, Martin, and Motomura 1997a, 227–54.

Hollifield, James. 1991. "Immigration and Modernization." In *Searching for the New France,* ed. James Hollifield and George Ross, 113–150. New York: Routledge.

———. 1992. *Immigrants, Markets, and States: The Political Economy of Postwar Europe.* Cambridge, MA: Harvard University Press.

———. 1994. "The Migration Challenge: Europe's Crisis in Historical Perspective." *Harvard International Review* 16(3): 26–32.

Homze, Edward L. 1967. *Foreign Labor in Nazi Germany.* Princeton, NJ: Princeton University Press.

Hönekopp, Elmar. 1987. "Rückkehrförderung und Rückkehr ausländischer Arbeitnehmer: Ergebnisse des Rückkehrförderungsgesetzes, der Rückkehrhilfe-Statistik und der IAB-Rückkehrbefragung." In *Aspekte der Ausländerbeschäftigung in der Bundesrepublik Deutschland,* ed. Elmar Hönekopp, 287–341. Nuremberg: Institut für Arbeitsmarkt- und Berufsforschung der Bundesanstalt für Arbeit.

———. 1997. "The New Labor Migration as an Instrument of German Foreign Policy." In Münz and Myron Weiner 1997, 168–182.

Hrbek, Rudolf. 1997. "Die Auswirkungen der EU-Integration auf den Föderalismus in Deutschland." *Aus Politik und Zeitgeschichte* 24(97): 12–21.

Huber, Bertold. 2001. "The Application of Human Rights Standards by German Courts to Asylum Seekers, Refugees and other Migrants." *European Journal of Migration Law* 3(2): 171–84.

Hucko, Elmar M., ed. 1987. *The Democratic Tradition: Four German Constitutions.* New York: Berg Press.

Hughes, Michael L. 1999. *Shouldering the Burdens of Defeat: West Germany and the Reconstruction of Social Justice.* Chapel Hill: University of North Carolina Press.

———. 2000. "'Through No Fault of Their Own': West Germans Remember Their War Losses." *German History* 18(2): 193–213.

Human Rights Watch. 1992. "'Foreigners Out': Xenophobia and Right-Wing Violence in Germany." New York. http://www.hrw.org/reports/pdfs/g/germany/germany92o.pdf.

———. 1995. "'Germany for Germans': Xenophobia and Racist Violence in Germany." New York. http://www.hrw.org/reports/pdfs/g/germany/germany954.pdf.

Ibrahim, Salim. 1997. *Die "Ausländerfrage" in Deutschland: Fakten, Defizite und Handlungsimperative.* Frankfurt am Main: Verlag für Akademische Schriften (VAS).

IHF (International Helsinki Federation for Human Rights). 2005. "Intolerance and Discrimination against Muslims in the EU: Developments since September 11." http://www.ihf-hr.org/viewbinary/viewdocument.php?doc_id=6237.

Independent Commission on Immigration. 2001. "Structuring Immigration, Fostering Integration." Report by the Independent Commission on Migration to Germany. http://www.bmi. bund.de/nn_148138/Internet/Content/Common/Anlagen/Broschueren/2001/Structuring_ _Immigation____Fostering__Id__14626__en,templateId=raw,property=publicationFile. pdf/Structuring_Immigation_-_Fostering_Id_14626_en.

International Labour Office. 1959. *International Migration: 1945–1957*. Geneva.

Ireland, Patrick. 1994. *The Policy Challenge of Ethnic Diversity: Immigrant Politics in France and Switzerland*. Cambridge, MA: Harvard University Press.

_____. 2004. *Becoming Europe: Immigration, Integration, and the Welfare State*. Pittsburgh: University of Pittsburgh Press.

Jackson Preece, Jennifer. 1998. *National Minorities and the European Nation-State System*. Oxford: Clarendon Press.

James, Harold. 1989. *A German National Identity, 1770–1990*. New York: Routledge, Chapman, and Hall.

Jarausch, Konrad H. 1994. *The Rush to German Unity*. New York: Oxford University Press.

_____, and Volker Gransow, eds. 1994. "Volkskammer Declaration on German History, April 12, 1990." In *Uniting Germany: documents and debates, 1944–1993*, trans. by Allison Brown and Belinda Cooper, 138–39. Providence, RI: Berg Publishers.

Jeffery, Charlie and William Paterson. 2003. "Germany and European Integration: a Shifting of Tectonic Plates." *West European Politics* 26(4): 59–74.

Joeres, Annika. 2004. "CDU will Multi-Kulti beenden." *die tageszeitung*. May 14.

Johnson, Paul, and Klaus Zimmermann, eds. 1993. *Labour Markets in an Ageing Europe*. Cambridge: Cambridge University Press.

Joly, Danièle. 1996. *Haven or Hell? Asylum Policies and Refugees in Europe*. New York: St. Martin's Press.

Jonderko, Franciszek. 2002. "Interethnische Beziehungen in Oberschlesien, 1945–1989." In *Die Grenzen der Nationen. Identitätenwandel in Oberschlesien in der Neuzeit*, ed. Kai Struve and Philipp Ther, 203–224. Marburg: Herder-Institut.

Jones, Philip. 1990. "Recent Ethnic German Migration from Eastern Europe to the Federal Republic." *Geography* 75(328): 249–252.

Joppke, Christian. 1996. "Multiculturalism and Immigration: A Comparison of the United States, Germany, and Great Britain." *Theory and Society* 25(4): 449–500.

_____. 1999. *Immigration and the Nation-State: The United States, Germany, and Great Britain*. Oxford: Oxford University Press.

_____. 2001. "The Evolution of Alien Rights in the United States, Germany and the European Union." In *Citizenship Today: Global Perspectives and Practices*, ed. T. Alexander Aleinikoff and Douglas Klusmeyer, 26–62. Washington, DC: Carnegie Endowment for International Peace.

Judt, Tony. 2000. "The Past Is Another Country: Myth and Memory in Postwar Europe." In *The Politics of Retribution in Europe: World War II and its Aftermath*, ed. István Deák, Jan T. Gross, and Tony Judt, 293–323. Princeton, NJ: Princeton University Press.

_____. 2005. *Postwar: A History of Europe since 1945*. New York: Penguin Press.

Juss, Satvinder. 2005. "The Decline and Decay of European Refugee Policy." *Oxford Journal of Legal Studies* 25(4): 749–792.

Kamusella, Tomasz. 1999. "Ethnic Cleansing in Silesia 1950–1989 and the Ennationalizing Policies of Poland and Germany." *Patterns of Prejudice* 33(2): 51–73.

_____. 2000. "Upper Silesia 1918–45." In Cordell 2000, 92–112.

_____. 2002. "Language and Construction of Identity in Upper Silesia During the Long Nineteenth Century." In *Die Grenzen der Nationen. Identitätenwandel in Oberschlesien in der Neuzeit*, ed. Kai Struve and Philipp Ther, 45–70. Marburg: Herder-Institut.

Kanstroom, Daniel. 1993a. "Wer sind wir wieder: Laws of Asylum, Immigration, and Citizenship in the Struggle for the Soul of the New Germany." *Yale Journal of International Law* 18: 155–211.

_____. 1993b. "Shining City and the Fortress: Reflections on the Euro-solution to the German Immigration Dilemma." *Boston College International and Comparative Law Review* 16: 213–243.

Kanther, Manfred. 1996. "Deutschland ist kein Einwanderungsland." *Frankfurter Allgemeine Zeitung.* November 13.

Karpen, Ulrich, ed. 1988. *The Constitution of the Federal Republic of Germany.* Baden-Baden: NomosVerlagsgesellschaft.

Kastoryano, Riva. 2002. *Negotiating Identities: States and Immigrants in France and Germany.* Princeton, NJ: Princeton University Press.

Katzenstein, Peter J. 1987. *Policy and Politics in West Germany: The Growth of a Semisovereign State.* Philadelphia: Temple University Press.

_____. 1997a. "The Smaller European States, Germany and Europe." In Katzenstein 1997b, 251–304.

_____, ed. 1997b. *Tamed Power: Germany in Europe.* Ithaca, NY: Cornell University Press.

_____. 1997c. "United Germany in an Integrating Europe." In Katzenstein 1997b, 1–48.

Kaya, Ayhan, and Ferhat Kentel. 2004. "Euro-Turks: A Bridge, or a Breach, between Turkey and the European Union?" Research Report presented at the OSCE conference "Tolerance and the Fight against Racism, Xenophobia and Discrimination." Brussels. September 2004.

Kelek, Necla. 2005. *Die fremde Braut: ein Bericht aus dem Inneren des türkischen Lebens in Deutschland.* Munich: Goldmann.

Kershaw, Ian. 1995. "The Extinction of Human Rights in Nazi Germany." In *Historical Change and Human Rights: The Oxford Amnesty Lectures 1994,* ed. Olwen Hufton, 217–246. New York: Basic Books.

Kessler, Judith. 1999. "Identitätssuche und Subkultur. Erfahrungen der Sozialarbeit in der Jüdischen Gemeinde zu Berlin." In *Ein neues Judentum in Deutschland. Fremd- und Eigenbilder der russisch-jüdischen Einwanderer,* ed. Julius H. Schoeps, Willi Jasper, and Bernhard Vogt, 140–162. Potsdam: Verlag für Berlin-Brandenburg.

Kirchner, Emil J. 1996. "Germany and the European Union: From Junior to Senior Role." *Developments in German Politics 2.* In Smith, Paterson, and Padgett 1996, 15–170.

Kitschelt, Herbert. 1997. *The Radical Right in Western Europe: A Comparative Analysis.* Ann Arbor: University of Michigan Press.

Klauder, Wolfgang. 1992. "Deutschland im Jahr 2030: Modellrechnungen und Visionen." In *Deutsche im Ausland—Fremde in Deutschland: Migration in Geschichte und Gegenwart,* ed. Klaus J. Bade, 455–464. Munich: C.H. Beck.

Klimt, Andrea. 1989. "Returning 'Home': Portuguese Migrant Notions of Temporariness, Permanence, and Commitment." *New German Critique* 46: 47–70.

_____. 2002. "The Myth of *Heimkehrillusion.*" *German Politics and Society* 20(2): 1–48.

Klingst, Martin. 1993. "Es fehlt nur der Wille." *Die Zeit.* June 18.

Klopp, Brett. 2002. *German Multiculturalism: Immigrant Integration and the Transformation of Citizenship.* Westport, CT: Prager.

Klusmeyer, Douglas. 1996. *Between Consent and Descent: Conceptions of Democratic Citizenship.* Washington, DC: Carnegie Endowment for International Peace.

_____. 2005. "Hannah Arendt's Critical Realism: Power, Justice, and Responsibility." In *Hannah Arendt and International Relations: Readings across the Lines,* ed. Anthony F. Lang and John Williams, 113–178. New York: Palgrave MacMillan.

Klusmeyer, Douglas, and Sophie Pirie, eds. 1997. "Membership, Migration, and Identity: Dilemmas for Liberal Societies." Special issue, *Stanford Humanities Review* 5(2).

Koehl, Robert. 1957. *RKFDV: German Resettlement and Population Policy, 1939–1945*. Cambridge, MA: Harvard University Press.

Kohl, Helmut. 1984. "Speech before the Bundestag, June 22, 1983." In *Bundeskanzler Helmut Kohl, Reden 1982–1984*, 208–20. Bonn: Presse- und Informationsamt der Bundesregierung.

Kolinsky, Eva. 1984. *Parties, Opposition and Society in West Germany*. London: Croom Helm.

———. 2000. "Unexpected Newcomers: Asylum Seekers and Other Non-Germans in the New *Länder*." In *The New Germany in the East: Policy Agendas and Social Developments since Unification*, ed. Chris Flockton, Eva Kolinsky, and Rosalind Pritchard, 148–164. London: Frank Cass.

———. 2004. "Meanings of Migration in East Germany and the West German Model." In *United and Divided: Germany since 1990*, ed. Mike Dennis and Eva Kolinsky, 145–175. New York: Berghahn Books, 2004.

Koller, Barbara. 1994. "Social and Occupational Integration of Immigrants of German Origin in Germany." *IAB Labour Market Research Topics*, 9.

Komjathy, Anthony, and Rebecca Stockwell. 1980. *German Minorities and the Third Reich: Ethnic Germans of East Central Europe between the Wars*. New York: Holmes & Meier Publishers.

Kommers, Donald P. 1989a. *The Constitutional Jurisprudence of the Federal Republic of Germany*. Durham, NC: Duke University Press.

———. 1989b. "The Basic Law of the Federal Republic of Germany: An Assessment after Forty Years." In *The Federal Republic of Germany at Forty*, ed. Peter H. Merkl, 133–159. New York: New York University Press.

———. 1999a. "The Basic Law: A Fifty Year Assessment." In "Fifty Years of German Basic Law." Conference Report. American Institute for Contemporary German Studies, Johns Hopkins University. http://www.aicgs.org/publications/PDF/basiclaw.pdf.

———. 1999b. "Building Democracy: Judicial Review and the German Rechtstaat." In *The Postwar Transformation of Germany: Democracy, Prosperity, and Nationhood*, ed. John Brady, Sarah Wiliarty, and Beverly Crawford, 94–121. Ann Arbor: University of Michigan Press.

———. 2002. "Constitutional Politics in Germany." American Institute for Contemporary German Studies. Washington, DC. March 28. http://www.aicgs.org/at-issue/ai-kommers.shtml.

Koopmans, Ruud. 2004. "Migrant Mobilisation and Political Opportunities: Variation among German Cities and a Comparison with the United Kingdom and the Netherlands." *Journal of Ethnic and Migration Studies* 30(3): 449–470.

———, and Paul Statham. 1999. "Challenging the Liberal Nation State? Postnationalism, Multiculturalism, and the Collective Claims Making of Migrants and Ethnic Minorities in Britain and Germany." *American Journal of Sociology* 105(3): 652–696.

Koppenfels, Amanda Klekowski von. 2002. "The Decline of Privilege: The Legal Background to the Migration of Ethnic Germans." In *Coming Home to Germany? The Integration of Ethnic Germans from Central and Eastern Europe in the Federal Republic*, ed. David Rock and Stefan Wolff, 102–118. New York: Berghahn Books.

Korte, Herman. 1985. "Labor Migration and the Employment of Foreigners in the Federal Republic of Germany Since 1950." In *Guests Come to Stay: The Effects of European Labor Migration on Sending and Receiving Countries*, ed. Rosemarie Rogers, 29–50. Boulder, CO: Westview Press.

Koselleck, Reinhard. 1985. *Futures Past: On the Semantics of Historical Time*. Trans. Keith Tribe. Cambridge, MA: MIT Press.

Koslowski, Rey. 1998. "European Migration Regimes: Emerging, Enlarging and Deteriorating." *Journal of Ethnic and Migration Studies* 24(4): 735–749.

———. 2000. *Migrants and Citizens: Demographic Change in the European State System*. Ithaca, NY: Cornell University Press.

Krauss, Marita. 2000. "Das 'Wir' and das 'Ihr'. Ausgrenzung, Abgrenzung, Identitätsstiftung bei Einheimischen und Flüchtlingen nach 1945." In *Vertriebene in Deutschland: Interdisziplinäre Ergebnisse und Forschungsperspektiven,* ed. Dierk Hoffmann, Marita Krauss, and Michael Schwartz, 27–39. Munich: Oldenbourg Verlag.

_____. 2004. "Jewish Remigration: An Overview of an Emerging Discipline." In *Leo Baeck Institute Yearbook XLIX,* 107–120.

Kreitl, Nikolai. 2001. "Schröder hat keine Vision." *Focus.* August 9.

Kruse, Imke, Henry Edward Orren, and Steffen Angenendt. 2003. "The Failure of Immigration Reform in Germany." *German Politics* 12(3): 129–145.

Kuechler, Manfred. 1993. "Framing Unification: Issue Salience and Mass Sentiment." In *The New Germany Votes: Unification and the Creation of the New German Party System,* ed. Russell J. Dalton, 29–55. Providence, RI: Berg Publishers.

Kühl, Jürgen. 1976. "Die Bedeutung der ausländischen Arbeitnehmer für die Bundesrepublik Deutschland." In *Gastarbeiter,* ed. Helga Reimann and Horst Reimann, 23–40. Munich: Wilhelm Goldmann Verlag.

Kühn, Heinz. 1979. "Stand und Weiterentwicklung der Integration der ausländischen Arbeitnehmer und ihrer Familien in der Bundesrepublik Deutschland. Memorandum des Beauftragten der Bundesregierung." In *"Gastarbeiter" oder Einwanderer?* ed. Karl-Heinz Meier-Braun, 27–70. Frankfurt: Ullstein.

Kulczycki, John J. 1981. *School Strikes in Prussian Poland, 1901–1907: The Struggle over Bilingual Education.* East European Monographs, no. 82. Boulder, CO: Columbia University Press.

Kunig, Philip. 1988. "The Principle of Social Justice." In Karpen 1988, 187–204.

Kurthen, Hermann. 1997. "Antisemitism and Xenophobia in United Germany: How the Burden of the Past Affects the Present." In *Antisemitism and Xenophobia in Germany after Unification,* ed. Hermann Kurthen, Werner Bergmann, and Rainer Erb, 39–87. Oxford: Oxford University Press.

Landler, Mark. 2007. "Germans Split Over a Mosque and the Role of Islam." *New York Times.* July 5.

Langewiesche, Dieter. 2000. "Föderativer Nationalismus als Erbe der deutschen Reichsnation." In *Föderative Nation: Deutschlandkonzepte von der Reformation bis zum Ersten Weltkrieg,* ed. Dieter Langewiesche and Georg Schmidt, 215–242. Munich: R. Oldenbourg Verlag.

Larrabee, Stephen F. 1993. "Eastern Europe and East-West Migration." Report for Rand Project on Migration Within and From the Former Soviet Union, prepared for the Ford Foundation, no. DRU-566-FF. November.

Laursen, Finn, and Sophie Vanhoonacker, eds. 1992. *The Intergovernmental Conference on Political Union.* Maastricht: Martinus Nijhoff.

Lavenex, Sandra. 1999. *Safe Third Countries.* Budapest: Central European Press.

_____. 2006. "Shifting Up and Out: The Foreign Policy of European Immigration Control." *West European Politics* 29(2): 329–350.

Lederer, Harald W., and Axel Nickel. 2000. *Illegale Ausländerbeschäftigung in der Bundesrepublik Deutschland.* Bonn: FES Library.

Leenen, Wolf R. 1992. "Ausländerfeindlichkeit in Deutschland: Politischer Rechtsruck oder Politikversagen." *Deutschland Archiv* 10: 1039–1054.

Lefebvre, Edwige Liliane. 2003. "Republicanism and Universalism: Factors of Inclusion or Exclusion in the French Concept of Citizenship." *Citizenship Studies* 7(1): 15–36.

Legge, Jerome S., Jr. 2003. *Jews, Turks, and Other Strangers.* Madison: University of Wisconsin Press.

Leise, Eric. 2007. "Germany to Regularize 'Tolerated' Asylum Seekers." Migration Information Source. Washington, DC. April 1. http://www.migrationinformation.org/Feature/display.cfm?ID=593.

Lemberg, Hans. 1999. "The Germans and Czech Statehood in the Twentieth Century." In *The German Lands and Eastern Europe: Essays on the History of their Social, Cultural and Political Relations*, ed. Roger Bartlett and Karen Schönwälder, 182–197. New York: St. Martin's Press.

Lendl, Egon. 1959. "Wandel der Kulturlandschaft." In *Die Vertriebenen in Westdeutschland*, Band 2, ed. Eugen Lemberg and Friedrich Edding, 455–501. Kiel: F. Hirt.

Leonardy, Uwe. 1996. "The Political Dimension, German Practice, and the European Perspective." In *Federalizing Europe? The Costs, Benefits, and Preconditions of Federal Political Systems*, ed. Joachim Jens Hesse and Vincent Wright, 73–100. New York: Oxford University Press.

Leonenko, Irina. 2006. "Germany." In *The European Constitution and Its Ratification Crisis: Constitutional Debates in the EU Member States*, ed. Nina Eschke and Thomas Malick, 79–83. Bonn: Center for European Integration Studies.

Lepsius, M. Rainer. 1985. "The Nation and Nationalism in Germany." *Social Research* 52: 43–64.

Levy, Carl. 2005. "The European Union after 9/11: The Demise of a Liberal Democratic Asylum Regime?" *Government and Opposition* 40(1): 26–59.

Levy, Daniel. 1999. "Remembering the Nation: Ethnic Germans and the Transformation of National Identity in the Federal Republic of Germany." Unpublished PhD diss., Columbia University.

⸻. 2002a. "The Transformation of Germany's Ethno-cultural Idiom." In *Challenging Ethnic Citizenship: German and Israeli Perspectives on Immigration*, ed. Daniel Levy and Yfaat Weiss, 196–220. New York: Berghahn Books.

⸻. 2002b. "Integrating Ethnic Germans in West Germany: The Early Postwar Period." In *Coming Home to Germany? The Integration of Ethnic Germans from Central and Eastern Europe in the Federal Republic*, ed. David Rock and Stefan Wolff, 19–37. New York: Berghahn Books.

Lichter, Matthias. 1955. *Die Staatsangehörigkeit*. 2nd ed. Berlin: Carl Heymanns Verlag.

Liebig, Thomas. 2003. "Recruitment of Foreign Labor in Germany and Switzerland." In *Migration for Employment—Bilateral Agreements at a Crossroads*, ed. OECD, 157–186. Paris.

Lindemann, Michael, and Christopher Bobinski. 1995. "Kohl Visit to Help Ties with Poland." *Financial Times*. July 6.

Linek, Bernard. 2000. "Polish and Czech Silesia under Communist Rule." In Cordell 2000, 131–148.

⸻. 2002. "Deutsche und politische nationale Politik in Oberschlesien, 1922–1989." In *Die Grenzen der Nationen. Identitätenwandel in Oberschlesien in der Neuzeit*, ed. Kai Struve and Philipp Ther, 137–167. Marburg: Herder-Institut.

Link, Jürgen. 1988. "Medien und 'Asylanten': Zur Geschichte eines Unworts." In *Flucht und Asyl*, ed. Dietrich Thränhardt and Simon Wolken, 50–61. Freiburg im Breisgau: Lambertus-Verlag.

Lohr, Eric. 2003. *Nationalizing the Russian Empire: The Campaign against Enemy Aliens during World War I*. Cambridge, MA: Harvard University Press.

Long, James W. 1988. *From Privileged to Dispossessed: The Volga Germans, 1860–1917*. Lincoln: University of Nebraska Press.

⸻. 1992. "The Volga Germans and the Famine of 1921." *Russian Review* 51(4): 510–525.

Luckau, Alma. 1941. "German Counterproposals of May 29, 1919: Comments by the German Delegation on the Conditions of Peace." In *The German Delegation at the Paris Peace Conference*, 306–406. New York: Columbia University Press.

Luedtke, Adam. 2005. "European Integration, Public Opinion and Immigration Policy." *European Union Politics* 6(1): 83–112.

Lumans, Vadlis O. 1993. *Himmler's Auxiliaries: The Volksdeutsche Mittelstelle and the German National Minorities of Europe, 1933–1945*. Chapel: University of North Carolina Press.

Lutz, Wolfgang, and Sergei Scherbov. 2006. "Future Demographic Changed in Europe: The Contribution of Migration." In *Europe and Its Immigrants in the 21st Century: A New Deal or a Continuing Dialogue of the Deaf?* ed. Demetrios Papademetriou, 207–222. Washington, DC: Migration Policy Institute.

Lyall, Sarah, and Stephen Castle. 2008. "Ireland Derails a Bid to Recast Europe's Rules." *New York Times.* June 14.

Mahlmann, Matthias. 2003. "Religious Tolerance, Pluralist Society and the Neutrality of the State: The Federal Constitutional Court's Decision in the Headscarf Case." *German Law Journal* 4(11): 1099–1116.

Mahony, Honor. 2003. "Germany Calls to Keep Veto in Immigration Policy." *EUObserver.com.* July 2.

Majer, Diemut. 2003. *"Non-Germans" under the Third Reich: The Nazi Judicial and Administrative System in Germany and Occupied Eastern Europe, with Special Regard to Occupied Poland, 1939–1945.* Trans. Peter Thomas, Edward Vance Humphrey, and Brian Levin. Baltimore, MD: Johns Hopkins University Press.

Mancini, G. Federico. 1992. "The Free Movement of Workers in the Case-Law of the European Court of Justice." In *Constitutional Adjudication in European Community and National Law,* ed. Deirdre Curtin and David O' Keeffe, 68–77. Dublin: Butterworths.

Markovits, Andrei S., and Philip Gorski. 1993. *The German Left: Red, Green, and Beyond.* Oxford: Oxford University Press.

Marrus, Michael R. 1985. *The Unwanted: European Refugees in the Twentieth Century.* New York: Oxford University Press.

Marshall, Barbara. 1992. "German Migration Policies." In *Developments in German Politics,* ed. Gordon Smith, William E. Paterson, Peter H. Merkl, and Stephen Padgett, 247–263. Durham, NC: Duke University Press.

———. 2000. *The New Germany and Migration in Europe.* Manchester: Manchester University Press.

Marshall, T. H. 1950. *Citizenship and Social Class, and Other Essays.* Cambridge: Cambridge University Press.

Martin, David A. 2005. *The United States Refugee Admissions Program: Reforms for a New Era of Refugee Resettlement.* Washington, DC: MPI Publications.

———, and Kay Hailbronner, eds. 2002. *Rights and Duties of Dual Nationals: Evolution and Prospects.* The Hague: Kluwer Law International.

Martin, Philip. 1994. "Germany: Reluctant Land of Immigration." In *Controlling Immigration: A Global Perspective,* ed. Wayne A. Cornelius, Philip L. Martin, and James F. Hollifield, 189–225. Palo Alto, CA: Stanford University Press.

———. 1998. "Germany: Reluctant Land of Immigration." *German Issues* 21. Washington, DC: American Institute for Contemporary German Studies. http://www.aicgs.org/publications/PDF/martin.pdf.

———. 2004. "Germany: Managing Migration in the Twenty-First Century." In *Controlling Immigration: A Global Perspective,* 2nd ed., ed. Wayne A. Cornelius et al., 221–253. Stanford, CA: Stanford University Press.

Martiniello, Marco. 2000. "Citizenship of the European Union." In *From Migrants to Citizens: Membership in a Changing World,* ed. T. Alexander Aleinikoff and Douglas Klusmeyer, 342–382. Washington, DC: Carnegie Endowment for Peace.

Mayer, Franz. 2006. "The European Constitution and the Courts." In *Principles of European Constitutional Law,* ed. Armin von Bogdandy and Jürgen Bast, 281–334. Oxford: Hart Publishing.

Mazower, Mark. 1999. *Dark Continent: Europe's Twentieth Century.* New York: Alfred A. Knopf.

———. 2004. "The Strange Triumph of Human Rights, 1933–1950." *Historical Journal* 47(2): 379–398.

McNeill, William. 1986. *Polyethnicity and National Unity in World History*. Toronto: University of Toronto Press.

Meier-Braun, Karl-Heinz. 1987. "Einwanderungsland Europa: Die Ausländerpolitik der EG-Mitgliedstaaten am Beispiel der Bundesrepublik Deutschland." In *Ausländerrecht und Ausländerpolitik in Europa*, ed. Manfred Zuleeg, 37–68. Baden-Baden: Nomos.

_____. 1988. *Integration und Rückkehr? Zur Ausländerpolitik des Bundes und der Länder, insbesondere Baden-Württembergs*. Mainz/Munich: Mattias Grünewald Verlag/Christian Kaiser Verlag.

_____. 1991. "Auf dem Weg zur multikulturellen Gesellschaft?" *Zeitschrift für Kulturaustausch* 41: 9–26.

Meindersma, Christa. 1997. "Population Exchanges: Individual Law and State Practice, Part I." *International Journal of Refugee Law* 9(3): 335–653.

Mendel, Meron. 2004. "The Policy for the Past in West Germany and Israel: The Case of Jewish Remigration." In *Leo Baeck Institute Yearbook XLIX*, 121–36.

Menges, Walter. 1959. "Wandel und Auflösung der Konfessionszonen." In *Die Vertriebenen in Westdeutschland*, Band 3, ed. Eugen Lemberg and Friedrich Edding, 1–22. Kiel: F. Hirt.

Merkl, Peter. 1963. *The Origin of the West German Republic*. New York: Oxford University Press.

_____. 1993. *German Reunification in the European Context*. University Park: Pennsylvania State University Press.

Mertes, Michael. 1994. "Germany's Social and Political Culture." *Dædalus* 123(1): 1–32.

Migration News. 1995. "Dual Citizenship Initiative Fails in Germany." 2(3). http://migration.ucdavis.edu/mn/more.php?id=589_0_4_0.

_____. 1996. "Germans Consider Immigration Policy." 3(7). http://migration.ucdavis.edu/mn/more.php?id=994_0_4_0.

_____. 2000a. "Germany: Green Cards?" 7(4). http://migration.ucdavis.edu/mn/more.php?id=2068_0_4_0.

_____. 2000b. "Germany: 'Green Cards.'" 7(6). http://migration.ucdavis.edu/mn/more.php?id=2116_0_4_0.

Migration News Sheet. 1995a. "Agreement with Hanoi on the Repatriation of 40,000 Vietnamese." February.

_____. 1995b. "Suspension of Deportation of Kurds Extended Again." March.

_____. 1996. "Germany: No Claim to Asylum for all Turkish Kurds Rules Federal Administrative Court." May.

Migration und Bevölkerung. 2006. "Abschiebschutz für Tschetschenen." March.

Milner, James. 2000. "Sharing the Security Burden: Towards the Convergence of Refugee Policy and State Security." Refugee Studies Centre Working Paper No. 4. Oxford University.

Minkenberg, Michael. 2001. "The Radical Right in Public Office: Agenda-Setting and Policy Effects." *West European Politics* 24(4): 1–21.

Mitchell, Maria. 1995. "Materialism and Secularism: CDU Politicians and National Socialism, 1945–1949." *Journal of Modern History* 67: 278–309.

Moeller, Robert G. 2001. *War Stories: The Search for a Usable Past in the Federal Republic of Germany*. Berkley: University of California Press.

Monar, Jörg. 2006. "The Project of a European Border Guard: Origins, Models and Prospects in the Context of the EU's Integrated External Border Management." In *Border Security and Governance: Managing Borders in a Globalized World*, ed. Marina Caparini and Otwin Marenin, 147–189. Geneva: DCAF.

Moravcsik, Andrew. 1998. *The Choice for Europe: Social Purpose & State Power from Messina to Maastricht*. Ithaca, NY: Cornell University Press.

Motomura, Hiroshi. 1997. "Family and Immigration: A Roadmap for the Ruritanian Lawyer." In Hailbronner, Martin, and Motomura 1997a, 79–120.

Mühlum, Albert. 1993. "Armutswanderung, Asyl und Abwehrverhalten: Globale und nationale Dilemmata." *Aus Politik und Zeitgeschichte* 7: 3–15.

Münz, Rainer. 2004. "New German Law Skirts Comprehensive Immigration Reform." *Migration Information Source.* August 1. http://www.migrationinformation.org/Feature/display.cfm?id=241.

———. 2007. "Aging and Demographic Change in European Societies: Main Trends and Alternative Policy Options." Social Protection Discussion Paper 0703. March.

———, and Rainer Ohliger. 1998. "Long-Distance Citizens: Ethnic Germans and Their Immigration to Germany." In Schuck and Münz 1998, 155–202.

———, Wolfgang Seifert, and Ralf Ulrich. 1999. *Zuwanderung nach Deutschland. Strukturen, Wirkungen, Perspektiven.* Frankfurt am Main: Campus Verlag.

———, and Ralf Ulrich. 1997. "Changing Patterns of Immigration to Germany, 1945–1995." In *Migration Past, Migration Future,* ed. Klaus J. Bade and Myron Weiner, 65–199. New York: Berghahn Books.

Murray, Laura M. 1994. "Einwanderungsland Bundesrepublik Deutschland? Explaining the Evolving Positions of German Political Parties on Citizenship Policy." *German Politics and Society* 33: 23–56.

Nagle, John David. 1970. *The National Democratic Party: Right Radicalism in the Federal Republic of Germany.* Berkeley: University of California Press.

Naimark, Norman M. 2001. *Fires of Hatred: Ethnic Cleansing in Twentieth Century Europe.* Cambridge, MA: Harvard University Press.

Nathans, Eli. 2004. *The Politics of Citizenship in Germany: Ethnicity, Utility and Nationalism.* New York: Berg.

Neugebauer, Gero, and Richard Stöss. 1996. *Die PDS: Geschichte, Organisation, Wähler, Konkurrenten.* Opladen: Leske and Budrich.

Neuman, Gerald. 1990. "Immigration and Judicial Review in the Federal Republic of Germany." *Journal of International Law and Politics* 23(1): 35–85.

———. 1993. "Buffer Zones Against Refugees: Dublin, Schengen, and the German Asylum Amendment." *Virginia Journal of International Law* 33: 503–526.

———. 1998. "Nationality Law in the United States and the Federal Republic of Germany: Structure and Current Problems." In Schuck and Münz 1998, 247–298.

Neumann, Franz. 1968. *Der Block der Heimatvertriebenen und Entrechteten, 1950–1960.* Meisenheim am Glan: Hain.

Neunreither, Karlheinz. 1959. "Politics and Bureaucracy in the West German Bundesrat." *The American Political Science Review* 53(3): 713–731.

Newland, Kathleen. 1995. *U.S. Refugee Policy: Dilemmas and Directions.* Washington, DC: Carnegie Endowment for International Peace.

———. 2001. "Refugee Protection and Assistance." In *Managing Global Issues: Lessons Learned,* ed. J. Simons and Chantal de Jonge Oudraat, 508–533. Washington, DC: Carnegie Endowment of International Peace.

———. 2003. *No Refuge: The Challenge of Internal Displacement.* New York: UN Office for the Coordination of Humanitarian Affairs.

Nielsen, Jørgen S. 2004. *Muslims in Western Europe.* 3rd ed. Edinburgh: Edinburgh University Press.

Niessen, Jan. 1996. "Introduction." In *The Developing Immigration and Asylum Policies of the European Union,* ed. Elspeth Guild, 3–66. The Hague: Kluwer Law International.

———. 2000. *Diversity and Cohesion: New Challenges for the Integration of Immigrants and Minorities.* Strasbourg: Council of Europe.

Nipperdey, Thomas. 1986. "Der Föderalismus in der deutschen Geschichte." In *Nachdenken über die deutsche Geschichte.* Munich: C.H. Beck.

_____. 1990. *Deutsche Geschichte, 1866–1918.* Vol. 1. Munich: C.H. Beck.

_____. 1992. *Deutsche Geschichte, 1866–1918.* Vol. 2. Munich: C.H. Beck.

Nugent, Neill. 1999. *The Government and Politics of the European Union.* 4th ed. Durham, NC: Duke University Press.

Oberpenning, Hannelore. 1999. "Zuwanderung und Eingliederung von Flüchtlingen, Vertriebenen und Aussiedlern im lokalen Kontext—das Beispiel Espelkamp." In *Aussiedler: deutsche Einwanderer aus Osteuropa,* ed. Klaus J. Bade and Jochen Oltmer, 283–313. Osnabrück: Universitätsverlag Rasch.

O'Brien, Peter. 1988. "Continuity and Change in Germany's Treatment of Non-Germans." In *International Migration Review* 1(3): 109–34.

OECD (Organisation for Economic Co-operation and Development). 1993. *Trends in International Migration.* Continuous Reporting System on Migration (SOPEMI), *Annual Report 1993.* Paris: OECD.

_____. 1995. *Germany's Report on International Migrations (SOPEMI) to the OECD.* Federal Ministry of Labour and Social Affairs.

_____. 2004. "Germany: Increasing the Capacity of the Economy to Create Employment." *OECD Economic Surveys* 12: 97–125.

Oltmer, Jochen. 2001. "Migration and Public Policy in Germany, 1918–1939." In *Crossing Boundaries: The Exclusion and Inclusion of Minorities in Germany and the United States,* ed. Larry Eugene Jones, 50–69. New York: Berghahn Books.

_____. 2005. *Migration und Politik in der Weimarer Republik.* Göttingen: Vandenhoeck & Ruprecht.

Oppitz, Catharina. 2007. "Neues Wort im Hort: 'Mama lernt Deutsch' seit sieben Jahren großer Erfolg." *die tageszeitung.* March 24.

Oschlies, Wolf. 1988. *Rumäniendeutsches Schicksal: 1918–1988.* Cologne: Böhlau.

Østergaard-Nielsen, Eva. 2003. *Transnational Politics: Turks and Kurds in Germany.* New York: Routledge.

Padgen, Anthony, ed. 2002. *The Idea of Europe: From Antiquity to the European Union.* Cambridge: Cambridge University Press.

Papademetriou, Demetrios. 1988. "International Migration in North America and Western Europe: Trends and Consequences." In *International Migration Today,* Vol. 1: *Trends and Perspectives,* ed. Reginald Appleyard, 123–209. Paris: UNESCO Press and University of Western Australia Press.

_____. 1996. *Coming Together or Pulling Apart? The European Union's Struggle with Immigration and Asylum.* Washington, DC: Carnegie Endowment for International Peace.

_____. 2003a. "Reflections on Managing Rapid and Deep Change in the Newest Age of Migration." Paper presented at the Greek President's conference "Managing Migration for the Benefit of Europe," Athens. May.

_____. 2003b. "Policy Recommendations for Immigrant Integration." *Migration Information Source.* October. http://www.migrationinformation.org/Feature/display.cfm?ID=171.

_____. 2005. "The Past, Present and Future of International Migration and Its Relationship to Aging Societies." Testimony given before the Social Security Advisory Board. Dirksen Senate Office Building. September 7.

_____, ed. 2006. *Europe and Its Immigrants in the 21st Century: A New Deal or a Continuing Dialogue of the Deaf?* Washington, DC: Migration Policy Institute.

_____, and Kimberly A. Hamilton. 1995. *Managing Uncertainty: Regulating Immigration Flows in Advanced Industrial Countries.* Washington, DC: Carnegie Endowment for International Peace.

_____, and Werner Weidenfeld. 2007. "The Children That Europe Forgot." *European Voice.* September 20.

Passerini, Luisa. 2002. "From the Ironies of Identity to the Identities of Irony." In Pagden 2002, 191–208.

Patton, David. 1996. "The Allied Occupation and German Unification Compared: A Forgotten Lesson from the 1940s." *German Politics and Society* 14(4): 1–22.

_____. 1998. "The Party of Democratic Socialism: An Ossie-BHE for the 1990s?" Conference paper presented at the 24th New Hampshire Symposium. June 24–July 1.

Pearson, Raymond. 1983. *National Minorities in Eastern Europe, 1848–1945*. London: MacMillan Press.

Peel, Quentin. 1994. "Germany's Coalition Faces a Mauling in the Year of the Voter." *Financial Times*. March 11.

Penninx, Rinus. 2003. "Integration: The Role of Communities, Institutions, and the State." *Migration Information Source*. October. http://www.migrationinformation.org/Feature/display.cfm?ID=168.

_____. 2006. "Integration of Migrants: Research Findings and Policy Lessons." In *Europe and its Migrants in the 21st Century: A New Deal or a Continuing Dialogue of the Deaf?* ed. Demetrios Papademetriou, 31–52. Washington, DC: Migration Policy Institute.

PEW Research Center. 2007. *The PEW Global Attitudes Project*. Washington, DC: PEW Research Center. October 4.

Pinkus, Benjamin. 1986. "The Germans in the Soviet Union since 1945." In Fleischhauer and Pinkus 1986, 103–153.

Piotrowicz, Ryszard. 1998. "Facing Up to Refugees—International Apathy and German Self-Help." *International Journal of Refugee Law* 10(3): 410–443.

Plender, Richard, ed. 1997. *Basic Documents on International Migration Law*. 2nd rev. The Hague: Martinus Nijhoff Publishers.

Pond, Elizabeth. 1993. *Beyond the Wall: Germany's Road to Unification*. Washington, DC: Brookings Institution.

_____. 2001. "A New Constitution for the Old Continent?" *Washington Quarterly* 24(4): 29–40.

Portes, Alejandro, and Rubén Rumbaut. 1996. *Immigrant America: A Portrait*. Berkeley: University of California Press.

Pratsch, Kristina, and Volker Ronge. 1989. "Ganz normale Bundesbürger? Zur Integration von DDR-Übersiedlern nach fünf Jahren im Westen." *Deutschland Archiv* 22: 904–912.

Preuss, Ulrich K. 2003. "Citizenship and the German Nation." *Citizenship Studies* 7(1): 37–56.

Prümm, Kathrin, and Stefan Alscher. 2007. "From Model to Average Student: The Europeanization of Migration Policy and Politics in Germany." In *The Europeanization of National Immigration Policies: Between Autonomy and the European Union*, ed. Thomas Faist and Andreas Ette, 73–92. New York: Palgrave Macmillan.

Pulzer, Peter. 1996. "Model or Exception—Germany as a Normal State?" In Smith, Patterson, and Padgett 1996, 303–316.

Quint, Peter E. 1997. *The Imperfect Union: Constitutional Structures of German Unification*. Princeton, NJ: Princeton University Press.

Rady, Martyn. 1999. "The German Settlement in Central and Eastern Europe during the High Middle Ages." In *The German Lands and Eastern Europe: Essays on the History of their Social, Cultural and Political Relations*, ed. Roger Bartlett and Karen Schönwälder, 11–47. New York: St. Martin's Press.

Rae, Heather. 2002. *State Identities and the Homongenisation of Peoples*. Cambridge: Cambridge University Press.

Ramelsberger, Annette. "Metin Kaplan darf nicht ausgeliefert werden." *Süddeutsche Zeitung*. May 28.

Rau, Johannes. 2001. "Plea for a European Constitution." http://www.germany.info/relaunch/politics/speeches/040401.html.

Reermann, Olaf. 1997. "Readmission Agreements." In Hailbronner, Martin, and Motomura 1997a, 79–120.

Remennick, Larissa. 2005. "'Idealists Headed to Israel, Pragmatics Chose Europe': Identity Dilemmas and Social Incorporation among Former Soviet Jews who Migrated to Germany." *Immigrants & Minorities* 23(1): 30–58.

Renzsch, Wolfgang. 2002. "Challenge and Perspectives for German Federalism." In *German Federalism: Past, Present, Future*, ed. Maiken Umbach, 189–205. New York: Palgrave.

Rist, Ray. 1978. *Guestworkers in Germany: The Prospect for Pluralism*. New York: Praeger Publishers.

Ritter, Gerhard, and Merith Niehuss. 1991. *Wahlen in Deutschland: 1946–1991*. Munich: C.H. Beck.

———. 1995. *Wahlen in Deutschland: 1990–1994*. Munich: C.H. Beck.

Rogers, Rosemarie. 1993. "Western European Responses to Migration." In *International Migration and Security*, ed. Myron Weiner, 107–148. Boulder, CO: Westview Press.

Rogge, Heinrich. 1959. "Vertreibung und Eingliederung in Spiegel des Rechts." In *Die Vertriebenen in Westdeutschland*, Vol. 1, ed. Eugen Lemberg and Friedrich Edding, 174–245. Kiel: F. Hirt.

Ronge, Volker. 1990. "Die soziale Integration von DDR-Übersiedlern in der Bundesrepublik Deutschland." *Aus Politik und Zeitgeschichte* 1–2: 39–47.

———. 1993. "Ost-West Wanderung nach Deutschland." *Aus Politik und Zeitgeschichte* 7: 16–28.

Rosamond, Ben. 2000. *Theories of European Integration*. New York: St. Martin's Press.

Roshwald, Aviel. 2005. "Ethnicity and Democracy in Europe's Multinational Empires, 1848–1918." In *Political Democracy and Ethnic Diversity in Modern European History*, ed. André W. M. Gerrits and Dirk Jan Wolfram, 65–77. Stanford, CA: Stanford University Press.

Ross, Ronald J. 1998. *The Failure of Bismarck's Kulturkampf: Catholicism and State Power in Imperial Germany, 1871–1887*. Washington, DC: Catholic University Press of America Press.

Rotte, Ralph. 2000. "Immigration Control in United Germany: Toward a Broader Scope of National Policies." *International Migration Review* 34(2): 357–390.

Rubio-Marín, Ruth. 1998. "Equal Citizenship and the Difference that Residence Makes." In *European Citizenship: An Institutional Challenge*, ed. Massimo La Torre, 201–228. The Hague: Kluwer International Law.

———. 2000. *Immigration as a Democratic Challenge: Citizenship and Inclusion in Germany and the United States*. Cambridge: Cambridge University Press.

Rudden, Bernard, and Derrick Wyatt, eds. 1993. *Basic Community Laws*. 4th ed. Oxford: Clarendon Press.

Rudolph, Hedwig. 1998. "The New German Guest-Worker Schemes and Their Implementation." Paper presented at "Conference on Dilemmas of Immigration Control in a Globalizing World," European University Institute. June 11–12.

Runge, Irene. 1995. *Ich bin kein Russe: Jüdische Zuwanderung zwischen 1989 und 1994*. Berlin: Dietz Verlag.

Schatz, Klaus-Werner. 1974. *Wachstum und Strukturwandel der westdeutschen Wirtschaft im internationalen Vergleich*. Tübingen: J.C.B. Mohr.

Scheuing, Dieter H. 2004. "The Approaches to European Law in German Jurisprudence." *German Law Journal* 5(6): 703–719.

Schlötzer, Christiane. 2000. "Streit über Kommission für Zuwanderung." *Süddeutsche Zeitung*. June 26.

Schmeidl, Susanne. 2001. "Conflict and Forced Migration: A Quantitative Review, 1964–1995." In *Global Migrants, Global Refugees: Problems and Solutions*, ed. Aristide R. Zolberg and Peter M. Benda, 62–94. New York: Berghahn Books.

Schmidt, Manfred G. 2003. *Political Institutions in the Federal Republic of Germany*. New York: Oxford University Press.

Schmitt, Carl. 1970. *Verfassungslehre*. 5th ed. Berlin: Duncker & Humblot.

_____. 1996. "Preface to the Second Edition (1926)." In *The Crisis of Parliamentary Democracy*, trans. Ellen Kennedy. Cambridge, MA: MIT Press.

Schnapper, Dominique. 1994. "The Debate on Immigration and the Crisis of National Identity." *West European Politics* 17(2): 127–139.

_____. 1998. *Community of Citizens: On the Modern Idea of Nationality*. Trans. Severine Rosee. Somerset, NJ: Transaction Publishers.

Schneider, Christian. 1988. "Aus Fremden werden Mitbürger und Landsleute." *Süddeutsche Zeitung*. September 10–11.

Schneider, Hans-Peter. 1999. "German Unification and the Federal System: The Challenge of Reform." In *Recasting German Federalism: The Legacies of Unification*, ed. Charlie Jeffrey, 58–84. New York: Pinter.

Schoenberg, Hans. 1970. *Germans from the East*. The Hague: Martinus Nijhoff.

Schönekäs, Klaus. 1990. "Bundesrepublik Deutschland." In *Neue Rechte und Rechtsextremismus in Europa*, ed. Franz Gress, Hans Gerd Jaschke, and Klaus Schönekäs, 218–311. Opladen: Westdeutscher Verlag.

Schönwälder, Karen. 1996. "Migration, Refugees and Ethnic Plurality as Issues of Public and Political Debates in (West) Germany." In *Citizenship, Nationality and Migration in Europe*, ed. David Cesarani and Mary Fulbrook, 159–178. New York: Routledge.

_____. 1999. "Persons Persecuted on Political Grounds Shall Enjoy the Right of Asylum—But Not in Our Country: Asylum Policy and Debates about Refugees in the Federal Republic of Germany." In *Refugees, Citizenship and Social Policy in Europe*, ed. Alice Bloch and Carl Levy, 76–90. New York: St. Martin's Press.

_____. 2006. "The Difficult Task of Managing Migration: The 1973 Recruitment Stop." In *German History from the Margins*, ed. Neil Gregor, Nils Roemer, and Mark Roseman, 252–267. Bloomington: Indiana University Press.

Schoeps, Julius H., Willi Jasper, and Bernhard Vogt. 1999. "Jüdische Zuwanderer aus der DDR—zur Problematik von sozio-kultureller und generationsspezifischer Integration." In *Ein neues Judentum in Deutschland. Fremd- und Eigenbilder der russisch-jüdischen Einwanderer*, ed. Julius H. Schoeps, Willi Jasper, and Bernhard Vogt, 13–139. Potsdam: Verlag für Berlin-Brandenburg.

Schreiber, Sylvia, 2003. "Club der Willigen." *Der Spiegel*. July 21.

Schuck. Peter H. 1997. "Refugee Burden-Sharing: A Modest Proposal." *Yale Journal of International Law* 22: 243–97.

_____, and Rainer Münz. 1998. *Paths to Inclusion: The Integration of Migrants in the United States and Germany*. Providence RI: Berghahn Books.

Schulze, Rainer. 1997. "Growing Discontent: Relations between Native and Refugee Populations in a Rural District in Western Germany after the Second World War." In *West Germany Under Construction: Politics, Society, and Culture in the Adenauer Era*, ed. Robert G. Moeller, 109–134. Ann Arbor: University of Michigan Press.

Scott, James C. 1998. *Seeing Like a State*. New Haven, CT: Yale University Press.

Sheehan, James J. 1981. "What is German History? Reflections on the Role of the Nation in German History and Historiography." *Journal of Modern History* 53: 1–23.

_____. 1989. *German History, 1770–1866*. Oxford: Oxford University Press.

Sinn, Annette, Axel Kreienbrink, and Hans Dietrich von Loeffelholz. 2006. *Illegal aufhältige Drittstaatsangehörige in Deutschland: Staatliche Ansätze: Profile und soziale Situation*. Nürnberg: Bundesamt für Migration und Flüchtlinge.

Sinn, Gerlinde, and Hans-Warner Sinn. 1992. *Jumpstart: The Economic Unification of Germany*. Trans. Juli Irving-Lessmann. Cambridge, MA: MIT Press.

Skran, Claudena M. 1995. *Refugees in Inter-War Europe: The Emergence of a Regime*. Oxford: Clarendon Press.

Slaughter, M. M. 1994. "The Multicultural Self: Questions of Subjectivity, Questions of Power." In *Constitutionalism, Identity, Difference, and Legitimacy*, ed. Michel Rosenfeld, 369–380. Durham, NC: Duke University Press.

Smith, Anthony D. 1998. *Nationalism and Modernism*. New York: Routledge.

Smith, Gordon, William E. Patterson, and Stephen Padgett. 1996. *Developments in German Politics 2*. Durham, NC: Duke University Press.

Smith, Helmut Walser. 1995. *German Nationalism and Religious Conflict: Culture, Ideology, Politics, 1870–1914*. Princeton, NJ: Princeton University Press.

Smith, Jeremy. 1999. *The Bolsheviks and the National Question, 1917–23*. New York: St. Martin's Press.

Smith, Rogers. 1997. *Civic Ideals: Conflicting Visions of Citizenship in U.S. History*. New Haven, CT: Yale University Press.

_____. 1998. "The Policy Challenges of American Illiberalism." Occasional paper no. 2, Carnegie Endowment for International Peace, International Migration Policy Program. Washington, DC.

Smyser, W. R. 1994–1995. "Dateline Berlin: Germany's New Vision." *Foreign Policy* 97: 140–158.

Snyder, Jack. 2000. *From Voting to Violence: Democratization and Nationalist Conflict*. New York: W.W. Norton & Co.

Sollors, Werner. 2004. "Goodbye, Germany." Paper presented at the conference "Goodbye Germany? Migration, Culture, and the Nation State." Berkeley, CA. October 28–30.

Sonntag-Wolgast, Cornelie. 1994. "Die Ausländerpolitik der Bundesregierung—Chronik der Versäumnisse." Press release from the Social Democratic Party of Germany. July 7.

Soysal, Yasemin Nuhoglu. 1994. *Limits of Citizenship: Migrants and Postnational Membership in Europe*. Chicago, IL: University of Chicago Press.

Spencer, Sarah. 2003. "The Challenges of Integration for the EU." *Migration Information Source*. October 1. http://www.migrationinformation.org/Feature/display.cfm?ID=170.

_____. 2006. "The Challenge of Integration in Europe." In *Europe and Its Immigrants in the 21st century*, ed. Demetrios Papademetriou, 1–30. Washington, DC: Migration Policy Institute.

Spevack, Edmund. 1997. "American Pressures on the German Constitutional Tradition: Basic Rights in the West German Constitution of 1949." *International Journal of Politics, Culture and Society* 10(3): 411–436.

Spoerer, Mark, and Jochen Fleischhacker. 2002. "Forced Laborers in Nazi Germany: Categories, Numbers, and Survivors." *Journal of Interdisciplinary History* 33(2): 169–204.

Steiner, Niklaus. 2000. *Arguing about Asylum: The Complexity of Refugee Debates in Europe*. New York: St. Martin's Press.

Stirn, Hans. 1964. *Ausländische Arbeiter im Betrieb*. Frechen and Cologne: Bartmann-Verlag.

Stolleis, Michael. 1998. *The Law under the Swastika: Studies on Legal History in Nazi Germany*. Trans. Thomas Dunlap. Chicago, IL: University of Chicago Press.

Stöss, Richard. 1989. *Die Extreme Rechte in der Bundesrepublik*. Opladen: Westdeutscher Verlag.

_____. 1990. *Die "Republikaner."* Cologne: Bund-Verlag.

Stråth, Bo. 2000. "Multiple Europes: Integration, Identity and Demarcation of the Other." In *Europe and the Other and Europe as the Other*, ed. Bo Stråth, 385–420. Brussels: PIE Lang.

_____. 2002. "A European Identity: To the Historical Limits of a Concept." *European Journal of Social Theory* 5(4): 387–401.

_____. 2005. "Methodological and Substantive Remarks on Myth, Memory and History in the Construction of a European Community." *German Law Journal* 6(2): 255–271.

Stricker, Gerd. 2000. "Ethnic Germans in Russia and the Former Soviet Union." In *German Minorities in Europe: Ethnic Identity and Cultural Belonging*, ed. Stefan Wolff, 165–179. New York: Berghahn Books.

Süddeutsche Zeitung. 1997a. "Kohl lehnt doppelte Staatsbürgerschaft ab: Widerstand gegen Forderung der FDP." October 27.

―――. 1997b. "Doppelte Staatsbürgerschaft entzweit Koalition Liberale bestehen auf erleichterter Einbürgerung: FDP-Generalsekretär Westerwelle nennt Kohls Warnung vor stärkerem Zuzug sachlich falsch und irreführend. 'Weitere Verhandlungen sinnlos'/CSU spricht von Grundsatzfrage für Fortbestand des Regierungsbündnisses." October 28.

―――. 1997c. "CDU-Politiker kritisieren Kohl: Parlamentarier für doppelte Staatsbürgerschaft 'Kein starker Ausländer-Zustrom zu befürchten.'" October 30.

―――. 2000a. "Schily will Henkel und Stihl." July 1.

―――. 2000b. "CDU kritisiert Süssmuths Zusage an Schröder Berufung in Zuwanderungskommission." July 27.

Süssmuth, Rita. 2006. *Migration und Integration: Testfall für unsere Gesellschaft*. Munich: Deutscher Taschenbuch Verlag.

―――, and Werner Weidenfeld, eds. 2005. *Managing Integration: The European Union's Responsibilities Towards Immigrants*. Washington, DC: Migration Policy Institute.

Süssner, Henning. 2004. "Still Yearning for the Lost *Heimat*? Ethnic German Expellees and the Politics of Belonging." *German Politics and Society* 71(22): 1–27.

Terkessidis, Mark, and Yasemin Karakasoglu. 2006. "Gerechtigkeit für die Muslime!" *Die Zeit*, no. 6. February 1.

Ther, Philipp. 1998. *Deutsche und polnische Vertriebene: Gesellschaft und Vertriebenenpolitik in der SBZ/DDR und in Polen, 1945–1956*. Göttingen: Vandenhoeck & Ruprecht.

―――. 2002. "Schlesisch, deutsch oder polnisch? Identitätenwandel in Oberschlesien, 1921–1956." In *Die Grenzen der Nationen. Identitätenwandel in Oberschlesien in der Neuzeit*, ed. Kai Struve and Philipp Ther, 169–202. Marburg: Herder-Institut.

―――. 2005. "The Homogeneous Nation-State and the Blockade of Democratization: Germany and East-Central Europe." In *Political Democracy and Ethnic Diversity in Modern European History*, ed. André W. M. Gerrits and Dirk Jan Wolfram, 78–93. Stanford, CA: Stanford University Press.

Thierse, Wolfgang. 2001. "Vorwort." In *Einwanderungsland Deutschland: neue Wege nachhaltiger Integration*, ed. Ursula Merhländer and Günther Schultze, 7–9. Bonn: Dietz Verlag.

Thornberry, Patrick. 1991. *International Law and the Rights of Minorities*. New York: Oxford University Press.

Thränhardt, Dietrich. 1984. "Ausländer als Objekt deutscher Interessen und Ideologien." In *Der gläserne Fremde*, ed. Harmut M. Griese, 115–132. Leverkusen: Leske and Budrich.

―――. 1995a. "The Political Uses of Xenophobia in England, France and Germany." *Party Politics* 1(3): 321–343.

―――. 1995b. "Die Reform der Einbürgerung in Deutschland." In *Einwanderungskonzeption für die Bundesrepublik Deutschland*, Gesprächskreis Arbeit und Soziales Nr. 50., 63–116. Bonn: Friedrich Ebert Stiftung.

―――. 1999. "Germany's Immigration Policies." In *Mechanisms of Immigration Control: A Comparative Analysis of European Regulation Policies*, ed. Grete Brochmann and Tomas Hammar, 29–58. New York: Berg Press.

―――. 2000. "Conflict, Consensus, and Policy Outcomes: Immigration and Integration in Germany and the Netherlands." In *Challenging Immigration and Ethnic Relations Politics*, ed. Ruud Koopmans and Paul Statham, 162–186. Oxford: Oxford University Press.

Tilly, Charles. 1975. "Reflections on the History of European State-Building." In *The Formation of National States in Western Europe*, ed. Charles Tilly, 3–83. Princeton, NJ: Princeton University Press.

―――. 1992. *Coercion, Capital, and European States*. Oxford: Blackwell Press.

Tress, Madeleine. 1995. "Soviet Jews in the Federal Republic: The Rebuilding of a Community." *Journal of Jewish Sociology* 37(1): 39–54.

———. 1997. "Foreigners or Jews? The Soviet Jewish Refugee Population in Germany and the United States." *East European Jewish Affairs* 27(2): 21–38.

Turkish Daily News. 2005. "More Than 20,000 Turkish-German Barred From Voting." September 18.

Ulbrich, Rudi. 1993. "Wohnungsversorgung in der Bundesrepublik Deutschland." *Aus Politik und Zeitgeschichte* 9: 16–31.

Ulrich, Ralf. 1998. "Grau oder bunt? Zuwanderungen und Deutschlands Bevölkerung im Jahre 2030." In *Migration und Gesundheit: Zustandsbeschreibungen und Zukunftsmodelle*, ed. Mattias David, Theda Borde, and Heribert Kentenich, 17–32. Frankfurt am Main: Mabuse.

Umbach, Maiken. 2002. *German Federalism: Past, Present, Future*. New York: Palgrave.

United Nations. 2000. *Replacement Migration*. New York: United Nations Department of Economics and Social Affairs Population Division.

———. 2005. *World Population Prospects: The 2004 Revision*. New York: United Nations Department of Economics and Social Affairs Population Division.

United States Committee for Refugees. 1996. "German Court Upholds 'Safe Third Country' Restrictions on Asylum." *Refugee Reports* 17(5): 7–8.

United States Department of State. 1950. "London Six-Power Conference, February 23–June 2, 1948." In *Germany, 1947–1949: The Story in Documents*. Washington, DC: US Government Printing Office.

Vitorino, Antonio. 2000. "Migrations: Scenarios for the 21st Century." Speech given at the EU conference "Towards a Common Migration Policy for the European Union." Rome. July 12–14.

Völker, Gottfried E. 1975. "Labor Migration: Aid to the West German Economy?" In *Manpower Mobility across Cultural Boundaries: Social, Economic and Legal Aspects*, ed. R. E. Krane, 3–45. Leiden: E.J. Brill.

———. 1976. "More Foreign Workers—Germany's Labour Problem No. 1?" In *Turkish Workers in Europe: 1960–1975*, ed. Nermin Abadan-Unat et al., 331–345. Leiden: E.J. Brill.

———. 2004. "Second-Class Citizens? Restricted Freedom of Movement for *Spätaussiedler* is Constitutional." *German Law Journal* 5(7): 761–789.

Walzer, Michael. 1983. *Spheres of Justice: A Defense of Pluralism and Equality*. New York: Basic Books.

Wasmer, Martina, and Achim Koch. 2003. "Foreigners as Second-Class Citizens? Attitudes Toward Equal Civil Rights for Non-Germans." In Alba, Schmidt, and Wassner 2003, 95–118.

Weber, Max. 1973a. "Die 'Objektivität' sozialwissenschaftlicher und sozialpolitischer Erkenntnis." In *Gesammelte Aufsätze zur Wissenschaftslehre*, ed. Johannes Winckelmann, 146–214. Tübingen: J.C.B. Mohr.

———. 1973b. "Der Sinn der 'Wertfreiheit' der soziologischen und ökonomischen Wissenschaften." In *Gesammelte Aufsätze zur Wissenschaftslehre*, ed. Johannes Winckelmann, 489–540. Tübingen: J.C.B. Mohr.

Week in Germany, The. 1997. October 31. New York City: German Information Center.

Wehler, Hans-Ulrich. 1970. "Von den 'Reichsfeinden' zur 'Reichskristallnacht': Polenpolitik im Deutschen Kaiserreich 1871–1918." In *Krisenherde des Kaiserreichs, 1871–1918*, ed. Hans-Ulrich Wehler, 181–199. Göttingen: Vandenhoeck & Ruprecht.

———. 1995. *Deutsche Gesellschaftsgeschichte*. Vol. 3: *Von der "Deutschen Doppelrevolution" bis zum Beginn des Ersten Weltkrieges, 1849–1914*. Munich: C.H. Beck.

Weil, Patrick. 2001. "Access to Citizenship: A Comparison of Twenty-Five Nationality Laws." In Aleinikoff and Klusmeyer 2003, 17–35.

Weiler, J. H. H. 1995. "Does Europe Need a Constitution? Reflections on Demos, Telos and Ethos in the German Maastricht Decision." *European Law Journal* 1(3): 219–258.

———. 1999. *The Constitution of Europe*. Cambridge: Cambridge University Press.

Weiss, Karin. 2004. "Between Integration and Exclusion: Jewish Immigrants from the Former Soviet Union in Germany." In *United and Divided: Germany since 1990*, ed. Mike Dennis and Eva Kolinsky, 176–194. New York: Berghahn Books.

Weizsäcker, Richard von. 1994. In *Demokratische Leidenschaft—Reden des Bundespräsidenten*, ed. Eberhard Jäckel. Stuttgart: Deutsche Verlags-Anstalt.

Wiener, Antje. 1998. "Promises and Resources: The Developing Practice of 'European' Citizenship." In *European Citizenship: An Institutional Challenge*, ed. Massimo La Torre. The Hague: Kluwer International Law.

Wille, Manfred. 2001. "Compelling the Assimilation of Expellees in the Soviet Zone of Occupation and the GDR." Trans. Sean Ward. In *Redrawing Nations: Ethnic Cleansing in East-Central Europe, 1944–1948*, ed. Philipp Ther and Ana Siljak, 363–383. New York: Rowman & Littlefield Publishers.

Wilpert, Czarina. 1977. "Children of Foreign Workers in the Federal Republic of Germany." *International Migration Review* 11(4): 473–485.

Wingen, Max. 1995. "Immigration to the Federal Republic of Germany as a Demographic and Social Problem." *International Migration Review* 29(3): 710–721.

Wolff, Stefan. 2000. "Changing Priorities or Changing Opportunities? German External Minority Policy, 1919–1998." In *German Minorities in Europe: Ethnic Identity and Cultural Belonging*, ed. Stefan Wolff, 183–203. New York: Berghahn Book.

———. 2003. *The German Question since 1919*. Westport, CT: Praeger.

———. 2005. "The Politics of Homeland: Irredentism and Reconciliation in the Policies of German Federal Governments and Expellee Organizations toward Ethnic German Minorities in Central and Eastern Europe, 1949–99." In *The Heimat Abroad: The Boundaries of Germanness*, ed. Krista O'Donnell, Renate Bridenthal, and Nancy Reagin, 287–312. Ann Arbor: University of Michigan Press.

Wong, Diana. 1992. "Fremdheitsfiguren im gesellschaftlichen Diskurs: Am Beispiel der Asylzuwanderung nach Deutschland." In *Zwischen den Kulturen? Die Sozialwissenschaften vor dem Problem des Kulturvergleichs*, ed. Joachim Matthes, 405–419. Göttingen: Schwartz.

Worbs, Suzanne. 2003. "The Second Generation in Germany: Between School and Labor Market." *International Migration Review* 37(4): 1011–1138.

Wüst, Andreas M. 2004. "Naturalized Citizens as Voters Behavior and Impact." *German Politics* 13(2): 341–359.

Yoder, Jennifer A. 1999. *From East Germans to Germans? The New Postcommunist Elites*. Durham, NC: Duke University Press.

Yurdakul, Gökçe. 2006. "State, Political Parties and Immigrant Elites: Turkish Immigrant Associations in Berlin." *Journal of Ethnic and Migration Studies* 32(3): 435–453.

Zekri, Sonja. 2007. "Einmal rein, einmal raus; Zaimoglu, Kelek, Ates—wer spricht für die deutschen Muslime?" *Süddeutsche Zeitung*. April 27.

Zimmermann, Klaus F., Holger Bonin, René Fahr, and Holger Hinte. 2007. *Immigration Policy and the Labor Market: The German Experience and Lessons for Europe*. Berlin: Springer.

Zlotnik, Hania. 1994. "International Migration: Causes and Effects." In *Beyond the Numbers: A Reader on Population, Consumption, and the Environment*, ed. Laurie Ann Mazur, 359–377. Washington, DC: Island Press.

Zolberg, Aristide R. 1985. "The Formation of New States as a Refugee-Generating Process." In *Refugees and World Politics*, ed. Elizabeth G. Ferris. New York: Praeger Publishers.

———. 2001. "Introduction: Beyond the Crisis." In *Global Migrants, Global Refugees: Problems and Solutions*, ed. Aristide Zolberg and Peter M. Benda, 1–18. New York: Berghahn Books.

———, Astri Suhrke, and Sergio Aguayo. 1989. *Escape from Violence: Conflict and the Refugee Crisis in the Developing World*. New York: Oxford University Press.

Index